GEORGE WILLIAM FEATHERSTONHAUGH

George William Featherstonhaugh, from a portrait belonging to his descendant, James D. Featherstonhaugh, Duanesburg, New York [Print courtesy of the McKinney Library, Albany Institute of History & Art]

History of American Science and Technology Series

General Editor, Lester D. Stephens

The Eagle's Nest: Natural History and American Ideas, 1812–1842
by Charlotte M. Porter

Nathaniel Southgate Shaler and the Culture of American Science
by David N. Livingstone

Henry William Ravenel, 1814–1887: South Carolina Scientist in the Civil War Era
by Tamara Miner Haygood

Granville Sharp Pattison: Anatomist and Antagonist, 1781–1851
by Frederick L. M. Pattison

Making Medical Doctors: Science and Medicine at Vanderbilt since Flexner
by Timothy C. Jacobson

U.S. Coast Survey vs. Naval Hydrographic Office
by Thomas G. Manning

George William Featherstonhaugh: The First U.S. Government Geologist
by Edmund Berkeley and Dorothy Smith Berkeley

George William Featherstonhaugh

The First U.S. Government Geologist

EDMUND BERKELEY
AND
DOROTHY SMITH
BERKELEY

The University of Alabama Press
Tuscaloosa and London

Library of Congress Cataloging-in-Publication Data
Berkeley, Edmund.
  George William Featherstonhaugh

  (History of American science and technology series)
  Bibliography: p.
  Includes index.
  1. Featherstonhaugh, George William, 1780–1866.
2. United States—Biography. 3. Geologists—United
States—Biography. 4. Diplomats—United States—
Biography. I. Berkeley, Dorothy Smith. II. Title.
III. Series.
CT275.F429B47 1988   973.5'092'4 [B]   87-5006
  ISBN 0-8173-0365-0
British Library Cataloguing-in-Publication Data available

This book is gratefully dedicated to the memory of the late
George W. White
who, for more than twenty years, generously gave us both
advice and assistance with our research

Contents

Illustrations

Preface

"A book-length study should be made of George William Featherstonhaugh who lived several lives," wrote the late George W. White, to whom this biography is dedicated.[1] Featherstonhaugh did indeed have a most unusual career. He was very much involved at various times in agriculture, diplomacy, geology, literature, and railroads. His name was familiar to many people in public life in the United States, England, and France during the early and middle years of the nineteenth century. His contemporaries attested to his abilities by electing him to membership in many prestigious societies both in the United States and in England. Although a number of short accounts of his life have been written there has been no previous book-length biography.

Having repeatedly encountered Featherstonhaugh in the course of other biographical studies, we reached the same conclusion as Dr. White. When we decided to undertake this work we were encouraged to do so, not only by Dr. White but by Whitfield J. Bell, Jr., the late Joan M. Eyles, and Leonard G. Wilson, all of whom had been interested in Featherstonhaugh. We are indebted to them for both encouragement and assistance.

As we look back over the years devoted to our investigation of Featherstonhaugh's life, we think of many people who have helped us in divers ways. Unfortunately, only a few of them can be mentioned here, but we hope that we have expressed our appreciation adequately to all of them. Fundamental to any biography is, of course, the availability of sufficient source material. We have been extremely fortunate in this respect. In the early 1900s Featherstonhaugh's daughter, Georgiana, sent a large collection of papers from England to the family in New York. Mr. James D. Featherstonhaugh, of Albany, New York, gave his family papers to the Albany Institute of History and Art. We are very much indebted to Mr. Featherstonhaugh, to Miss Daryl J. Severson, of the institute, and to Miss Ruby J. Shields of the Minnesota Historical Society, which lent us microfilms of these papers, enabling us to study them in detail. Other major sources of information have been Featherstonhaugh's scientific papers, which Georgiana Featherstonhaugh presented to Cambridge University, and the many letters housed at Cambridge University Library and at the Codrington Library of All Souls College, Oxford. We are indebted to Mr. A. E. B. Owen, of the former, and to Mr. J. S. G. Simmonds, of the latter, for making copies of these letters available to us. We recall many pleasant days spent in the impressive new facilities of the British Public Record Office at Kew and the courtesy and efficiency of the staff in providing us with an extensive number of records involving Featherstonhaugh.

We appreciate the courtesy of all of the following in kindly giving us permission to quote from manuscripts in their collections: Albany Institute of History and Art; Alderman Library, University of Virginia; the Warden and Fellows of All Souls College, Oxford; Bodleian Library, Oxford, Department of Western Manuscripts; British Library; British Museum (Natural History); Cambridge University Library; Columbia University, Rare Book and Manuscript Library; William R. Perkins Library, Duke University; Haverford College, the Quaker Collection; the Historical Society of Pennsylvania; Massachusetts Historical Society; John Murray (Publishers) Ltd.; Public Record Office, London.

Numbers of people in England went to great trouble to help us as we investigated Featherstonhaugh's background. We think particularly of Mr. Ian A. McKee of Chapman and Hall, publishers, at Methuen Educational, Andover; and of Brian Merriman, Alan

Dearden, Marie Belfitt, and Irene Newham at the Scarborough Public Library. To all these people and a great many others in England and the United States we wish to express our sincere appreciation and hearty thanks.

GEORGE WILLIAM FEATHERSTONHAUGH

Early Life

A second child and first son was born to George and Dorothy Simpson Featherstonhaugh on 9 April 1780 in London. The infant was christened George William at Saint Saviour's Church.[1] His sister, Ann, was then two years old. The children's paternal great-grandfather, William, came from Northumberland. He was said to have been a wealthy gentleman descended from the family that once owned Fetherston Castle near the village of Haltwhistle. Enjoying the sporting life, he ran through a fortune and left his family destitute when he died. His eldest son, the children's grandfather, also William, was taken to London by two maiden aunts who owned substantial property there, including the two Fetherston Buildings. Young William felt that they treated him more like a servant than a relative, however, and so he ran away to York, where he made his home with some of his mother's family. In time he became innkeeper of the White Swan in Petergate, York.[2] Dorothy Simpson's husband was his eldest and only surviving son.[3]

George Featherstonhaugh, then thirty-six, was in partnership with two friends, Machell and Johnson, as "lead dealers, shot makers and colour makers," with a place of business on Bank Side, Southwark.[4] Soon after his son's christening, the business required that Featherstonhaugh make a trip to Norwich. By the

Dorothy Simpson Featherstonhaugh, a pastel from the British School, belonging to James D. Featherstonhaugh, Duanesburg, New York [Print courtesy of the McKinney Library. Albany Institute of History & Art]

time he reached that town he was extremely ill and was alarmed when he was unable to find lodgings. A Doctor Catford had a bed made up for him in his own home and tended him there. After a few days, Featherstonhaugh felt well enough to write to his wife of his illness. He tried to avoid worrying her, confidently asserting that there was now "no danger and all symptoms favorable," but in fact he was far from being out of danger. Not long after writing, he suffered a relapse and died on 2 May. He was buried at All Saints Church, Norwich, with only a small group of acquaintances present.

Dorothy Simpson Featherstonhaugh had been named executrix of her husband's will, and she inherited all his money and his share of the stock of his business. His only other bequests were for the purchase of mourning rings for Charles Barrow, Esquire, Sir Richard Machell, and Sir John Fearn, in memory of their friendship for him. The will was proved in early June and soon afterward Dorothy took steps to dispose of her share of the business.[5] She had decided to return to her native Scarborough, where she had been married on 14 January 1777[6] and where her parents, George and Ann Stephens Simpson still lived. She would need their assistance in supporting herself and caring for her children. As soon as she was able to make all the arrangements, she returned home and invested funds in a millinery shop.[7]

Scarborough is an ancient city on the North Sea, 221 miles from London and 43 from York. Towering above the town are the ruins of ancient Scarborough Castle, which stands on a hill that rises some three hundred feet from the sea.[8] This headland, known as Castle Hill, was one of a number of coastal signal stations during the latter part of the Roman occupation of England. From its beginnings in the twelfth century the castle had a long history of capture and recapture.[9] By the late 1700s Scarborough was a popular spa. It had some of the finest beaches in England and an even greater attraction: medicinal springs thought to be beneficial in the alleviation of a variety of human ailments. After their discovery, in 1620, the town had capitalized upon them by constructing a large and spacious hall for assemblies, balls, plays, and other entertainments. A great number of the more affluent members of British society flocked there to enjoy the resort atmosphere and the waters.[10]

It was to one of the houses on St. Nicholas Cliff that Dorothy Featherstonhaugh brought her children. Her father owned property there, and in 1791 she purchased from Richard Courteen the house that she was occupying.[11] As very young children, Ann and her brother spent many happy hours playing on the terrace of the Cliff House from which there was a beautiful view of the strand below and the North Sea beyond. When the sea was calm, the little boy thought that the road to heaven might be where it ended, but when it was stormy, it made him realize "the deceitfulness of the fairest looking things." Every day the children went for walks along the beach. There was always something to watch on the waterfront, the focus for most activity.[12]

Sea bathing was very popular all over England at the time, and

"Bathing Machines" from John Cole's *Curiosities of Scarborough* [Courtesy of the Scarborough Public Library]

Scarborough was an ideal place for it. Bathing was segregated by sexes, the men going out some distance in boats and swimming without suits. The ladies bathed from "machines," which were essentially cabanas on wheels, drawn by horses. A lad, riding the horse, drove out to the desired depth while the ladies undressed in the machine and put on their bathing costumes. Steps were let down and two women, standing up to their waists in the sea, helped the ladies down.[13]

The children and their friends, as well as some adults, explored the exposed sands for clams, shells, carnelians, fossils from the cliff, or anything else left behind by the receding waters. The firm beaches were favorite places for horseback riding and for a display of carriages of all descriptions. Horse races were even held there. The large number of summer visitors attracted a varied assortment of entertainers. Fairs brought the usual sideshow attractions with their universal appeal to children. Featherston, as young George William's friends called him, was especially fascinated by an Irish giant he saw in one such sideshow.[14] Another visitor to Scarborough who made a long-remembered impression on Featherston was the prizefighter "Gentleman Jackson," who gave boxing lessons to young men and boys. Featherston was an eager pupil and thrilled when the pugilist became champion of England soon afterwards.[15] Traveling dramatic groups frequently presented matinees, and for adults there were balls every evening, a faro bank, a hazard table, and fair chance, cards and billiards. Of more importance to Featherston was the bookstore in Long Room Street, where out-of-town newspapers could be bought and, for an annual subscription of five shillings, books could be taken home.[16] By the time he was six, he was an avid reader.

On Sundays, Mrs. Featherstonhaugh and her children attended services at the Church of Saint Mary the Virgin, located on a high hill near the castle. This, too, had an ancient history, having been founded during the Roman occupation and reconstructed at intervals since 1180.[17] Numbers of townspeople took an interest in both the history and the natural history of Scarborough. Among those interested in the latter was the Featherstonhaughs' neighbor, Dr. William Belcombe, who published a chemical analysis of the spa waters. The ocean cliffs abounded in fossils of various kinds. Dr. William Travis, a surgeon, had a fine collection of them and another of minerals, which had been given him by a gentleman "eminent in mineralogy." Possibly this was the Mr. Drury to whom Featherston later sent mineral specimens and who was responsible for arousing the youngster's interest in geological matters.[18] Scarborough was clearly a very stimulating place for an intelligent child with an enquiring mind, and Featherston certainly found it so.

Summer visitors brought their children to Scarborough from many parts of Great Britain. They mingled with local children at school, at church, and at play, adopting the same democratic manner their parents assumed in the relaxed resort setting and making many enduring friendships. Featherston's first school was one recommended by a close family friend, the Reverend George Dodsworth, rector of Saint Mary the Virgin. The school was run by a Yorkshireman, the Reverend Robert Howard, at Throxenby, a small village not far from Scarborough.[19] Featherston soon spoke the Yorkshire brogue so broadly that even his mother had difficulty understanding him. During the long holidays he joined in the town sport of collecting the eggs of sea birds from their nesting places on the cliffs that fronted the sea.[20] During the nesting season these eggs were harvested in considerable quantity by "clemmers," boys and young men who attached ropes to stout stakes at the top of the cliffs and lowered themselves with baskets to gather the eggs. There was a ready market for this delicacy even as far away as London.[21]

Featherston continued his education as one of a hundred boarders at Stepney House, a private school, whose brick buildings stood among green pastures two miles southwest of Scarborough.[22] Here he received a sound basic education with particular emphasis on the classics and history. He became adept at expressing himself, both orally and in writing, and his natural facility for languages was greatly augmented. Once, during his school holidays, three ships loaded with priests fleeing the French Revolution entered Scarborough Harbor. Although the town was primarily Protestant, the priests were welcomed into private homes. One from Morlaix was quartered with the Featherstonhaughs. Featherston honed his French by talking with the priests and listening to their accounts of the revolution, which fascinated him.[23]

Featherston's deeply enquiring mind and almost photographic memory made him a successful student. Unfortunately, however, his mother was not financially able to send him to a university, and she worried about a vocation for him. In the meantime, she permitted him to undertake further study of Latin and Greek under the guidance of the Reverend Thomas Irvin, who taught the classics "with great and merited celebrity."[24] When not studying or reading, Featherston rambled the beaches collecting fossils and indulging his interest in mineralogy and natural history. As he walked, he wondered if he would ever be able to travel. Would he always live at Scarborough, "vegetating in obscurity," until buried at Saint Mary's? He yearned to visit many historic places in England and in Europe, but the grand tour, then popular with young gentlemen, was beyond his family's means.[25] Quite unexpectedly, an exciting opportunity for travel presented itself. One of Featherston's relatives had married a son of Admiral Sir Hugh Clobury Christian. Her husband was also a British naval officer and had recently received command of a naval vessel. The younger Christian suggested that Featherston sail with him to Gibraltar, Italy, and perhaps the Levant and Egypt. Featherston needed no urging and joined the ship at Plymouth, though in what capacity is not clear.[26]

The ship sailed south, across the Bay of Biscay and along the western coast of Spain. Very early in the trip Featherston wished he had been less hasty. He proved a very poor sailor, miserably seasick most of the way and very glad to reach Cadiz. There, he went with Christian to call on the British consul, and they were entertained at some of the best houses. When the ship was about to sail again, Featherston became seriously ill and had to be left behind. A kindly priest undertook to treat him with doses of rhubarb and rum, while terrifying him with accounts of how many people had recently died of yellow fever. In time Featherston went to recuperate at a country place, spending long hours studying Spanish. At last he continued to Gibraltar, on horseback rather than by ship.

There he rejoined Christian, and the two men fully enjoyed the next two months. One day they visited St. Michael's Cave. It was Featherston's first experience with such a cavern. The two were ill equipped for spelunking, but they returned a second day, outfitted with ropes, and explored the cave thoroughly, delighted by its stalactites, stalagmites, and freshwater pools. Unfortunately, Featherston, still a little weak from his illness, had difficulty in climbing out and had to be rescued.[27]

From Gibraltar the ship sailed to Naples, which Featherston found a great contrast to Spain. He was amused by such sights as gentlemen dressed in fine silk coats carrying umbrellas to protect their elaborate coiffures. The British minister introduced the captain and his protégé to a number of interesting people, and the two men did as much sightseeing as possible. They visited Pompeii and Herculaneum and, with the aid of guides, struggled to the top of Mount Vesuvius. Peering into the great crater, they imagined rumblings and vibrations, and later they were awakened from sleep by a genuine earthquake. Since the ship had no orders to proceed, they made a trip to Rome. This was an exciting experience for one fond of history, and Featherston made the most of it. He was not very favorably impressed by the people they met but was pleased to feel that his mind was "expanding and spreading itself."[28]

After their trip to Rome, the two men went with the ship to Trieste. They were able to make a brief visit to Venice before the ship was ordered back to England. Featherston felt reluctant to leave the Continent, and Christian advised him to stay on as long as his limited finances would permit. It was possible that Featherston could earn a living representing merchant firms abroad. With this in mind, he left Christian and went to Leghorn, where he reached some agreement with an importing firm owned by a man named Philip Jaume.[29] Featherston continued his travels, returning to Scarborough in 1801 for six months with his family. While there he made further commercial arrangements with at least two

British import-export firms and persuaded his friend John Bielby
to return with him to the Continent.[30]

During the next several years the two young men visited many
parts of Europe as Featherston's business required. Making use of
letters of introduction, they met a number of socially prominent
and interesting people and made new friends. They enjoyed opera
and other musical events and visited cathedrals, museums, and
places of historic interest. They improved their command of several languages and even took music lessons.[31]

There was ample time for indulging their interest in geology,
collecting fossils and mineral specimens that made holes in their
pockets. While the term *geology* was not generally used in the late
eighteenth century, it was not for lack of interest in the subject,
especially mineralogy. There were many avid amateur and professional collectors, and a number of books had been published on
the subject, perhaps the best known being *Von den ausserlichen
Kennzeichen der Fossilen* by Abraham Gottlob Werner in 1774.[32] It
seems likely that Featherston and Bielby depended on Dru Drury's
Thoughts on the Precious Metals. . . . Although an entomologist,
Drury had written on collecting gold, precious metals, and other
natural riches, "from the rough diamond down to the pebble-
stone" for travelers.[33] In August, Featherston wrote Ann that "Mr.
Drury may expect to see some fine mineralogy" and that he had
just purchased a hammer to use in the Pyrenees. He and Bielby
visited Madrid's cabinet, or specimen repository, of natural history
and found the mineral collection excellent. In Rome they searched
the ruins for bits of jasper, porphyry, and other stones. All these
and some fossils would soon enrich Drury's collection.[34]

Featherston's business affairs proved less fortunate and gradually
deteriorated. The Scarborough merchant he represented, Richard
Courteen, went bankrupt, owing Featherston money he badly
needed. Then came the more serious failure of Philip Jaume, who
owed not only Featherston but also the British merchants to whom
Featherston had recommended him.[35] It was a disappointing end to
his Continental business career, but Featherston had in any case begun to question the advisability of continuing his travels. The years

on the Continent had been rewarding and valuable in many ways. Now, however, it seemed time to find a career with more promise for the future. In 1804 he borrowed money from Bielby to pay his passage home.[36]

Featherston found that his family affairs had altered during his absence. His grandfather Simpson had died not long before his return.[37] His mother was upset over the death and over his sister's engagement. Ann's fiancé was Charles Bourne Lawton, whose family had long owned Lawton Hall in the village of Lawton, near Newcastle. Two of the Belcombe girls, with whom Ann and her brother had grown up, had married men from the Lawton area, and Charles, a graduate of Trinity College, Cambridge, might seem to have been an eminently suitable marriage prospect for Ann. He was, however, a younger son, who lived with his mother and elder brother, and his only income was an allowance from his mother. If his brother married, Charles would have no financial prospects. Featherston agreed with his mother in opposing the match, but to no avail.[38]

The years in Europe had given Featherston some experience in the business world, so he decided to try life in London. Exactly what his occupation was there is not known, but he had some association with Thomas Dickason & Company. Featherston found it difficult to settle down. After only two years in a London office, he felt restless. For some time he had thought of visiting the United States, encouraged by young Tom Dickason, a good friend and fellow worker, who had spent some time in Boston. Featherston thought that he might be able to make a study of the languages of North American Indians. How long he might stay would depend again upon finances. He had inherited a hundred pounds from his grandfather, and he could arrange some commercial commissions, perhaps with the Dickason firm. In August 1806 he sailed for Boston on the *Crocker* from Liverpool.[39]

When he landed, Featherston was suffering from the rheumatism that had troubled him in London. He went on to New York, thinking the milder climate might help him, and he soon felt better. By December he was enjoying some social life when he received a letter from W. H. Nevitt, the elder Dickason's nephew, reporting that his uncle had received Featherston's letter announcing his safe arrival. Nevitt and other friends missed him at their musical parties. Tom Dickason thought he could picture Featherston "with frosty blue nose, sans chapeau, and understockings, playing the Gallant to the Boston Ladies at the Assembly, and charming with your agreeable small talk."[40]

Featherston was less sure than Tom about his ability to charm Americans. Like many other newly arrived Englishmen he seemed to be unconsciously offending his hosts. The mercantile houses tended to send young, inexperienced men who talked too much of "Lord this and My Lady that" and spoke "in raptures of Richmond Hill and Kew Garden." He had not realized how much he was doing this sort of thing until he was quietly deflated by one of his new acquaintances. Having imbibed a little too freely of Madeira at a social gathering, he had spoken of British superiority in various things until this gentleman asked him if it was true that the moon "was larger and rounder in England."[41]

Featherston soon made a number of friends and began enjoying a pleasant social life. He was often a guest at the home of Mrs. Duane, widow of James Duane, who had been mayor of New York and a federal judge. Upon his death, each of his four daughters and his son, James, had inherited a large tract of land near Schenectady. Featherston was particularly attracted by Sarah, or "Sally," a lively, pretty woman, then thirty-two years old. She had been educated at Mrs. Belle Graham's "polite establishment of female culture" in New York. She shared Featherston's interest in languages and music, played the harp, and painted in both oils and watercolors.[42]

Among Featherston's new acquaintances were two men who were unusually congenial and soon became good friends, Archibald Bruce and William James MacNeven. Their principal common interest was mineralogy, by then a well-established science in Europe and receiving increased attention in the United States. Bruce, the son of a Scottish medical officer in the British army and a physician himself, with an M.D. from the University of Edinburgh in 1800, had just been appointed professor of mineralogy and materia medica at the College of Physicians and Surgeons in

New York. He had spent two years in France, Italy, and Switzerland, studying minerals and meeting the leading European mineralogists. His wife, Judith Bayard Van Rensselaer, was a relative of the Duanes. MacNeven, according to John C. Greene, "was an Irish patriot. Born in County Galway, Ireland, in 1763, he received an excellent medical education at the University of Vienna. . . . Returning to Ireland, MacNeven played a leading role in planning the Irish rebellion of 1798, was arrested for sedition, and spent four years in prison. After serving two years in the Irish Brigade of Napolean's army . . . he emigrated to the United States, arriving in New York on July 4, 1803."[43] Bruce and MacNeven welcomed this new friend who shared their interest in the study of mineralogy.

In the late spring of 1807, Featherston made a trip to Canada. On his way north he visited the Duanes at Schenectady and was impressed by the beauty of the area.[44] In May he joined a friend, Edward Ellice, whose father was a director of the Hudson's Bay Company and founder of Inglis Ellice & Company.[45] Edward had been educated at Winchester and Marischal College and had worked as a clerk in his father's London office, where Featherston probably met him. Edward was now involved in the fur trade for his father. He and Featherston were congenial, and they spent the next six months traveling together. They found Quebec interesting and imagined that the Plains of Abraham had been little changed since General Wolfe took the city a half century earlier. They called on Sir John Caldwell, a member of the Legislative Assembly, and visited the Falls of Chaudière near his home.[46]

After an extended visit in Montreal, the two men explored some of the Indian territory to the west in the region known as Upper Canada. Featherston spent as much time with the Indians as he could, trying to learn something of the languages. Wildlife in the woodland near their homes particularly appealed to him. He was astonished by some of the sights. One day there were great hordes of glossy black squirrels "with singularly bushy tails" moving north from Lake Huron. He theorized that a food shortage might have caused the migration. Another day he and some Indians came upon a multitude of wild pigeons. He had heard of them and had supposed the accounts to have been exaggerated, but he later wrote of "the woods loaded from top to bottom with their nests for a great number of miles, the heaviest branches of the trees broken and fallen to the ground, which was strewed with young birds dead and alive, that the Indians in great numbers were picking up to carry away with their horses. . . . A forest thus loaded and half destroyed with these birds, presents an extraordinary spectacle which cannot be rivalled."[47]

While in Canada, Featherston visited Niagara Falls and found it even more impressive than he had anticipated. He was particularly interested in the erosive effect of the falls and would later write about the continuous recession of land caused by "the constant moisture, the violent concussion and the strong current of air."[48] He left Montreal in October, hoping to rejoin Ellice at Schenectady, but the latter, an "admittedly changeable animal" went on to New York, and Featherston remained in Schenectady for much of the following year.[49] It is possible that he served as an instructor or tutor at Union College, since he soon numbered among his friends several of the Union faculty who shared his interests. Among these were Dr. Eliphalet Nott, the president, just beginning a sixty-three-year career in that office; Nott's brother-in-law, Benjamin Allen, professor of mathematics and natural philosophy; and Count Pierre G. Reynaud, a refugee from the French Revolution, who taught French. The only traveling Featherston is known to have done during this year was to Bethlehem, Pennsylvania, where he spent a week visiting the Moravians and gathering information from them about the Indians they had befriended.[50]

Featherston was undoubtedly enjoying his friends at Union College, but he also had another reason for lingering at Schenectady. He was very much in love with Sally Duane, and they became engaged in October 1808. Featherston had no means of supporting a wife, but it had been agreed that he would undertake the farming of her undeveloped land at Duanesburg, where they planned to build a home. Marriage articles were drawn up for them on 5 November, stating that it was Featherston's desire that Sally's estate should be separate and distinct from his financial affairs. All her property was placed in trust to her brother-in-law,

General William North, husband of her sister Mary, for Sally's benefit. The two then married, on 6 November 1808, at Saint George's Episcopal Church.[51]

Featherston and Sally began their married life in Philadelphia. Plans were being drawn for the house they wanted to build, but construction could not begin before spring. They rented a small house and settled in for the winter. Despite such distractions as marriage and planning a home, Featherston continued to be absorbed in the language studies that had always attracted him. Fortunately Sally enjoyed them too, or so General North believed. He wrote that he pictured them sitting before their cottage fire "poring over Greek, Hebrew & Indian Mss."[52] Other friends had similar ideas. Count Reynaud wrote to them in Spanish. Benjamin Allen reported that he had acquired a book containing the Lord's Prayer in 172 languages. He thought it might satiate even Featherston's "philological voracity." Featherston wrote to borrow a Sanskrit grammar from the Union College Library. One of his friends wrote that he thought Featherston must be acquainted "with all the languages which have existed since the destruction of Babylon." This and other interests soon took him to the great Logan Library, of Philadelphia. The librarian asked him to prepare a list of books that he thought should be added to their collections.[53]

In early April the Featherstons went to Duanesburg to oversee the construction of their "Baronial Castle," as Peter S. DuPonceau, a Philadelphia friend, called it. They would miss Philadelphia and their many friends. One of the first letters Featherston received after leaving was the official notice of his election to membership in the American Philosophical Society, whose meetings he had enjoyed. It was accompanied by DuPonceau's personal congratulations and hope that the new member would favor the society with communications from time to time. He valued Featherston's friendship and would miss him but hoped to pay them a visit the following summer when the house would be finished. He still automatically offered his snuff box as if his friend were still there.[54]

The house the Featherstons were to occupy while their own was being built was not fully furnished when they arrived, and so they sat on their trunks and ate with forks Featherston cut from hazel twigs with a pocketknife. Although Sally had inherited large tracts of land, she had not owned that on which they wanted to build, about a mile from the Norths' house. They had acquired it by exchanging some acreage with the owner. They had located the house on a high hill overlooking a small lake, with an "enchanting 200 mile view." There was a great deal of work to be done on Featherston Park, as they had decided to call their estate, and they were soon completely absorbed by it. A large vegetable garden had to be laid out and prepared. Stables and other outbuildings had to be both planned and built. General North had purchased a chaise and a pair of "star-gazing horses" for them, but a lot of additional livestock would be needed as soon as preparation could be made for it. Featherston was unused to the strenuous physical labor in which he was soon involved, but he enjoyed it thoroughly.[55]

From time to time there were letters from England bringing Featherston up-to-date on family and friends there. Ann, who had married Charles Lawton, reported that the Belcombes' daughter Harriet was about to make them grandparents. Ann wondered if Sally was yet expecting. Sally was, and her husband was somewhat worried about her. He was not favorably impressed by what he heard of local doctors and so wrote to Dr. Bruce, who regretted that the distance prevented him from attending Sally. He suggested that it would be wise to take her to Albany. Featherston's concern proved justified for Sally had a difficult labor and their child died. Their distress was then prolonged by congratulatory letters from England received long afterward.[56] The Featherstonhaughs' house was completed in 1810. His mother thought they had been far too ambitious but Featherston and Sally were eager for a large family. After the loss of their first child they were extremely happy when a healthy son, George William, was born 8 October 1811.[57]

The following year on 18 June the United States declared war on England, placing Featherston in an awkward position. By March 1813 he found it necessary to ask his lawyer friend William Johnson how new State Department restrictions would affect him.

Johnson informed him that only those "alien *enemies*" residing within forty miles of New York City would be restricted. Featherston could visit Albany without a passport. He was, however, uncomfortable about the war, as he explained to Ann. He carefully refrained from making any remarks about "the Unhappy War," feeling that "it would be dishonourable and dishonest" for him "to wish any evil to a Country from which he had received nothing but good." On the other hand, his "undivided affections belonged to England," and he felt concern for her welfare. He had nothing but scorn for those British subjects in North America who, "to curry favour" with Americans, execrated "every thing good in England." Such Englishmen were, he believed, "despised and mistrusted by all honest men here." He saw no hope for peace "until Bonaparte's nails are cut and his Teeth drawn."[58]

His letter to Ann was sent in care of friends, Mr. Jeffrey, "leading manager of Edinburgh *Review,*" and his wife, the former Miss Wilkes. She was the daughter of his friend Charles Wilkes and great-niece of "John Wilkes of Famous political memory." The Jeffreys were returning to Edinburgh and took with them not only the letter but a copy of Spafford's *Gazetteer of the State of New York.* The map was so small, Featherston wrote, that Ann would not find Duanesburg shown, but she would find her brother mentioned. He particularly called her attention to pictures of Lake George, which he thought "one of the most beautiful lakes in the world. . . . you will see Fort George mentioned: the ruins of this Fort are important in British American history: I have purchased the surrounding Lands, to preserve them from entire dilapidation, and I intend to build a fishing lodge there."[59]

Mrs. Featherstonhaugh sent her son a portrait of herself in 1813. Though he had not yet received it when he thanked her in March of that year, he had reciprocated by having a minature of Sally done by the artist G. Baillie Brown when they were last in New York. There were delays in receiving the minature, which Dr. Bruce had promised to have packed. He finally sent it to Featherston and Sally in late February. Featherston did not wholly approve of it. He wrote his mother that he had told Brown to draw Sally's bust "in the most chaste manner and not to attempt to

Sarah Duane Featherstonhaugh, from a miniature belonging to
James D. Featherstonhaugh, Duanesburg, New York [Print courtesy
of the McKinney Library, Albany Institute of History & Art]

describe anything but what he actually saw." He did not think that the artist had followed his instructions, and his mother might think there was "too much for a modest Woman to expose." Sally, on the other hand, commented when her husband sent the portrait that she had "never in the morning of life been so handsome."[60]

The Featherstonhaughs had been ambitious in planning not only their house but their farm as well. Featherston had hitherto spent his life in cities, and although Yorkshire was a region noted for fine farms, he had had little or no personal experience with farming. Nonetheless, if he was going to take it up, he intended to do so in impressive fashion. A house for a farm manager or steward was constructed about a quarter of a mile from the main house and barns, and other outbuildings were built near it. Additional land was acquired by purchase and exchange, and within a few years Featherston was farming fifteen hundred acres and contemplating the addition of five hundred more. He employed twelve farm laborers as well as a gardener and house servants. Although he raised a variety of crops and acquired many farm animals, he had elected to concentrate on sheep raising and did so on a grand scale. Within three years of the completion of their house he had a flock of five hundred breeding ewes and planned to increase that number to three thousand. At that time he was also raising approximately fifteen hundred bushels of grain a year.[61]

Although he employed a steward and laborers, Featherston was personally involved in all the activities entailed in sheep raising: buying, selling, feeding, shearing, doctoring, and even bottle feeding. He was not content to merely follow accepted local farming practices but wanted to improve them in every way possible. He provided more shelter and better feeding than was customary and culled his flock with care. He found that there had been little attempt to improve the basic breeds of livestock being raised in the New York area, and he decided to set up his own breeding program. He purchased the finest English Bakewell-Teeswater rams he could afford and bred the best of his Merino ewes to them. In time, he developed a strain that came to be called the Bakewell-Merino sheep, which attracted wide attention. He won prizes at fairs for the size and vigor of his sheep and the quality of their wool. Leading farmers and farm journals congratulated him on the success of his operation, and his breeding stock was in great demand.[62]

Encouraged by his success in improving the quality of sheep in his area, he undertook to do the same with cattle. In 1820 he attracted even more attention for the Holderness cow he imported from England. She arrived on the *Martha* from Liverpool. Captain Sketchley, the master of that vessel, had taken great pains to procure for Featherston as fine an animal as England produced. Soon her picture appeared in the *Plough Boy,* a leading agricultural journal. Two years later, the same journal gave a report of the October Schenectady Fair: "The stock which Mr. Featherstonhaugh exhibited, and which was numerous, was, in every branch, decidedly superior to everything else shown."[63]

It should come as no surprise that Featherston was also responsible for the presence at the fair of the famous stallion Janus, bred by General Wade Hampton. Again, the *Plough Boy* publicized his efforts: "The breeders of horses are informed that *Janus,* a horse of the highest celebrity for blood and character, has been brought from South Carolina into this state at a very great expense and will stand this season in the counties of Schenectady and Albany. Mr. Featherstonhaugh introduces this horse with the view to improve the breed in this state."[64]

In the space of a few years and with no prior experience to guide him, Featherston had established himself as a very accomplished and successful farmer and had earned a well-deserved reputation as a benefactor to farming in his part of New York state. His efforts, however, had required not only a great deal of hard work on his part but the expenditure of large sums, and the Featherstonhaughs found themselves in serious financial difficulties. He wrote to his mother of his "principal part in this great reformation which is taking place. As to practise, I think no man in this country farms on so large a scale, nor do I know of anyone with such fine breeds of Horses, Cattle and Sheep. I have betwixt one and two thousand acres in my own Farm which I cultivate, and I shall soon have one thousand of it in the first rate condition, but the want of capital prevents my turning it to the best account and distresses me cruelly at times."[65]

The financial difficulties went well beyond a mere lack of capital. They were seriously in debt. Featherston's problems were not entirely his own fault, although he freely acknowledged that he had been too ambitious. The War of 1812 and the depression that followed it found him overextended at a time when land values were low and money scarce. In 1815 land in New York City, for which he and Sally had refused twenty-five thousand dollars could not be sold for five thousand. Creditors began to press them, and they were constantly worried about money. Featherston economized in every way he could think of, even firing his steward and undertaking all supervision himself. In this last he was pleasantly surprised to find that he seemed to get along better. He also attempted to collect money owed him by Richard Courteen for representing him in Europe but could get no reply to his letters, even though Courteen was reputed to be prospering. Meanwhile, Bielby wrote to remind him of the money borrowed in Italy, and Featherston was forced to ask his mother to pay it with interest.[66]

His struggles to reduce their debts continued for a long time and were very painful to Sally as well. She wrote him once while he was away attending a meeting of the state legislature that she felt the humiliation of their financial situation deeply but relied upon his "unremitting diligence to extricate us from these unpleasant embarrassments so that at last we may once more enter the 'bowers of ease and repose in the shades of security.'" Featherston would have been very well pleased by what he had accomplished in the United States had it not been for his debts. He found it "impossible to be in Debt and to be happy at the same time," and he often felt "more like a slave than a Freeman."[67]

New Interests and
Undertakings

2

Although farming occupied most of his time, Featherston did not abandon his long-held interest in mineralogy. When he was able to visit New York, he spent as much time as he could with Archibald Bruce and James MacNeven and tried to keep informed about new developments in both mineralogy and geology. He often spent time, too, with the family of James Renwick, who in 1813, became "instructor in natural and experimental chemistry" at Columbia College.[1]

Featherston and Bruce were particularly close. They dined together, attended plays and meetings, and visited people who shared their interest in mineralogy. It was Bruce who in 1810 had founded the *American Mineralogical Journal,* which, as John Greene has pointed out, was "the first specialized scientific periodical in the United States apart from medical journals." It found a ready readership among others with similar interests, and contributors included David Hosack, Samuel Latham Mitchill, Benjamin Silliman, and George Gibbs. Although the journal was well received, not only in the United States but in Europe, Bruce only published four issues, from 1810 to 1814, when failing health forced him to discontinue it. Featherston's association with Bruce continued until the latter's untimely death in 1818. An account of their activities in July 1816 may give some idea of their relationship. On the sixth they were joined at dinner by General Solomon Van Rensselaer. On the tenth they went to visit Colonel George Gibbs at his estate on Long Island. The colonel had one of the finest mineral collections in the United States and had contributed articles to Bruce's journal. On the following day, Bruce, Gibbs, and Featherston dined together before attending a meeting of the New York Literary and Philosophical Society, at which Featherston was proposed for membership.[2]

In October 1814 Ann died in childbirth. It was a hard death for Featherston to bear, for he and his sister had been singularly devoted. He and Sally had named their second surviving child, born 21 June, for his sister. For a long time Featherston complained that his mind was overwhelmed with melancholy.[3] To express his feeling of desperate loss, he composed a poem, "On a Beloved Sister," which was published in *Port Folio*.

The poem was not his introduction to the literary world, for Featherston had already begun to occupy himself with writing when his farm work permitted. In the fall of 1814 he spent many hours preparing an edition of Sir Walter Scott's *Romance of Sir Tristam*. He sent his copy to James Eastham, a New York bookseller, who promised to publish it as soon as Featherston completed his corrections and additions.[4]

When an article entitled "Papers on the Irish Language," by Thomas Cooper, appeared in two parts in the October and November issues of *Port Folio*, Featherston could not resist challenging Cooper's views with his own. Cooper was an Englishman and Oxford graduate, who came to the United States with Joseph Priestley in 1794 and practiced law at Northampton, Pennsylvania. At this time he was, or was about to become, professor of chemistry at Dickinson College. He was brilliant but highly eccentric.[5]

In his reply to Cooper's essay, published in the April 1815 issue of *Port Folio*, Featherston adopted a self-deprecating pose, describing himself as but "a Country farmer . . . more conversant with esculents than with Hebrew and Irish roots." He then proceeded to make it evident that he was very familiar with previous efforts, both ancient and modern, to trace the origins of the Irish language. He cited the "opinions of General Vallancey on the supposed affinity of the ancient Irish to the Phoenecian or Punic language." He discussed the opinion of a number of Irish historians that the original ancestors of the Irish people were "the three daughters of Cain" and noted "the favorable reception which these and a thousand equally wild relations have obtained amongst the warm-hearted sons of Erin." He then contended that he did not doubt but that "an ingenious person equally competent to the task, might produce words out of the Tartaric, Icelandic, Finnic, and Welsh," which would be quite as convincing as the collation of General Vallancey. For his part, Featherston was "prepared to acknowledge and to demonstrate, if required, that the Hyberno-Celtic is cognate with the ancient Carthaginian; but this is a different position from one which asserts the Irish to be descendants of Carthaginians, and their language to be 'exactly the same with the ancient Carthaginian.'" He defended his position at great length, concluding: "Leaving therefore, the fabulous to their fables, and all men else to their fancies, who have cast nations into countries afar off, I know not how; I will follow herein the relation of Moses and the prophets; to which truth there is joined both nature, reason, policy, and necessity; and to the rest neither probability nor possibility."[6]

Encouraged by editor Charles Caldwell's reference to his "learned and able communication" and to the importance to *Port Folio* of such "able pens" as his, Featherston attacked another article that had disturbed him. The June 1815 number of the journal contained his "Observations on a Paper in the March Number of the *Port Folio,* Touching the Peopling of the Continent of America." He started his essay by pointing out that the Bible had often been used "to derive aid to the various historical, etymological, or physical hypotheses, which the fertility of the human mind is continually engendering. Sectarians respectively find in the holy scriptures every illustration and confirmation, which they can desire for their conflicting doctrines. Theological theories, altogether hostile to each other, can be clearly affirmed and sustained upon the authority of the Bible." Featherston was an ardent churchman, and he was quarreling not with the "imperfections of the instrument but with . . . the ignorance and perversity of the workmen."

He thought, however, that even such poor laborers encouraged others to study for themselves and "thus the knowledge of the true religion will be forwarded even by the labours of a superficial Volney, a conceited Priestley, and a blasphemous Paine."[7]

Featherston did not limit his literary efforts to writing articles. He took great pleasure in translating Dante's *Inferno* into blank verse. After some practice he found that he could put a whole canto into verse between breakfast and dinner if he had no interruptions, but there were few days when he had so much free time. Even on Sundays there was service to attend at the church James Duane had built in Duanesburg. In the absence of the minister, Featherston, as senior warden, often read prayers and even gave a sermon. Then there were meetings of the Bible and Common Prayer Book Society, of which he was a member.[8] His limited time for translating the *Inferno* protracted the project for several years, but by 1821 he had completed it. He wrote to Edward Everett, editor of the *North American Review,* who had asked him to write an article on another subject: "Your Review ought to be supported by those who can write, but there are few men of leisure here. . . . As to the Dante, the Lord preserve us. I should like very well to make myself immortal if I could cheap but as to running the risk of losing two or three thousand Dollars, to pass for a bad Translator—. . . . I will give you a specimen or two, and for which I ask your unreserved Opinion." He enclosed his version of the twenty-fourth canto, adding that he would have included a passage from the *Purgatorio* had he not feared that it would cost Everett double postage. He had always thought blank verse a "proper Frame to put a picture of Dante in" and had been more careful to give his meaning than anything else. Neither Everett's opinion nor Featherston's manuscript have survived, but Peter DuPonceau, who read the translation, thought Featherston a "Potential genius" in verse making.[9]

The Featherstonhaughs' desire for a large family was partly fulfilled by the birth of another son, James Duane, on 8 August 1815 and another daughter, Georgiana, 8 March 1817. His growing family, his farming, and his writing should have been enough to occupy Featherston, but in 1819 he became president of the newly reorganized Duanesburg Agricultural Society for Schenectady County, whose principal objective was to hold an annual fair. The same year saw the fruition of a much more ambitious under-

Stephen Van Rensselaer, from a portrait by A. Dickinson in Joel Munsel's *The Annals of Albany*, III, 280 [Courtesy of the Alderman Library, University of Virginia]

taking. The New York legislature established the New York Board of Agriculture, the first such board in the United States, and appropriated ten thousand dollars for its expenses over a five-year period. Featherston had played a major part in the promotion of this legislation, being familiar with the accomplishments of a similar board in Great Britain, and he was very much involved with the New York board from its beginning. It was to be composed of representatives from each of the county agricultural societies and was authorized to elect its own officers, establish rules of procedure, and distribute an annual report. The organizational meeting was held early in 1820.[10]

Featherston's friend and his wife's distant relative Stephen Van Rensselaer was elected president. The "Patroon," as he was known, owned some 700,000 acres of land. He had served in the state assembly and state senate and as lieutenant governor of New York. The other officers of the board were James LeRay Chaumont, vice-president; Solomon Southwick, recording secretary; and Featherston, corresponding secretary. Southwick was the editor of the *Plough Boy,* which was made the official publication of the board. As the first order of business following the election of officers, Featherston was appointed chairman of a committee to propose a statement of policy under which the board should operate. His committee recommended, among many things, that it should follow the example of European boards and avoid rigid rules. The *Plough Boy* referred to the report as "a document of no small importance," adding that "no tribute of thanks from any public body was ever more deservedly conferred than that to Mr. Featherstonhaugh."[11]

The board consumed Featherston's time but also involved him in a number of activities that he enjoyed. It allowed him to write about agricultural matters and to correspond with such interesting and important people as James Madison, Albert Gallatin, Henry Clay, and Oliver Wolcott in the United States and Sir John Sinclair and others abroad. Featherston's first act as corresponding secretary was to prepare a report of the establishment of the New York board and to send it to influential people concerned with agricultural matters in this country and overseas, requesting their correspondence and the exchange of publications.

It had been intended that the annual report of the board would contain communications of general interest from each of its county societies. When the general committee met to plan the first report, however, very few such articles had been received. All the committee members were embarrassed, but Southwick was perhaps most chagrined. He had contemplated an annual report of six hundred pages. Thanks very largely to Featherston's efforts, they were fortunate enough to produce one of five hundred pages, comprising the act of the legislature that had established the board; a report of a geological survey of Albany County by Amos Eaton, the New York naturalist, and Dr. Lewis C. Beck, a physician interested in chemistry, botany, mineralogy, and geology; a letter to Featherston from Sinclair, originator and president of the British board, with extracts from his correspondence with George Washington; and an address by James Madison to the Albemarle County, Virginia, Agricultural Society, of which he was president. The remaining several hundred pages were provided by Featherston, who wrote an essay entitled "Principles and Practices of Rural Economy."[12]

In the preface of his essay Featherston praised the geological survey report of Eaton and Beck and urged all the county agriculture societies to sponsor their own surveys. His farming experience and his reading had intensified his interest in geology, and both he and Van Rensselaer recognized the need for geological studies in the United States. Featherston stressed "the connection betwixt Botany, Chemistry and Mineralogy with Agriculture." He recognized that New York farmers were not great readers, partly, he thought, because they lacked sufficiently elementary books on agriculture. Many people had told him that it would not be possible to explain to ordinary farmers the principles of chemistry and geology basic to agricultural practice. He did not agree, having gained great respect for the basic intelligence of even the less educated among them. All that was necessary was for the writer to express the principles in terms familiar to them. This he undertook to do, beginning with the fundamental importance of soil as a natural resource. He noted that substances removed from it must be returned to it and explained that the structure of soil was as important as its chemical composition. He wrote about crop requirements for, and tolerance of, water and gave practical instructions for constructing inexpensive drainage ditches and farm ponds for livestock. He advised farmers on what kinds of crops and livestock to raise and how to manage them for profitable results. Throughout, he emphasized practical suggestions and simple language.[13]

The board at its next meeting expressed appreciation to Featherston for "the distinguished services performed by him in his official duties and particularly for the extraordinary labors generously and gratuitously bestowed in composing an essay."[14] The annual report, or *Memoirs* as it was called, was well received. The *New York Statesman* recommended it to its readers. The *American Farmer* did likewise and published excerpts from it, prefacing them with the statement: "To the Secretary of the board, Mr. George W. Featherstonhaugh, a learned, enterprizing [*sic*], and practical farmer, the people of New York, and of this union, are under heavy but grateful obligations for his persevering and successful efforts, to unfold the principles and correct the precepts of our rural economy."[15]

Southwick was succeeded as recording secretary of the New York board by Jesse Buel in 1822. Buel was an experienced farmer; the *Plough Boy* called his the "best organized farm in Albany County." He and Featherston worked well together in preparing a second volume of the *Memoirs,* which appeared in April 1823. This time Featherston had succeeded in obtaining a number of articles by practical farmers and had contributed one himself on the use of turnips in sheep husbandry, which was reprinted in the *American Farmer.*[16] The report received many gratifying compliments. One reader wrote that the book was "a rich treat." Another considered it the best book he had ever seen on agriculture and declared that the entire United States was indebted to them. Van Rensselaer, familiar with Featherston's work with the board as well as his early attempts to improve New York agriculture, bestowed on him the sobriquet of "Hercules in Agriculture." The *Memoirs* also attracted the attention of other organizations, and Featherston was unanimously elected to the board of the New York Horticultural Society and to the Albany Lyceum of Natural History.[17]

Sometime during the summer of 1821 he had a visit from Colonel James Perkins of Boston, who had befriended him when he first came to the United States. Perkins was accompanied by Everett, who needed all the help he could get with the *North American Review*. Featherston promised to provide him with an account of the Erie and Champlain canals, which were then nearing completion. Everett wrote him in late August to remind him of his promise and to let him know that he and the "venerable Colonel" had arrived safely in Boston. Since then Everett had been amusing young friends with Featherston's stories about Yankees, just "as if my father had not been of Dedham, and my mother of Boston. I want an account of your C-A-N-A-L for the next number of the N.A. Review."[18]

Featherston was reluctant, thinking an article might be premature, but the January issue of the *Review* contained his twenty-page commentary on three recent publications concerning New York canals. He considered the advantages of canals so obvious as to need little discussion, but he summarized them briefly. He touched on their history in England, beginning with the seven-mile canal that the duke of Bridgewater had constructed in 1758–1759, the forerunner of over three thousand miles of canals presently in use there. Turning to this country, he mentioned Albert Gallatin's "Report on Public Roads and Canals," made to the United States Senate when he was secretary of the treasury. Featherston then reported the history of the New York canals, as given in the three publications he was reviewing.[19]

The year 1820 proved a very emotionally disturbing time for Featherston and Sally. Both had always been extremely ambitious for their children and felt that any real success could only be achieved by a thorough education starting at an early age. By the time George was four he had been introduced to Latin, Greek, and Hebrew. His English grandmother protested that so many languages would only perplex a child and asked Featherston if he intended his son to be a bishop or the pope. Her remarks did little to discourage Featherston's educational plans for his son, however. When the boy had his ninth birthday, his father thought it would be wise to send him to an English preparatory school, but Sally was distraught at the thought of sending her young son so far away. It took her husband a full year to obtain her very reluctant consent.[20]

When the time came for Featherston to take George to New York there was a heartrending scene with Sally, who was already depressed by the recent death of her mother. They left her in a state of "absolute despair." On 5 June George sailed in the care of Captain Sketchley on the *Martha* for Liverpool. There he stayed with one of Ann's friends, a Miss Buchanan, until he could be safely conducted to Scarborough.[21] By 1 August he had been with his grandmother long enough for her to report that she was finding him a handful. She could not keep him from the seaside, and she had made more trips down there since his arrival than in the previous seven years. After much debate, she sent her grandson to Stepney House. He seemed to be happy there, and the headmaster, the Reverend Herbert Phillips, wrote favorable reports of his progress.[22]

Having already turned his hand to writing poetry and essays, as well as translating Dante into blank verse, Featherston now undertook playwriting. This new venture was inspired by his having met the English actor, Edmund Kean, on board the *Martha*. Six months later he wrote to Kean that he was working on a play expressly for him. Featherston proposed sending it, on completion, to the actor, who could decide whether or not it was suitable for production at Drury Lane.[23]

Agricultural concerns had involved Featherston in both local and state politics, and he became increasingly interested in the influence of the federal government on agricultural prosperity. His close association with Van Rensselaer on the New York Board of Agriculture had stimulated this interest, for Van Rensselaer had just been elected to Congress.[24] Featherston came to feel that government policies had favored manufacturing over agriculture and that farmers must try to exert more influence in Washington. His concern was personal as well as altruistic. The profits of his large-scale sheep farming were dependent on the price of wool. He thought it high time that duties were imposed on imported wool and other products that competed with those produced in the

United States. In 1823 he decided to do whatever he could to promote protective tariff legislation. With dependable farm laborers, who had little to do in winter but care for livestock, he was free to travel.

Before going to Washington, Featherston made a quick trip to Boston to see friends and then to New York where he hoped to improve his still-precarious financial situation. He wanted to arrange a mortgage on the home farm at Duanesburg to enable him to consolidate some of the debts. It had been necessary for Sally to appear personally before a commissioner to testify that she approved of the mortgage, since the property had remained in her name in accordance with the marriage agreement. Featherston was able to arrange a mortgage of fifteen thousand dollars. His evenings were spent dining with friends, one of whom was Mrs. William Renwick. Returning home only to attend the annual meeting of the New York Board of Agriculture, he was off again within a week.[25] Although Washington was now his destination, he spent ten days in New York and then went to Philadelphia, accompanied by Mrs. Renwick's son, William. There, Featherston had a grand reunion with other friends. He went with Joseph Hopkinson to call on Count Survilliers (Joseph Bonaparte, the exiled king of Spain) and next day dined with the count and accompanied him to a play. On another night he had dinner with the Hopkinsons, and there he met Senator Langdon Cheves of South Carolina and Daniel Webster.[26]

After a three-day stay at Philadelphia, Featherston continued on to Wilmington, Baltimore, and Washington, accompanied by Renwick, Cheves, and others. The roads were bad, and the coach passengers had to get out and walk at times. Crossing the Susquehannah in a boat, they had to break ice ahead of them as they went. Such delays provided Featherston with an opportunity to discuss with Cheves the possibility of acquiring United States citizenship by the introduction of a bill in Congress. Featherston was very favorably impressed with Baltimore and thought Barnum's Hotel there the best inn he had seen in America.[27]

He thoroughly enjoyed his week in Washington. He had breakfast with Van Rensselaer and listened to debates in Congress. Van

Rensselaer and Cheves introduced him to many important people. He wrote his mother that he attended several social gatherings, including a Presidential Drawing Room where President Monroe showed him "marked attention." He enjoyed most a party at the home of Senator James Brown, a native of Virginia but now of New Orleans, whose wife was one of Henry Clay's sisters. Monroe had just appointed Brown ambassador to France. Featherston was impressed by Clay, with whom he had corresponded as secretary of the Board of Agriculture. He called on the secretary of state, John Quincy Adams, who invited him to a party at his home, which Featherston found gay but not fashionable. Since the objective of this trip was to lobby for a protective tariff for farm products, he lost no opportunity to express his views to people of influence. He found far more occasions to do so than he had anticipated and noted in his journal that he was very pleased by the "vigorous tone of thinking and talking that prevails here." On his return trip he again lingered for several days at both Philadelphia and New York, although admitting some concern about having left his wife so long with both children and farm responsibilities.[28]

Sally had kept everything under control at home. The weather was bitterly cold, and there was heavy snow when Featherston returned. He was soon very much involved in helping his farm workers care for the lambs that were arriving daily. In May, Sally left him in charge of the two younger children, James and Georgiana, while she, her sister Kitty, and daughter Ann, traveled to Philadelphia. They did not arrive home until 13 June, by which time Featherston was "exceedingly put out."[29]

Featherston was very pleased by the progress the children were making under a tutor and well he might have been. His six-year-old daughter, Georgiana, had already completed the first six books of Vergil's *Aeneid* and was starting to read Greek. With James's education in mind, Featherston made a trip to the United States Military Academy at West Point, where he was received with great cordiality. On a trip to Albany, he dined with Joel R. Poinsett and Colonel Drayton of South Carolina. He enjoyed their company so much that he decided southern gentlemen, on the whole, were quite superior to northerners. His kindly feeling was reinforced when Poinsett visited Featherston Park and complimented its beauty.[30]

In mid-September, Featherston was faced with a new and serious problem. He received word that his friend and attorney, John Wells, had died suddenly. The death of a friend was a blow, but this death was even more devastating since Wells had been handling Featherston's defense in a suit brought against him in the New York Chancery Court by merchants he had represented in Europe twenty years previously. They had instituted the suit in 1821, but it was just now coming to trial. The merchants contended that Featherston had entered into an agreement with them in 1801, under which they were to ship goods to Leghorn. Featherston and the three men would each provide one-fourth of the cost. Since Featherston had no funds, the others had made up his fourth. The goods had been shipped to Philip Jaume & Company of Leghorn on Featherston's recommendation. Jaume had sold the goods and remitted money until he went bankrupt.[31]

The full details of the matter are not entirely clear, but Featherston's comments about it in letters shed some light. In a long letter to one of the merchants he wrote that "the only commercial connection we ever had together (I allude to the marbles) was proposed by yourselves, and that I never had anything to do, directly or indirectly, with the matter now in question; and if it had fulfilled your most sanguine Expectations I should never have been in the least benefitted by it, for I was in no manner concerned in the interest which Mr. Jaume had in the cargo. It is true that I was the dupe, with many others, of his affairs, and innocently misled you." He referred to his youth at the time and added that they were mistaken if they thought him prosperous. Every bit of land he owned was mortgaged, and New York laws protected his wife's property. When he mentioned the suit to his mother, he wrote, "Do not fear the result. They cannot recover anything from me." In spite of his apparent optimism, it was a deep source of worry for almost two years. Wells had advised the appointment of commissioners in England and at Leghorn to take statements from witnesses. This had been done and had involved a great deal of time-consuming correspondence, delay, and expense.[32]

When Featherston reached New York in mid-September he arranged for Peter Jay to represent him. He knew that Wells had been preparing a meticulous defense against the suit and had felt confident of winning it. Now he felt much less certain. He still believed that he did not owe a cent to the merchants but thought that it might be wise to compromise. He asked Jay to deny that he owed $8,773 and to attempt to settle for $2,030, which Jay was able to do. Featherston was relieved to see the matter ended but bitter about the treatment he had received from people he had once thought to be his good friends.[33]

While the state legislature was in session, Featherston spent much of his time in Albany. He fought the partition of Duanesburg into two parts, contending that it would leave no memorial to Judge Duane. He opposed a movement, led by Jesse Buel, to repeal the agricultural improvement laws that had created the Board of Agriculture. He suspected that Buel wanted to suppress the board in order to promote his own pet project, an agricultural school. Featherston never lost sight of his primary objective, to obtain a protective tariff for wool, and spent hours with state lawmakers, seeking their support with members of Congress. He approached several congressmen directly to urge the introduction of a tariff bill. James Wadsworth declined, but Henry Clay and others supported the idea. A bill was introduced and passed the House in April 1824.[34]

Clay was to be one of the candidates in the 1824 presidential election. For all practical purposes there had been only one party, the Republican party, since 1812. It had been completely dominated by what had come to be known as the Virginia Dynasty. This time, however, other sections of the country were rebelling; they were vigorously supporting candidates of their own in opposition to the heir apparent, William H. Crawford of Georgia. His opposition now included such prominent candidates as John Caldwell Calhoun of South Carolina, Andrew Jackson of Tennessee, and John Quincy Adams of Massachusetts, as well as Clay.

Though Featherston had spent only limited time with Clay in Washington, he became an ardent supporter. Very early in discussions of the forthcoming election, Featherston had informed Martin Van Buren, leader of Crawford supporters in the New York legislature, that in a contest between Crawford and Clay he could only support Clay and would not change. As an English citizen, Featherston was not able to vote, but he worked energetically on Clay's behalf. He wrote frequently during the year, advising Clay of the political situation in New York state. In May, he thanked Clay for sending him a copy of a speech he had made in support of the tariff and commented on the speech of another: "I certainly admire my friend Mr. Webster, as all men must who have had the opportunities of judging the vigor of his capacious mind, but his speech is a plea for his Boston Constituents, he is against it because of them." In late May, Clay wrote to congratulate Featherston on the final passage of the tariff bill.[35]

By mid-November, Featherston was in Albany campaigning hard for Clay throughout late maneuvering in the legislature. He reported from there to Cheves that the voting had gone as he expected: "Not one Crawford Elector is elected. Seven Clay men who were on the Crawford Ticket are elected, and twenty-five Electors for Mr. Adams—four more remain to be elected." His count was only approximately correct. The final official tally gave twenty-six electors to Adams, five to Crawford, four to Clay and one to Jackson. Much of Clay's opposition in New York had been led by Van Buren, as Featherston had predicted. Clay was unable to account for it, writing Featherston that Van Buren had repeatedly told him and his friends that he would be equally satisfied with Clay or Crawford. When Van Buren prepared to return to Washington, his campaign for Crawford a shambles, Featherston told him that he would be "shot to pieces" as soon as he arrived there. He sent Van Rensselaer a suitable epitaph to erect over the fragments:

> Here, by some gross mismanagement of Fate
> Lies one, in management esteemed too great.
> He had a knack to turn him every way
> But death alone could turn him unto Clay.[36]

Van Rensselaer wrote Featherston that he expected Clay to give his support to Jackson, but instead he supported Adams. As many had predicted, the election was thrown into the House where Van

Rensselaer cast the deciding vote that gave the election to Adams. The latter made Clay his secretary of state. Featherston also preferred Adams to Jackson, believing that a man "should have something more in his favour than a '*veni, vidi, vici,*' and being called 'Old Hickory' to be elected President." When the election of Adams had been announced, Professor James Renwick wrote Featherston that he feared the Englishman would now "get no foreign embassy." The failure of Clay's election left Featherston "indifferent to all publick matters."[37]

In spite of his remark, there was one matter in which Featherston retained a keen personal interest. He was disappointed when Governor De Witt Clinton in his message to the legislature in January 1826 mentioned almost everything except railroads. The latter were very much on Featherston's mind. He was having Elisha Williams prepare a bill that would bring the subject before the legislature. If they should pass it, he wrote Van Rensselaer, it would be "a great Event."[38]

Featherston's interest in railroads was not new. As early as 1811, he had been thinking about George Stephenson's invention of the steam locomotive. "In that year," writes George Roberts, "Chancellor [Robert R.] Livingston, who was associated with Robert Fulton in the invention of the steamboat, received a letter from some 'wild hair-brained [*sic*] individual,' asking his opinion of the practicality of railroads. After giving the matter due consideration, the worthy Chancellor replied that besides being too dangerous, it would be impossible to build rails that would sustain so heavy a weight as you propose moving at the rate of four miles an hour on wheels." The "wild hair-brained individual" was Featherston. He also wrote at least one article on the subject, which produced more ridicule than support.[39]

In 1820 Lewis Jenkins of Canandaigua, New York, congratulated Featherston upon his agricultural accomplishments and added that "the great work you have now undertaken, the new *Rail Way,* will be a lasting benefit." Just what Jenkins had read or been told is not clear but what Featherston wanted to propose to the legislature in 1825 is well documented. He wanted to construct a railroad sixteen miles long, between the Mohawk and Hudson rivers, connecting Schenectady with Albany. He had made a long and detailed study of the subject, obtaining much of the information available about railroads constructed in England. These were all short roads connecting mines and quarries with canals or the sea, the trains being drawn by horses or mules. One drawn by a steam locomotive was expected to be in operation in 1825. Featherston prepared a detailed cost estimate of the road he proposed and a comparison with canal transportation to show the time and money that could be saved by such a railroad and the probable return on the investment required. He had persuaded Van Rensselaer to support his proposal and to serve as one of the three commissioners should a charter be granted.[40]

Although Featherston had indicated to Van Rensselaer that he was having a bill prepared, he did not actually present it to the legislature in 1825. Sally became very ill in January, and Featherston was kept close to home. When he had some time for thought, he began considering another transport proposal. He had the idea of operating steam-propelled boats on the Hudson between Albany and New York to provide commodious accommodations for "genteel people." Each would have a cabin seventy feet long with large square windows and furnished with comfortable chairs and tables. For those who wished to view the scenery from outside there would be a sheltered piazza on deck. If such a ship, having room for 140 passengers, could average 100, at a net profit of four dollars per passenger, Featherston estimated it would pay its initial cost in one year.[41]

All thoughts of such things as railroads and steamboats gave way to continuing worry over his family's health. As Sally showed signs of slight improvement, the children came down with scarlet fever. Ann and Georgiana died within two weeks of each other in March, and James continued seriously ill. The distress of Featherston and Sally over the loss of both daughters and their concern over James made all other matters unimportant. Featherston, who had had to carry much of the burden of nursing, was also desperately worried about the effects of this emotional devastation on Sally, who was still very sick. He feared for her life and sanity. It was not until early May that he dared to take her and James to a small house near the Battery in New York. As they slowly recuperated, Featherston tried to make plans for the future. Since returning to Duanesburg, he felt, would be torture for all of them, he wanted to go to England to live, but he would have to arrange to pay all or most of their debts before leaving, for he doubted that they would return. He decided to try to sell all their property except the home estate, which he thought to advertise in England.[42]

The only property from which he had a chance of raising the amount of money he would need was in New York City. He and others petitioned the city council to open Twentieth Street between Bloomingdale Road and Third Avenue so their land might be developed. A more immediate source of money appeared to be the Gramercy property, jointly owned by all of James Duane's heirs. Featherston wrote to each of them, seeking approval of a sale. James, Jr., agreed, but somewhat reluctantly. He admitted that it was not his business to advise Featherston and his sister, but he thought they would be very unwise to sacrifice their estate to such a move. If they were determined to leave America, he would want to be paid the approximately three thousand dollars they owed him and would expect Featherston to pay the note at the Mohawk Bank that James had endorsed. Then all thought of the sale of the Gramercy property had to be abandoned when General North wrote that his children would not agree to it. Having no other place to turn for the amount of money he would require, Featherston was forced to postpone any thought of leaving. It was not until November that he and Sally could face returning to Duanesburg.[43]

While still in New York, Featherston had noticed some interesting landscapes of the Hudson River displayed in a shop and met the artist, Thomas Cole, a young Englishman who had come to the United States with his family in 1821. Featherston suggested that Cole spend some time painting views of Featherston Park and its surroundings, for he wanted to have a few pictures of his home to show friends in England. He would pay twenty to thirty dollars for each painting, and of course, the artist would have no living expenses. Cole was still struggling to establish himself. He had sold but four pictures that summer, none for more than twenty-five dollars and one for considerably less. He was, therefore, very interested in the proposition. After the Featherstonhaughs returned home in November, they made definite arrangements for Cole's visit around 1 January.[44]

Featherston, to his regret, saw little of Cole during his stay, for he was forced to spend much of January and February in Albany on business. In mid-January he wrote Van Rensselaer that he was delighted with the "fine things" the artist had already painted. Van Rensselaer, too, was impressed and asked Featherston to select a painting for him.[45] Cole returned to New York in March to carry out two commissions, taking two of Featherston's paintings, *Schoharie Views,* with him to complete when he finished his other work. Cole had left three in Duanesburg, one of which was to be sent to the governor in chief of Canada, George Ramsay, earl of Dalhousie. The other two Featherston would send down to New York in time for an exhibition. Cole's landscapes were handsome. There were, according to Noble, "the mountain summits, unmistakably American, with their infinity of tree-tops, a beautiful management of light, striking forms of trees and rocks in the foreground, and a certain lucid darkness in the waters below."[46]

On 28 December 1825 Featherston inserted a notice in the *Schenectady Cabinet* that an application would be made to the legislature for an act to incorporate the Mohawk and Hudson Rail Road Company for construction of a railroad between the Mohawk and Hudson rivers, with capital of three hundred thousand dollars, to be increased to five hundred thousand dollars if necessary. At that time an act of the legislature was required for incorporation. Featherston and Van Rensselaer presented their petition in mid-February. At first it was considered a very popular undertaking, and even the canal commissioner approved. When the bill Featherston had composed came up for discussion early in March, however, criticism emerged. One Schenectady man ridiculed the idea. "Did you ever hear of such a wild idea?" he asked. "Why, the cars couldn't be made to go fast enough between here and Albany to keep the mosquitoes from eating the passengers."[47]

The formal opposition, led, as expected, by the Turnpike Company and the Albany Basin Company, surfaced on 10 March. The opponents began by calling the proposal visionary but soon went to the opposite extreme, accusing Featherston and his fellow commissioner of "a deep laid plan to make an enormous Fortune." Their arguments gained little support from other members of the legislature, who had the highest regard for Van Rensselaer and were disinclined to question Featherston's motives in view of his past exertions for the public good. Seeing that they would not be able to block the proposal, the opponents then sought to require that the road be constructed along a particular line, to be specified. Featherston countered this tactic by saying that the commissioners were indifferent to the precise location of the road but advising that this be determined by competent engineers. He no longer worried about passage of the bill but feared he would have to accept a provision under which the railroad would be turned over to the state if it began to make money.[48]

Meanwhile, a Mr. Lush, representing the Turnpike Company, recognizing that they were losing their fight in the legislature, appealed directly to Van Rensselaer. He contended that the city would be ruined and that trade would all be moved to land owned by Van Rensselaer near the proposed terminal. Van Rensselaer beat a surprisingly hasty retreat, offering to withdraw his name from the bill if necessary and appealing to Featherston to help him out of his difficulty. Featherston was startled but thought too highly of his friend to be willing to cause him embarrassment. Although the majority of the prominent citizens of Albany were supporting the bill, Featherston swallowed his pride and went to call on Lush, telling him that he would make any sacrifice to avoid unpleasantness for Van Rensselaer. Much to his astonishment, he found Lush very agreeable, and they were able to work out a mutually acceptable compromise. Lush then promised to support the bill, and Van Rensselaer did not withdraw his name.[49]

Featherston managed to shepherd his bill through the legislature to ultimate passage on 29 March 1826 by a vote of ninety-nine to eight. The bill became law on 17 April, allowing Featherston, Van Rensselaer, and their associates to incorporate. It gave them "an Exclusive privilege" for fifty years. As Featherston had feared, the bill had acquired seventeen or more amendments along the way. Most were acceptable to him, but if numbers fifteen and seventeen could not be removed by a subsequent legislature, they would certainly kill the project. The fifteenth amendment provided that the stockholders and directors be personally liable for all debts contracted by the corporation or its agents and permitted them to be sued. The seventeenth allowed the state to take over the railroad at any time within five years of its completion, reimbursing the company for its construction expenses with interest, less the amount of tolls received. It did not even provide for the deduction of what might be several years of operating expenses. Prospective purchasers of stock would hardly find it attractive to invest in an enterprise that the state would take over if it became profitable.[50]

In spite of the amendments, the corporation began to take shape. Commissioners were Featherston, Van Rensselaer, and Lynde Catlin, cashier and later president of the Merchant Bank in New York City. Featherston would have preferred Charles Wilkes to Catlin but worried about giving the commission too English a character. Catlin could be helpful in selling stock and would not be especially objectionable in other areas. Stock was made available in Albany on 29 June and in New York City early in July. On 27 July five directors were elected, the three commissioners plus Peter Augustus Jay and Andrew Edmiston, an English friend of Featherston's. When the directors met two days later, they appointed Catlin treasurer and Peter Fleming engineer, giving them one-year terms at salaries of fifteen hundred dollars each. Even before the bill had passed, Featherston had approached Fleming, who was examining the navigation of the Hudson River. The directors asked Fleming to go to England immediately to study the "construction and Management of railways" and agreed to pay his expenses up to seven hundred dollars.[51]

When Featherston found it necessary to confer with Van Rensselaer in May 1826, he took his wife and son to Washington, where Congress was still in session. Sally and James visited Mount Vernon and heard the celebrated John Randolph speak in Congress. The little boy was thrilled to meet President Adams and, later, Count Survilliers, who took them all driving through his

Bordentown estate in his "best barouche" and entertained them at dinner. They spent eleven days in New York before returning home and Sally seemed to be helped by the trip.[52]

The previous year Featherston had been ready to return to England permanently and would have done so had he been able to sell sufficient property. Now that he had succeeded in organizing his Mohawk and Hudson Rail Road Company, he still wanted to go to England, but only temporarily. He had not seen his mother for twenty years, and Sally had never met her. Both of them also wanted to see George, who had been in England for five years. Featherston was sure that the development of the railroad would benefit greatly if he joined Fleming in studying railroads. He also wanted to make a firsthand study of British agricultural practices for the New York board.

Last, and by no means least, Featherston was eager to learn all he could about the science of geology, which had been developing abroad during his years in the United States. As Robert Hazen has pointed out, "The science of geology, as we know it today, was largely a European development." America lagged behind. As Featherston later expressed it: "When we cast our reluctant eyes upon the state of geological knowledge in our own country, and observe the total want of combination of talent for the illustration of this great subject; we feel as every ardent naturalist must, depressed in spirit, while we see the rich resources of this extensive country laying dormant upon our hands, and the period deferred, perhaps, beyond our own existence, at which the value of geological knowledge will be properly felt among us." In spite of this gloomy view, it was, as George Daniels has pointed out, in the years following the end of the War of 1812 that "American science got its start. During that period American scientists evolved from a disorganized group of amateurs without common goals or direction into the professional body that they had become by midcentury."[53]

It was the middle of August before Featherston had completed preparations for sailing. A Mr. Cady would run the farm and Andrew Edmiston would take charge of business affairs. Edmiston had returned from England to his home in Cooperstown in late March, bringing letters and packages from George and his grandmother. He agreed to lend Featherston seventy-five hundred dollars, much of which would go to pay a debt. Then another tragedy intervened, and the sailing had to be postponed once more. On 17 August, Edmiston and his nephew Robert were visiting at Featherston Park to receive final instructions from Featherston and his power of attorney. After dinner, Edmiston walked with Robert and James down to the lake while their host talked with a neighbor who had come to the door. Soon afterwards Featherston heard screams from James and ran to the lake. Here he found that Edmiston had dived into the lake to rescue Robert who he thought was drowning. He had managed to save Robert but he himself was drowned.[54]

When Featherston had time to recover from his grief, he realized that he not only had to find someone else to act for him in his absence but would have to act as his friend's executor. Edmiston had left his extensive property in Oswego and Chenango counties to Featherston in trust for a sister in England, and there were many other complications. The railroad board of directors met on 7 September. They appointed a former New York City alderman, Nicholas Fish, to fill Edmiston's place on the board and elected Van Rensselaer president and Featherston vice-president. Thus, it was not until 16 November that the Featherstons embarked on the *Canada* for Liverpool.[55]

Old and New Friends in England

3

Featherston had been worried about Sally's reaction to ocean travel, remembering how little he had enjoyed the crossing when he came over. He was somewhat chagrined to find that she was a far better sailor than he. She was even thrilled by the great speed of the vessel, which alarmed him considerably. The ship maintained full sail, even in the dark of night. Featherston was astonished to have his family comfortably established at the Adelphi Hotel in Liverpool on 4 December. Although all three Featherstons were eager to reach Scarborough, he kept them at Liverpool for several days. There had been little time to improve his wardrobe at New York, and he had preferred to do so in England. He had no desire to appear the unfashionable colonial to his old friends there. As soon as they were well settled at the Adelphi, he hurried out to do some shopping.[1]

While the suits he had ordered were being made, Featherston began his study of railroads. He visited the Steam Engine Manufactory, a flourishing concern already employing seven hundred people, where he learned much that interested him. His most valuable experience, however, came from visits to the offices of the Liverpool and Manchester Railway Company. He was welcomed there with the utmost cordiality, far more than he had anticipated. The director permitted him to study all their plans, drawings, and estimates. Moreover, the company had spent fifty thousand

44

pounds acquiring all known information pertaining to railroad construction, and Featherston was allowed to study any of it he wished. Within two days, he realized that he had already learned enough to enable his own company to avoid many costly mistakes. He had thought himself to be fairly well informed on the subject when he left home, but it was clear that railroads in England had made great strides during the past year from which he would be able to benefit. He collected drawings, models, and information as quickly as he could, making many sketches as well. Fleming arrived for a brief conference, and Featherston was very favorably impressed with what he had accomplished.[2]

There were other things to be done in Liverpool. Featherston exchanged some American gold eagles for English pounds. He and Sally called on Ann's friends the Buchanans to thank them for all their kindness to young George when he had arrived in Liverpool. In spite of its thriving bustle, Featherston found the city an "ill built, dirty, rainy place," where the sun apparently shone only on Sundays. He was delighted to depart for Scarborough. As they traveled he was struck by the lush greenness and perfection of the English countryside. Every pasture had far more grass than any of his own and was capable of supporting five times as many sheep. He wrote General Theodore Sill of his determination to find out the reasons for this verdure before he returned home "like a Bee with my thighs loaded with all sort of things useful to our country."[3]

The great reunion at Scarborough took place on 10 December. Featherston's mother, then seventy-six, had long feared that she might never see him again. Young George, now fifteen, had not seen his parents for five years. All hands were ecstatic and scarcely calmed down before Christmas. Old friends came to see Featherston and to meet his family. He escorted Sally and the boys around the town, greeting acquaintances and visiting boyhood haunts, and spent as much time as he could talking with his mother. When comparative calm permitted, he wrote to friends at home, reporting his railroad observations and urging action to persuade the legislature to repeal the objectionable amendments to the railroad authorization bill.[4]

He had given a great deal of thought to how he should budget his time abroad, but he soon found schedules impossible. He was not sure how long he could stay or how long any of his objectives might take to accomplish. He wanted to see as much as possible of his relatives and friends and to show Sally as many parts of the British Isles as he could and possibly some of the Continent. He wanted to find a school for George and, of course, he wanted to study English agricultural practices, railroading, and geology. He intended to meet as many British and European geologists as possible, for although he was, as one of them expressed it later, "already a good mineralogist," he felt very inadequately informed about recent developments in geology.[5]

Featherston's mother would not tolerate his leaving her before the holidays and did so reluctantly afterward. Early in January, he and Sally left both boys with her and went to Scotland. Fleming was waiting at Glasgow for another conference with Featherston and a meeting with the directors of the railroad there. During this time, Featherston had his first ride on a train. Its twenty-four cars and locomotive weighed one hundred tons, and it was drawn uphill by steam at a speed of eighteen miles an hour. On the return trip Featherston hung on the "knee" of the last car as it gathered velocity downhill and found it "really terrific."[6]

After Fleming's departure, Featherston and Sally spent nearly six weeks in Scotland. Winter was not an ideal time for touring, and stormy weather limited their time in northern Scotland to a few days. The remainder was spent in Edinburgh where they stayed at the Waterloo Hotel and "saw all the Lions of the Day," thanks in great part to Sir John Sinclair, who had long corresponded with Featherston. The two men were immediately congenial. Featherston gratified him by telling him how much United States agriculture was indebted to the British board. Sinclair asked Featherston to put his laudatory comments in writing so that they might be transmitted to other members of the board. Featherston was happy to do so, and thereafter Sir John could not do enough for him and Sally.[7]

Featherston's first direct encounter with a geological controversy that had been raging for forty years came at Edinburgh. In the course of his reading of the *Edinburgh Philosophical Review* at home he had come to entertain "very reverential ideas" of the knowledge and ability of the geologist Robert Jameson, one of its coeditors. He was introduced to Jameson by Sinclair and had the privilege of holding a number of discussions with him. He soon found himself rather disillusioned to learn how rigidly Jameson adhered to the geological views of the great Saxon mineralogist-geologist Abraham Gottlob Werner concerning the origin of the crust of the earth. These views had been under attack by adherents of the opposing view, first clearly expressed by a Scottish physician, farmer and geologist, James Hutton.[8] Featherston later summarized this debate:

When, in 1787 and in 1788, Werner and Hutton published their opinions, the first in his "Kurze Klassification," the second in his "Theory of the Earth," the mineral condition of our planet had been very much attended to, and a vast accumulation of geological facts collected. The important fact, that the crust of the earth was composed of mineral beds superimposed one upon another, in a regular series, and that an equivalent bed, a thousand miles off, was always found in the same relative position with its type, as to the rocks above it and beneath it, had been established and received as the basis of geological knowledge. The departures from this regularity, in the order of succession, which were occasionally observed . . . became so many interesting problems for geological ingenuity to solve, in accordance with physical laws, such as were supposed to have governed the mineral substances during the formation of the crust of the earth. Out of these observed facts, the two celebrated theories of the aqueous and igneous origin of the mineral beds arose.

The world is greatly indebted to Werner for the energetic awakening which his opinions produced, and which were disseminated successfully in Europe by a numerous class of intelligent disciples. . . . bending all his great powers to the propagation of mineral knowledge, and his own particular theories, he announced, in the most oracular manner, the law of the formation of the crust of the planet, with scarce any other basis for his opinion than the limited phenomena about his little den of Freiberg. He taught that all rocks were formed by chemical precipitation from a terraqueous fluid, which at one time formed the whole globe; so that the mountains were caused by deposition, and the oceans, by the retreat of waters that had deposited their minerals.

The theory of Dr. Hutton, supposes the superficial form of the earth to depend upon the expansive force of a central fire, which elevates continents from the bed of the ocean, to be again degraded, and worn down, by the influence of external circumstances; their ruins, carried into the ocean by the agency of rivers, are consolidated by the subterranean heat and superincumbent pressure of water, to be again raised into new continents. It is a theory of eternal degradations and renewals, and presents the earth to us as a pure self-acting machine. This hypothesis comes recommended to the mind by great simplicity of character. It contains an adaptation of causes and effects, that we look in vain for in Werner's chaotic fluid, with its incomprehensible crystallizations and precipitations, effected in the very teeth of physical laws.[9]

Geologists had become polarized as Wernerians or Huttonians. Featherston was returning to England at a time when Huttonian views were becoming more generally accepted, but he would encounter a number of the better-known adherents of both schools. At Edinburgh he found himself in better sympathy with Jameson's coeditor, David Brewster, F.R.S., a physicist, mathematician, and author of many articles on optics, who was also interested in geology. Another man whom Featherston found congenial was Major General Joseph Straton.

In addition to the Hutton–Werner controversy other important developments had occurred in European geology during the early years of the nineteenth century. As Cecil Schneer has written, "At this point in our history . . . geology underwent a profound transformation destined to produce major changes in the geological world view. A new dimension was added to geology by the work of William Smith, Cuvier and Brongniart. . . . It was Smith who observed the similarities of the sequence of the strata of southern England persisting from place to place through changes in the inclination and thickness of the beds, making his identifications positive by cataloguing the fossil contents. . . . At almost the same time, the classification, sequential ordering, and paleontological determination of the Tertiary strata of the Paris Basin were being carried out by Cuvier . . . and Brongniart." Joan Eyles noted that "it has sometimes been suggested that Smith in England and Brongniart and Cuvier in France were pursuing similar paths quite independently." She, however, has found reason to believe that Brongniart should have been aware of Smith's work.[10]

The travelers returned to Scarborough in mid-February to relax a bit and spend some time with the family. They remained there two months, making only short trips. Featherston carried on an extensive correspondence, much of it concerning possible schools for his son. Finding one proved more difficult than he expected. He also gathered all the railroad information he thought necessary and relayed it to Nicholas Fish and others. Featherston had long wanted a painting of Fetherston Castle and now arranged to have one done by Thomas Miles Richardson, who had painted many of the castles along the border between England and Scotland. Featherston had hoped that this painting might be hung at the annual exhibition of the Royal Academy but it was not completed in time.[11]

Soon after his return to Scarborough, Featherston made the acquaintance of a man he had long hoped to meet. In August 1818 he had read in the journal *Port Folio* a review copied from the *Edinburgh Review* of the *Geology of England* by William Smith. Three years earlier, Smith, who in 1795 had begun to use fossils to identify geological strata, had published a map of much of Great Britain, showing the strata. Now Featherston was delighted to learn that Smith was living in Scarborough and had been giving a series of lectures on geology with the assistance of his nephew, John Phillips. Furthermore, Smith had given individual lessons in geology. Few things could have excited Featherston more, and he hastened to meet Smith and arrange for tutoring. As he later wrote, he spent "many a happy day" in the field with "the venerable and amiable man." Smith made extensive use of the famous cliffs at Scarborough in his lectures, pointing out the fossils typical of each of the visible strata. According to Eyles, he later commented that Featherston had "recommended to me to name the beds of this rock by the fossils of which they are characterized and indeed almost entirely composed." Smith undertook this work but quickly decided that he was "incompetent to the task."[12]

Featherston was so interested in his lessons and in all that Smith had told him of other British geologists that he began to weaken in his plan for leaving England in the spring. His mother, eager to persuade him to prolong his visit, offered to sell some bank stock to help him if he would stay, even though he did not plan to remain at Scarborough. She had no difficulty in convincing him. Having decided to postpone their departure, the Featherstonhaughs moved to London in mid-April. Both James and George were sent to Sunbury for tutoring by the Reverend W. G. Fitz-Thomas. Featherston brought with him all the fossil and mineral specimens he had collected at Scarborough and elsewhere. In London he added some 1,750 specimens, purchased for £115 from George Brettingham Sowerby, artist, conchologist, and dealer in shells. These had been collected by James Parkinson, F.G.S.[13]

Soon after coming to London, Featherston called upon Albert Gallatin, then United States minister to Great Britain. They had corresponded previously and may also have met before. Featherston was not surprised to find Gallatin very much interested in the railroad proposal and promised to write to him fully on the subject. Featherston did so at some length later in the summer, emphasizing that the time and cost required to deliver produce to market was of prime importance in comparing various methods of transportation. He then reviewed the problems of canal boats pulled by horses—the delay from crowded canals and burst banks and the ice that made the canals unusable in winter. Unlike canals, railroads can be run in a straight line, often halving the distances covered. Featherston admitted that there were still many problems to be overcome in railroad construction, including the beveling of the wheels and their adjustment to friction, the best form for the rails, and the most practical wagon. Since most of the men working on these questions were primarily surveyors rather than engineers, solutions would take time and experimentation.[14]

Once he was well settled in London, Featherston made the most of his contacts and letters of introduction to enlarge his circle of acquaintances. Among the first of these was Charles Babbage, a mathematician with broad interest in science, including geology, who was then working on designs for mechanical calculators. He was extremely cordial and helpful. To express his appreciation, Featherston presented him with the second and third volumes of the *Memoirs* and promised a copy of the first volume when it was reprinted.[15]

Another new acquaintance, and a very important one for Featherston, was Dr. William Henry Fitton, then president of the Geological Society of London. It was Fitton who had called attention to the importance of Smith's work by a glowing tribute to him in the review Featherston had read in 1818. His house in London, according to Archibald Geikie, "formed a pleasant centre for the geologists of town." A few weeks after his arrival in London, Featherston received a letter from Fitton, expressing his pleasure at having made his acquaintance and thanking him for copies of the *Memoirs*. More important, Featherston was soon attending meetings of the Geological Society and visiting in Fitton's home; at both places he met a number of the more important English geologists.[16]

The Geological Society was relatively young. After its founding in 1807, there had been attempts to make it a branch of the old and prestigious Royal Society of London. The geologists had resisted and finally received a royal charter in 1825. Featherston found the meetings not only impressive but instructive. The secretary, Roderick Impey Murchison, who had succeeded Charles Lyell in 1825, would read a memoir, exhibiting any accompanying geological or topographical illustrations as well as specimens of rocks or fossils. After this, the president would ask for observations on the memoir. Then, Featherston later wrote, "by one or more of the leading members—[the memoir] is attacked and defended, warily but sometimes zealously. The disputants feel all the importance of an acute and vigilant audience; everyone who takes the floor, knows that he is to be marked 'an creta an carbone.' These discussions are warmest between the most cordial friends, and strangers have sometimes thought they were carried on at the expense of friendship—but the members have the wisdom to make the geological society a school of mutual instruction. As men, there is not a band of firmer friends in the world: as geologists, they sometimes take different roads in the pursuit of truth."[17]

The president at that time was the Reverend William Buckland of Oxford University. He had been tutored in his student days there by two friends of William Smith. He became reader in mineralogy in 1813 and later was made canon of Christ Church, Ox-

Roderick Impey Murchison [Courtesy of the Palaeontology Library, British Museum (Natural History)]

ford. His lectures included geology, and he had done extensive fieldwork in Great Britain and on the Continent. In 1822 he published his cavern researches, for which he was awarded the Copley Medal of the Royal Society. He came up from Oxford to London to attend meetings of both societies. Every year, in early June, Buckland took his geology students for a horseback field trip around the hills of the Oxford area. The reputation of his lectures had spread, and his class had been augmented by members of the Geological Society, others who came from a distance for the occasion, and a number of local people. At the Geological Society or perhaps at Fitton's home, Featherston met Buckland and expressed a desire to participate in his famous annual excursion.[18]

On 1 June, Buckland wrote to tell Featherston that the excursion was planned for the following Tuesday. He said that he would be happy to have Featherston attend and hoped that he and Sally would dine with the Bucklands that night. The following day, however, Buckland postponed the excursion until June 14. He had been summoned to the opening of another hyenas' den near Maidstone but hoped to see Featherston the following evening at Dr. Fitton's house. Buckland's earlier studies of the fossil bones found in an ancient hyenas' den in Yorkshire had attracted wide attention.[19]

Among those who went to Oxford for the outing was Roderick Murchison. He had recently become interested in geology and had studied with Smith the previous year. Murchison was a Scot who had made a career of the army before his marriage. His wife, the former Charlotte Hugonin, had persuaded him to resign his commission. They had spent two years on the Continent, and after their return to England, he had devoted himself almost entirely to hunting foxes and pheasants. In time, he became bored and permitted his friend, Sir Humphry Davy, to persuade him to come to London to study chemistry. He had also attended meetings of the Geological Society and had immediately become a dedicated student of geology. Although younger than Featherston, Murchison quickly found that they greatly enjoyed each other's company.[20]

It was about noon when nearly a hundred "noblemen and gentlemen" on horseback followed Buckland onto the London Road.

William Buckland [Courtesy of the Palaeontology Library, British Museum (Natural History)]

For several hours they visited gravel pits, swampy areas, and other interesting geological formations on which Buckland lectured.[21] During the course of a very pleasant evening at the Bucklands' house, the discussion turned to the problems being encountered in the construction of the Thames Tunnel between Wapping and Rotherhithe, a project of much interest to scientists and the general public. The river had broken through the tunnel, and Marc Isambard Brunel, the engineer, and his son, Isambard Kingdom, were attempting to repair it and expel the water. Someone suggested that geologists would seem the proper people to offer advice and proposed that a group of them should visit the tunnel to see if they could offer any helpful suggestions. Featherston and Murchison were among those who volunteered to take part. Both later wrote accounts of what took place. They agreed that a third party had been Charles Lucien Bonaparte, Napoleon's nephew, but their reports differ as to the identity of the fourth member of the group. Murchison wrote:

> The first operation we underwent (one which I never repeated) was to go down in a diving-bell upon the cavity by which the Thames had broken in. Buckland and Featherstonhaugh, having been the first to volunteer, came up with such red faces and such staring eyes, that I confess I felt no great inclination to follow their example, particularly as Charles Bonaparte was most anxious to avoid the dilemma, excusing himself by saying that his family was very short-necked and subject to apoplexy, etc.; but it would not do to show the white feather; I got in, and induced him to follow me. The effect was, as I expected, most oppressive, and then on the bottom what did we see but dirty gravel and mud, from which I brought up a fragment of one of Hunt's blacking bottles. . . .
>
> The first folly was, however, quite overpowered by the next. We went down the shaft on the south bank, and got, with young Brunel, into a punt, which he was to steer into the tunnel till we reached the repairing shield. About eleven feet of water were still in the tunnel, leaving just enough space above our heads for Brunel to stand up and claw the ceiling and sides to impel us. As we were proceeding he called out "Now gentlemen, if by accident there should be a rush of water, I shall turn the punt over and prevent you being jammed against the roof, and we shall then all be carried out and up the shaft!" On this C. Bonaparte remarked "But I cannot swim!" and just as he said the words, Brunel, swinging carelessly from right to left, fell overboard, and out went the candles, with which

he was lighting the place. Taking this for the *sauve qui peut,* fat C. B., then the very image of Napoleon at St. Helena, was about to roll after him, when I held him fast, and, by the glimmering of light from the

Adam Sedgwick [Courtesy of the Palaeontology Library, British Museum (Natural History)]

entrance, we found young Brunel, who swam like a fish, coming up on the other side of the punt, and soon got him on board. We of course called out for an immediate retreat, for really there could not be a more foolhardy and ridiculous risk of our lives, inasmuch as it was just the moment of trial as to whether the Thames would make a further inroad or not.[22]

They might well have been nervous. In the sixteen years required to complete the tunnel, there would be many breaks and seven men would drown. Inasmuch as Featherston wrote his account of the adventure in a letter to Buckland, however, it is obvious that the fourth member of the party was not the Oxford professor. Featherston identified him as the Reverend Adam Sedgwick, another of England's more prominent geologists. Sedgwick was Woodwardian Professor of Geology at Cambridge University, an able field geologist, and an active member of the Geological Society of London. Featherston was off to a very good start with his plan for meeting the leading English geologists and learning as much as he could from them.

Soon after returning to London he met an equally interesting man, but an American. On 22 June he accompanied Charles Bonaparte, the naturalist Nicholas Aylward Vigors, and the British Museum mineralogist John George Children on a visit to John James Audubon, whose "portfolios were opened before this set of learned men." Bonaparte, an able ornithologist, had been one of those at Philadelphia who encouraged Audubon when he had met a cool reception there in 1824.[23]

In July, Buckland extended an invitation to Featherston and General Straton to accompany him to his new hyena cave. His invitation was eagerly accepted and the three men traveled by stage to Maidstone, where they apparently remained a week. While there they paid an unexpected call on another well-known geologist, Dr. Gideon Algernon Mantell, at his home at Lewes. They arrived at his house at five o'clock in the afternoon and were so fascinated by their host's collections that they did not leave until two o'clock in the morning. Mantell had long been collecting fossils from the chalk around Lewes and the Weald of Sussex. His first paper on the subject had been published in the *Transactions* of

Gideon Mantell [Courtesy of the Palaeontology Library, British Museum (Natural History)]

the Linnean Society of London in 1814, and he had published many since. Featherston wrote to Mantell a few days later, expressing his pleasure at having made his acquaintance and his great admiration for Mantell's accomplishments. He told him that his writing was well known and respected in America, where there was a great field for similar pursuits. All that was needed were specimens to illustrate Mantell's work, and these Featherston hoped to take home with him. Some of Parkinson's specimens were applicable. Featherston had visited the Cuckfield Quarries, hoping to collect more, but had been disappointed, finding very few. Mantell had offered to give Featherston some of his duplicates and the latter hoped that he might be able to reciprocate. He was particularly interested in the chalk and its substrata, for such formations had not yet been found in the United States. He asked Mantell if he might purchase copies of his books for a friend and whether he could do anything for the doctor on his upcoming trip to Paris. Mantell replied promptly, sending the books and welcoming a correspondence with Featherston, promising to send the duplicate specimens in a few days.[24]

Featherston employed the naturalist Henry Rowe Stutchbury to help catalogue and pack his mineral specimens and fossils. There were over four thousand of them, and Featherston thought they would finish within a week. Stutchbury's brother, Samuel, had just returned from New Holland and the Polynesias with a collection of shells and corals, which were to be sold by Sowerby. Featherston was not ordinarily a shell collector but felt the need of some present-day analogues to help illustrate his fossils, which were often imperfect. He offered to make purchases for Mantell and Buckland at the sale. Buckland accepted the offer and indicated the items that interested him on the catalogue his friend had sent. Welcoming Featherston's offer to serve him in Paris, he sent a package to deliver to Alexandre Brongniart, French geologist, mineralogist, and zoologist, hoping that Brongniart might give Featherston a book to bring back for him. Mantell had consulted Buckland as to how he might safely send eleven of his best fossil fishes to Georges C. L. D. Cuvier, French paleontologist. Buckland thought that they could arrive without injury if sent by water and if Cuvier could arrange with French customs officials that the boxes not be opened until they reached the Jardin du Roi at Paris. Buckland wanted Featherston to discuss such exchanges with Cuvier and learn from him how the boxes must be marked when shipped.[25]

At Sowerby's sale Featherston purchased corals and shells for

Lava figure of female deity named Aroonoona, from Raivavai, Austral Islands, Polynesia, presented by Featherstonhaugh to the Ashmolean Museum, Oxford [Courtesy of the Pitt Rivers Museum where it is now deposited]

Buckland and a number of items for himself. He soon had second thoughts about one of his purchases, a Polynesian idol from Riavai. The statue, carved from lava, depicted Aroonoona, a Tiki, or god, once believed to have great power but deposed when Christianity was introduced to the island. The local king had given it to Stutchbury. Over three feet tall, the idol was rather large to ship to New York and was, in any case, better suited to a museum. Featherston sought Buckland's advice about whether to give it to the British Museum or the Ashmolean Museum at Oxford. Buckland urged him to send the piece to the Ashmolean, since the British Museum would have many more chances of acquiring others. Buckland himself accepted happily for Oxford and sent instructions for packing and shipping.[26]

Sometime before the middle of August, Featherston reached Paris; Sally had left for Naples. It was not until 19 August that he found time to write to Mantell. Featherston had found the savants so busy with their own affairs and with politics that it was not an easy matter to get even a conversation with them at first. Fortunately, he found that they mellowed on further acquaintance, perhaps because he spoke their language. When he was able to share their leisure hours, he found them very obliging men. He had supped with Baron Cuvier the previous day and spent the evening with him. That morning he had visited with Alexandre Brongniart and his son Adolphe. He had politely reproached all of them for their neglect of Mantell and told them that unless they did him justice, he might block all "future monsters" from leaving Tilgate Forest. To this, Cuvier had hastily replied "Ne doit pas être." The senior Brongniart, whom Featherston found charming, admitted that Mantell's last two letters were among the two hundred unanswered ones on his desk. He was very apologetic but had been overwhelmed by multitudious affairs. Cuvier professed to be astonished that Mantell had not heard from him but refrained from actually saying that he had written. The younger Brongniart did produce a letter that had earlier been written to Mantell but had been waiting for someone like Featherston, going to Great Britain, who would deliver it.[27]

Cuvier agreed with Buckland that the safest way for Mantell to send his fossil fishes would be by water, and he gave Featherston instructions as to how they should be marked. Featherston cheerfully told Mantell that he might reasonably expect to have his fossils returned in three or four years—the usual time for those borrowed in Paris. He did not neglect other missions he had promised to perform for Mantell. He purchased a set of Byron's works for him and tried to obtain the casts that Mantell wanted, though he could not promise to succeed. Before leaving London, he had made arrangements that he hoped would provide Mantell with an iguana. Now he found that several had been brought there recently but had died. Their bodies, which would have provided Mantell with skeletons, had unfortunately been thrown away.[28]

Ambassador Brown gave a dinner in Featherston's honor and included several scientists, but Featherston did not limit his activities to social affairs. He began studying Brongniart and Cuvier's *Essai sur la géographie minéralogique des environs de Paris,* published in 1811 "together," wrote Eyles, "with a memoir in which the use of fossils in identifying the different strata was emphasized." They had also published brief accounts of their work in 1808. Featherston, having studied with Smith, was, of course, interested in the technique of using fossils to identify strata, which Smith had been employing since 1795. Unfortunately, no comment by him on the subject has survived.[29]

By early September, Featherston was back in England and wrote to Buckland from Brighton, where he delivered his letters and purchases to Mantell. Buckland hastily replied, urging Featherston to come to Oxford on Monday morning. George Bellas Greenough and Henry Warburton, founding members of the Geological Society, would be there to discuss Italian geology before Greenough's impending departure for that country. Buckland also mentioned the latest curiosity, fossil footprints found in the new red sandstone in southern Scotland. He was certain that they had been made by quadrupeds and thus, obviously, reptiles. By way of testing this hypothesis, he had made live crocodiles and tortoises "gallop" over some soft dry sand and, on the basis of these modern footprints, had decided that the fossil ones were made by tortoises. Exactly how he had made this test is not known, but it is

probable that Featherston accepted his invitation. He seems to
have been in London during most of September but was planning
another trip, this one to study geological formations along the
coast between Portsmouth and Land's End while Sally was away.
Buckland was planning a trip to Devon to introduce his wife to old
friends. He hoped that he and Featherston would meet there, although his day-to-day locations would be as difficult to predict as
Featherston's. He advised his friend to put himself under the guidance of Mary Anning at Lyme and "the Red Man McEnery" at
Torquay, the only person who might be able to supply Featherston
with a series of bones from hyena caves.[30]

Murchison wrote from Scotland on 6 October at great length,
thanking Featherston for his most recent "amusing and agreeable
letter," which had reached him at Edinburgh. His own was equally
entertaining. He gave a general account of observations he and
Sedgwick had made in Scotland, where they had found "every
branch of geology in a state of somnolency." Having received
from Featherston an account of the reptilian footprints, casts of
which were displayed by Buckland, they went to Rothwell to visit
Dr. Duncan, who had sent them. Murchison and Sedgwick had
been skeptical before their visit and were no less so afterward but
asked Featherston not to tell Buckland that they were "unbe-
lievers." Workmen at the quarry assured them that "not only turtles but . . . *Lions, Tigers, Crocodiles and Squirrels*" had left their
footprints in the sandstone. "Sedgwick found one so original that,
as our work was done on a Sunday morning, he was bound to
christen it the devil's hoof & explain to the pious sawneys that we
intended to shoe the arch fiend to prevent further mischief and
scratching—Conceive mon cher all these wonderful animals crawl-
ing and romping upon very incoherent red sandstone [sloped] at
38°!" Featherston was equally amused and replied, "Oh my poor
dear Turtle footsteps on New Red—what a fine race they must
have had up a plane at 38°! And oh my still dearer Buckland who
has given in his adhesion in writing to them. I shall observe your
caution, but my affection for him is so great that I hope you will
write him a note 'Post Office, Plymouth' to stop the matter where
it is." In spite of his unbelief, Murchison had collected many sam-

ples of rock containing the supposed footprints and had cause to regret doing so. "Curse the trotters and petit toes," he wrote, "for in loading my pormanteau with them, I have broken an invaluable bottle of strong *water* 25 years old."[31]

In the course of their travels Featherston and Buckland were able to join forces at Sir Thomas Ackland's house, from which Buckland dragged Featherston "through all of the morasses and caves in Devonshire, during eight days of rain," he wrote Murchison. For three days they had "kept company with nothing but bones in the Torquay Cave, disputing with the good natured priest McEnery about two diluviums he makes out." Featherston was not complaining, for he had been able to collect "a complete series of Bones of nine animals: Bear, Rhinoceros, Tiger, Wolf, Stag, Fox, Hyena, Deer, Elephant!!! Most *charmingly* gnawed as Buckland says." Murchison would find him "particularly learned in Cave Bones when we meet, of which I give you due notice and therefore when you charge me with any particular prancer you may happen to ride at this moment, Expect me in the Lists upon Ursus curtidens, armed with the Femur of an antediluvian Rhinoceros." Murchison had joked about Charles Lyell's method for determining the age of fossil bones: he had made Sedgwick and Murchison test their "adhesiveness to the tongue." Featherston, who had met Lyell, replied: "And as to adhesiveness, know that we allow a few privileged recent Bones to have lost their gelatin— but *all* our Bones are in that situation, which is not the Case with the wretched things produced since the Deluge. What do you think of a man's riding from Torquay to London with the Tibia of a Bear sticking to his Tongue all the way! Will Lyell's Bones do that? I remember Lyell and his two Diluviums!!!" Buckland's cave discoveries, important though they were, inspired a great deal of humor among his friends and in the press.[32]

Before returning to London, Featherston had traveled all the way to Land's End. At St. Michael's Mount, that "precious stone set in the silver sea," as Featherston later wrote of it, the sheriff of Cornwall, Sir John St. Aubyn, M.P., F.R.S., had made him, he wrote Murchison, "*entire* and sole master of the castle whilst in the neighborhood." St. Aubyn was repaying the kindness shown his

Mary Anning [Courtesy of the Palaeontology Library, British Museum (Natural History)]

son in New York. Featherston had written letters of introduction for the young St. Aubyn to Clay, Van Rensselaer, and Count Survilliers. This ancient castle, located on a steep, rocky island that rises abruptly from the sea a short distance offshore near Penzance, had belonged to the St. Aubyn family since 1659. Sir John, a keen mineralogist himself, gave Featherston permission to collect. He found the island a fascinating place and was able to add some interesting specimens to his own collection. He discovered that on the "sides of some masses of granite that had been separated from the rock for a great period of time, but which had never evidently been the wall of a fissure or vein . . . amidst a profusion of small crystals of quartz, several hundreds of small white topazes were apparently forming. . . . The rocks there contain very curious minerals, but they are all contained, as the fine blue crystals of apatite are, in small veins. The topazes, on the contrary, were spread indiscriminately over the surface of immense fragments of granite, anciently separated from the mountain mass."33

Featherston spent a delightful Sunday morning with that "very clever funny Creature," Mary Anning, at Lyme. She was a carpenter's daughter, who as a child had enjoyed collecting fossils with her father on the cliffs there. These they displayed and sold at a curiosity table. After his death in 1810, she continued to collect and sell the fossils to help her mother. Accompanied by her small dog, which guarded her finds, she spent many hours searching the cliffs. When she discovered the skeleton of a creature so huge she had to hire men to help extract it, she called it a crocodile. It was a sensation in Lyme, and everyone urged each other to "come and see what Mary Anning has found." A Mr. Henley bought the skeleton for twenty-three pounds, and it was eventually acquired by the British Museum. The scientific world was startled by her discovery, for it was a previously unknown fossil skeleton. After much study by Buckland, Cuvier, and others, Cuvier identified it as an *Ichthyosaurus.*34

Since Sally was still in Naples when Featherston returned to London in late October, he accepted the Murchisons' invitation to visit them at Petersfield. Murchison had promised to arrange for Featherston to visit his neighbor Sir Henry Fetherstonhaugh, sec-

Uppark [Courtesy of The National Trust Photographic Library]

ond baronet of Uppark. Despite the variation in the spelling of their names, Featherston was convinced that he and Sir Harry were related. The latter was the only son of Sir Matthew Fetherstonhaugh of Northumberland, who had inherited a large fortune in 1746 from a kinsman, Sir Henry Fetherstonhaugh. Uppark stands in the high Sussex hills, from which the land slopes gently across the South Downs toward the Solent. From the upper part of the house it is possible to catch glimpses of the sea twenty miles away.[35]

Sir Harry had attended University College, Oxford, and had been twenty when his father died and he inherited the estate. He had quickly acquired a reputation as a sport. He loved hunting and horse racing and rode his own horses at Newmarket, Goodwood, and elsewhere. He lavishly entertained his sporting friends, among whom was the Prince Regent. In short, according to the *Craftsman,* Uppark became "the Rendezvous of all that is gay and fashionable in the country." Sir Harry served as MP for Plymouth from 1782 to 1796. He had remained unmarried until he was past seventy. Then, in 1825 he shocked his friends by marrying Mary Ann Bullock, his head dairymaid. The old man sent her to Paris to be educated. The Murchisons took Featherston to meet Sir Harry, and both enjoyed the visit.[36]

Not long after his return to London, Featherston made a hurried trip to Norwich. He had intended to visit his father's grave while he was in England, and Buckland had urged him to go to Norwich to meet Richard Cowling Taylor, whose paper on the geology of East Norfolk had just been published. Featherston visited his father's grave and copied the inscription, went to see Taylor, and then found himself with a little time to kill before returning to London. Someone had mentioned to him some curious discoveries made by well diggers on Heigham Hill several years previously, so he went there to see for himself. The workmen had suddenly sunk into a deep hole, or vault, which led into a series of galleries eight feet high and from two to five feet wide, extending sixteen hundred feet. After careful study, Featherston concluded that the galleries had been made to extract the flints that had been extensively used in the construction of the ancient buildings and walls of the city. The miners had removed the nodules of flint, leaving the chalk. The entrance to these tunnels had become covered over and forgotten, and current residents were unaware of their existence. When the original entrance was again opened, the name of a workman and the date 1571 were found on an inside wall. Featherston reported his observations in a letter to Dr. Fitton.[37]

After they parted and Featherston returned to London, Buckland had continued his travels and performed some good offices for his friend. At Lyme and Charmouth he purchased a number of fossils for him and reported that Mary Anning was extracting a large mass of pentacrinite for Featherston, providing she did not break her neck in the process. Buckland asked the lord bishop of Bath and Wells to send Featherston a series from the Banwell Cave for his American collection. The bishop promised to do so, but Buckland thought it advisable for Featherston to write, expressing his appreciation of the bishop's good intentions and stressing that the bones were intended to promote the cause of transatlantic science. He added that the bishop might send a more impressive collection should Featherston chance to be acquainted with the bishop's brother, Thomas Law, "a half crazy man," reputed to have made a fortune in India and to have spent much of it in Washington where he now lived. Featherston and Sally had indeed known the brother as early as 1810.[38]

Sally was seriously ill when she returned from Naples at last. She was anxious to go on to New York as soon as possible. Dr. Charles Bell attended her in London but could do little for her. Featherston hastily took passage for the family on the *Napoleon,* sailing from Liverpool on 24 November.[39]

Tragedy and Disillusionment

4

The Featherstonhaughs reached New York on 9 January. The trip home had taken twice as long as the crossing to England and had been a frightening experience for all of them. Featherston was a poor sailor at best, and Sally had been seriously ill before leaving London. They spent ten days at the Park Place House in New York to give her time to regain her strength, but New York doctors, like Dr. Bell in England, held out little hope for her recovery.[1]

Although his primary concern was the state of Sally's health, Featherston also had to decide what to do with all the boxes and barrels of specimens he had brought home. It was natural that he should think of depositing them, at least temporarily, at the Lyceum of Natural History. The lyceum had evolved from the Literary and Philosophical Society, whose membership, according to John C. Greene, "was dominated by devotees of natural history. . . . In January and February 1817 several of them held a series of meetings at the College of Physicians and Surgeons to discuss 'measures for instituting a *Cabinet of Natural History.*' The outcome was the formation of the Lyceum of Natural History of New York, named after Aristotle's illustrious research organization." Its formation had weakened the Literary and Philosophical Society, and the New-York Historical Society had turned over its natural history collections to the lyceum. Featherston was quite familiar with the lyceum and knew that his specimens would be more appreciated there than anywhere else in the state. He attended the January meeting, at which the president announced that Featherston had just returned from England and the Continent with a superb collection of eight thousand fossils and minerals. Among them were a series of fossils from Tilgate Forest, illustrating Mantell's work; from Yorkshire and Lyme there were organic remains from the lias, or blue limestone; encrinites and pentacrinites demonstrated the work of one Mr. Miller of Bristol; the English rock formations were extensively represented. The collection was temporarily stored with the cabinet of the lyceum whose rooms were already crowded. Featherston offered to transfer his to a geological institution should one be established by the New York legislature.[2]

Benjamin Silliman, editor of the *American Journal of Science and Arts* and a member of the Yale faculty, sent Featherston a tear sheet from the next number of his journal, describing the collection. Silliman offered to propose him as a member of the American Geological Society. The long-talked-of society had finally been authorized by "an act of the Connecticut legislature constituting George Gibbs, Benjamin Silliman, Parker Cleaveland, J. W. Webster, Robert Hare, Robert Gilmor, Jr., and their associates a body politic and corporate, by the name of THE AMERICAN GEOLOGICAL SOCIETY" on 31 May 1819. Silliman had been very active in its formation although he contended that "Colonel G. is the real father of the G. S." At its first meeting in September 1819, William Maclure had been elected president, and Gibbs, Hare, and Silliman were among seven vice-presidents. The high hopes of its founders had not materialized, however, and by 1828, the society had "tended to become an adjunct of Silliman's program at Yale." When Featherston wrote to thank Silliman, he remarked on the confusion in regard to the Secondary Formation, mainly promulgated by Amos Eaton, an enthusiastic Wernerian, who had written about it in the last issue of the journal. Featherston professed to be a great admirer of Eaton's accomplishments and loath to hurt his feelings. Nevertheless, if Eaton was correct, North American geology must be far different from that of Europe, and this hypothesis Featherston could not accept. The editor suggested that Featherston comment on the article and give Eaton an opportunity to read his remarks in order to answer them in the same number of the journal. Featherston, however, decided not to send any communication on the subject, for he did not want to offend either Silliman or Eaton.[3]

To stimulate interest in geology among a wider audience, Featherston began to distribute some of his specimens to various scientific societies. He hoped to enlist people from every state to collect specimens, either voluntarily or for a small premium. There was much opportunity for collecting in New York state, where the digging of canals and mines constantly exposed new specimens, but little collecting was being done in other states. He asked James Madison if he could suggest any men interested in sending him materials from Virginia. To show his earnestness, Featherston casually mentioned having met all of the first-rank geologists while overseas. He enclosed an excerpt from the 1827–1828 *Proceedings of the Geological Society of London,* in which there was a reference to his letter to Fitton on the Norwich flints, which Murchison had read to the society. Madison had to admit that geology was practically an unknown subject in his state. He could suggest only one possibility, the state engineer, Claudius Crozet, but he had not met him.[4]

To his friend, Henry Clay, now secretary of state, Featherston praised the kind reception he had received both at the Court of St. James and at Paris. He was still hopeful that Congress would pass a tariff protecting the farmers. Clay replied that the one now being framed was so prejudicial to New England manufacturers that it would dangerously divide the country during the coming election. While in New York, Featherston sought out Buckland's brother, Henry, whom he was astonished to find living most luxuriously at an expensive hotel among wealthy acquaintances and associating with rather questionable characters. They were helping him to spend, at a rapid rate, the limited resources supplied by his brother. Featherston urged Henry to move to less costly lodgings at once and to seek employment. Though Henry seemed to agree with this advice, he remained at the hotel, much to his brother's disgust. Buckland felt that Henry's compulsive weakness had always been his tendency to live above his station.[5]

Sally was well enough to return to Duanesburg in late January, but her condition continued to worsen. As she became weaker, her husband became most reluctant to leave her for any length of time. He hid his distress as best he could by immersing himself in various affairs, mainly in correspondence. He was doubly grateful for the distraction of letters from abroad and was pleased to learn that he had been elected a member of the Geological Society of London on 7 December. Buckland's letters dealt primarily with his problem brother, but Murchison's were lengthy and full of geological news and general chatter—all related with his inimitable humor. Even dignified meetings of the Geological Society and the Royal Society were described with a comic touch. At Featherston's request, Murchison had been to see Sir Thomas Lawrence, president of the Royal Academy of Arts, about exhibiting the Cole landscapes of Featherston Park that Featherston had given to Buckland and Murchison. Murchison discovered that it would be necessary for the artist himself to send an application and asked Featherston to get one.[6]

Sally died in early May. Although Featherston had known for many months that there was no hope for her recovery, her death was still heartbreaking. Losing her so soon after Ann and Georgiana left him feeling desolate. He took what comfort he could from the survival of his two sons. It was not until October that he received letters of condolence from Buckland and the Murchisons. The latter had been in Paris, where they presented Featherston's letter of introduction to Ambassador Brown and were gratified by the attention shown them. Brown entertained in their honor at an elegant dinner at which General Lafayette and members of his family were fellow guests. Lyell had joined the Murchisons at Paris for a summer of geological fieldwork in central France and Italy.[7]

Featherston did not neglect geology during what he later referred to as his months of "melancholy leisure."[8] From time to time he arranged exhibits at the lyceum. He presented a new mineral, haytorite. In June he gave a talk on the fossil deposits at

Stonefield and Tilgate Forest, illustrated with specimens. He was not satisfied to discuss European geology but began to draw a corollary to that of North America. He showed a transition limestone specimen found at Duanesburg that was identical "in arrangement, composition and fossil contents with the Dudley limestone of England." He commented on the Floridian and Cuban specimens presented by Dr. Swift of the United States navy. Such activities led to his election as a corresponding member of the lyceum.[9]

He devoted many hours to the preparation of a paper, "On the Series of Rocks in the United States," addressed as a letter to Murchison, who protested: "Pray, my dear friend, do not send such ponderous dispatches by the post. Your 2 last cost me *One pound five shillings*! or about 3 times as much as your box of minerals!" The memoir was read at the first meeting of the Geological Society in the new year, 1829. It was critical of one by Eaton, which had appeared in a recent issue of the *American Journal of Science*, entitled "Geological Nomenclature for North America." Featherston could not reconcile the order of succession of North American rocks as given by Eaton with the order as recognized in the British Isles. He believed that they did follow the same order. He also noted that "neither the oolite, nor indeed any of the beds which are in England higher in the series than the coal measures, are to be found in North America, at least, north of 40° north latitude." Joan M. Eyles has called attention to this paper and commented that "Featherstonhaugh's attempt at a trans-Atlantic comparison deserves more commendation than it has hitherto received from American geologists. Before its publication very few attempts had been made to compare European and American strata." Featherston's paper was not published until later, but Eaton learned of his criticism and countered with what Featherston considered "a very coarse publication" about him, which was printed in the *Troy Register*. When Featherston protested, Eaton admitted that he had had no provocation for his "offensive conduct," as Featherston called it. He was now persuaded that perhaps strata of both continents were in general conformity but went no further than this, offering no formal apology.[10]

Buckland sent plaster casts of the mastodon that had recently been found at Ava in the East Indies and asked Featherston to present them to the American Geological Society. Thus it seems likely that Featherston attended the November meeting of the society, which proved to be its last. If he did, he met the elderly and infirm president, William Maclure. Commenting on this meeting, Greene wrote: "Maclure's best days as a geologist were over, but he had done much for American geology and would continue to support it throughout his life. He had traced in the field the rock structures of the United States, compared them to those in Europe, and delineated them in one of the earliest geological maps. He had given freely of his time, money, books, and specimens to American scientific societies, especially the Academy of Natural Sciences of Philadelipha, and had subsidized and inspired many young scientists. Not without reason has he been called 'the father of American geology.'" In 1809 he had published his *Observations on the Geology of the Unites States* with a colored geological map of the regions east of the Mississippi River. At the time of the last meeting of the Geological Society he was also president of the Academy of Natural Sciences of Philadelphia, an office he held for twenty-two years. He was on his way to Mexico to spend the winter, as he had the previous one. It was at this meeting that Featherston was elected to membership.[11]

Featherston continued to be interested in languages. Believing that there was no English translation of Cicero's *Republic,* he spent much of the fall and early winter making one, which was published in early 1829 and dedicated to Murchison. The work was well received in this country, and Featherston sent copies to various friends, including Madison. Buckland wrote that he had read it "with extreme satisfaction" and added that he could not but think that it would do "very great service for the American public for whose benefit you have translated it & if it induces them finally to settle into the form of mixed government so strongly recommended at page 75, you will have placed yourself in the next rank to Washington amongst the great Benefactors to the United States."[12]

When Featherston returned from England, he found that his fellow officers and directors of the Mohawk and Hudson Rail

Road had accomplished almost nothing in his absence. The objectionable amendments to the act of authorization had not been repealed, and everything else was at a standstill. Van Rensselaer, the president, who had never done much but lend his name, had sold eighty-nine of his hundred shares. Immediate action was needed if the undertaking was to avoid failure. Featherston quickly mended his fences at Albany and succeeded in obtaining the repeal of the amendments. Meetings of the board of directors approved the route survey and authorized purchases of land and timbers, and the project began to gain momentum once more. Featherston's drive and enthusiasm, which had given the initial impetus, had been required to keep things moving.[13]

Unfortunately, he was not able to keep it up. He missed some meetings during Sally's illness. Her death and subsequent financial problems forced him to sell his six hundred shares in the railroad, a one-fifth interest. He found it impossible to sell them profitably, however, because John Jacob Astor, a newly elected board member, had circulated rumors that he could obtain the shares at cost or less. In a state of disgust, Featherston offered them to the board, and his offer was accepted. The railroad had been his idea, and he had worked hard to promote it. He withdrew from it with a feeling of bitterness, suffering, he told Fish, "the humiliation of seeing others triumph over my rights, and enriching themselves with a Stock that never would have been Created but for my exertions." After Featherston's last push, the railroad construction was able to continue to completion. On 9 August 1831 the first train, three passenger coaches drawn by a small locomotive named the De Witt Clinton, inaugurated the route. Crowds thronged the right of way to see it depart. Featherston's brainchild, the Mohawk and Hudson, was the beginning of what eventually became the New York Central.[14]

For him, this winter became a time to seek a new direction to his life. Only two years before, he had been able to view the future with optimism. For nearly twenty years he had immersed himself in agricultural affairs and the raising of a family. In spite of painful problems, he had good reason to feel great pride in what he had accomplished. He had built a fine home and developed a large and

De Witt Clinton Engine and Train, from Ulysses Prentis's *A History of Agriculture in the State of New York,* page 254 [Courtesy of the Alderman Library, University of Virginia]

impressive farm. He had made substantial contributions toward the improvement of New York agricultural practices and had earned wide public respect for them. He numbered among his friends many men of importance in public affairs, and he had involved himself in political matters on both state and national levels. He had conceived of railroad development for New York and had persuaded the legislature to authorize the first step. He could foresee a great future for railroading in North America and a prominent part in its development for himself. But the deaths of Ann and Georgiana from which Sally had never fully recovered, had begun the series of tragedies that would deprive his accomplishments of their savor. During the year spent in England he had become deeply committed to the pursuit of his fascination with geology, but he had imagined continuing his studies while maintaining his establishment at Duanesburg and promoting his railroad concerns. With Sally's death, he found that everything at Featherston Park had come to represent tragedy for him. The intense pleasure he had derived from its development and from his plans for it had been lost.

Featherston began to consider his future. He concluded that it would be best for his sons' careers if he remained in the United States rather than returning to England, but as 1829 began he was still uncertain about just what should form his main interest and occupation. There were still financial problems to solve. Writing and geology were his dominant preoccupations. He promised to give several lectures as part of the year's program for the New York Lyceum. John Torrey, the noted botanist and professor at the College of Physicians and Surgeons, would lecture on chemistry, and Featherston would discuss geology. The discussions, held in the chapel of Columbia College, proved extremely popular. Featherston used a twelve-foot copy of Sir Henry De la Beche's *Tabular View* of geological phenomena and other illustrations to clarify the subject. At five dollars a head for the course, the crowded house brought in a tidy sum, which he donated to the lyceum to help reduce its debt. He was urged to give a full course the following winter. [15]

While preparing and giving his lectures, he saw a great deal of Major Joseph Delafield, president of the lyceum, and other officers and members. Many of them thought New York should have its own scientific journal. This may have been an idea planted by Featherston, or he may simply have encouraged it. There can be no doubt that he thought it might very well be possible for him to edit such a journal and that such work would enable him to combine his literary and scientific interests.

The lyceum had long been publishing its proceedings in Silliman's journal. Clearly, therefore, any proposal for another scientific periodical would be of no little concern to Benjamin Silliman. In 1828, he, Featherston, and Delafield had talked of an expedition to Pennsylvania's coalfields. Featherston wrote to Silliman on 29 April to ask if the editor still wished to join the excursion. Having reported the success of his geological lectures and the rapidly increasing interest in natural science in New York, he mentioned that he thought this interest would soon manifest itself in an experiment establishing a quarterly journal of science. Of course, the experiment might not succeed, but the pride of New York was very much involved. He felt that he must inform Silliman that he heartily supported the proposal and would try to enlist the backing of his European friends. His own great personal regard for Silliman induced him to inform him of their intentions. To what extent did Silliman think the proposal would interfere with his journal? Everyone involved had the greatest respect for him and had no unfriendly feelings.[16]

Within the week, Silliman wrote to Delafield, offering to publish all the papers that the lyceum might want printed, under their own volume and series numbers, not to exceed two hundred pages per year. Reprints would be furnished for the cost of paper and binding. Those papers he published would be credited to the lyceum's *Annals* and would appear before the journal. In writing to Featherston the next day, Silliman gave several reasons why he did not think the proposed quarterly a good idea. One scientific journal was enough, and since his was not just a local journal but a national one, it certainly had priority. Silliman felt sure that salesmen for the projected quarterly would preempt his present subscribers, and he noted that many years were needed to build up a subscription list sufficient to finance such a project. Having listed the arguments against the new quarterly, he admitted that he was willing to relinquish his journal for a financial consideration.[17]

In reply, Featherston wrote that they would rather purchase the journal than have any ill feeling and asked what amount would satisfy Silliman. In the course of further correspondence, the editor indicated that he would expect to be paid the three thousand dollars that he had invested in stock on hand, in addition to his selling price. In the meantime, Featherston heard from Dr. Robert Hare of Philadelphia, a member of the first geological society in the United States and a close friend of Silliman's who had sent him Featherston's letter. Hare did not think there was any need for a second journal. When Featherston wrote to Silliman that they would not consider buying his stock on hand but just wanted to know the number of subscribers and his price, the latter informed Hare, who suggested that the whole correspondence be published. Silliman disagreed but sent copies for Hare to show to his friends and to the Philadelphia academy in the event that they might be interested in purchasing. In a letter to Featherston he declined to sell without payment for stock in hand and noted that he considered their negotiations at an end. To this Featherston agreed, but he assured Silliman of his good will and that he would gladly resume correspondence at any time on scientific subjects.[18]

The proposed New York journal did not materialize, and in the midst of the correspondence about it, Featherston suffered another crushing blow. The house at Featherston Park caught fire. He and his two sons escaped, but the house burned to the ground. Only a few portraits and paintings were saved. The accumulation of years disappeared within hours, and with the house went the last tie that bound Featherston to Duanesburg. As soon as he was able to make arrangements for his sons and for the care or disposal of his livestock, he left, writing his mother: "My situation is quite a disconsolate one. I am deprived of all the comforts that made life agreeable, My Family, My Home, all perished. . . . I reside no more in Duanesburg and wish never to see it again. It has been the tomb of all my Prosperity." By September he was living in New York City. George, Jr., a handsome young man, as tall as his father, made his home with his Aunt Kitty. He was being tutored in mathematics in hope of receiving an appointment to West Point. James was doing well at a good academy.[19]

As a distraction from his problems that summer of 1829, Featherston again turned to geology and wrote a thirty-one-page critique of the first American edition of Robert Bakewell's *Introduction to Geology,* published by Silliman. This book, written in popular style, had first appeared in England in 1813 and had gone through five editions. It was outdated by 1829, making no mention of the use of fossils in the correlation of strata. In his review, Featherston summarized the views and theories of geology and how they had evolved. "This science has positive merits. . . . they consist in its long and patient researches, its bold and determined spirit of inquiry, its enlarged and interesting relations, and, above all, in its close adherence to the principles of the inductive philosophy. . . . Its faithful adherence to the Baconian philosophy, and the successful results which it has thereby obtained, form one of its noblest features." Featherston clearly shared the views of his friend, Edward Everett, who wrote in 1823, "The *Baconian* philosophy has become synonymous with the *true* philosophy."[20]

The supposed effects of the deluge on the American continent had long fascinated Featherston. He had studied them for years in the New York area, particularly the land drained by the Hudson but also that around Niagara Falls. Now he found himself caught up in the diluvial controversy among his English friends. When Murchison and Lyell had returned from their field trip to Auvergne and Italy "red hot Huttonians," Buckland suspected that they would be attributing the great geological changes to the work of volcanoes and earthquakes rather than to any deluge. They would explain the deposits of fossils as "the piddling produce" of flooding rivers and overflowing lakes. Buckland was certain that such could not explain the detritus left behind and urged Featherston to send him information on the subject from America.[21]

Murchison reported to Featherston that his and Lyell's summer work made it impossible not to see that there had been many diluviums rather than the one great one espoused by Buckland and others. These could not be distinguished in England. Any general hypotheses based solely on conditions found in England must fail when those of other countries are studied. Sedgwick, who had been a diluvialist, was one no more. The latest memoir of Elie de Beaumont, wrote Murchison, "proves at least one great elevation of mountain chains posterior to Buckland's Diluvium par excellence." Elie de Beaumont was professor of geology at the Ecole des Mines at Paris and had been preparing a geological map of France. He postulated that the mountain ranges of the earth had been elevated abruptly by a series of internal revolutions.[22]

Featherston was eager to enter the fray for he had found diluvium a hundred feet thick, which could in no way be explained by mere flooding of a river. He was disturbed that Murchison, Sedgwick, and Lyell might be implementing a geological schism. From his observations of primitive rocks, Featherston inclined to agree with Murchison on igneous fusion but definitely disagreed with his friend if Murchison no longer accepted the mighty deluge of Noah. Both Featherston and Buckland were strong churchmen, brought up in strict eighteenth-century interpretation of the Bible, but it was not just his religious training that influenced Feather-ston. He was convinced that no series of small fluvia could have deposited so much detritus. That summer he spent two weeks exploring the area around West Point, where the detritus con-firmed what had been reported in other parts of the United States. Much of it was around fourteen hundred feet above sea level, and some was at sixteen hundred feet. The rivers were apparently small remnants of the draining of that immense flood, which had been held in pockets by the mountains. Great boulders of primi-tive rocks attested to the torrential violence.[23]

During the summer Featherston wrote an article on the general geology and drainage of North America for the Geological So-ciety of London, incorporating his studies and observations. A year later, after further field trips, he wrote a much longer article which was published in the United States. In it, he said, "The bed of the Hudson River then is to be considered as the contracted Drain of an immense body of Water held up by a Chain of Hills with Floors of different levels; and the waters flowing in the Drain have cut their way through the universal sediment, which was Contemporaneously deposited when the general Deluge covered the whole Country. It is in such a manner probably the whole Continent has been drained." To his conclusions on the drainage, Featherston added a short account of the erosion caused by the river at Niagara Falls in answer to those who contended that streams "have no appreciable erosive action, upon the rocks over which they run." By coincidence the artist George Catlin hap-pened to be in New York, building a model of the falls from trigonometrical surveys he had made. He allowed Featherston to include a plan of the model in his paper.[24]

News from England helped alleviate Featherston's depression. Buckland was disappointed that his brother had still not found a niche in the New World, but his own family was well and rejoicing in a new daughter. Murchison's letters contained much humor over Buckland's "Cloaca Maxima," his new science of fossil feces, or coprology. Murchison swore that his friend introduced the sub-ject as freely as so many sausages but declared that the study was not all that new, since Mary Anning had earlier identified certain black fossils at Lyme as crocodiles' feces. When Featherston sent Mrs. Murchison a box of fossilized shells, she, too, entered into the fun about Buckland's new obsession, describing how he ran around with a green collecting bag. She hoped that Featherston would send him some mastodon's coprolites![25]

While Murchison was away with Sedgwick for five months' study of the geology of various parts of Germany, Mary Anning visited his wife for a week. It was her first trip to London, in fact her first out of Lyme. The two ladies had a fascinating time visiting the museums. Charlotte Murchison was also a fossil enthusiast and quite an expert on ancient shells. Anning's immediate financial worries were over. The previous year she had discovered the first skeleton of a *Pterosaurus,* or flying lizard, to be found in England and had sold it to the British Museum for a hundred pounds. She asked her hostess to convey her respects to Featherston and to ask if there was anything she could get for him. Others enquired about him, too; whenever Mrs. Murchison visited Uppark, Sir Harry and his wife wanted to know the latest news of him.[26]

Sir Harry was pleased by a mark of respect from his kinsman across the Atlantic early in the new year. Having received no encouragement from Edmund Kean in regard to his play, *The Death of Ugolino,* Featherston had had it published in Philidelphia, dedicating it to Sir Harry. In the preface, he gave an account of the Pisan war, which a critic in the *American Quarterly Review* considered much better written and far more interesting than the tragedy itself, strongly recommending that the author stick to history in the future. He considered the work more of a narrative poem and entirely too tedious for a drama. He had thought it impossible for anyone to write of this stirring tale without touching the reader's feelings: "But our author has achieved this wonder. The most melancholy portions of the piece are the comic scenes." Fortunately, Featherston never attempted the role of playwright again. Although he had sent copies of the play to Murchison and John Gibson Lockhart, editor of the London *Quarterly Review,* no comments on it seem to have survived, which is perhaps just as well.[27]

Young George entered West Point in 1830, straining his father's finances once more. Featherston's small income would have been barely sufficient for one yet had to cover his sons' expenses as well as his own. Featherston thought of settling all he owned on them until they were self-supporting. He was certain that he would be able to earn an income adequate for his own needs. With this in mind, he moved to Philadelphia, which he had enjoyed when he and Sally lived there. He had always found it stimulating and still had friends there. He began attending meetings of the American Philosophial Society, where his friend DuPonceau presided. Soon Featherston was serving on various committees. He found many of the members most congenial. The Quaker merchant Isaac Lea was an enthusiastic mineralogist and conchologist. Through Featherston he sent Mrs. Murchison a box of shells from his collection, enclosing a list of specimens that he desired.[28]

Lea, Reuben Haines, and Robert Griffith proposed Featherston as a member of the Academy of Natural Sciences of Philadelphia, to which he was duly elected 23 February. The academy had been founded since Featherston and Sally had lived in Philadelphia. It was organized in 1812 and given a charter by the Pennsylvania legislature in 1816. The first president had been the Dutch scientist, Gerard Troost, then operating a pharmaceutical and chemical laboratory in Philadelphia. Troost had been succeeded as president in 1817 by Maclure who had continued in that office ever since, even though he was frequently away from Philadelphia for extended periods. It was Maclure's leadership and his generous gifts of books, money, and specimens that established the academy as an important scientific society. Featherston was soon serving on committees, including one to examine a "Description of Fossil Bones of a Megalonyx . . ." and a paper on a fossil of the *Fucoides* family. He began to feel a part of the scientifc world once more.[29]

Being otherwise unemployed, Featherston at last had time for both reading and writing during the early part of 1830. He needed any money he could earn from writing. By April he had completed what purported to be a review of two books: Andrew Ure's *A New System of Geology* and William Thomas Brande's *Outline of Geology*. Actually, however, only six pages of his long essay were devoted to the review. Most of Featherston's article was a summary of the history of geology as an introduction to a description of the present status of the science in Great Britain and on the Continent. To this he added his own observations made in this country, emphasizing the similarity between the various American formations and those abroad. As he had in his lectures, he wrote in a simple manner that could be understood by and would appeal to the general public.[30]

Brande's book, based on his lectures at the Royal Institute, Featherston found pleasing although somewhat inaccurate. He complimented Ure's publication for its appearance and general information but strongly objected to the author's attempt to make all geology agree with the biblical account of creation. He ridiculed Ure's statement that no animals known today had descended from those saved by Noah. Perhaps, he wrote, "Noah and his friends ate them all up, spiders and all. . . . Now, if taking liberties with the Bible be irreligious, we say unhesitatingly that all the irreligion which has been introduced into geology, has been by religious writers, or men who are anxious to be distinguished as such." Featherston vigorously castigated other authors with views similar to Ure's but had to moderate his criticism at the request of the editor. One item deleted was an epigram:

> Your book, most learned Dr. U,
> Is filled with things original and new
> And admirable indeed, were they but true!
> Yet you have given us fact most true;
> And I could praise your work, 'twixt me and you,
> If but the new was true, the true was new.

Even the toned-down review was sufficient to kill the sales of Ure's book at Philadelphia.[31]

Less than a month after the publication of Featherston's article in the June *American Quarterly Review,* he received a copy of Sedgwick's address on Ure's book to the Geological Society of London and was delighted to find that he and Sedgwick were in agreement. He wrote his friend that he only wished that he had read Sedgwick's paper before he had written his and sent him a copy of the deleted epigram. Sedgwick was amused but suggested that the laugh was really on Ure's side, since he had written the book to sell and had made five hundred pounds.[32]

English friends were impressed by how Featherston had "seized so rapidly upon all the recent advances in our science," as Murchison later put it. He pronounced the essay "an excellent review of 'Geology and its Progress.' This article, which developed in a masterly and clear manner, conveyed to the American public an accurate view of the true order of succession of those formations which were marked out by William Smith, [William Daniel] Conybeare and others, and ably tabulated by De la Beche. Nor does he omit to do full justice to [John] McCulloch and those who so well illustrated the power exercised by the eruption of rocks of igneous origin and the structure of such rocks." Buckland thought it "not only in the highest degree creditable" but also "such as I sh'd have been proud to be the author of."[33]

There had been more than one motive for writing the review. During the past year Featherston's desire to return to England permanently had been growing. The previous fall Murchison had mentioned that the geological chair at the new University of London was vacant. He had even gone so far as to speak to Warburton about appointing Featherston to the position, but Warburton had been unenthusiastic. In January, Murchison had spoken to Leonard Horman, the warden of the university, on Featherston's behalf, and he was quite agreeable. If Buckland also put in a word, Murchison was convinced the position was Featherston's, for none of the English geologists were interested. Before making such a move, Featherston wanted more details about the permanency of the situation and what he could expect in the way of a salary. Murchison had to admit he would lecture only part of the year, and lecture fees would constitute his only financial remuneration, as the university gave no salary. Moreover, some of the schools, such as Eastern languages, had no students at all, although classes in European languages, botany, and chemistry were very popular. At least Featherston would be "in an agreeable situation" that would connect him with all his friends.[34]

Featherston sought Buckland's advice. He was aware that his own knowledge was small compared to Buckland's but was confident that his diligence would soon overcome his deficiencies. Judging by the popularity of his New York lectures, he really did not think he would lack students. Could Buckland inform him if the post was worth having, and if so, could his friends get it for him? He enclosed copies of his geological article to be given to Warburton as well as to his more intimate friends. Buckland was quite frank in his reply. He did not think the university would continue more than three years, for their income the previous year had been £3,500, but expenses had been £5,500. Moreover, not a penny of interest had been paid on the £150,000 borrowed for the buildings and their furnishings. The zoology professor, "an able man," had had only three students, and only the lectures leading to medicine, chemistry, and botany were full. Buckland had talked to Warburton, who had made no bones about how he felt. If any promising position appeared, Buckland would certainly remember his friend. Buckland was not alone in his doubts. Both William Jackson Hooker and John Lindley had declined to seek the botany chair, thinking that such a post would be precarious with no guarantee of a minimum income. Charles Babbage had been offered the mathematics chair but had commented: "They have no dignity to confer as yet, they have their reputation to make. I have not. If, as they admit, they wish to get some from me, why they ought to buy it, and pay for it." Featherston gave up all thought of lecturing at the University of London when he received Buckland's letter in October and felt doubly justified in his decision when the university's annual report showed a decrease of fifty students.[35]

To relax a bit and forget his problems for a time, Featherston spent a month at New Brighton on Staten Island in midsummer 1830. It was a very pleasant resort named for England's seacoast town. The Pavilion Hotel there reminded him of similar unpretentious inns at Scarborough. He often took the ferry over to Manhattan, five miles away, where he still felt that he knew almost everyone. During his stay at New Brighton, he became more sociable than he had been since Sally's death. There were a number of attractive families among the summer visitors, one of which was that of the poet Bernard Moore Carter, a scion of the well-known Carter family of Virginia. His father was Charles Carter of Shirley, and his mother a granddaughter of Governor Alexander

Spotswood. Bernard Carter's wife, Lucy Grymes Lee, was a daughter of General Henry Lee. Featherston was attracted to the youngest of the Carters' four daughters, eighteen-year-old Charlotte Williams. Although she was about the same age as his son James, she returned his affection, and the two were married on 28 January 1831 by the Reverend Dr. James Abercrombie, rector of Christ Church, Philadelphia.[36]

Featherston received about one dollar a printed page for his reviews, but the work was sporadic and scarce, and his financial situation continued precarious. In late December, he had to borrow five hundred dollars for thirty days from Nicholas Fish when something delayed expected funds and his wedding was imminent. He started lecturing at the Franklin Institute in Philadelphia as he had in New York. The American Philosophical Society allowed him to use their geological specimens, which were a helpful addition to his own. Again, his lectures were extremely popular, and the fees made a welcome addition to his income. He used any money he could spare to pay people to bring him geological specimens. He was eager to encourage the formation of new geological societies. He wrote Sedgwick that the only American society, the one at New Haven, had been a farce, for there was no meeting room nor were there any books or fossils. The society's head, Silliman, had "carried it & all its property about with him in his Belly." Silliman believed that "granite was formed out of the Chaotic Abyss of Genesis, and that it is still a doubtful matter whether Trap is of igneous origin." The "battering ram" Featherston employed against this theory was lecturing, and even though he was "considered by hundreds of his pious friends, as in a fine state of preparation for either turning—or being turned about the devil's spit—" he was "making a great party here, and the thing is attracting prodigious attention."[37]

His geological crusade included exposing Amos Eaton's empiricism. Eaton was now science professor at Rensselaer School in Troy, New York, and his *Geological Textbook* had been published the previous year. Featherston had lost no time in writing a review of the book, for he wished, he wrote Everett, "to stop, as quick as possible, a System of Quackery, that is poisoning the very fountains of knowledge here, and making the Character of this Country, for Natural History, painfully ridiculous abroad." The editor evidently did not feel the same urgency about publishing Featherston's review, and it did not appear in Everett's *North American Review* until April 1831.[38]

Again Featherston devoted a great part of his review to the general subject of geology before turning to the book reviewed. He did not mention it until the twelfth page of the nineteen-page review. First he dealt with the progress of justice and reason in overcoming bigotry and ignorance in the history of science since the time of Galileo. He discussed the virtues of geology as a field of scientific study and the almost universal attention it was receiving in Europe. By contrast, among publications on American geology, only Maclure's *Sketches* was of any value. Featherston recognized that there were many intelligent Americans interested in natural history, as attested by geological collections of the New York Lyceum and the studies of Thomas Say, Isaac Lea, Isaac Hays, and others. Unfortunately, few Americans had the leisure to pursue scientific studies. He was pleased to see more attention being given to the study of natural history in American colleges and praised the work of Silliman at Yale and Edward Hitchcock at Amherst.

He began his devastating critique of the object of the review with the statement that Americans interested in natural history were familiar with Eaton's "chemical, botanical, and above all, his geological notoriety." The professor claimed to have already taught seven thousand students, and Featherston shuddered at such widespread dissemination of false information. Eaton, in his preface, had invited "the most rigorous criticism" of his book, which Featherston did not hesitate to supply. He attacked the nomenclature the author had introduced and quoted from a French geological journal, in which the writer remarked of Eaton that "the nomenclature of all the European and American geologists, appears unsuitable to him, and he believes that his queer names, and his little wood-cuts, colored like the deposits, are the ne plus ultra of clearness and true Geology." Featherston criticized Eaton's system of dating by the mineral character of rocks rather than by their organic remains. The illustrations of the world cut into two halves received a heavy dose of sarcasm: "Six little fires, with chimneys to them, are nicely built around the edges of one of the hemispheres. The fires are burning very briskly and the smoke is coming out very prettily." As to the fire under the Atlantic Ocean, if it "should break through, as the Thames did into the Tunnel, it strikes us that the packets running to Europe would be in great danger. We by no means desire to alarm the public, but we advise the proprietors to look to it, and to consult Mr. Amos Eaton before his second edition appears." In regard to Eaton's espousal of Werner's ideas, Featherston remarked that "Werner was singularly happy in two things: one, that he did not outlive his reputation; the other, that he died before Mr. Eaton applied his views to American earth." Eaton's elucidation of Buckland's discoveries was likewise pilloried, and quite justly, for according to Featherston, Eaton stated that mastodon bones were found in caves with openings but two feet wide. In a letter to the *American Journal of Science and Art,* Van Rensselaer formally protested Featherston's statement that Eaton had not taken advantage of his opportunities while surveying for him. On the contrary, he had been well satisfied with the professor's work.[39]

Featherston found much better things to say of another book published in 1830, Charles Lyell's first volume of *Principles of Geology,* which emphasized the uniformity of geological changes. Featherston had only one reservation about the book. Lyell held that the human species was "a deviation that tends to destroy our Confidence in the uniformity of the order of nature, both in regard to time past and future." Featherston admitted that there was a great difference between the structure of infusorias and that of human beings, but unlike Lyell, he was not alarmed by the implications. In fact, he considered a progression from "animal stages as preparatory to intellectual power." In England there was some criticism of Lyell's doctrines as being opposed to the Scriptures, yet his appointment to King's College had the approval of both the bishop of London and the archbishop of Canterbury. It was quite different in the United States. In an American review, Featherston did not dare approve the author's doctrines. Lyell was amused. "So much" he said "for toleration of Church Establishment and no Church Establishment countries." Lyell's English colleagues were far more critical of his book than was Featherston. Buckland reported that Sedgwick, in his speech as retiring president of the Geological Society, had made a "flagellating" attack on the book. Buckland, Conybeare, William Whewell, and others also disapproved.[40]

New Developments in American Geology

5

Featherston's lectures and writing were received so enthusiastically that, as he wrote Sedgwick, he was urged to write a textbook. He planned to do so as soon as he could collect enough American examples with which to illustrate the principles. He thought that the American reading public numbered close to fifteen million, most of whom were interested in natural history. From the early eighteenth century on, Europe had had a strong influence in developing this interest in the United States, largely through the European medical schools in which American students were enrolled. There, exceptional faculties, physic gardens, journals, and museums all had their part in inspiring students to continue the study of natural history after they returned home. The University of Edinburgh medical school, where 139 American students received their M.D.'s between 1749 and 1812, was particularly influential. It was a period in which "natural philosophy" was being transformed into "science." Scientific societies were becoming numerous, and "there was a state of mutual dependence between the scientific society and the scientific journal," as Daniels has pointed out. If there were to be more geological societies, as Featherston hoped, they would need a journal of geology to encourage them.[1]

Featherston had ample opportunity to consider his next moves during the severe winter of 1831. Snow filled the streets from

January to March, making travel difficult, and at the end of that month he was confined to bed for four weeks. Finally he reached a decision and began negotiations for the publication of a monthly journal. He received great encouragement and offers of assistance. Mathew Carey, the printer and publisher, sent him a cost estimate for two thousand copies of approximately fifty pages monthly. Publication would be through Dr. Henry H. Porter, publisher of the *Journal of Law* and the *Journal of Health,* who had already established channels of distribution.[2]

A prospectus for the *Monthy American Journal of Geology and Natural Science* was printed 20 May. In it, Featherston stressed the need for scientific education, particularly in geology, evidenced in the recent reports sent abroad of the discovery of "huge antediluvian lizards," which proved to be only the skeletons of the common spermaceti whale. His new journal would include other branches of science, as well as remarks on remains of aborigines and discussion of Indian languages. There would be reports of new scientific discoveries abroad and reviews of scientific books. To reach as many readers as possible, Featherston made the price of a year's subscription only $3.50. He realized his main competitor would be Silliman's journal, which, he remarked to Sedgwick was but "a weak performance made up with scissors." Perhaps he was prejudiced by "the many reports of mermaids observed between New York and Havre" interspersed between "splendid scientific articles," as William Smallwood has commented. Featherston decided to publish monthly both to avoid too direct a challenge to Silliman and to anticipate and scoop current news. He hoped, too, to receive letters from his English geologist friends that would give him another edge.[3]

He sent a copy of the prospectus to Sedgwick by his friend Charles Vaughan, England's minister plenipotentiary, who was returning home on leave after six years in the United States. He also sent one to Buckland, who had been impressed by the glowing newspaper accounts of Featherston's lectures. Buckland thought these would certainly have laid the ground for a favorable reception of the journal, but he thought the price was so modest that it would hardly pay expenses, much less realize a profit. He offered to circulate the prospectus if Featherston would send additional copies.[4]

The first issue of the *Monthly American Journal* appeared in July 1831 and was sent to 63 subscribers. Within three months the number reached 201 and included not only President Andrew Jackson but most government departments. One of the principal articles in this first issue was Featherston's "On the Drainage of North America," which he had prepared for the Geological Society of London, illustrated by Catlin's scale drawing of Niagara Falls. There was a naturalist's diary kept at the Bartram Garden by John B. Carr. The editor had also inserted several short pieces on such things as geological nomenclature and the award of the Wollaston Medal to William Smith. A report from the New York Lyceum on the bones found at Big Bone Lick was followed by a brief review of John Lindley's book on the natural order of plants, which included notes by John Torrey. Featherston intended to narrow the focus of his journal gradually, but first, he felt, he must interest his readers. He would begin to educate them in geology when the journal could concentrate on that science.[5]

Perhaps the most important contribution in the next ten issues of the journal was a series of six articles called "An Epitome of the Progress of Natural Science," written by the editor "so that the great principles, from which philosophical views of the arrangements and operation of nature are drawn, may be lucidly brought forward." The first essay began with a history of the deluge as presented in ancient accounts by Herodotus, Pythagoras, and others, moving on to science in the time of the Romans. In discussing Greek science, Featherston concentrated on biology. In describing Italian science in the Middle Ages, he emphasized its early recognition of the importance of fossils. In dealing exclusively with geology, he gave a brief resume of the work of John Ray, Hutton, Woodward, Werner, Thomas Burnet, and others, recommending Lyell's *Principles of Geology* for collateral reading. In an additional article, he reviewed the current scientific journals in the United States and abroad. George W. White, discussing American geological writers in the period 1803–1835, considered Featherston to have been "the most geologically knowledgeable and critical."[6]

One of the most important contributors to the new journal was John James Audubon. Soon after his move to Philadelphia, Featherston made, or renewed, a friendship with Dr. Richard Harlan, the city's leading authority on comparative anatomy. Among Featherston and Harlan's mutual acquaintances was Audubon, with whom Harlan was then corresponding. Featherston may have been doing the same, or perhaps Harlan had written of Featherston's interest in his work. In any case, Audubon was preparing to return from England to the United States, relishing his triumphal reception abroad and hoping for a more enthusiastic one at home. He wrote to Harlan in June: "I wish you would ascertain on what grounds the Philadelphians are so virulent towards me. . . . I have some hopes that affairs will turn rather more favourable to me in America and Philadelphia, more especially when I have written three more volumes and my Life—assisted by yourself, [Dr. H.] McMurtrie and Featherstonhaugh."7

Audubon arrived at New York in early September. He had been honored abroad by election to membership in ten of the leading scientific societies and had been acclaimed in not only the European press but also that of New York. Nevertheless, he was coolly received at the New York Lyceum. William Cooper, writing to Charles Bonaparte at the time, commented that, although Audubon seemed to be regarded as a great naturalist in Scotland and England, the lyceum had not even permitted him to borrow bird skins. Not surprisingly, he did not linger long at New York. In Philadelphia he was more kindly received but by no means unanimously. Both the American Philosophical Society and the Academy of Natural Sciences subscribed to his work, and the former elected him to membership. His enemies were losing ground rapidly, and fine reviews of his work were appearing. One of those reviews was a very laudatory one written by Featherston for the September issue of his journal. Of the *Ornithological Biography,* he wrote: "To say that this is one of the handsomest books ever reprinted in America, is to assert one of its slightest merits." He referred to *The Birds of America* as "that most magnificent of all works" and quoted Cuvier's remark to the French Royal Academy of Sciences, which had asked him to comment on it, that it was "the most magnificent monument which had hitherto been raised to Ornithology."[8]

In a later issue of the *Monthly American Journal,* Featherston discussed the controversy that had produced a mixed reception for Audubon at Philadelphia. Some scientists had faulted the accuracy of Audubon's observations. These criticisms, he said, had originated in "the spirit of Jealousy" on the part of some friends of the ornithologist Alexander Wilson "who did not view, with the most Cordial Spirit, those evidences of transcendent merit, which others willingly accorded to Audubon's drawings. . . . Opinions were industriously circulated that Audubon had, in many instances, attempted to impose upon the credulity of the world, by inventing stories which had no foundation in truth." Featherston discussed the classic example of this supposed imposition, Audubon's *"mocking birds defending their nest from a rattlesnake."* His detractors, by denying the ability of rattlesnakes to climb trees, tried, wrote Featherston to "ruin the reputation of one of the most remarkable men America ever produced."[9]

Audubon left Philadelphia to travel through the southern Atlantic coastal states, hoping to continue to Mexico and the Pacific Coast. Before leaving, he promised Featherston to write accounts of his travels from time to time for publication in the *Monthly American Journal.* Featherston announced this proposed series in the December issue, reporting that Audubon had been well received in both Washington and Richmond. He had written Featherston that the birds had gone south to Florida, and he was doing the same. The first of the promised letters, written on 7 December from St. Augustine, duly appeared in the *Monthly American Journal,* as did two later ones from Florida. Audubon wrote to his wife on 8 December: "F. has written a tremendous Review of my work for the North American Review which will appear on the 1st of Jany next," but it did not come out until the following April.[10]

In the meantime the controversy over the habits of rattlesnakes continued. Colonel John James Abert, head of the United States Topographical Bureau of the War Department, wrote at length to Harlan on the subject, and Featherston published his letter in the November issue. Abert had talked with Audubon at Washington,

Mockingbirds and Rattlesnake, by John James Audubon
[Courtesy of the Alderman Library, University of Virginia]

admired his plates of birds, and thoroughly enjoyed his "anecdotes of the habits of animals" as he had observed them in the wilderness. He had urged Audubon to include such observations in his publication but the latter had some reservations after all the criticism of his mockingbirds defending their nest. Abert took note of this criticism and cited a number of reports by others who had observed rattlesnakes in both shrubs and trees. Audubon was delighted by Abert's supporting evidence when Featherston's journal reached him in Florida and thought it might shut the mouths of his city critics who had no opportunity for making their own observations.[11]

Featherston's promised review of Audubon's *Ornithological Biography* and *Birds of America* for the *North American Review* occupied forty-one pages of its April 1832 issue. Like all his reviews, it was more of an essay on the subject involved than a review of the particular book. Although entitled "Audubon's Biography of Birds," the greater part of it was a tribute to those bold spirits who, like Audubon, forgo the quiet life of home and family for one of danger and adventure and the marvelous diversity and charm of his subject, American birds. Although he was no ornithologist, Featherston left no question about his enthusiasm for both topics. It was clear that the exacting, if lonely, life of the adventurer in the wilderness had a tremendous appeal for him and equally clear that interest in all aspects of natural history had long included observation of birds and their habits. The two subjects gave wide scope to his talents as a writer, and he was at his eloquent best.

Of exploring he wrote: "Some esteem it a privilege to be frozen up during three quarters of the year, in the dead night-calm of a polar sea; others spring forward to seize the fortunate chance of leaving their bones whitening on the sands beneath the red heat of an African sun; some are enchanted with the idea of tracing the course of rivers, which, according to the best authorities, have neither beginning nor end; others can die contented when they have scaled the tops of mountains, where they stand, petrified with cold, several inches higher than man ever stood before."[12]

Having pointed out that any careful scientific study of a subject increases its fascination for the student, he continued: "This explains how men of great ability are so engaged in what are often ignorantly regarded as little things; how they can watch with the gaze of a lover, to catch the glance of the small bird's wing, or listen to its song, as if it were the breath of a soul; how the world and every thing in it looks so spiritually bright to them, when to others the bird is but a flying animal and the flower only the covering of a clod."[13]

Having expounded upon these two themes at some length, Featherston turned to the subject of American birds, noting that he found it "surprising to see how few of all the birds which annually visit us, are known by name, and how little their habits are understood." It became evident that his remarks did not apply to himself as he wrote about a great many different ones to be seen in New England. He depicted them vividly—"the blue jay, one of the earliest of our visitors, who comes sounding his penny trumpet as a herald of spring, and either amuses himself by playing pranks upon other more serious birds, or entertains them by acting to the life, the part of an angry Frenchman," or "the snow-bird, that comes riding from the Arctic Circle upon the winter storm,—and the baltimore, or golden-robin, that glances like a flame of fire through the green caverns of foliage." He also debunked various misconceptions about birds, noting, for example, that "we hear complaints annually from all parts of the United States, that some insect or another is destroying the fruit, and proposing to offer a large reward to any one who will discover a remedy. Lest we should be anticipated in our design, we would say that we mean to contend for that prize, and to secure orchards and gardens by protecting the birds, and offering a handsome bounty for the ears of those who shoot them."[14]

Featherston discussed the work of Wilson as well as that of Audubon and the relationship between them. Finally, he concentrated on Audubon himself, giving an account of his life, a description of the man, and a summary of many of his experiences. He gave his own evaluation of his work and a list of some of the new birds discovered, described, and named by Audubon. Finally, he praised the ornithologist for having written for the enjoyment of the general public rather than the scientist. "If Mr. Audubon had contented himself with Linnean descriptions, he would have had the honour of discovering more birds than readers." The review pleased Audubon who wrote his wife, "The North American Review is come out and is a good one."[15]

Another important item in the *Monthly American Journal* was the first printing of the journal of Colonel George Croghan, American Indian agent, the original of which Featherston possessed. He hoped that similar manuscripts would be offered for publication. Expectations of many contributions from the English geologists never materialized, although he published extracts from their letters from time to time. The main result of his appeal for support from his English friends was a letter written on 18 June, expressing high hopes for the success of the new journal and great confidence in the editor. It was signed by Murchison as president of the Geological Society of London; Davies Gilbert, vice-president of the Royal Society; Conybeare, Sedgwick, Buckland, and Greenough.[16]

The journal developed a controversial aspect in its second issue. Featherston had been criticized in the July issue of the Franklin Institute's journal. Dr. Isaac Hays accused him of attacking the late Dr. John Davidson Godman's reputation in his lecture on 13 May. Godman had been anatomy professor at Rutgers Medical College, editor of various journals, and author of *American Natural History* and other books. Featherston had stated that fossil bones belonging to the American Philosophical Society, which he showed, were not those of a new genus, as had been claimed, but were those of a young mastodon. In the August issue of the *Monthly American Journal* he minced no words, calling Hays's statement "a deliberate falsehood" and adding that he had "been strongly solicited to expose the previous moral obliquities of that mendacious little individual." Several such missives were exchanged, as well as letters to the newspaper, culminating in Hays's demand for an apology or a duel. This choice, Featherston said, was "as presumptious [*sic*] as it is ridiculous," and he gave a detailed history of the affair in his September issue. Godman's new animal had been recently described at the American Philosophical Society and published in its *Transactions*. New York naturalists had rejected the claim that it was a new animal, as had Dr. Richard Harlan, whose reasons had been published in the *Bulletin des Sciences Universelles* in 1830. When Featherston had exhibited these fossils, he had never referred to Godman by name, and he produced evidence through a newspaper report of his lectures that demonstrated the invalidity of Hays's accusations. Featherston's exposure of Dr. Hays's conduct was evidently accepted, for there was no further reference to it.[17]

Featherston stirred controversy again over Eaton's textbook. He employed the indignation aroused by his criticism of the book in the *North American Review* to promote a lively discussion by supporting the "anonymous" reviewer in his own journal. Again, he demolished Eaton's system and nomenclature in his August issue.

Another instance of controversy ended in much embarrassment, however. In his July issue Featherston printed an account of *Rhinoceroides alleghaniensis,* "a new genus of the order Pachydermata," which he had provisionally named after studying what he took to be a fossil fragment of its jaw. The article consisted of a copy of a letter he had written to Buckland on 3 April 1831, describing the fossil jaw that had been sent to him fourteen months previously by Benjamin Wright. It had been given to Wright by Robert Fulton, who reported that it had been found three feet below the surface of the soil, beneath the roots of a fallen oak, in Somerset County, Pennsylvania. Both Featherston and Dr. Harlan had made measurements, comparing the fragment with the jaw of a modern rhinoceros, which Harlan had obtained from India, and they found it to be nearly twice as large. Featherston asked Buckland to present his description and a wax cast of the fossil to the Geological Society. He had hesitated about naming and describing this fossil because of some features he recognized as very unusual, if not unique. These should have aroused his suspicions but did not. The mineral composition of the fossil had "nothing of the nature of bone about it, excepting the form: the whole substance, the teeth included, being constituted of an agregate of small quartzose particles; and presenting the appearance, not of a gradual substitution by mineral infiltration, to osseous matter, but a cast of a part of a jaw and teeth, formed by small quartzose grit."[18]

Even though he had only the wax cast to examine, Buckland

was very skeptical about the supposed jaw, but he took it to a meeting of the society and discussed Featherston's description of it with several friends. He reported that they shared his opinion that "some artifice had been employed in fabricating the original specimen." None of them had ever heard of a fossil in which all of the bone had been replaced. Moreover, the form of the teeth and the places where they had been worn down were unlike any they had ever seen. The substance he had described as now composing the jaw was what might be expected to have been used in "fabricating a false specimen." They urged that Featherston have a chemist analyze a bit of the material to see if it contained any phosphate of lime, which must be present if any bone had been involved, although it could also have been added if the material was artificial.[19]

Featherston was chagrined, to say the least, particularly in view of his remarks about pseudoscientific accounts that had reached Europe from America. Only the portion of Buckland's letter dealing with other matters appeared in the next issue of the journal. Still, Featherston was not prepared to give in too easily. He wrote Sedgwick that there would be "an end to all working if Fossils are to be turned to the right about because they are unique," and he sent Buckland the original specimen. When the specimen reached him in late April of 1832, Buckland knew at once that it was, as he had thought, an obvious hoax. To convince Featherston of this, he asked his friend Mr. Clift to examine it confidentially. Clift found the "bone" to be a form of iron sandstone, and the "teeth" composed of sand, cement, and some limestone. He wrote Buckland, declaring that he was grateful for "a sight of this wonder of the new world, & shall not hereafter despair of seeing the sea serpent himself." Since the original was now in England, it could disappear or, better still, Buckland suggested, Featherston could withdraw it himself, pleading the absence of collections with which to compare it. If he could discover the author of the hoax, Featherston could show him up, even if he is "a good fabricator of cement," but Featherston was never able to determine who had made the "fossil." This was not the last of the unfortunate "rhinoceros."[20]

On 22 February 1832 the Geological Society of Pennsylvania

was established, to Featherston's great satisfaction. Judge John Banister Gibson was elected president, and Lieutenant Colonel Stephen Harrison Long one of the vice-presidents. Dr. Harlan and Featherston were two of the three curators. A committee drew up a circular to be distributed entitled *Queries on the Geology of Pennsylvania,* and Featherston reprinted it in the March issue of the *Monthly American Journal,* which the society had chosen as its official organ. This was a series of twenty-eight questions designed to arouse an interest in geology through individual study of local environments and the collection of mineral and fossil specimens. Seven pages of the May issue were devoted to the April meeting of the society, at which Featherston read a paper by R.C. Taylor and presented a sketch of the area around the Blue Ridge from the Susquehanna to the Mississippi. He did not forget the Geological Society of London either. He sent them casts of a scaphite and of a saurian tooth. The former had been found sixty feet below the surface during the digging of the Chesapeake and Delaware Canal, in a formation resembling one that he had seen at Speetown Cliff near Scarborough. Similar casts were sent to Murchison and Buckland.[21]

In this same month, Featherston learned of the failure of his publisher, Henry H. Porter. The subscription payments for the *Monthly American Journal* were lost in the bankruptcy. Rather than fail his subscribers, who had paid for a year's subscription, Featherston undertook to finance the March issue and the remaining three numbers of Volume 1 himself, at a cost of fifteen hundred dollars. It was a cruel and costly ending to a journal that had been well received both in the United States and abroad. There had been highly complimentary reviews in London's *Philosophical Magazine* and the *London Monthly Review* as well as extremely favorable reports in newspapers in Philadelphia, Boston, New York, and Washington. Featherston made one last effort, too little and too late. He dispatched a package of circulars about the journal to Buckland so that he could distribute them at the meeting of the British Association for the Advancement of Science, of which he was president. Featherston had already sent him twenty copies of the April number. In the June issue, the editor thanked his readers and apologized for the poor circulation during Porter's regime. He hoped to resume publication sometime in the winter with a series of articles on American gold mines after a personal investigation in the fall.[22]

The last few issues of his journal involved Featherston with the able but eccentric Constantin Samuel Rafinesque. He had come to the United States in 1802, already a knowledgeable naturalist. He had then returned to Europe and remained there for ten years before he again came to the United States. He had subsequently become professor of natural history at Transylvania University, where he was known for his stimulating lectures. Extremely versatile in his interest and an avid collector in almost every aspect of natural science, he had completed a major work on fishes and had contributed many articles to Silliman's journal. He had also edited one of his own, the *Western Minerva*. In 1826 he had left Transylvania and settled in Philadelphia.[23]

Featherston had commented briefly in his January issue on the continuation of Rafinesque's French essay on Ohio River bivalve mollusks, which had been published in Belgium in 1820. In the February issue, Featherston had published Rafinesque's account of his 1821 visit to Big Bone Lick, and C. A. Poulson's translation of the bivalve essay was reviewed in depth. The reviewer pointed out that many of the new species discovered and described by Rafinesque had been rediscovered by others and claimed without recognition of Rafinesque's priority. Dr. Charles Wilkins Short, who had succeeded him at Transylvania, was among the few who had not been guilty of such misappropriation. After all this attention, Rafinesque had reason to feel kindly toward Featherston. If so, the May issue of the *Monthly American Journal* was something of a shock. This contained reviews of Rafinesque's *Enumeration* of his cabinet, published the previous November, and of his new *Atlantic Journal,* the first issue of which had just appeared. Featherston's comments on both were caustic. In the *Enumeration* Rafinesque had displayed "an entire ignorance of even the outlines of the science" of geology. The twenty advertisements contained in the first issue of the *Atlantic Journal* were impressive for a new publication until one learned that all of them had been composed by the editor. The new periodical was "a perfect museum of curiosities," well worth the twenty-five cents it cost. To make matters worse, Featherston published a letter from Harlan, who claimed that Rafinesque had borrowed a fish from him, had failed to return it, and had described it as a new genus in a letter to Cuvier that Rafinesque had quoted in his new journal.[24]

Not surprisingly, Rafinesque returned the compliment with a scathing attack on both Featherston and Harlan in his *Atlantic Journal*. His comment about it in a later letter to John Torrey expresses his satisfaction: "The Atlantic journal produced me the enmity of FEATHERSTONHAUGH and HARLAN, who published a journal of geology, fancying that I would interfere with them, and because I belonged to the French School of Natural Science and Geology, instead of praising like them the English system of Geology based exclusively upon their Island. They picked up a quarrel with me, and I had to expose their blunders in my journal upon a rolled stone, puffed up into a Rhinoceros jawbone! Harlan could not forgive me to have seen the fossils of CLIFFORD before him." His reply to Featherstonhaugh was "but a just defense. I have exploded his Rhinoceroides any how . . . & his only discovery."[25]

The final number of the *Monthly American Journal* was not published until mid-July. In spite of this delay, Audubon's letter dated 15 April was not included in the journal. Perhaps it arrived too late. His communication from Charleston, to which city he had returned, reveled in anticipation of his imminent second visit to Florida, where he knew he would be "scorched" by the sun and half eaten by flies but would find pelicans' eggs, catch boobies, discover fish and perhaps an immense pearl. Such a jewel would be easier to find than ready subscribers for either his or Featherston's publications. Audubon sympathized with his friend's financial troubles but added, "What is money after all but Senseless matter?" Buckland, too, commiserated with Featherston. Even his agent in London had not been cooperative in supplying copies of the journal. Featherston wrote Buckland that Silliman had told a Yale class that he would consider anyone who supported the *Monthly American Journal* inimical to his own journal.[26]

During the late summer and early fall, the Featherstonhaughs accepted the hospitality of the Madisons at Montpelier for a long visit while Featherston explored various parts of Virginia. The former president was now eighty-two, somewhat feeble phys- ically but as alert and interested as ever. Featherston marveled at the old gentleman's remarkable intelligence and knowledge as well as the gentle, unstinting care of his wife. He told her son, John Payne Todd, that he had had such an enjoyable visit that he would certainly return, for the Madisons made him feel as if they were old friends. Their conversation ranged widely. Several times they discussed slavery, and Madison told Featherston that he could never die in peace if he thought slavery would continue perma- nently. He had once called his slaves together and offered to free them immediately, but they had refused his proposal, saying that he had always provided for them. If they were free, where could they go and who would protect them?[27]

During his stay at Montpelier, Featherston made a trip to Rich- mond, where he was impressed by the beautiful view of the James River from the upper part of the town; it reminded him of the English Richmond-on-Thames. He was delighted with fossil de- posits along the river and those on the hill where the courthouse stood. It was the coal deposits, however, that he made his par- ticular study. He traced the veins from outcroppings and found them to lie northeast to southwest. They apparently ended just below Petersburg, where the Appomattox River empties into the James. To the north they ran approximately thirty miles. He found it difficult to determine the width but thought it might be fifteen miles. The depth of the vein varied greatly, depending on its gran- ite foundations. Four hundred feet down Heath's Maidenhead Mine, the seam was almost thirty feet thick. Some places were being mined as deep as six hundred feet. When Featherston and Charlotte returned home, he composed a poem praising the Madisons and Montpelier, which he sent to them.[28]

Featherston was interested not only in coal mining but in the possibilities for gold. In 1830 he had written Sedgwick that in geological studies "an active and clear headed man might make himself a fine reputation. The gold formations in the southern parts of the U.S. are going to be very valuable. I am preparing materials from every quarter." In March 1832 the *American Quarterly Review* published a lengthy account entitled "Gold Districts," ostensibly a review of two books on the subject, which strongly resembles Featherston's work. The first thirty-four pages are mainly devoted to the history and methods of gold mining in the United States. The last twelve actually review the two books. Featherston had also discussed gold with Matthew Rhea, of Columbia, Tennessee, who had made a geological map of his state, which Featherston had promised to note in the June number of his journal. He tried to pin down the rather vague terms Rhea had employed in the map. Exactly what beds were involved in the secondary formation and in the transition? If he had samples, Featherston could draw up the succession. He was curious about Rhea's location of the gold region north of the Great Smoky Mountains; it would be most unusual to find gold there. Was it in veins or could it be an alluvial deposit?[29]

Once again Featherston found it necessary to seek a new means of occupying himself and supporting his dependents. Having become completely absorbed in geology, he naturally continued to look for opportunities in this field. It would not be difficult to find things that should be done but to find something financially adequate would be another matter. In his 1830 article in the *American Quarterly Review* he had compared the problem of Americans who were interested in natural science with those of their counterparts abroad: "In England, the field is occupied by men of education and fortune; they have wealth, and they seek for noble modes of expending it." Americans, however, "are almost universally prevented by personal occupations . . . from contributing largely to any of those branches of science, which only flourish where wealth and leisure assert their influence." As Daniels has pointed out, one obvious solution to this problem might have been government support for scientific investigations, but this had not been a politically popular idea. There had been some such support for exploring expeditions like those of Lewis and Clark and Major Long, but even these had been criticized as inadequate.[30]

Since Featherston's return from England, he had been thinking of the need for geological surveys in the United States. In fact, he had had them on his mind for some time before his visit to England. His interest in geological surveying and mapping of the United States had been encouraged by the response to his journal, and he had used the journal to promote the idea. The September issue had carried his article "On the Value of Geological Information to Engineers," in which he suggested that some of the many military men and engineers who were enthusiastic about his journal might start some surveys. There was a particular lack of information about the physical geography of the West. One who heartily agreed with Featherston's ideas and who encouraged his efforts to promote them was Richard C. Taylor. He had been working for some months on a survey of the Pennsylvania coalfields when Featherston asked him for information about them. His reply, accompanied by an excellent section of the Allegheny Ridge, showing the coal strata, formed the lead article in the April issue of the *Monthly American Journal* and had excited much attention. Featherston had stressed the importance of geology in establishing boundaries. He cited the case of the dispute over the boundary between Maine and New Brunswick, which he thought could have been settled in 1783 had geologists been involved.[31]

In December 1832, he made a move that he hoped might produce financial support both for his journal and for the national geological survey he had so long been eager to undertake. He presented a memorial requesting such support to the United States Senate, which referred it to Lewis Cass, secretary of war. Cass made the requested report on 17 January 1833. He praised Featherston's journal and recognized its cultural contribution, but he did not see how the War Department could justify any financial assistance to it other than the purchase of a number of copies to be distributed to military bases. The survey was another matter. Cass praised Featherston's attempts to promote a geological survey and emphasized the value of such an investigation. He was strongly in favor of a complete geological survey of the United States and thought it could, and should, be carried out through the Military Academy at West Point. Army officers, trained by a professor of geology and mineralogy there, could be required to make such studies as part of their duties at all military posts; their efforts would add greatly to the geological knowledge needed for a map.[32]

Cass had asked Featherston to write a more detailed account of his suggestions, and it was included with his own report. Featherston stated that he had been studying the mineral resources of the United States for many years, both in fieldwork and in correspondence. He pointed out that a geological map had already been made of Great Britain and that others were in progress in Germany and France. He suggested that Congress might accomplish what he was urging by authorizing the employment of a competent individual to work with the Topographical Bureau. Such a man might spend seven or eight months of each year making field studies and the remaining months at the bureau. As part of his duties he might be required to deliver an annual course of lectures upon the geology of the United States during the session of Congress. Featherston had been encouraged by both Lieutenant Colonel Abert and Colonel Stephen Long of the Topographical Bureau.

Featherston did not expect any immediate action by the Senate. He wrote Edward Livingston, secretary of state, on 28 December 1832 that the proposal for a federally sponsored geological survey, about which they had talked, would be presented to Congress in a few days. His friends all advised him that it would probably not be acted upon at the current session and that he might have to wait a year or more before he knew the result. In the meantime he planned to continue his geological investigations insofar as his limited finances would permit.[33]

The Featherstonhaughs spent the winter of 1832–1833 in Washington so Featherston could continue to promote the survey. He was able to persuade the congressional committee appointed to consider it to adopt his reports and to get an appropriation to start the project under Cass's direction, with the help of the Topographical Bureau. Jackson's cabinet members were enthusiastic. In their report to the president, they recommended that Featherston be put in charge. Nevertheless, his problems were not yet over. Legal questions had to be resolved before an appointment could be made, and these would involve a long delay. He was grievously disappointed, writing to Murchison that in England this postponement would never have occurred after an appropriation had been made.[34]

On 4 July 1833, Featherston wrote from Shirley to the Virginia planter Edmund Ruffin, editor of a new publication, the *Farmer's Register*. Featherston had seen the first number and had read with pleasure an article entitled "General Description of Virginia." Whether he had seen Ruffin's *Essay on Calcareous Manures,* published the previous year, is not known. Richard Sheridan has called Ruffin "the most influential leader of southern agriculture in the antebellum period," and many others have written accounts of his career. Ruffin, at this time thirty-eight years old, had, since 1818 or earlier, been ardently advocating the use of marl and other calcareous materials for the improvement of soils. Featherston in his letter used the opportunity to promote more attention to the geology of the state and to stress its importance to farmers, who, he thought, might get tired of always reading about barnyard manure. Virginia had been remiss in not yet having authorized the production of a geological map of the entire state as Maryland had done. The failure was particularly regrettable as Virginia was probably richer in minerals than any other state, even aside from her coal deposits and the marl beds in the Tidewater. In conclusion, he quoted Long's description of the natural bridge in Scott County in toto, since one of the *Register*'s articles had deprecated it. He was emphasizing his belief that writers should actually examine the things whereon they wrote: *"Veni, vidi, vici."*[35]

Gold mines and a general study of the gold regions were Featherston's special projects that summer. He spent much time in the woods west of Fredericksburg, where the rounded hills were cut by alluvial streams into small valleys. He would go out early in the morning, as he later wrote, and "many a time, when wandering by one of these murmuring brooks, and listening to the rich and varied melody of the Mocking-bird, whose favorite breeding place is in the groves, have I dipped out the auriferous gravel, washed it in a pan that I carried about with me, and thus collected in the course of the day native gold of the value from five to ten shillings." At night he returned to a clean room in the cabin of a settler who shared his bread, bacon, milk, and tea with Featherston. In Louisa County he visited one mine where miners had taken ten thousand dollars' worth of gold from the stream in six days before locating the vein, a quartz studded with knobs and lamina of gold in contrast to the waterworn alluvial gold. He found that the gold-carrying quartz veins lay from the northeast to the southwest. In a few places gold was alloyed with silver, and in several there was tellurium, but usually the gold was almost pure at 23 or 23½ carats. Nowhere in Europe had he seen gold as rich and beautiful, the finest of it being found in Orange, Spotsylvania, and Culpeper counties. By the end of his two-year tour, he had visited every gold mine in Virginia. Everywhere, the miners and mine owners had been most cordial and had extended every facility for his investigations.[36]

In September he took a brief trip to Philadelphia, where he happened to see Andreas del Rio, a fellow member of the American Philosophical Society and former professor of mineralogy in Mexico. He had been shown two small diamonds by Don Vincente Guerrero (later president of Mexico), who had found them in geodes given him by some Indians. Guerrero had visited the place in the Sierra Madre where they had been discovered and found many imbedded in such very hard rock that pickaxes were necessary to get them out. Some geodes contained amethysts, others rock crystal, and a few of them diamonds. Featherston was inclined to be amused at the story but del Rio was so serious that he decided to see what he could learn. He had just received a welcome letter from Maclure, who seldom wrote his friends since he had taken up residence in Mexico. Featherston immediately answered the letter, hoping that Maclure could discover whether there was any truth to the del Rio story. If so, perhaps he could send some of the geodes and a piece of the rock in which they were to be found. He added that he was trying to keep flying the "geological flag" Maclure had first hoisted. He reported that his journal had only survived a year but that he and his friends had founded the Geological Society of Pennsylvania. Unfortunately, he noted, it had more enemies than friends. Among the former was the American Philosophical Society, which looked on it as a rival. He had deposited geological specimens with the Geological Society but had no money to purchase minerals needed to complete the collection.[37]

Back in Fredericksburg in November, Featherston was busy writing an essay entitled "Mineral Resources of Virginia," in response to Madison's request. This was published in the *United States Telegraph* immediately and reprinted in the *Richmond Enquirer* and the *Farmers' Register.* The Virginia governor had just recommended a geological survey of the state, which gave Featherston a welcome opening for his remarks. He gave a brief review of the rather casual American interest in mining since 1619, except for coal; then he summarized Great Britain's use of her mineral resources, which had contributed much to her present prosperity. Now that it was felt that much of the state's arable land was somewhat exhausted, agricultural practices were improving, but a study of available minerals could also bring great profits. He recounted his own investigations, with particular emphasis on gold, but added that there were indications of iron, silver, copper, lead, and other ores. A complete geological survey like the one the governor had suggested could locate them. In regard to gold, more systematic mining would yield far more, but such mining would require a greater knowledge of metallurgy, more labor, and more capital. The $150,000 invested by northerners was far from sufficient. There should be more incorporated companies to spread the risk among many, and money should be sought from abroad. Twelve to fifteen million pounds had been invested in South American mines. If ten million pounds were invested in Virginia, the resulting wealth would affect the whole state. Seventy thousand dollars' worth of bullion had passed through a Fredericksburg bank in this year alone. The value of real estate would rise and labor would be in demand.[38]

Before Featherston left Fredericksburg on 28 December, friends urged him to write to Joseph Carrington Cabell about the governor's proposed geological survey of Virginia. He did so from Washington 4 January 1834. He hoped that such a bill would be submitted to the state legislature under Cabell's auspices, since he

was known for his interest in the improvement of the common-
wealth. Would Cabell be interested in doing it? The Chesapeake
and Ohio Canal Company had already approached Cass about a
federal geological survey to be made of the Potomac Valley. If
Congress approved, perhaps it could be made a joint survey with
Virginia's. He recalled how DeWitt Clinton had overcome many
difficulties before the Erie Canal was an actuality, and now Clinton's name would never be forgotten because of his stubborn support of the project. Cabell did not think that it was an appropriate
time to bring the question of a state survey before the legislature
because of another undertaking. If and when Cabell did bring up
the idea, Featherston volunteered to supply the practical means of
its execution. His move to Washington was to lobby again for his
survey proposal. He already knew a number of members of Congress and obtained introductions to others, including James K.
Polk. When not involved in promoting the United States survey,
he passed the time translating Alessandro Manzoni's *Betrothed
Lovers,* which was published by the District of Columbia publisher, D. Green, that same year. Again Featherston was more or
less scooped when Andrew Norton published a translation very
early that year in New York.[39]

The First Geological Survey Begins

6

On 28 June 1834 Featherston's aspiration became a reality. Congress passed an act authorizing examination of the elevated country between the Missouri River and the Red River and appropriated five thousand dollars for the survey. Ten days later Abert wrote Featherston that he was "directed by the Honorable Secretary of War to inform you, that you have been selected, as principal Geologist, to aid in carrying into effect the directions of the law in relation to Geological and Mineralogical research." His compensation would be six dollars per day and twelve cents per mile for transportation. Within four days Featherston had accepted the "appointment of Geologist to the U.S."[1]

His first orders from Abert, addressed to him as "U.S. Geologist," 16 July, directed that he proceed to the northern boundary of the Territory of Arkansas, arriving there by early October. The government wanted to acquire "accurate information of the Mineral and Metallic Resources of that territory." At Little Rock, he was to make "a general reconnaisance of the geological formations of the adjacent country, noting the mineral and metallic deposits with the accuracy requisite to the transfer of your information to a geological map of the Territory to be hereafter constructed." He was to return to Washington to report to the bureau by 1 February 1835. He would probably not be able to make a complete and detailed survey in the time allowed, but Abert desired that he give particular attention to "all the high lands and water sheds of the tributaries of Red River and the Canadian, as well as the Arkansas comprehended by those highlands called the Ozark or Messerve Mountains."[2]

Abert did not want Featherston to limit his report to the survey he was ordered to make. He specifically directed that, "although by these instructions you are limited to the Territory of Arkansas, and the adjacent public land, it is nevertheless desirable that in the report to be made by you on your return to this City whatever geological information you may possess, which can be usefully applied to the investigations you are about to make, and which may aid in developing the resources of the country you are directed to examine and their connexion elsewhere, should be fully stated for the information of the government." This was a suggestion Featherston was unlikely to overlook.[3]

He had known for some time which region Abert wanted him to study and had made broad plans, but until the orders came, he had not been able to make a detailed schedule or to equip himself for an expedition. His son George, who had left the United States Military Academy, would make the trip with his father. Charlotte would accompany them as far as Nashville, Tennessee, where she would visit friends from the French embassy, Mr. and Mrs. Pageot. Featherston decided that he could more easily obtain some of his supplies in Baltimore than in Washington. He needed no excuse to spend a few days at Barnum's Hotel. He had acquired a taste for the canvasback duck there and indulged it whenever an opportunity arose. A few days after receiving his orders, the Featherstonhaughs went by train to Baltimore. They spent ten days there while Featherston was acquiring the chemicals he needed, some of which had to be sent from Philadelphia.[4]

The excursion began from Baltimore on 1 August and took them by railroad to Frederick, Maryland. From there they were to go by stage to Harpers Ferry, which was then in Virginia, and down the Shenandoah Valley into the Allegheny Mountains to the medicinal springs. He discovered very early on the first day that travel, even in these long-settled regions, was beset with many problems and aggravations. His first shock came when his carefully packed box of chemicals was dropped from the coach that took them from the hotel to the train. Fortunately, a druggist at Frederick was able to help him replace most of the chemicals that had been lost. There were compensations as well. When the train stopped for breakfast at Ellicot's Mills, Featherston "mounted the top of the railcar" and maintained his "ground there in the teeth of a column of smoke loaded with sulphurated hydrogen." The railroad followed the Patapsco River through an interesting ravine, and he "was delighted at being wheeled with the velocity of a locomotive through a singularly picturesque road, where such a variety of primitive rocks presented themselves" (12. See Note 4).

At Harpers Ferry, where the Potomac River is joined by the Shenandoah, he found evidence to support his belief that river channels passing through mountains have not been preceded by fissures but have been made by the rivers themselves. Although he had previously thought Thomas Jefferson's descriptions of the gorge through which the Potomac passes here somewhat extravagant, he was impressed by it and thought the issue of the Shenandoah from its ravine "very grand." Soon after leaving Harpers Ferry they entered the limestone region of the Shenandoah Valley, which Featherston had not previously seen. He looked for fossils when they stopped for breakfast but found none. He thought the limestone to be contemporaneous with that of New York and to be "subjacent to the old red sandstone" (13).

Taking pains to establish cordial relations with the stage driver, Featherston was able to persuade him to make occasional stops to rest his horses while he made quick geological observations. At regular stops he used his limited German to converse with some of the many people of German extraction who had settled the valley. They were mostly thrifty farmers, some worth as much as $300,000, and yet superstitious and clannish. The roads were rough and travel tiring, so the Featherstonhaughs were pleased to find the landlords where they stopped, attentive and obliging. They kept rather strange hours since, traveling by stage, they were sometimes called from their beds at half past three in the morning, as they were when they left Staunton on 4 August. At that point they had traveled 130 miles on the Valley Pike. Now the way led to the west into the foothills and mountains, and the coach slowed to three and a half miles an hour, giving Featherston even more opportunities for geological and other natural history observations. He and his son often got out to walk, easily keeping up with the coach, for it made frequent stops. When they paused to dine at a tavern, he found that he received "rational and obliging answers" to his questions. He enjoyed the stories some of the old hunters told him but took them with a grain of salt. He found that "the traveler who takes such an interest in the country he is passing through, gets through it in a friendly manner, and gleans a great deal of information" (16), and this philosophy served him well throughout his life.

He walked up the eastern slope of Warm Springs Mountain at a leisurely pace and found it "difficult to do justice, either with the pencil or language, to the magnificent objects that were continually presenting themselves. . . . [The mountain] created an impression of grandeur too lofty to be scanned by aught living save 'The lordly eagle.'" He elected to ride down the mountain but soon regretted his decision. The driver of the coach, having locked one wheel as a brake, nonetheless drove down "at speed." The passengers arrived at the hotel, thankful to have reached it alive. Feeling dirty and disheveled, the Featherstonhaughs were somewhat embarrassed by the scrutiny of an assemblage of elegantly clothed guests on the verandah. The ladies were well corseted, some with bustles, and all had elaborate hair styles; the arrogant-looking gentlemen smoked, chewed, and spat.

Although the hotel accommodations left much to be desired, Featherston liked the rather unusual proprietor, Colonel Fry, who did his best to make them comfortable. There were not nearly enough servants to attend to the wants of the guests, and so there was great confusion, especially before meals. Featherston was highly amused by some of the protests he overheard: "Waiter, there ain't not a drop of water in my pitcher" or "Waiter, who under arth has taken the towel out of my chamber?" or "Waiter, I swar you've brought me two odd boots; one's considerable too little and the t'other's the most almighty big thing what I never seed" (17).

Food was always plentiful, if not always well cooked, and there was "plenty of excellent milk, and lumps of beautiful transparent ice to put into it, a luxury which is universal in the pleasant state of Virginia" (17). The real excitement was the dinner hour. Place cards were on the plates, and latecomers were seated at the bottom of the table and then moved up as other guests left. Various overdone meats were already on the table, and to one side would stand Colonel Fry, clad in a blue-checked pinafore, to carve the mutton roast. When any lady rose to leave, he would bound over to her, offering his left arm while his right still brandished the carving knife. In the evening, everyone retired to the so-called ballroom where one fiddler provided the music. Fry and his son waited at the door to drag each lady over to the benches along the side. When the quadrille started, the two Frys would grab two of the most recently arrived ladies, usually protesting, and haul them to the dance floor. The ladies usually submitted "with all the resignation of a bird in the talons of a hawk" (18). Although Fry's actions astounded Featherston and others from out of state, the Virginians were accustomed to such behavior in their host and esteemed him highly.

The thermal baths and the beauty of the Warm Springs region delighted Featherston, and he decided to remain there for a week. He thought the water of the springs to be unrivaled in its beauty; "not even the waters of the Rhone where they issue from the Lake of Geneva" were as beautiful. It was his practice to rise at dawn and occupy himself "wading through a burning sun, climbing the rugged mountain's side, hammering rocks." When he returned, laden with specimens, he thought a bath in the sparkling waters of the springs "the greatest enjoyment in the world . . . next to *Champagne frappé de glace*" (18). The main bath was thirty-five feet in diameter and five feet deep. It was deserted at this hour, having been used alternately by the sexes every two hours since four in the morning. Sometimes as many as twenty shared it.

Featherston found his geological tramps rewarding. The limestone of the Warm Springs Valley particularly interested him. He found fossils not far from the hotel that closely resembled fossils found in the Dudley limestone in England and in calcareous rocks from near Lake Erie. From the highest point of Warm Springs

Mountain he had George make a sketch of the view to the west, in order to include Warm Springs Valley and the ridges beyond. One of the latter, Backbone Ridge, or Allegheny Mountain, was of special interest as a watershed. Streams arising on its eastern slope flow eventually into the Atlantic Ocean and those on the west into the Gulf of Mexico.

From Warm Springs the Featherstonhaughs traveled by coach to White Sulphur Springs on 12 August. Although these attracted more visitors than Warm Springs, Featherston had been warned to expect poorer accommodations and less attention there. He determined to go anyway; Charlotte had not been well and had accompanied Featherston partly to benefit from the medicinal properties of the water there. He thought that he had been promised accommodations at White Sulphur, having written to friends who had assured him they had arranged it, but this illusion was rudely ended when the hotel manager told him, "Look ye, Mister, I han't room for a cat" (22). Featherston finally found a room of sorts in the badly overcrowded home of a local blacksmith, who had, wrote Featherston, "abandoned the anvil for the vocation of entertaining company, for which he was as much fitted as we were for making horse shoes" (23).

After five dreadful days at the blacksmith's abode and many threats to the manager, Featherston finally got a dismal room in a cottage at the hotel. To his dismay, he found it little better: "In this establishment, that might be as unrivalled in its comforts as in its natural advantages and beauty, everything is alike, a scene of dirt and confusion; and a charming rural retreat from the heats of the summer is thus disgraced with all of the filth and nastiness of a badly conducted hospital" (27). There seemed ample evidence that the waters had the curative properties claimed for them, and they attracted some of the most distinguished families of the state. Some of the "White's" popularity was due to the bar, which offered "gin slings," "gum ticklers," "phlegm cutters" (28), and other cocktails from early morning to late at night, and to the ballroom, where a good orchestra played lively tunes. The men who ran the gaming table and other gambling devices were not too much in evidence. Although there were 150 slaves to wait on the 300 guests, the service was poor and the food impossible. A cavernous kitchen opened directly on the dining room, and the slaves ran about over the filthy floors in the gloom, tending fires that blazed like subterranean furnaces. In spite of the prodigious waste of food, the innkeeper's profits were well over thirty thousand dollars a year.

Featherston was amused by several titles he acquired at White Sulphur. One man, seeing his collection of specimens, called him Doctor. Most other acquaintances called him Colonel, and the hotel servants addressed him as Judge. He found this practice of conferring honorary titles widespread in the United States, where people professed to "abhor titles of every kind." In New England, "the plainest farmer, as soon as he is elected to the State Legislature, is metamorphosed into 'The Honorable Mr. Slick!'" Young lawyers in New York, given political appointments as "Inspector-General of the Militia, an office without duties," acquired the title of General for the rest of their days. This obsession with titles was even greater in Virginia, where "almost every person of the better class is at least a colonel, and every tavern-keeper is at least a major" (29).

The geology of the Alleghenies interested Featherston not merely for its local aspects but as part of a mountain range extending from a "southwestern-termination" northeastward "far into that part of Canada which lies north of the St. Lawrence," a distance of nearly seventeen hundred miles. Especially interesting was "the great limestone valley, which more or less accompanies it throughout its extent, and which is most conspicuous in Pennsylvania, and in that valley of Shenandoah in Virginia" (29). He enjoyed visualizing the great upheaval that had produced not only the immense mountain range and the accompanying valley but also the varied springs of this region. He found the waters of the White Sulphur Springs similar to those at Harrogate in England and "like them . . . not particularly agreeable to the taste." He "only drank them once, and not being fond of nasty things, never had the curiosity to taste them again" (30).

Before going to White Sulphur and while he was there, Featherston consulted with competent physicians who regularly took

their families to the springs about the curative properties of the
waters. He found general agreement among them that the waters
were beneficial to people suffering from a variety of ailments.
Having grown up next to medicinal springs himself, Featherston
had no illusions about some of the miraculous cures claimed. He
thought it probable that the visitors were equally benefited by
leaving the rather unhealthful climate of the Tidewater for "the
invigorating air of a salubrious region, the fine exercise enjoyed in
the hills, and a relief from the cares of business." He thought it "a
providential dispensation that there should be a mountainous region
containing so many precious resources so happily situated—mid-
way, as it were, between the inhabitants of the low lands of the
Atlantic Ocean, and those of the basin of the Mississippi" (31).

Examining the "dry beds of mountain brooks," Featherston
found "quantities of fossil impressions on sandstone," but he did
not find their main source until he and his son undertook to climb
White Rock Mountain southwest of White Sulphur. There was no
path up the mountain, and one local resident advised them that if
they succeeded in getting up, they "should not be worth sixpence"
when they got down. Such comments did not deter them, but
they understood them better before they returned. They climbed
for two and a half hours before reaching the summit. Although
they found the view "exceedingly fine," they remained only long
enough to make a sketch. About a hundred feet from the top they
found horizontal beds of rock that "turned out to be the red ferruginous sandstone with fossils in situ" (30), which they had only
found before in the stream beds of wet-weather brooks. They had
started their climb at nine o'clock in the morning and got back to
the hotel eleven hours later with their clothes in tatters.

The Featherstonhaughs were happy to leave White Sulphur for
the Sweet Springs, eighteen miles away at the foot of Peter's
Mountain. Everything there was in sharp contrast to what they
had left, and the family began to enjoy themselves again. The
cabins were scattered about under the cool shade of huge oaks that
gave them some precious privacy. The landlord set an excellent
table, and all soon recovered. Featherston reflected, "What a delightful country this would be if there were none but well-behaved

people in it" (32). The baths he found invigorating, and he re-corded temperatures and other data concerning them. He believed the sweetish taste of the water was probably due to the presence of magnesium carbonate.

The geological feature that most interested him was the traver-tine deposits (crystalline calcium carbonate), which he was able to study in both recently formed and ancient deposits. He could find the beginning of it within a hundred yards of the overflow from the springs. Two miles downstream he found a waterfall over a dam of travertine 550 yards wide. The stream, "now only a few yards broad, had once covered the whole surface of the valley" (32). He was surprised by this evidence that the volume of water had formerly been so much greater. Checking the flat land below the dam, he found travertine extending far beyond the present stream on both sides. He enjoyed picturing the geological history of the valley from the time of its formation to the present "fertile valley capable of producing 10,000 bushels of maize annually: an-other beautiful instance of the beneficent manner in which provi-dent Nature operates in favour of man" (33).

He collected many fine specimens of travertine along the stream. One day, as he was returning to his cabin with some of these, he met the landlord, Mr. Rogers, who was interested in his collections and his explanation of them. He told Featherston that several years previously he had seen similar rock formations not in the valley but high in the hills above. Featherston persuaded Rogers to show him what he had found. The two spent the morn-ing looking for the place. Featherston finally became convinced that his guide was confused about what he had seen and suggested that they give up, but Rogers wanted to make one more try. He found the spot almost immediately. It was on the side of Snake-Run Mountain, some 350 feet above the level of the springs. Feath-erston was astonished to recognize a "huge mural escarpment of ancient travertine, skirting the brow of a hill," and resembling those that he had seen in the valley. He had clear evidence "that a stream of mineral water of great breadth, loaded with carbonate of lime, had for a length of time passed over this brow, and formed this very ancient escarpment." As he contemplated this "extraordinary phenomenon," he found it "to be susceptible to no other explanation than that the level of the valley was, at some remote period, much higher than it is now, and that the Sweet Springs were then at the same level with this ancient travertine" (33).

With only a few days left for his investigations, Featherston explored the area adjacent to the springs fairly thoroughly and found much to interest him. He even found "anthracite coal cropping out in a ferruginous sandstone, on the left bank of a stream called Fork Run." Ferruginous deposits were abundant in the mountains and those near the top of Sweet Springs Mountain he thought contained more than 50 percent iron. The combination of iron, coal, and limestone with very fertile soil held great promise for "a thriving population establishing itself here" (34).

The plan to have Charlotte accompany her husband as far as Nashville had to be abandoned when a letter informed them there was a serious epidemic of "bilious fever" there. However, a Commodore and Mrs. Rogers were returning to Washington and would be happy to have Charlotte join them. They planned to spend a day with the Madisons on their way. Featherston wrote Madison that Charlotte was looking forward to seeing them. If convenient, she would like to have a longer visit with Dolley provided she had a satisfactory way of going on to Baltimore and Philadelphia. 5

Featherston and George left Sweet Springs on 3 September, their immediate destination Fincastle, twenty-nine miles away. They sent their luggage on by stage and then set off on foot, recording geological observations as they went. Early on their walk they noted an impressive and undisturbed bed of anthracite coal at the bottom of Pott's Mountain. Having walked twenty-five miles since eleven o'clock, they reached a tavern a few miles from Fincastle long after dark. Next morning, they continued their journey, making frequent stops for observations and sketches.

The small town of Fincastle was, on the whole, pleasing to the travelers. It was full of activity since court was in session. Featherston was amused by the conversation of lawyers at their dinner table at the inn. He recorded some of his observations of the Virginia political scene there and elsewhere, and of Virginians in general. With few exceptions, the influential men were all lawyers; they filled the state legislature and represented the state in Congress. All professed "to be most religiously devoted to the maintenance of the Constitution of Virginia" (35) but had many ways of interpreting it. They were equally eager to maintain their devotion to Jeffersonian doctrine. Featherston then gave a commentary on Jefferson, whose views and influence he abhorred, despite his admiration of and friendship for Madison. Jefferson had been responsible for the exchange of "a Federal Government resting for its maintenance upon character and property" for "one based upon free thinking and universal suffrage, two grand incarnations of fancied virtue totally without the principles they stood in place of" (36). Always the aristocratic federalist in his point of view, Featherston seldom lost an opportunity to discourse upon the evils of universal suffrage

Featherston and George continued by stage down the Valley of Virginia to Christiansburg. Early next morning they reached a crossing of the New River. As they approached, they came to a scene utterly abhorrent to them, which reminded Featherston of the coffles in Africa, described by Mungo Park, the Scottish explorer who examined the sources of the Niger. Slave drivers, on their way to Natchez with some three hundred Negro slaves, had camped near the river, which they were preparing to cross. There were women resting on logs, children warming themselves at a fire, and two hundred men chained together like so many animals. Featherston thought he "had never seen so revolting a sight before. Black men in fetters, torn from the lands where they were born, from the ties they had formed . . . driven by white men, with liberty and equality in their mouths, to a distant and unhealthy country, to perish in the sugar-mills of Louisiana, where the duration of life for a sugar-mill slave does not exceed seven years" (36–37). Standing around laughing and joking were the slave drivers, white men who rode in carriages and wagons, which also carried the black children and lame adults. Slave drivers had learned from cases of slave revolt during such trips to be ever vigilant. They used experienced blacks to help drive the new slaves and to amuse them with stories and singing. Food was generally

Featherstonhaugh's sketch of "Slave Dealers" from his *Excursion
Through the Slave States,* I, Frontispiece [Courtesy of the Alderman
Library, University of Virginia]

good and plentiful. Each year fewer slave gangs went by land,
however, for they were easier to control at sea. The demand for
their labor had increased with the purchase of Louisiana and the

price for a slave had gone from five hundred to a thousand dollars.

Featherston wrote at length about the evils of slavery, every aspect of which he loathed, but he clearly recognized the problems of owners who wanted to free their slaves. The abolitionist who demanded that a planter immediately free his slaves was not only asking the planter to accept financial ruin for his family but was offering no provision for the freed slaves. Featherston thought that emancipation could only be accomplished at "national expense." The rapid increase in the slave population, already amounting to approximately two million, raised serious questions for the future.

The route Featherston had chosen to follow took them south through Wytheville to Abingdon. As they traveled he noted that the Alleghenies were composed of the transition formation that Murchison called Silurian, while the Blue Ridge rocks were older, preceding fossil-bearing ones.[6] At Abingdon they were welcomed by General Francis Smith Preston, who lent them horses for an excursion to visit his saltworks at Saltville. Colonel William King, who leased the property, put them up for a day or two while Featherston studied the geological formations in the area. The salt was secured from a reservoir of salt water some two hundred feet underground. When not diluted by recent rains, it yielded as much as fifty pounds of salt from twenty-four gallons of water pumped to the surface. Gypsum was also mined from a quarry there. Featherston supposed this to have been the location of an ancient lake, formed by the elevation of the surrounding land and "fed by saline and gypseous springs" (40).

The Featherstonhaughs resumed their Tennessee journey. On the stagecoach to Blountville a fat young man of about thirty amused himself by baiting Featherston, "the Englishman." At the tavern that night he again undertook to attract attention in the same way and made the mistake of calling Featherston a "_____ rascal." It had been nearly forty years since he had been "an eager pupil of the then celebrated pugilist Jackson," but Featherston's reaction was instantaneous: "It was literally Scarborough warning he got—a word and a blow" (44). The man was knocked to the floor. He reached for dirk and pistol. Whereupon Featherston jumped on him, the landlord jumped on Featherston, and George on the landlord. When order was restored, the young man rose with swollen cheeks and blackened eyes. The atmosphere was a bit tense for a time, but Featherston was treated with greater deference. Later, he apologized to the landlord and company for losing his temper, shook hands with his tormentor, and explained that he had never before been called a rascal.

They traveled by way of Kingsport, Rogersville, and Knoxville to Campbell's Station. Here Featherston was astonished to see President Jackson sitting by a window in the tavern, smoking a pipe. Greeting the Featherstonhaughs cordially, he laughed when they apologized for their dirty appearance. He told George, "If you were a politician you would have dirty work upon your hands you could not so easily get rid of" (45–46). Featherston told the president that he had seen a box addressed to him at a tavern in Virginia and had learned by chance that it had been there for several weeks. It had not been prepaid and the local representative, no admirer of Jackson, had declined to forward it. Featherston had taken the liberty of taking charge of it and had it with him. Jackson was greatly indebted to him, as the box contained his favorite saddle, which he had feared lost. He asked that Featherston take it along with him until he reached the Hermitage at Nashville and insisted that they should call on him at the White House as soon as they returned to Washington.

Their route, which had been south, now turned westward toward Nashville through Kingston, Crab Orchard, and Sparta. Soon after parting with the president, Featherston identified a man who had been traveling with them and who seemed familiar. He finally recognized him as one of the slave dealers he had seen at New River. The man, attired in a white hat with a black mourning band like the president's, loudly proclaimed his admiration for Jackson. Featherston could not resist asking for whom he was in mourning. He was somewhat startled to learn that it was for "Marcus Layfeeyate." He suggested to the man that the general, "who had gloried in making all men free" (46), would not appreciate his mourning and that his ghost might come some night and set free all the slaves. The man made no comment, but George and the man's Negro servant, Pompey, roared with laughter. Pompey was immediately threatened with later punishment and hastily explained that he had not intended to laugh at his master. They parted company when they came to the "fearful and irritating spectacle" of the slave encampment (47). At Kingston, Featherston and George were joined by a far more agreeable companion. He was a French silk merchant from Philadelphia named Nidelet, who was attempting to collect large debts owed to his firm. He had traveled in this part of the United States for many years and seemed to be known by all sorts of people. He had heard of Featherston at Philadelphia, was delighted to meet him, and when they parted at Sparta, gave him a letter of introduction to his father-in-law at St. Louis.

Finding the country around Sparta interesting, Featherston decided to stay for a bit and explore. The innkeeper provided horses, which they rode to the summit of the Cumberland Mountains, collecting fossils along the way. Next day, they went on foot to investigate the graves of a tribe of supposed pygmy Indians at a place called Hickory Valley. A great many of these curious graves had been found when farmers cultivated newly cleared land. The "caskets" were made of six slabs of limestone—top, bottom, side, and end pieces—and inside each was found an Indian skeleton. The odd feature of these caskets was that none of them were more than twenty-four inches long. A book had been written about them, which Featherston had either seen or heard of. He and his son visited farms belonging to Turner Lane and a Mr. Doyle, where hundreds of these graves had been found. Featherston was even permitted to open one of them himself and to take measurements of it. All the skeletons were found lying on their right sides with the knees drawn up. Under the neck, there was always a pot made of clay and particles of unio shells (freshwater clams or mussels). Perforated shells and stones, probably from necklaces, were also commonly found. Featherston, skeptical about pygmies, made the mistake of calling Doyle's attention to the size of the skulls, which were as large as his own. These seemed unusually large for pygmies. He told Doyle that a number of western Indian tribes made a practice of exposing the bodies of their dead on scaffolds until only the bones remained. These were then buried in short graves. Doyle did not appreciate being so enlightened. He not only stuck to his belief in pygmies but suggested rather strongly that Featherston talk about something else when he got to Nashville. Featherston resolved that in future he would be "as careful about interfering betwixt a man and his pigmies as I would be betwixt a man and his wife" (49). Later he recalled that "in the ancient British barrows the stone coffin, too, or kistvaen, is composed of six pieces of stone." The Featherstonhaughs left Sparta on 19 September and reached Nashville the next day, having stopped at the Hermitage to leave Jackson's saddle.

Featherstonhaugh's sketch of a Fort near Nashville, from his *Excursion Through the Slave States*, I, 53–54 [Courtesy of the Alderman Library, University of Virginia]

Nashville appeared to be "the centre of civilization of the western country" (51), and Featherston found so much of interest that he and his son spent two weeks there. He called on Dr. Gerard Troost, with whom he had corresponded but whom he had not previously met. He was quite familiar with Troost's career and his geological studies of the Nashville area. Charlotte Porter has said that "Harlan may well have suggested this collaboration [with Troost] for, as Rafinesque bitterly complained, the well-known British-born editor had no qualifications whatsoever as a field researcher." Rafinesque, however, was hardly an unbiased commentator. Featherston had in fact been introduced to field research by such experienced workers as William Smith and William Buckland. This is not to say that he had nothing to learn from Troost. He undoubtedly did and was happy to do so.[7]

Troost was an able, if somewhat eccentric, scientist, then teaching chemistry, geology, and mineralogy at the University of Nashville (not the University of Tennessee). He also served as state geologist and mineralogist. A native of Holland, he had studied mineralogy under Werner. Later, as a surgeon in the Dutch army, he was commissioned to study the natural history of Java. Unfortunately, the English had taken it before he arrived there. As previously noted, he eventually settled for some years at Philadelphia where he had been the first president of the Academy of Natural Sciences, holding that office for five years. He had then joined Robert Owen and William Maclure at New Harmony, Indiana, for a time before coming to Nashville. He was an excellent chemist, geologist, and zoologist, with a particular interest in reptiles, especially snakes. He had a number of pet snakes, which sometimes startled other people by unexpectedly emerging from his pockets. He once caused the hasty evacuation of a stagecoach in which he was traveling when the heads of two rattlesnakes appeared from a basket in his lap, although he attempted to reassure his fellow passengers, saying: "Gendlemen, only don't let dese poor dings pite you, und dey won't hoort you" (51).

Featherston visited Troost many times, finding him very friendly and helpful. They did geological fieldwork together, and Featherston attended a public examination of the professor's students, which he found impressive. Another of Troost's interests was Indian relics, of which he had a fine collection. Featherston saw a resemblance between some of these and Mexican idols he had seen. He was familiar with Troost's geological studies of the Nashville area and grateful for his assistance in making his own

observations. Fossils were abundant in various strata, and Featherston found one type that he had previously seen in the limestone
along the Saguenay River in Canada. With Troost's guidance, he
was able to examine strata from the level of the rocks along the bed
of the Cumberland River, to those of Harpeth Ridge, high above
the city, where one could see "a good section of some of the beds
of the vicinity" as they had once more generally existed before
many of the upper strata were worn away. Featherston was able to
distinguish principal strata of the region and to record a table
showing the approximate depth of each, its general composition,
and the more conspicuous fossils, if any. James Corgan has recently questioned why Featherston spent more time in Nashville
than in other southern cities, suggesting that he may have "pirated
his data from Troost."[8] It is an allegation that appears to be completely unfounded. Undoubtedly, Featherston spent more time at
Nashville than elsewhere because he had the benefit of assistance
from an able and congenial geologist thoroughly familiar with the
region.

Featherston added many fossil specimens to his collections as
well as some from the Columbia River, including beautiful unio
shells, which were particularly fine and abundant there. He found
it interesting that these mollusks were much more plentiful in
streams that empty into the Gulf of Mexico than in those emptying into the Atlantic. He carefully packed his collections in casks
to be shipped to New York via New Orleans.

Tennessee in general, and Nashville in particular, amazed Featherston. Since he had arrived in New York in 1806, when Tennessee
was hardly mentioned, it had grown to a population of 700,000,
had become a state, and had even provided a president of the
United States. The first log cabin had been built at Nashville in
1780. It was now an impressive town of 7,000 people. Rather
reluctantly Featherston made stagecoach reservations for Louisville, Kentucky, on 4 October. They passed near Mammoth Cave
but did not have time to visit it. Featherston was beginning to be
concerned about the passage of time, and he had previously visited
various caves abroad, as well as the Helderberg in New York.
Featherston found the Ohio River magnificent, imagining what it

must have been like when it had once covered several more miles than it now did.

They found Louisville an attractive and prosperous city, beautifully located, with every resource needed for continued prosperity. Featherston considered the citizens more thoughtful and less given to demagoguery than those in many southern cities and towns. He suspected that they were greatly influenced by his old friend Henry Clay. Being tired of coach travel, Featherston thought to go by water on the next leg of their journey. There were small steamers carrying both passengers and freight between Louisville and St. Louis. He booked passage on one that professed to be sailing that day. When the embarkation was repeatedly postponed, he decided that the captain was a pathological liar, who had no intention of sailing until he had a full complement of passengers. Featherston gave up, and they traveled by coach through Indiana and Illinois.

They left Louisville on 13 October, traveling west to the old French settlement of Vincennes, on the Wabash River. Featherston was interested in the Indian mounds he could see on a ridge of sandstone hills. They reminded him of tumuli he had seen on the Yorkshire wolds. He had another interest in Vincennes, having published the journal of Colonel Croghan, who had been sent from Pittsburgh in 1765 by the British government to attempt to strengthen peace with the Indians and to explore the country along the Ohio River. Indians attacked the party, killing five men and wounding Croghan. The prisoners were taken to Vincennes where the French settlers had shared the plunder with the Indians. The citizens of French origin there when Featherston arrived seemed to have little to do with the more recently arrived Americans. He visited with some of them and talked with one man whose father had been there when Croghan was brought in.

After crossing the Wabash River, their stagecoach traveled through Illinois prairies, which Featherston found incredibly beautiful. Comparatively level, smooth roads were a great relief to the travelers. They were able to enjoy these for approximately 140 miles before descending to the former bed of the Mississippi River. They crossed some six miles of this before reaching the river itself, an awesome sight. They could see the steamships, wharves, and church steeples of St. Louis across the great expanse of river and realized that they had safely reached the end of stagecoach travel. They did not feel quite so safe as they crossed over, for the river was surprisingly rough. Featherston, remembering Father Hennepin's travels and the adventures of La Salle, had thought a strong French influence would still be evident at St. Louis. When they reached the main street, he was greatly disappointed to find little or nothing of what he had expected. He found stores filled with eastern merchandise and bearing comparable names. He commented digustedly that the "La Sales [*sic*] had given way to Doolittle & Co" (64).

Featherston and George spent a week at St. Louis. After the initial disappointment, they found it an interesting and thriving place. One reason for its prosperity was that it was a center for the far western fur trade. Featherston was directed to a tavern that he found "in every sense inferior to that at Louisville." The barroom was filled with a rough and rowdy crowd of "idle-looking fellows, drinking, smoking and swearing *American:* everything looked as if we had reached the terminus of civilization." He had scarcely arranged to book rooms when "an exceedingly fine gentleman, superbly dressed, his jowls covered with hair, and a gold watchguard magnificently streaming across his chest, came out from the knot of smoking fashionables in the bar-room, and with his face beaming satisfaction, extended his right hand most lovingly" to Featherston. "It was *'Colonel Smith, of the British army!'* who had formerly served at Waterloo" (64) and whom he had met at White Sulphur Springs. Instead of shaking the "colonel's" hand, he asked the landlord if he might speak to him in private. Featherston told the latter that the so-called colonel was in fact a "runner" of Negroes. The landlord returned to the barroom and remarked that the latest arrival had told him that two Virginia planters were arriving on the next stagecoach, looking for a man who had cheated them. Half an hour later the "colonel" caught a steamer just sailing for New Orleans.

Runners practiced a form of fraud in which they would sell a Negro as a slave. The black man would run away and rejoin the runner, who would resell the man as many times as he thought safe. The proceeds of the sale were supposed to be shared, but the Negro seldom received much and often was killed when he became troublesome.

Not long after his arrival Featherston drove out to Jefferson Barracks, about ten miles south of St. Louis, to pay his respects to General Henry Atkinson, the commanding officer, whom he had met previously. The Sixth Regiment of the United States Infantry was then stationed at the barracks, which were located on a high bluff overlooking the river. The buildings were substantial and well planned, the grounds were attractive, and everything possible to make life pleasant for officers and men seemed to have been done. There was even a library of some three thousand volumes. The general spoke of remarkable fossils he had seen on the west bank of the Missouri River, not far from where it was joined by the Yellowstone, a petrified forest extending for twenty to thirty miles, with trees and limbs on the ground and stumps of trees all turned to stone. Featherston was shown samples of the silicified trees and thought "the phenomenon must be admitted to be one of the most extraordinary facts in the history of mineralogy."

On another day Featherston recrossed the Mississippi to visit a coal mine in the Illinois bluffs. He found an eight-foot seam of coal, lying under a bed of light gray limestone. He had hoped to find fossil plants but found none. He did collect some good specimens of fossil brachiopods, "producta and terebratula." This mine was the principal supplier of coal for the city, to which it was hauled by oxen. Featherston suggested to the contractors that they could save two-thirds of the cost by constructing six miles of railroad at a cost of about thirty-five hundred dollars per mile. He doubted that they would take his advice, however, for the slovenly character of the mining operation did not suggest much ambition. Coal was also found on the west side of the river, and there appeared to be a more or less continuous deposit extending eastward almost to Vincennes.

There were a number of Indian mounds not far from the coal mines east of the river. Featherston saw at least sixty of these mounds in a variety of shapes and examined the largest in some detail. His belief that they must be burial mounds was confirmed by General William H. Ashley, a celebrated fur trader with many years' experience in the west. He assured Featherston that mounds were also to be found far from the river. He showed him pottery and weapons, which were consistently found with Indian skeletons when the mounds were opened. It was evident that they "were to the Indians what the pyramids were to the ancient Egyptians, and the barrow to the races that inhabited England in times of yore" (67). Featherston marveled that the Indians not only constructed mounds comparable to the ancient English barrows but placed in the graves pottery vases that strongly resembled in ornamentation and form those so placed by the English, differing mainly in the materials available. He had owned a number of specimens of the English vases, and the Indian ones he acquired were strikingly similar.

At St. Louis, Featherston particularly enjoyed visiting the elderly General William Clark, of the Lewis and Clark expedition. The general, his daughter, and her husband, Lieutenant Colonel Stephen Watts Kearney of the United States Dragoons were most cordial. The same was true of many of the French families to whom he was introduced by General Pratte, Mr. Nidelet's father-in-law. At the Featherstonhaughs' inn there were trappers from the Rocky Mountains who astonished the Englishman by the quantities of food they consumed. Some of them had spent many years in the Far West; a few had even been in California. Featherston delighted in talking with them of their experiences, particularly with the various Indian tribes. He gathered that there had been a great deal of overtrapping. As a result, the American Fur Company was no longer receiving the number and quality of furs it once did. The trappers had a higher regard for the Hudson's Bay Fur Company. Many of them thought they might eventually settle in the Willamette Valley of Oregon, where the climate was mild and the soil fertile, but Featherston thought it very unlikely that the United States would ever attempt to establish a colony so far away as the Columbia River and was quite certain that the British would never surrender the mouth of that river.

A New Mode of Travel 7

When they left St. Louis, the Featherstonhaughs entered territory where stagecoaches did not venture. They purchased a wagon called a dearborn and a fine young gray horse sired by one of the wild stallions of the prairies. Fortunately Missouri, as the Featherstonhaughs decided to name him, showed none of his sire's wildness. Even so, they decided to try him on a short trip before they really set out. They went first to St. Charles, perhaps twenty miles downriver, to call on Major Henry H. Sibley, to whom Featherston had a letter of introduction. Sibley, one of the commissioners who laid out the traders' road to Sante Fe, had been a United States Indian agent for many years. The Featherstonhaughs put up at a poor tavern where they left Missouri and the wagon, and walked about a mile and a half to Sibley's house. They would have been happy to bivouac in his garden for the night, but he persuaded them to occupy two very comfortable rooms in his house. Sibley's extensive knowledge of Indian customs and languages made him fascinating to Featherston, and they held prolonged conversations on the subject. When they left the next morning, Featherston and George paid a brief visit to what the French had called Mammelles, points of land on the bluffs of the plateau.

Featherston did not want to leave St. Louis without visiting at least part of the mining area downriver, so on 26 October he and

George headed toward Herculaneum, their ultimate objective being the Mexican border some five hundred miles away. Their belongings were comfortably accommodated in the dearborn, to which they added a top to provide shelter from rain. Missouri's harness was in good order, and he was well rested—in fact, too well rested. As they "drove through the streets, Missouri became exceedingly restive and gave sundry signs of dissatisfaction by plunging and elevating his hind heels rather too much above the level of the shafts to promise any good to the general concern" (72). Featherston feared they might be wrecked before they even got out of St. Louis. Missouri was, however, only disturbed by some cannon firing; he settled down once he no longer heard the noise. The Featherstonhaughs spent their first night at Jefferson Barracks. The next day they collected fossils from the limestone beds along the Mississippi.

On 28 October they continued downriver to visit the lead mines of the region, stopping at Herculaneum. This town, on the river's edge, faced a semicircular cove "where the edges of the strata of limestone are worn so as to resemble the seats of an ancient amphitheatre" (73). This feature had suggested the name of the town to its founder, Moses Austin. They spent the night here and started on next morning but did not progress very far before encountering their first serious mishap. On the ferry crossing of the St. Joachim River, a Mississippi tributary, an important part of their wagon was broken. They had anticipated minor problems and had equipped themselves with hammers, nails, cords, and other hardware, but this repair required a forge. Fortunately, there was a blacksmith at Herculaneum, to which they returned.

Having time to kill, they set out to examine the imposing bluffs nearby, which provided a fine view of the very beautiful river scenery below. Great blocks of limestone, filled with chert, had fallen from the bluffs, leaving large grottoes. These formations reminded Featherston of some of the chalk, filled with flint, he had encountered in England. There was a large island in front of the town with a sandbar large enough to make a racetrack. At night, it was occupied by tens of thousands of cranes, the scourge of the cornfields, whose "whirring and croaking" disturbed the evening quiet. There were also large flocks of wild geese, whose honking together with the noise of the cranes and the many passing steamboats, created a bedlam of sound. All of this gave Featherston a feeling of taking part in a scene from the "Arabian Nights."

The entire region he had been observing raised basic geological questions in Featherston's mind. He rejected Werner's views and accepted Hutton's only with reservations. He was familiar with the geological debate then going on in Europe between those who believed in a historical *"general aqueous catastrophe,* similar to that recorded in the scriptures," and those who "look to the effects of causes now in action, to the abrasions, and wearings, and deposits which floods and rivers are producing daily, and have always produced." There were impressive names in both groups. In England Buckland, De la Beche, Warburton, and Greenough were catastrophists, and Lyell, Murchison, Sedgwick, and Fitton were uniformitarians. Featherston had friends in both groups. He regretted that "none of those powerful minds who have espoused" the uniformitarian view had ever visited the United States. His immediate concern was how to explain the entire basin of the Mississippi as sedimentary. As he had earlier asked, "But where are the roots of the rocks that have furnished the mineral matter of which the whole basin of the Mississippi and hundreds of miles of contiguous territory, comprehending an area as large as Great Britain? And what a stretch of the imagination does it not require to contrive the destruction of a continent of such extent! It would seem to be a much more simple process, and one capable of fulfilling all the conditions of the problem, to suppose a great portion of the solid contents of the existing strata to have once been in solution in subterranean depths, and to have been sent to the surface loaded with calcareous matter, as in the case of the Sweet Springs in Virginia, and with siliceous matter, as in the case of the Geysers, as they are exhibited in our own day" (74).[1]

The Featherstonhaughs lingered at Herculaneum until the morning of 1 November, when, with the wagon repaired, they made their way to Vallee's Mines. They found this operation to be more of a quarry than a mine. The smelting of the galena was carried on in small outdoor furnaces by French workmen. Featherston and George then went on to Taplitt and Perry's Mines, where a young miner invited them to share his quarters. He proved to be one of the managers and invited them to join in the evening meal that had been prepared for him and some of his miners. They provided such a pleasant evening that Featherston brought out a bottle of brandy he had brought along for "emergencies only." Next morning, the miners took Featherston down in a bucket 110 feet into a mine shaft. He was able to observe the horizontal veins of "sulphuret" of lead as they descended. He also saw many pockets, or cavities, in the calcareo–siliceous rock similar to those he had seen in Virginia gold mines. But what gave him the "greatest satisfaction was coming at length to a vein *almost vertical* containing a breadth of about eighteen inches of compact galena." After careful study, he concluded that all the horizontal veins had arisen as jets from the molten vertical lode "which rising from below had injected the horizontal bands into the rock" (76) in a manner comparable to the injection of trap into sandstone, which McCulloch had observed at Trotternish, Scotland.

The whole mining operation, capable of bringing up five thousand pounds of ore a day, impressed Featherston most favorably. The "sulphuret" they were bringing up was so free of impurities as to yield the 65 percent pure lead of commerce, and hence it was extremely valuable. The Featherstonhaughs spent the next night at the village of Farmington and the following day visited Iron Mountain, one of the much-talked-of curiosities of this part of Missouri. Featherston found it to be "one of the rarest metallic spectacles" he had ever observed. It consisted of two adjacent hills about 350 feet in height, covering a base of perhaps five hundred acres. There were a few trees, but the surface of the hills "had the appearance of being paved with black glossy-looking pebbles of iron," beneath which there seemed to be a "solid mass of micaceous oxide of iron," extending north and south for perhaps half a mile (77).

On 3 November they visited Mine la Motte, an Old French village of miserable huts. The mining operations in this region again proved to be more quarrying than mining. Featherston made what observations he could and went on to Fredericktown.

With Arkansas their destination, the Featherstonhaughs soon left civilization to spend the next month in the interminable forest and rich, marshy bottoms between the Missouri and Red Rivers. The few settlers in the region had been drawn from the very poor of Kentucky, Tennessee, and Louisiana. Most of them were weak and emaciated from malaria. When the man was a hunter, the cabin was poor, there was no cleared land, and the woman and six or seven children were left by themselves. One pitiful, dirty woman told them that her husband had "gone to help a neighbor to hunt up an old painter that's been arter the pigs; he ain't been hum in a week." When the man was a farmer, he usually cultivated 160 acres of bottomland, but the family still ate poorly. In the thick woods there were buffalo, deer, panthers, wolves, elk, and wild turkeys. At night, the baying of the wolves made Featherston's horse restless.

The dearborn was often mired, once almost adrift in the river, and once it turned over. Much of the time Featherston and George walked, sometimes through burned-out areas. One day their own cooking fire started to spread so rapidly that it was only by a half hour's hard work that they were able to put it out. In spite of the problems, Featherston was at last giving free rein to the spirit of adventure for which he had long envied Audubon, Murchison, and others. He wrote to his mother: "We suffer a good many privations it is true, but this life, being so new, has many attractions, and I confess I like it; especially as it affords me so fine an opportunity of indulging my propensity for geological rambling, and scientific investigation. George is in his Element, he looks like a German Hussar in his shooting dress, and a beard that has not been shaved these 15 days."[2]

Current River, in Arkansas, was deep and filled with fish, even salmon up to thirty pounds. They were relieved to find a "Military Road" had been cut. The trees were blazed, and there was a fine wooden bridge from which they studied the interesting strata exposed by the river: quartz, chert, "agatized flints," and hornstone. After fourteen miles of this carefree travel, they suddenly realized that they had been following the wrong road for several miles when they drove up to a settler's cabin. It seemed that there had been much disagreement as to the route of the Military Road, and several people had cut roads to their own cabins with blazes resembling the official ones.

One afternoon, tremendous flocks of pigeons obscured the daylight with flight after flight. Their motion created "a wind, and produced a rushing and startling sound, that cataracts of the first class might be proud of" (88). Missouri stood trembling in his harness. Settlers had warned the Featherstonhaughs about the dangers on the road from the many rascals thereabouts. They were not reassured one day to find that they were being followed by two rough-looking characters. Featherston decided that they had better plan for the possibility of attack, so he crept silently into the woods, leaving his son on the wagon. After seeing no one for two miles, he rejoined George only to spot the two men ahead of them. Urging Missouri into a trot and with rifles at the ready, they passed the two armed men at a rapid pace.

They reached Little Rock on 15 November, having traveled eighteen hundred miles since leaving Virginia. The city was a funnel through which drained immense numbers of riffraff, and some criminals, on their way to Mexico. Few people went unarmed. The Featherstonhaughs found pleasant lodgings at a clergyman's house on the outskirts of town. They visited the pyramid-shaped Mammelle Mountain. Leaving the horses two-thirds of the way up, they clambered over the naked sandstone blocks, some lying at a seventy-five-degree angle. It was a desolate peak with not a plant, but the view was worth the climb. To the northwest could be seen Mount Cerne and Magazine Mountain, the highest point in the territory at 2,753 feet. The meandering of the Arkansas River could be readily observed. Its extensive bottomland might be cultivated if protected by levees, Featherston thought.

On 27 November they left for Hot Springs, spending the night at a tavern where the hotel staff consisted of but one small black woman named Nisby. Things were a bit informal. She and her mistress prepared dinner for six. When the latter stopped cooking for a minute to inspect the table, Nisby played her part in what seemed a well-rehearsed conversation used to cover up the inn's inadequacies. When asked where she had put the forks, Nisby replied: "I ha'nt put no forks nowhar. I niver seen no forks but them ar what's on the table; thar's five on'em, and thar's not no more; thar's *Stump Handle, Crooky Prongs, Horny, Big Pewter,* and *Little Pickey,* and that's jist what thar is and I expec they are all thar to speak for themselves. . . . and Nisby," Featherston noted, "was right. *Stump Handle* was there, and was by far the most forkable-looking concern, for it consisted of one prong of an old fork stuck into a stumpy piece of wood. *Crooky Prongs* was curled over on each side, adapting itself in an admirable manner to catch cod-fish, but rather foreign to the purpose of sticking into anything. *Horny* had apparently never been at Sheffield or Birmingham, as it was a sort of imitation of a fork made out of a cow's horn. *Big Pewter* was made of the handle of a spoon with the bowl broken off; and *Little Pickey* was a dear interesting looking little thing, something like a cobbler's awl fastened in a thick piece of wood" (105). Fortunately, the Featherstonhaughs carried their own tableware.

After such accommodations, they were glad to reach Magnet Cove, where they spent the night at the summer cottage of Colonel Conway, surveyor general of the territory of Arkansas. In the morning, Featherston climbed a nearby hill from which to view this twelve-hundred-acre cove of very rich land, where only deciduous trees grew on the decomposing greenstone. On the surrounding heights, composed of sandstone, there were only evergreens. Investigating this curious cove, he found a vein of strongly magnetic micaceous iron oxide similar to that at Iron Mountain in Missouri. There were other curious rocks and minerals: black tourmalines, syenite, and hornblende. Some arrowheads that he found were made of novaculite, a type of siliceous rock used for whetstones, but he could not find the rock from which they had been made. Later, a man who was using a piece of it to sharpen his razor, took Featherston to the ridges where it was abundant. He found the novaculite to be "of a pearly, semi-transparent nature, indeed quite opalescent in places, lying in vertical lamina so brittle and so packed together, that it was very difficult to detach a piece even six inches long without the aid of proper tools." The pits from which the Indians had taken the novaculite were sometimes as deep as thirty feet and had been dug with pieces of the greenstone.

Leaving the cottage 30 November, the Featherstonhaughs continued to Hot Springs, which they found to consist of four wretched cabins, into one of which they moved. Featherston thought a town in the narrow valley could well be supplied with hot water by gravity from the many springs that issued from the ridge above.

Unable to find a guide to Towson, the United States military post on the Mexican border 120 miles away, the Featherstonhaughs left 2 December to search on their own. They took a short cut to the Military Road and spent the night at the house of a settler named Mitchell. Here they left their wagon to be repaired and their trunks as surety for a borrowed horse and two saddles, and rode to the Caddo River. Overhead, the parrakeets screamed, and "the trumpet tone of the ivory-billed woodpecker was frequently heard" (115). The limestone bed of the Caddo River provided specimens of turritella, a marine mollusk, and other fossils. They crossed the Little Missouri River on a ferry but found that the flooded bayous beyond were traversed by nine bridges, five of which were of no use since the floor boards had not been secured and had floated away in the flood. The borrowed horse became lame, and it was decided that George would return it to its owner, who had offered to take the young man on a panther hunt.

Featherston continued to Judge Cross's home, where he presented a letter of introduction. He learned a great deal about the geography and mineralogy of the area from his host, whose jurisdiction extended two hundred miles to the west. For the first time in months he slept between spotless linen sheets in a room with plaster walls and a floor that had no spaces between planks and no squealing pigs beneath it. He was out early, feeling very rested. The cabin was in a beautiful setting, and the cultivated acres lacked the usual ugly stumps. The soil was a deep black but rested on limestone, for he found great numbers of fossils. The judge rode with him over to Washington where land sales were being held. There General Sam Houston was living a mysterious existence, sleeping during the day and awake all night. Ostensibly, he was gambling, but he was suspected of encouraging Texas settlers to revolt against the Mexican government.

Land sales, Featherston learned, were far from being a just and open way for settlers to acquire a farm. Congress had provided that public lands should be divided into sections of one square mile (640 acres). These, or subdivisions of them, would be sold at auction. If not purchased, they were "free to be entered at the minimum price established by law, of one dollar and a quarter" per acre, at the next auction. Many poor would-be settlers, foolishly thinking to establish a claim to a section, built cabins, cleared land, and planted crops, expecting to acquire title at the next auction. Instead, land speculators would give them a choice of bidding against them or permitting the speculator to take title and mortgage the land to the settler for as much as ten dollars per acre.

Two days later, Featherston reached Mexico, which had won independence only twelve years previously. For the first few years immigrants from the United States had been welcomed to the province of Texas, which was sparsely inhabited. Most of those who came were from the southern United States, and the most ardent promoter of Texas was Stephen F. Austin. Attracted by rich cotton land that could be bought for only a few cents an acre, almost twenty thousand white settlers and a thousand slaves were living in Texas by 1830, when Mexico realized that her hospitality was being abused. The government prohibited further immigration from the United States, as well as importation of slaves, and required the settlers to become Roman Catholics. At the time Featherston visited Texas, the settlers' dissatisfaction had reached a boiling point; there was much talk of a declaration of independence and of annexation by the United States. Featherston strongly disapproved of a United States annexation of Texas but remained quiet during the innumerable discussions of the subject.

In defiance of the Mexican laws, the settlers were still bringing in slaves. Featherston was even more shocked than he had previously been by their situation, for here the slaves were treated like livestock: "The horse does his daily task, eats his changeless provender, and at night is driven to his stable to be shut in, until he is again drawn forth at the earliest dawn to go through the same unpitied routine. This is the history of the slave in Texas," differing only in that a bit of salt pork was added to his diet of corn. At least in Maryland and Virginia, where slavery had become less profitable, the owners were more inclined to consider humane legislation.

As he rode back to the Crosses' home, he contemplated the effects of the annual flooding of the rivers. Particularly impressive were the great deposits of dead trees. One, called the Great Raft, had extended 150 miles up Red River, blocking a third of the channel and making it unnavigable. Under order of Congress, Captain Henry Miller Shreve had managed to clear the river, using floating steam sawmills, only to see the raft re-form every spring. This type of deflection, where whole rivers were diverted, could be of gravest importance. If the Mississippi ever regained its old channel, for example, New Orleans would be left high and dry.

Featherston rejoined his son at Mitchell's, and they left immediately for Little Rock, which they reached again after a month's absence. While they rested, they packed specimens, completed sketches, and wrote up their journals. They were unwilling to give up the patient and loyal Missouri and so decided that George would return east overland while his father took the riverboat to New Orleans and returned home by way of the Gulf States and the Creek Indian territory, Georgia, the Carolinas, and Virginia. This route would add many miles to his investigations.

Torrents of rain that fell on 22 December enabled a steamer to come up the Arkansas to within twenty miles of Little Rock and take on passengers at Eagle Bend. The voyage down the Arkansas was rather dull, for the river had eroded the land to a depth of 30 or 40 feet and, at Red Pine Bluffs, to 130 feet, and these banks blocked all views. Featherston, however, was interested in the parti-colored strata and the scars where great fractures had eroded the banks. He felt that a more careful study of the effect of recent floods could reveal much about ancient geology and might explain various mineral phenomena. The irregularity of these floods and deposits would not afford specific statistics and computations but could give a broad picture.

Featherston arrived in New Orleans on 4 January 1835. He

found the population of the city a mixed one; there were West Indians, Brazilians, Spaniards, French Creoles, blacks, and half-breeds of all sorts. No man, it seemed, lacked a cigar, and all were dark and piratical looking. The raggedly clad blacks were noisy and constantly screaming. Even on Sunday the markets and gambling houses were open. The latter were branches of a syndicate that ran such houses from White Sulphur Springs, Virginia, south and west. The old French Quarter was gloomy and partially deserted. The accommodations were poor, but there was excellent food. In the American part, houses and buildings were substantial, the streets wide and clean. During his week in the city, Featherston visited the legislature and the Exchange, as well as attending performances at the American theater and the French opera house.

Going by rail to Lake Pontchartrain, Featherston boarded the steamer *Otto* on 7 January. It was a rough voyage all the way to Mobile Bay, which was smooth under a benign sun. Thirty or more vessels were anchored just outside, for the bay was shallow because of alluvial deposits, but the city wharves were crowded with ships of shallow draft. Although he had been told that Mobile was anything but attractive, Featherston found the town quite charming. There were wide macadamized streets with fine sidewalks, the cleanest he had ever seen. Buildings were of brick or newly painted white clapboard, set on large lots with picket fences. Many citizens retired to the nearby plains during the worst season to escape the endemic yellow fever. Mobile was in sharp contrast to New Orleans, which stood in the middle of "a swamp, which is a magazine of malaria that explodes every autumn" (142).

When the steamer *Chippewa* departed up the Mobile River at midnight, Featherston was aboard. Some of the crew were Creek Indians whom he thought more efficient than blacks. Forty miles from Mobile, the ship started up the Alabama River. At Fort Claiborne, Featherston was able to collect some fossil shells from the 150-foot cliffs to send to Timothy Abbott Conrad, whom he considered the United States authority on fossil conchology. Because road conditions were poor in winter, mail was carried on horseback, and stagecoaches did not operate. Featherston, therefore, hired a carriage at Montgomery to take him to Columbus,

Georgia. The trip of only ninety miles cost him sixty-five dollars, and the road was so wretched that he had to walk most of the way.

When they crossed Oakfukee Creek they were in Creek Indian territory. In eleven of the twelve treaties the Creeks had concluded with the United States government they had given up land, a total of twenty-five million acres. Featherston was horrified to see the results of these treaties: execrable roads, miserable Indian cabins with poorly cultivated plots, and villainous looking whites, who sold whiskey and tobacco to drunken Indians. He conversed with many of the Creeks, though he was sickened by the filth and stench of their cabins. The inhabitants of one cabin included a black slave. Everywhere, there were the sick and listless, some begging; it was a shocking degradation of a proud and handsome race. The federal government was turning over jurisdiction of the territory to Alabama, and the interim period had brought no law and order. The few white settlers were understandably nervous. On the road, Featherston passed a number of planters' families, emigrating to the Deep South with their slaves. He saw at least a thousand of these miserable wretches, most of whom were walking the whole distance. On the fourth day he reached Columbus, a pretty little town, and left by mail stage the following morning, 17 January.

At Macon, Featherston collected some unios to compare with those from the rivers emptying into the Gulf of Mexico. He found them to be of the same species as those from farther north along the Atlantic Coast and far different from the beautiful species of the Gulf drainage. As the coach continued north and east, through Warrenton, Augusta, and on to Columbia, South Carolina, he was again struck by the similarity of southern towns. Each seemed to consist of "one endless street filled with small linen-drapers' shops or stores," selling ready-made clothes, boots, and shoes. Sometimes there were one or two bookstores. Always, there were "one hundred dram-shops and dirty taverns . . . crowded with men, all upon a level in greediness and vulgarity" (155).

Columbia and its inhabitants presented Featherston with a new picture of the diversity of his adopted country. It was a strange mixture of the Nullifiers and those who agreed to the Compromise Act. One of the most enthusiastic of the Nullifiers was Thomas Cooper. In 1834, when he was denouncing Christianity, he had been relieved of his position as president of the College of South Carolina and given a sinecure as a means of pensioning him off. Featherston found him living in a comfortably furnished villa, where Cooper received him cordially. Seldom had Featherston spent a more pleasant and amusing evening. When he brought up the subject of the Compromise Act, the elderly gentleman, "almost bent double like a hook," rose from his chair and pranced about, wielding the hearth brush like a sword and denouncing the act. He thought the Nullifiers should have challenged General Jackson in the field and concluded, "We have lost a fine opportunity, sir, of carrying this State to the highest renown" (157). When neighbors joined them for tea, Cooper was "constantly paddling about," chatting and paying "lively compliments," as the conversation ranged from geology to law but dwelled primarily on politics and religion.

The following day, Featherston was invited to dine with some gentlemen he had known in Washington. He was astonished by the liberal tone of the conversation in regard to both religion and politics. Unlike other Americans, who were voluble in praise of everything in their country, these men did not hesitate to denounce the Republic. They said frankly that there could only be good government when it was administered by gentlemen. Having kept quiet up to this point, Featherston suggested that Mr. Madison would certainly be considered a gentleman in any country. His hosts retorted that Madison was "a false hypocritical dissembler, that he was one of the favourites of the Sovereign People, and one of the worst men the country had produced." Discouraged by this pronouncement, Featherston kept silent until something so extravagant was said that he could not resist asking, "in a good natured way, if they called themselves Americans." One gentleman spoke for all: "If you ask *me* if I am an American, my answer is No, sir, I am a South Carolinian" (157).

The inconsistency of their liberality was blatantly brought home to Featherston when the mail coach he was to take arrived on 22 January. A black man was chained flat on the roof. He wondered how these liberal-minded southern gentlemen could condone such actions and remarked to his friends who were seeing him off, that the South would never be as prosperous as the North as long as southerners felt as they did about slavery. The reply of one of the men was so startling that Featherston could hardly believe his ears. He said that no one outside the slave states could understand how slavery "elevated the character of the master by comparison, made him jealous of his own, and the natural friend of liberty" (158). To this specious absurdity, the man added that the primogeniture practised in the South preserved them from the rapacious spirit of the North. Northerners divided their estate among their children, who then had to struggle to acquire wealth. Featherston boarded the coach only to find he was joining a murderer in chains and his guard. They had gone fifty-five miles when the coach turned over. Featherston received a blow on his head and decided to walk to Chesterville. There, he boarded the coach again and reached Charlotte, North Carolina, that night.

The town had achieved some fame recently for constructing mills to crush the gold ore that was abundant in the area. The town lay in part of what was known as the Gold Region, which extended southwest from the Potomac River in Virginia to the head of the Tallapoosa in Alabama. Featherston had studied part of this region in Virginia. The superintendent of the mills, J. Humphrey Bissel, took him out to see Capp's Mine. They went down the 160-foot shaft, and Featherston found that the "quartz vein was sheathed with a case of talcose slate" (161). Since most of the gold was associated with iron, it was seldom visible. One vein had some gold, but was extremely rich in copper, so Featherston thought that copper mining might soon be found to be more rewarding than gold in North Carolina. The next day, a half hour's walk from Charlotte, he came upon one of the most remarkable rocks he had seen in the United States. It was a pale-colored dike of felspathic siliceous rock, with stains of manganese oxide that looked like leopard's spots. It was appropriately known as leopardite, a quartz porphyry. He remembered that the Germans had named it *Weiss-stein,* or white stone. He was so fascinated by this rock that he arranged to obtain an eight-hundred-pound specimen of it.

Late in the evening of 27 January he arrived home, having traveled three thousand miles. Since both houses of Congress had called for his report, he worked hard and rapidly for the next three weeks. Its forty-two pages, addressed to Abert, were completed 17 February. The first fourteen pages gave a brief account of modern geology and its potential applications and benefits to the United States. He then gave a detailed account of his investigations, with particular emphasis on lead and iron mining. He touched on the possibility of piping the hot water of mineral springs into houses. He mentioned novaculite and the probabilty of anthracite deposits. He urged the building of levees to preserve the forests and the topsoil. In conclusion, he suggested that a geological survey of the entire United States should be made as soon as possible. The report, signed "U.S. Geologist," was submitted to the House by Secretary of War Cass on 18 February, and fifteen hundred copies were requested. Ten days later, Cass presented it to the Senate, which ordered a thousand additional copies to be printed. Congress adjourned 3 March, and Featherston spent the next three months preparing an enlarged version of his report, with details and elevations that had been omitted from the first. Its ninety-seven pages were published by Gales & Seaton on 6 June. The geological section, covering the area from the Atlantic at New Jersey, west and south to the Red River in Texas, was colored to show the various strata.[3]

Although the report may not have had as many geological details as some might have wished, it was quite influential in its way. The *Missouri Argus* and the *Missouri Republican,* as well as some Arkansas papers, published long excerpts from it, for it was by far the most detailed report of the region up to that time. The *Anzeiger des Westens* gave a summary of his investigations and hoped that there would be additional mineralogical studies, particularly of Iron Mountain. All this publicity did much to stimulate interest in developing mining in the area. Even Silliman's journal had kind words; after a long description of the report and the map, the reviewer remarked, "This report is a document which geologists, both at home and abroad, will consult with advantage, on account of the wide range it covers, the splendid features of the country and the scientific precision and perspicuity with which it is described." Featherston forwarded copies to friends. Madison considered it valuable, though he admitted he was not scientifically qualified to judge it. Buckland was so impressed that in September he exhibited Featherston's section at meetings of the Bremen Geological Society and at the German Naturfors at Bonn, giving his copy to a Professor Hoffman to take to Berlin.[4]

The appointment as United States geologist had inspired Featherston's friends to propose him for membership in the Royal Society of London in April 1835, and he was duly elected. The certificate referred to him as "a gentleman who has zealously promoted the cultivation of geology in the United States and who has recently been appointed by the Congress to conduct an extensive Geological and Mineral Survey of that Country under the title of 'Principal Geologist of the United States.'" It was signed by Murchison, Greenough, Buckland, Sir Henry Holland, and Sir John Franklin, the well-known Arctic explorer.[5]

Featherston's federal project was beginning to inspire state surveys. Joseph Cabell forwarded some Board of Works records that Featherston found interesting because they showed what the state of Virginia was doing. He sent a copy of his report to Cabell, drawing attention to several pages applying to the successful survey of any state. Featherston, now a government employee, felt that he could readily give disinterested advice. Senator John Tyler of Virginia approached him, saying that Cabell wanted information that might assist him in drawing up a bill to establish a survey. As president of the James River and Kanawha Canal, Tyler was naturally interested in such a project. Featherston wrote Cabell that Virginia was "like a slumbering Giant, and you have only to awaken it to see what immense power nature has endowed it with." The last session of the New York legislature was considering a survey. In April, Troost sent Featherston copies of the first few pages of his *Geology of Tennessee,* asking his friend when the Geological Society of Pennsylvania would publish a second volume of transactions, since his "Memoir" would appear in it.[6]

While in Washington, the Featherstonhaughs lived at Peter's Grove on Georgetown Heights, where Charlotte had stayed during her husband's absence. The mansion, built in 1808, was surrounded by more than eight acres of land, which made it a "comfortable retreat," as Featherston wrote to Madison. The present owner was Colonel John Carter, possibly a relative of Charlotte's. During their stay, their first child, Georgiana, was born.[7]

During his recent travels Featherston had kept in mind the official and formal report he was required to make. He had also given a good deal of thought to the possible publication of a popular account and had kept his travel notes accordingly. He sent copies of a portion of them to both Buckland and Murchison even before he reached home. Buckland had already received his copy when he wrote to Murchison on 5 February 1835. Featherston had asked Buckland to assist Murchison in promoting publication. The manuscript he had sent was heavy enough for Buckland to prefer carrying it to London rather than mailing it, Oxford not being "fertile in franks," as he put it. Murchison approached John Murray, Lyell's publisher, who was most excited about the whole idea.[8] In fact, he was so enthusiastic that Featherston was flabbergasted to read premature announcements of his proposed book in London periodicals. He sent a parcel containing his official report and a copy of his translation of Manzoni's *Betrothed Lovers* to Murray. The former would give him an idea of the proposed book and the latter Murray was free to republish, with no conditions attached. Featherston had been disappointed by the efforts of his Washington publisher, although the book had enjoyed such popularity that it had been reprinted in a miscellany in the United States. He added that he was not a "mercenary person but would not refuse an offer to share in any profits." It was just at this point that he received a new assignment from Abert, so he wrote Murray that the publication of the book would have to be postponed until after his return in December. At that time he would complete the manuscript but would like to know whether Murray planned one or two volumes and how many illustrations. As for Featherston's remuneration for the book, he would leave the amount to Murchison and Murray, adding frankly that his name was not yet well enough known to have any promotional value.[9]

Canoeing Up the Minnay Sotor 8

Abert's order of 7 July directed Featherston to travel to Green Bay in the Wisconsin Territory. He was then to proceed down the Wisconsin River, looking for both lead and copper and collecting specimens. At Prairie du Chien, he would go up the Mississippi to St. Peter's River and continue to the higher land known as Coteau des Prairies.[1] This area had never been examined closely, although French writers had reported copper there.

While he was in Washington, Featherston's salary had been two hundred dollars a month, but once he returned to the field he received the usual six dollars a day and twelve cents a mile. No longer was he financially worried. George had become an assistant civil engineer for the government in Michigan. James had graduated from Union College the previous year. Although not yet twenty-one he, too, was working as a government civil engineer, helping to run a ship canal around Niagara Falls. Featherston had little compunction about leaving Charlotte and the baby in such a congenial place as Peter's Grove.[2]

For this trip an assistant was appointed to help Featherston. Lieutenant William W. Mather was a West Point graduate who had taught geology, mineralogy, and chemistry at the military academy for six years. While on leave from the army in 1833, he had been geology professor at Wesleyan University in Connecticut and

153

had published a textbook, *Elements of Geology for the Use of Schools.* In 1834 he had made a geological survey of a Connecticut county. Mather had asked permission to accompany Featherston but had been refused by Major General Alexander Macomb. Abert himself then asked the general to detach Mather for the expedition. There was no other officer with the same qualifications: "known devotion to such pursuits, his many valuable communications which are to be found in the journal of sciences, his able digest of the reduction of iron and silver ores," and his paper on Connecticut geology. Such a man would be of great assistance to Featherston. Abert's orders to Mather were quite specific: "You will report to Green Bay Michigan Territory to aid in the Geological and Mineralogical investigations to be made between that place and the Coteau des Prairies, in relation to which you will receive and Conform to the instructions of G. W. Featherstonhaugh Esq."[3]

The expedition began in luxury. On a clear and sunny 8 July, Featherston and Mather boarded an eighty-five-foot iron boat on the Chesapeake and Ohio Canal at Georgetown. It carried a number of gentlemen who were superintending the building of the canal and who were going on a tour of inspection. They had invited the two geologists to accompany them as far as William's Port, where the canal ended. Colonel Abert was one of the group, which included General Tobias E. Stansbury and George C. Washington, the company's president. There was also a very jolly Virginia Quaker, who soon became the life of the party. Just past the Great Falls of the Potomac a delicious cold luncheon was served in the comfortable cabin. The accompanying Madeira, generously imbibed, produced great gaiety. Featherston could scarcely remember a happier day. That night and each succeeding one were spent at taverns along the way.

Featherston was charmed to be in such congenial company, particularly since they had no objection to his leaving the boat whenever he spotted some interesting geological subject. He examined John Lee's quarries, whose stone was being used in some of the public buildings in Washington. It was Silurian sandstone with traces of copper and anthracite seams that provided some excellent specimens of fossil plants. Not only was there the superb scenery to enjoy, but Featherston could not help but marvel at the

impressive canal construction. Eleven miles from Georgetown began a series of eleven locks, the west side of the canal requiring
masonry one hundred feet high. He was not surprised that the cost
had been many millions. Once, when they returned to the boat
after an inspection, Featherston enquired how far to the next lock.
The Quaker immediately responded, "Thee may'st put it down in
thy book, that it will take us just two bottles of Madeira to get
there" (1:7).

On 11 July, just beyond Shepherdstown, they came to an
eighty-five-foot limestone hill through which the canal had been
cut. To their right were the prosperous Maryland farms, settled by
the Pennsylvania Dutch, where the fertile land cost fifty dollars an
acre. The great prehistoric earth movements were apparent on the
eastern Alleghenies, where limestone beds "frequently dipped
both ways" and parts of an arch had been forced upright when the
movement subsided. Mather, as intrigued as Featherston, made a
sketch of the scene. At William's Port, slate appeared in sheets of
limestone, some of it bearing fossils. Here, a hundred miles from
Georgetown, the canal was still under construction.

On their way by stagecoach the next day to Cumberland, future
terminus of the canal, Featherston walked up North Mountain to
study the Silurian sandstone and then to Bath Springs in Berkeley
County. At Cumberland, the two geologists parted with their
friends and spent the day investigating the wonders of the gorge in
Will's Mountain. At Bedford Springs they paused for a day, roaming the area and noting the northeasterly direction of the Alleghenies, sometimes broken by intersecting ridges. Two day's
travel by carriage took them to Pittsburgh, a "dusty, dirty, coal-
hole-looking place" (1:33). The imperfect combustion of many
factories and forges caused a continual rain of soot flakes. All
laundry had to be done indoors. Across a fine bridge was the new
town of Allegheny where refugees from Pittsburgh's dirt were
settling. Featherston sketched the city and its two rivers, and Brad-
dock's Field, nine miles away. Having earlier read Washington's
journal and made a detailed study of the arrogant General Brad-
dock's disastrous campaign, he welcomed the chance to visit the
battlefield.

The travelers took the steamboat *Beaver* to the community of

Economy, eighteen miles below Pittsburgh, and found it in shin-
ing contrast to that city. Unlike the landings of other towns, Economy's had no taverns serving "half-and-half," the popular drink
that was "half whiskey, half cider-brandy, and no mistake," the last
word referring to water. Economy's founder, George Rapp, kept
the landing low-key to discourage the casual visitor. The inhabitants, immigrant German farmers, had a rather turbulent history.
Led by Rapp, they had left the Stuttgart area in the early 1800s,
seeking religious freedom. They had first settled in Pennsylvania,
then moved to New Harmony on the Wabash. Rapp had found
that situation not only unhealthful but inconvenient to the markets. He sold it to Featherston's acquaintances Robert Owen and
William Maclure in 1824 and purchased these three thousand acres
of bottomland on the Ohio.

Featherston could scarcely believe that Economy had reached its
high state of development in only eleven years. From every point
of view, it was idyllic. There was a commodious house for each
family, situated on the neatly right-angled streets. Each house had
its fine vegetable garden and fruit trees as well as vineyards. The
abundance reminded him of the lush gardens of Tuscany and Lom-
bardy, to which the often careless, weed-grown American ones
usually stood in such sad contrast. The wheat, corn, and oat fields
were also luxuriant, yielding excellent crops.

Featherston was equally interested in the silk industry, which
turned out lengths of cloth for waistcoats and handkerchiefs. Two-
thirds of the five hundred residents were engaged in making
blankets and cotton cloth, for which there was a ready market in
Pittsburgh, where they purchased coffee, sugar, tea, and other
items that they were unable to raise or make themselves. Economy
had a fine school as well as a library and natural history museum.
The German love of music was freely indulged, but overall, there
was the aura of a truly religious life, happily lived. The importance
their religion placed on subduing passion apparently forbade marriage and would eventually lead to the extinction of the community, but this possibility did not worry the members, who
considered themselves one happy family of brothers and sisters.
Featherston was granted an interview with the venerable founder

one afternoon, and Rapp's serenity and godliness deeply impressed the Englishman. Having complimented him on the excellence of his community, Featherston asked what chance there was for the success of the Socialist group at new Harmony. Rapp felt that the two communities were far different. His was based on leading a peaceful, godly life, while Owen's group wished to spread their ideas abroad and to convince others that their "religion, morals, laws, and manners" were wrong (1:87).

Mather and Featherston spent a continuous thirty-six hours in carriage and stagecoach before they reached Cleveland. There they boarded a steamer for Detroit, arriving 30 July. On Sunday, Featherston invited Mather to cross by ferry over to the British side to examine the area, but Mather declined. Instead, he attended the Presbyterian services. Featherston had thought an army man would be interested since the British might again be the enemy some day. He should not have been surprised, however, for Mather had missed seeing Fort Malden, explaining that he had been too sleepy. When Featherston asked him if he would like to go to the afternoon service at the Canadian church, the lieutenant replied that he was going to a Presbyterian meeting.[4]

The two men had other disagreements as well. Featherston had told Mather in Washington that theirs was not an army expedition; they would make their way to Coteau des Prairies as best they could, paying their own way. Indignantly, Mather declared that their supplies would be provided by the army quartermaster, and Featherston pointed out that they had no supply requisition. Nevertheless, Mather wanted to engage two canoes and crew and to buy all the "munition de Bouche" in Detroit. He persuaded Featherston to have a tent made, emphasizing the scourge of "Musquitoes, Gnats and god-knows-what" and bought many things on his own, saying he would draw a hundred dollars of his travel allowance in Green Bay.[5]

Featherston soon realized that he and Mather had little in common, but he assumed a mutual interest in geology. Even in that he was mistaken. Mather proved to be a pedantic mineralogist, as excited over a bit of talc as Moses was "about the ten Commandments when he found them fossilized on Mount Sinai." He had no interest at all in the broader aspects of geology. Featherston did not hide his feelings about Mather from Abert: "D———n such Assistants in geological matters—I have made a mistake—he is like a 56 pound shot hanging over my back." He had other reservations about his traveling companion as well. He admitted that Mather was respectful and kindly, but these virtues did little to make up for the fact that he was a deadly bore. He was uninterested in any politics beyond those at West Point. Even to the highly principled Englishman, Mather seemed a complete Presbyterian puritan. He was a Temperance Society member and, although so young, "would absolutely faint away, at the sight of any woman's legs excepting Mrs. Mather's." Featherston asked Abert what he was to do about the instructions that Mather was to return to Washington with him, if needed, to assist in making the report, adding that the young man could never suggest one idea for it. Perhaps General Macomb could think of another reason for Mather's return, possibly as chemistry professor in place of Lieutenant Hopkins, who had resigned this position at West Point.[6]

The two men left on 4 August by steamer for Fort Gratiot, which they reached that evening. They examined earth brought up by well diggers at stops along the way. Featherston deduced that the region had been covered by water fairly recently in geological time. The trip was uneventful except for one stop when a large number of pigs came squealing down to the landing place. It seemed that this island farm belonged to the ship's captain who dropped them swill as he passed. Major William Hoffman, commandant of the fort, invited them to stay there until a ship bound for Lake Huron came by. Featherston found the majority of army officers to be intelligent men, extremely interested in the surrounding country and the Indians. He learned much from their information and advice.

One day he dined with Lieutenant Amos B. Eaton, whose father's geological views he had criticized. This was not the only Eaton hospitality, for the lieutenant forwarded a box of specimens for Featherston, and Featherston spent the night of 7 August with the Eatons. He discovered that he was occupying his hosts' only bed and, rather than incommode them further, he had his tent pitched in the morning. He crossed to the British side where he visited the Methodist minister James Evans, missionary to the Ojibways. Evans told how he could always tell when his congregation would be increased: conjuror's drums, medicine bags, and other superstitious trappings would be left in his hall. He presented some of these to his guest.

The two geologists made a rough schooner trip to Mackinac Island. There they soon forgot their *mal de mer* when they enjoyed a superb breakfast featuring a thirty-pound salmon. Featherston immediately called on Henry R. Schoolcraft, the Indian agent, whom he knew. Sixteen years previously Schoolcraft had visited the same lead region of the Mississippi Featherston had recently investigated, and he had published a book on the natural history of the area. In 1832 he had taken part in a government expedition exploring the Mississippi Valley.[7] His advice was therefore valuable. Schoolcraft lived in an attractive lakeside house with his half-Indian wife, who had been educated in England. Featherston spent some time chatting with members of an Ojibway encampment nearby. A delegation of Indians from Lake Michigan amused him as they tried to talk the agent into giving them ammunition, blankets, and tobacco. When the tactful agent gave them some of the last, they were satisfied, since, as Schoolcraft knew, they had already received much from the British agent. Featherston had dinner with the Schoolcrafts and spent the rest of the day with them, learning much about the Ojibway language and being shown all over the neighborhood by his host.

One of the army officers took Featherston around the island by boat the next day. They landed several times so Featherston could look for specimens and make sketches. They even rifled some Indian graves, for which they received a just retribution within hours; the odor of the bones and trinkets was all-too reminiscent of a charnel house and more lasting. The next morning Featherston scrubbed with brushes and soap in the lake and liberally sprinkled himself with eau de cologne, wryly acknowledging that he well deserved such punishment for their desecrations. For the next three days, Schoolcraft helped him with the study of the Ojibway language he was making, particularly the pronunciation, for he had already accumulated a large vocabulary. It was a curious language, resembling such Semitic tongues as Hebrew in grammatical construction. Schoolcraft offered to send Featherston's specimens as well as the trinket and skull from the graves, on to Abert.

Featherston and Mather boarded the steamer *Monroe* for Green Bay. After an extremely violent storm that night, with terrifying displays of lightning "that seemed to have set the world on fire," all were ready to land at their destination the next afternoon. The surrounding land was so flat, Featherston remarked, that it would not "put a snail out of breath." They had now traveled twelve hundred miles but had nine hundred more to go by water and two to three hundred by land. Charlesvoix and others had claimed to find tidal action here, so Featherston set out sticks to test the hypothesis. He found that the water rose and fell about a foot in twelve hours and was told this occurred daily. General Cass, who had also observed this phenomenon, had attributed it to the action of the northerly winds, and Featherston agreed. General George Brooke, commandant of Fort Howard, took Featherston across to the island on his barge. The fort was surrounded by fine-looking vegetable gardens. Tomato plants on trellises were six feet tall with good fruit. Brooke, an ardent gardener, kept his men busy working the earth when they were not on duty, and thus they were able to supply their own needs. The general and other officers were helpful with advice as to what the geologists would need.

They spent several days in preparation. For fifteen dollars they bought a birchbark canoe that could accommodate eight people and a ton and a half of luggage. They engaged five voyageurs recommended by the trader Daniel Whitney. Each would receive his food and a dollar a day. This pay seemed extravagant to Featherston, but he had no alternative. Whitney advised Featherston never to allow the voyageurs to drink. As headman, Louis Beau Pré would be paid more than the other men. Featherston bought a barrel of pork, two barrels of biscuits, boxes of rice, flour, tea, sugar, candles, tobacco, presents for the Indians, and kitchen utensils. It seemed impossible that all this, plus a tent, gun, portfolio, and trunk of books, would fit into the canoe, but they did. Featherston even found room for the great bearskin on which he would sit, resplendent in his bright green mackinaw.

They left on 22 August. Mather was sporting a broad belt into which he had thrust a knife, a tomahawk, and a pair of loaded pistols. He had also slung a rifle over his shoulder and looked as if he expected to fight Indians all the way to Coteau des Prairies. Featherston warned him that he would have to be unarmed when they actually faced the Sioux, or they would all be in danger. He himself felt confident armed with only his fists, a geological hammer, and some prudence. He was already respectfully known among the Indians as the "Stone Doctor."[8]

The days slipped into a true routine. They would be up at four o'clock and would stop for breakfast at nine, after covering ten or fifteen miles. They omitted lunch. An hour before sunset they would stop to make camp. They would pitch the tent and line the ground under it with the soft tips of spruce branches, double where the beds were to be. These comprised an oilskin, then a bearskin, with blankets for cover. They would raise the canoe on poles to provide a shelter for the voyageurs. Even though ham and boiled potatoes fried together were not exactly gourmet fare, Featherston found this clean, outdoor life far preferable to the noise and dirt of the miserable frontier inns. It was surprisingly cold for August and raining every day, but nothing discouraged the stifling clouds of mosquitoes. Undaunted, however, the men, encouraged by Featherston, sang lustily, and he joined them in the choruses. He enjoyed talking with them, but Mather, who spoke no French, could not join in, nor could he take part in Featherston's attempts to converse with the Indians.[9]

In fact, the two geologists hardly spoke to each other, for Mather seemed to have no interest in literature, history, or general science and to know little and care less about the Indians or even the little-explored country through which they had passed. Such obtuseness exasperated Featherston, who was fascinated by everything, particularly whatever he could learn of the Indian languages. He felt a bit guilty about his attitude toward the young lieutenant, realizing that he was a "good" man, but could not resist adding, "as a sugar lump is good with nothing bad in it." He told

Mather that he had written on his behalf to General Charles Gratiot, chief army engineer and inspector at West Point, to see if he
could get Mather orders for West Point, where he could be with
his family; Mather only said that he would need additional appointments in order to afford living at the academy. [10]

One day Featherston and his party raced with several canoes of
mourning Menomineys, whose charcoal-blackened faces might
have emerged from Dante's Inferno, finally leaving them behind.
They passed through some fourteen thousand acres of wild rice,
with stalks up to ten feet high, in the Winnebago country. It was a
desolate land, inhabited only by red-winged blackbirds, rails, and
black watersnakes, of which Featherston snared a specimen. The
land was geologically uninteresting, but he was comforted to find
a few primary boulders. He reflected that the charm of geology
depended on the realization that even pebbles formed "an interesting link in the undefinable and rather awful world of existences to
which they belong and where man's intellect delights in roaming"
(1:181). Beyond the rice was tall wild grass, no longer kept down
by buffalo. They had been driven across the Mississippi by the
Indians who, driven by the whites, would soon follow the buffalo.
Featherston realized that "the scythe of what is called 'civilization'
is in motion, and everything will fall before it . . . substituting for
the unpretending barbarity of nature, the artificial government of
meum and *tuum,* with the improvements in fraud and vice" (1:188).

They reached Fort Winnebago on 29 August, after two hours of
dragging the canoe through a rice swamp. Major Nathan Clarke,
the commandant, and his officers were glad to have visitors, for
theirs was a post of utter isolation and boredom. After dinner, the
garrison's surgeon, Dr. Lyman Foote, walked with Featherston to
the nearby sandhills, composed of disintegrating sandstone with
horizontal red strata of iron oxide, reaching heights of sixty feet or
more. These were so similar to the formations in the Missouri lead
regions that Featherston thought the latter might extend into the
Wisconsin Territory. The doctor presented him with a large conch
shell taken from an old mound there, thought to have been made
by an Indian race preceding the present one. Since the Mexican
side of the Gulf of Mexico was the nearest place where conchs

could be found, it seemed likely that those ancient tribes came from there.

The portage to the Wisconsin River the next day took them from the waters emptying into the Atlantic to those flowing into the Gulf. Having struggled so long against the strong current of the Fox River, they found it delightful to float downstream, powered by a three-mile-an-hour current. Featherston and the voyageurs roared their songs joyously as they flew along toward the Mississippi. More and more red and yellow oxides appeared on the sand banks. At Helena, Featherston delivered a bag of silver money to David Whitney, nephew of the Green Bay trader, who took Featherston to see the two-hundred-foot shot tower, where Wisconsin lead was made into bullets. The top of the tower gave a fine view of the river and the rich valley on either side, formed by an ancient flood. Featherston had first observed such "wide margins and terraces" along the St. Lawrence in 1807 and, later, in the land around the Potomac and the James. He thought some of these valleys had been formed when the ocean receded and others by "an inland sea of freshwater."

In early afternoon, the travelers reached the Mississippi and paddling again became a chore as they made their way north. While they struggled upstream, Featherston contemplated the possibilities of the fertile land through which they passed as a future granary of a great agricultural nation. The grain crops, in turn, would feed large numbers of hogs. Canals and railroads would complete the superb natural waterways. They continued to Prairie du Chien where Colonel Zachary Taylor was commandant. He was most knowledgeable about the area and the Indians, and he and his officers gave a stirring account of their defeat of Black Hawk just three years previously.

Featherston and Mather left late in the day on 2 September, for most of the men were drunk. They were a sullen bunch when finally rounded up. Featherston was glad to have with them a sergeant from the fort, who had begged a ride to Fort Snelling. His presence reassured them when a passing Canadian said he had seen an Ojibway war party of forty men looking for the Sioux. Featherston and his friends had heard of another such party that had attacked and killed a white trader's crew. The Indians they met at an abandoned government blacksmith shop were friendly, however. They helped Featherston with his language study, even discussing theology with him. The next Indian village they visited had high scaffolds on which rested coffins of the tribe's most prominent deceased members. The bodies remained on the scaffolds until the bones fell apart. They were then buried in the ground with the lesser folk. On 5 September the travelers passed Prairie La Crosse, named by the French for the Indian game, which Featherston erroneously thought similar to golf. Aside from Indians, they met only Schoolcraft's half-breed brother-in-law, who was interpreting for surveyors running the line between the Sioux and the Ojibways.

They arrived at Fort Snelling on 12 September. Major John Bliss, the commandant, greeted them and ordered Featherston's luggage taken to a room in the fort. Featherston crossed the St. Peter's River to present his letter of introduction to the fur company's agent, Henry Hastings Sibley, who would later become the first governor of Minnesota. Sibley knew someone who would exactly suit his caller's requirement for a guide-interpreter, a man called Milor, whose father had been a French officer and his mother a Saukie. Milor was a fine-looking man of fifty-five, tall and muscular, and he spoke French, as well as several Indian languages, including Sioux. Featherston engaged him immediately so he might have the interpreter's advice concerning the area to which they were going. He found Milor excellent company and enthusiastic about the trip. Milor agreed to tutor Featherston in the Sioux language, and they began their lessons right away when rain postponed departure for several days. Milor presented a vocabulary of two hundred words with pronunciation. He had more information, too, about the country to which they were going than had the fort's officers, who had never been in the area. Even the United States Indian agent, Lawrence Taliaferro, could tell Featherston little about his charges.

It was a perfect day for traveling when they set off in their heavily laden canoe on 17 September. They crossed the river and entered "a world of adventure in a region unvisited by civilization,

and in advance of all the frontier posts of the United States."
Thrilled as he was to be exploring the little-known area, Featherston could not help having a few qualms. While the older Sioux
were men of reason, the young warriors were continually seeking
scalps of their enemies, the Chippewas, to prove their manhood.
Where these were not available, a few white scalps would as easily
impress their women. Many voyageurs had thus been killed in the
Yankton country to which they were going. Featherston carefully
concealed his apprehension from Mather, who was already so nervous that Featherston offered to send him to another area. Mather
declined and insisted on accompanying him rather than show "the
white feather." To occupy the young man and divert his anxieties,
Featherston had him map the St. Peter's River, for current maps
were abominable. Featherston determined to exercise great prudence, depending on his large supply of gifts for the Indians and
his growing knowledge of Nakota, a Sioux language. In spite of
the brave front he showed Mather, Featherston wrote Abert, asking him to look out for Charlotte and young Georgiana if anything happened to him.[11]

The Indians called the St. Peter's River the "Minnay Sotor or
Turbid Water." It ran through great prairies from which rose cov-
eys of grouse, reminding Featherston of the Yorkshire moors of
his childhood. He wondered at the solitude of these prairies, abandoned by Indian and white alike and yet so tempting for development. He found that Jonathan Carver's descriptions, which he had
followed as he went, were often inaccurate. From time to time,
they passed small Indian villages, mainly occupied by women and
children, for the men were gathering the rice harvest. The scenery
shifted from prairies to handsome forests and back again. Calcareous rocks and others similar to Missouri's lead-bearing rocks
began to appear. Throughout his travels, Featherston was interested in ornithology. Along the Minnesota he observed cliff swallows and was told they were gradually migrating east. One day the
men shot three cormorants, which they boiled with their pork.
There were often huge flocks of ducks and geese, the "gaudy-
crested" wood ducks being very common.

On the fifth day they reached a strange sight: an immense

prairie strewn with granite boulders of fifty to a hundred tons. Featherston climbed one to make a sketch, glancing warily around now and then, conscious that a Sisseton band would be eager to scalp an unwary loner. Although it was still September, the tent thermometer dropped to thirty-four degrees. There was ice on the river's margins. Dogwood and sumac showed scarlet, and the sugar maples were turning. The expedition explored the Blue Earth River, where Pierre Charles LeSueur had claimed to find copper in 1692. Since then, no one had checked, although Indians collected a blue paint somewhere in the vicinity. The river was only half as big as the Minnesota but the current was very strong. When they reached the bluff from which the Indians procured their paint, Featherston discovered it was only a seam of bluish-green silicate of iron in the limestone. He discounted the Frenchman's copper mine as well as his claim of retrieving fifteen tons of copper ore in twenty-two days. Milor agreed with him, adding that the Indians who were familiar with all these lands had never described such a mine.

Returning to the Minnesota, they found the current practically nonexistent in comparison to that of the Blue Earth. Nevertheless, Featherston realized, the voyageurs were becoming uneasy. It was getting colder, they had no tent, and they were reluctant to venture among the Sioux, having lived among the Ojibways. When asked his advice, Milor said they would all be perfectly safe if they acted prudently. Featherston persuaded the men to go on, but they became upset the next day by a broad trail with blazes. Again, Milor calmed them down, explaining that it was only the trail of some Sioux going south.

Calcareous rock gave way to a hard red sandstone, so worn that it appeared polished. Fields of wild rice replaced the sugar maples along the riverbanks and were replaced in their turn by beautiful open woodland. Fine days and the pleasant scenery revived the high spirits of the men. They literally screamed Canadian boat songs. On 25 September, the sandstone gave way to granite, the source of the boulders they had seen previously. A trader, Hazen P. Mooers, who was building a house and trading post, told Featherston that Coteau des Prairies was only fifty miles to the west and that it was formed of sandstone and limestone. Mooers had worked for the American Fur Company for a time but had now set up on his own. Sibley was planning to open a store opposite him. Featherston applauded this competition, which he thought would favor the Indians, who often had to pay sixty muskrat skins for one blanket.

The beautiful weather continued, but the river became so shallow that they made a cache of supplies to lighten the canoe. There were several portages but still the bottom of the canoe had to be gummed from time to time to repair injuries made by rocks. At the Grande Portage, they had to walk a mile and a half, carrying luggage and most of the provisions, leaving two men "to conduct" the canoe through three miles of rapids. It was the last day of September before they were again able to travel by canoe. The men expressed their *joie de vivre* by hallooing whenever they saw otters swimming among the wild rice. That night the sky was lit on all sides by numbers of prairie fires, often started by Indian campfires. They woke around two in the morning to find a roaring fire only a few hundred yards from them. Fortunately their camp was on a low bottom where the grass was juicy and green. Dawn revealed the stark black of the burned prairie beneath a pellucid blue sky.

After cutting through a series of fallen trees, they came to a clearing where a log cabin was being built. Three Indians came to greet them, two in frayed British uniforms, who said the hut was being constructed for a missionary. They immediately left for the Lac qui Parle mission to inform their friends of the canoe and its passengers. Featherston had hoped to reach their village before there could be a large assembly, but by the time they arrived, a hundred brawny braves had gathered. Some were decked out in buffalo robes, all were in war paint, and most were armed. They greeted the travelers with heart-stopping screams, yelling and brandishing their weapons. Featherston remembered saying to Abert that he could not understand why Major Stephen H. Long had run away from the Yanktons when he had a military escort. Now he understood. He felt as if

the curtain of some great theatre had suddenly drawn up, and discovered a stage filled with all sorts of grotesque diabolical figures—tall, insolent-looking young fellows, six feet two or three inches high, with wiry, black, coarse hair, clotted with bear's grease, and profusely rubbed with vermilion. Some of them had their faces entirely covered with it, whilst others had daubed their countenances with whiteish and blueish clay; and not a few of them were adorned with a broad ring of dirty white round each eye, the rest of their faces being completely blackened over with burnt wood. A few who were the most *recherchés* in their costume, had vermilion faces fantastically streaked with black and white lines. Dirty eagles' feathers were in great profusion on their heads. (1:341–42)

Realizing that they were in some danger and that only a quiet, relaxed approach could save them, Featherston told Milor to come ashore with him, unarmed. He ordered the men to take the canoe to midstream to avoid plundering. Milor hurriedly addressed the Indians, assuring them that they came in peace and that they were not of the military. Later, they discovered that the Sioux had thought they had come to arrest those who had murdered some Ojibways. Joseph Renville, the half-Indian agent of the American Fur Company, expressed his displeasure by refusing to greet the visitors.[12] He assumed that they were competitors who had come to trade.

Milor announced that Featherston would immediately call on Renville at the fort. Milor, who was known to some of the Sioux, calmed their suspicions, and the Indians accompanied the explorers to the fort. The Indians, knowing that the visitors were in their power, maintained their insolence, but now they were enjoying the unusual excitement of white visitors. Renville, who showed no indication of white ancestry, was far from cordial in his greeting. He said that the Indians disliked people who came to their country without informing them ahead of time. Featherston replied, "My principal object was to see so fine a people as the Sioux, of whom I had heard so many pleasing accounts. . . . I was also desirous of seeing whether there was any coal or lead in this country" (1:343). He added that after examining the Coteau des Prairies, he hoped to visit the Mandans, returning to the Mississippi by way of the Missouri. Renville, impressed by Featherston's sincerity and frankness, volunteered to act as interpreter at the gathering of the chiefs in the fort.

Featherston's speech was a diplomatic success. He said his only trade was to purchase some of the excellent Sioux tobacco, but not for his own use as it made him ill. It would be a gift to the chiefs, who loved tobacco. After this, his audience was completely with him and his remarks were greeted by "ungh, ungh, ungh" (hear, hear, hear). He added how widely he had traveled. Hearing what a fine race the Nakotas were, he had determined to visit them. He knew that every country had a very few wicked men but that the majority were good. If they were satisfied, he hoped the principal chief would shake hands. Renville interpreted that the visitor would shake hands with all the chiefs, and Milor told Featherston this, but he shook hands only with the two senior chiefs. He had learned that whites who shook hands indiscriminately lost caste in the Indians' eyes. It was most important that they recognize his independent strength. If he vacillated, they would not respect him, creating a dangerous situation.

A cart was provided to bring up the canoe, and the explorers were given sleeping accommodations in the fort. Featherston called on the Presbyterian minister Dr. Thomas S. Williamson, who invited him to breakfast the following day. There he met Alexander G. Huggins, who assisted the missionary, "an odd, long-legged, sharp-faced asparagus-looking animal, every portion of his body being as narrow as the head he bore on top of it" (1:348). Huggins had more information on the Indians, whom he called "critturs," than Williamson. He even used their grunts in place of yes and no. When asked why he had not married an Indian girl, he told Featherston, "Stranger, I allow tham thar young painted Jizzabuls aint just up to missionarying" (1:349).

Featherston ate with Renville, whose family included his Nakota wife, twenty-six-year-old son, two rather unattractive daughters, and a fifteen-year-old blond girl, daughter of a trader and an Indian woman. The meal of bear's meat, potatoes, and tea sweetened with maple sugar, was excellent. Featherston then climbed a small hill from which to view the lake surrounded by woods, as well as the village. Indian women were bent over, carrying heavy sacks of corn to a cave they had dug. Such work and continual childbearing aged the women to pathetic hags by thirty.

He returned to the town, where he called on the various chiefs with presents for their women: calico handkerchiefs printed with flags from all nations and, for the young girls, paste jewelry aping emeralds, rubies, sapphires, and diamonds, which had been especially made for the Indian trade.

After another meal with the Renvilles, he attended a scalp dance honoring the young men who had taken three Ojibway scalps. He was enraptured by the Indian singing, the finest he had ever heard: "It was a loud strain of glorification, accompanied with a sort of drum or tambourine. The music rose and fell, and was loud and low, both sexes singing in the most exact concert. Sometimes the men, after a bold sustained strain, would let it die away; and as their voices began to sink, the drum beating louder was a signal to the women who, taking the melody up with their soft and sweet voices, would continue it for awhile when the men joining in with them once more, the women would give from time to time a curious cluck with their voices, producing a peculiar sort of harmony, when the whole would be suddenly concluded for two or three minutes by a war whoop and yells on the part of the men, and a general laugh" (1:352).

Twenty painted warriors danced in a circle with thirty women adorned with red on their cheeks accompanying them in a restrained classical manner, hardly lifting their feet. Now and then even the children joined in. They treated the scalps with the same sort of casual, everyday attitude that might be shown toward an English boy's first partridges. So entranced was Featherston by the beauty of the music and the dance that he hardly noticed when Huggins came up to him, except to say, "Huggins, do you think you could manage to purchase those three scalps for me?" (1:356). The man departed abruptly.

Williamson had sent his assistant to invite Featherston to the prayer meeting, but Huggins had not delivered his message. When Featherston breakfasted with the missionaries the next morning, there was such a lengthy grace that he thought it wise not to mention his enjoyment of the Indian dance. Instead, he asked how successful the mission was. He learned that it was making little headway, for Renville never came to prayer meeting, at which remark all present glared at Featherston. Then he realized that he had involuntarily offended them by attending the dance instead; they thought his absence from prayer meeting would weaken their influence, fragile as it was. He hastened to assure Williamson that he would certainly have attended the meeting had he known, for he had always respected the objectives and values of missionaries. Williamson readily accepted his apologies, but Huggins was still mystified. He told Featherston, "It beats all creation . . . to see you so a-haunting after sich *complete* Philis*tines;* when you got the Doctor and me to talk to" (1:357).

The next day Featherston was permitted the unusual privilege of watching Renville's private security guards put on their paint for a dance in his honor. When he gave out the promised tobacco, he hastened to emphasize that he, the Sioux, and the Ojibways were all Wakan's children and should love one another. He had just remembered that his actions would be a little difficult to explain to any Ojibways they might meet later. That evening the women honored Featherston with another dance. By this time he considered the dances "as tedious as a ballet at a minor theatre," having to endure a fourth performance that night.

His assessment of Indians was becoming less favorable. Even the best of them, such as the Nakotas, were "idle, selfish, and insolent," with an unjustified claim to superiority. He felt that men in the wild state were anything but attractive, although the women were often obliging and civil. He was disgusted, for example, when a large band of Nakotas arrived. Their horses dragged only the tents, on which the children sat. The women, bent over with their burdens, carried everything else, while the men arrogantly strutted along with only a gun or a bow and arrows in their hands.

Featherston and Mather breakfasted with Mr. and Mrs. Williamson on 3 October, the day of their departure. The missionaries were living in Renville's building until their log house was completed. The reason for their impatience to move became apparent during the lengthy psalm singing, when the Indians competed with the noise by yelling and drumming. There was no doubt they did it on purpose. Featherston could hardly stifle his laughter when Huggins "screamed at the top of his voice," only to have the warriors shriek even louder. After farewells, Featherston mounted an old gray mare with foal following, which Renville had found for him. There was a horse-drawn charet to carry the luggage, and the rest of the party walked.

Featherston went ahead of the slower party, for Renville had told him that the horse had often been to Big Stone Lake and knew the way. Toward evening sleet began to fall. Mare and man became glazed with ice. Just as Featherston was certain that he was lost on this great prairie, he heard the approach of his party. Like him, they were covered with icicles. By this time the foal was tiring and the mare anxious, so he followed the charet. Soon the cart disappeared and he was left behind, again feeling lost. Visions of freezing to death haunted him until the weather began to clear, and the mare began to hurry again to catch up with the others. Even as camp was being made, he still felt half-frozen, clapping his numbed hands and running to help his circulation. With a roaring fire, strong tea, and food, he finally revived and even wrote his journal notes in the tent.

At Lake Travers the next day, Joseph E. Brown, factor for the American Fur Company, greeted them. His interpreter, François Frenier, advised Featherston on the surrounding area. The Coteau des Prairies was actually an upland, dotted with small lakes. It would take seven days to reach the Missouri. Brown displayed two of his rare furs, the skin of a yellow grizzly bear and a huge otter skin, which Featherston purchased. He also bought a bow of wood and bone and a quiver of arrows from a chief of the Assinboins, one of the Sioux tribes. As they approached the Coteau des Prairies, they saw more fire-blackened land.

They came to a great collection of buffalo skeletons. The ever-impoverished Indians were never content to kill a few of the animals but slew the whole herd for their skins in hopes of reducing their permanent debts to the local trader. As he viewed the skeletons, Featherston wondered whether "at some future geological period, when another deposit is made on this part of the terrestial surface, it may be that these remains may be discovered, and produce theories and conjectures as to the cause of the destruction that will greatly interest mankind, or whatever kind may then exist, until some Buckland *redivivus,* finding the barb of an arrow in the rib of one of them, will, with the same power of genius and fancy that once illuminated the obscurity of the Kirkdale Cave, people these prairies over again with the butchering Indians and flying buffaloes" (1:389).

Riding ahead in a northwesterly direction, Featherston soon came to great sandhills stretching into the distance. When he turned back he made his way to a wooded area where he thought the others would be likely to come, but it was several hours before they joined his fire. During that time he had pondered upon the likelihood that his scalp might enrich some wandering Indian's collection. The next morning the whole party went up what the Sioux called the Chhra Tanka, or Great Hills. Major Long had estimated their height at 1,000 feet but did so from thirty to forty miles away. Featherston thought it nearer 625. Small ponds, supporting a few trees, appeared here and there. The apparent absence of buffalo was not surprising in view of the paucity of grass. At this point, a wheel of the charet was disintegrating. The men were fearful of having to carry everything, including provisions, two trunks, the tent, hampers, and a large bag of minerals, through the rapidly approaching freezing weather and snow; they were, therefore, greatly relieved when Featherston decided to go no further. Personally, he was deeply disappointed, but at least he had penetrated that little-known wilderness. Ice on his pail of spring water in the tent convinced him that his decision had been correct.

They arrived back at Renville's to find that his son was taking a second wife, although his first was still young and good looking and had borne him several children. In spite of having demanded and received a good price for her daughter, the bride's mother was howling inconsolably. Featherston concluded that "a jumble of this kind could only be met with in such a state of society: a savage brought up by French missionaries singing canticles in the 96° of W. longitude, in North America, to the tune of 'God Save the King,' as a religious preparation for a bigamy; and a mother, after screwing all she could get out of him for her daughter, going to the woods to scream in the dark as if her heart was broken" (1:406). Renville's clerk confirmed Featherston's view that the Indians had lost their independence when they fell into permanent debt to the traders. The latter, in order to cover their financial risks, charged very high prices.

The Minnesota River was now so shallow that Featherston sent the guide on with the charet and the heavy luggage to Traverse de Sioux, under Mather's charge.[13] As Featherston and the rest of the party boarded the canoe at seven o'clock on the morning of 9 October, they received a hearty send-off. No doubt the handkerchiefs and beads he had distributed to the young girls had made them popular. They arrived at Fort Snelling a week later, Mather having rejoined them two days previously. They had been gone a month. The Blisses had a large room waiting for Featherston as well as letters from his family. It was the first time he had slept in a bed since 21 August. Soldiers' wives laundered his linen while he caught up with his correspondence and notes before a welcome open fire. Minerals and shells were carefully packed. Milor came twice a day to help him check his notes on the Nakota language, with particular reference to pronunciation, for which Featherston had devised his own system of accents. He had already found that his growing knowledge of the language was exceedingly useful when he rode ahead and met Indian families.

Featherston offered to take the Blisses' son, John, with him to their friends the Andersons in Pittsburgh to continue his education, and they accepted his proposal. Breakfast was a gloomy meal on 22 October when the travelers were about to embark. The whole complement of officers went down to see them off. John was so thrilled with the gay songs of the voyageurs and the excitement of the trip that he did not immediately feel any wrench at parting from his parents, perhaps not as much as Featherston felt at saying good-bye to Milor. It was so bitterly cold that ice formed in a ring around the paddle handles where they dipped into the river. Although John had been well bundled up, he began to shiver uncontrollably late in the afternoon, so Featherston decided to camp earlier than usual. After supper, he wrapped John up in bearskins and blankets. So excited was he over camping and sleeping on the ground that it was scarcely a minute before the lad was sound asleep, not waking once. Featherston, on the other hand, suffering from icy feet, hardly slept at all.

In the morning the two repaired to the river to wash, Featherston telling the boy, "If you had waited until one of the men
brought you water, he would very probably have dipped the basin
into the first mud-hole he found" (2:17). He pointed out that it was
far better to be independent and do for oneself, even cooking. He
recalled that one of the voyageurs called out once, "There goes the
third big blue bottle fly I have found in my soup this evening."
John reveled in cooking his own breakfast and in the dinners they
prepared. Great flocks of geese, swans, brants, and ducks were
migrating south. Nothing could rival dinners of duck fattened on
wild rice. Lake Pepin's glassy surface reflected "hundreds upon
hundreds of noble swans . . . floating with their cygnets, looking
at a distance like boats under sail" (2:19).

Although the voyageurs, under Featherston's supervision, were
always meticulous in cleaning up the camp site before they left,
they were hardly in the river before the wolf pack they had heard
in the night was hopefully scavenging. Beyond the lake, there was
no more snow, and the weather soon became perfect. On 26 October they reached Prairie du Chien, where family letters again
awaited Featherston. He stayed with the trader, Joseph Rolette,
while John was the guest of the commandant, Colonel Zachary
Taylor, with whom Featherston dined one day.

When the party left on 30 October, the voyageurs made a sorry-
looking crew: some were hung over and others still drunk, exhibiting black eyes and bruised faces. John realized that Featherston's
domineering manner was admirably suited to managing the voyageurs, but the boy preferred Mather's gentler comportment. He
felt Featherston was chiefly to blame for the noticeable friction
between the two men. Nevertheless, he had to admit that Featherston could not have been kinder or more thoughtful toward him.[14]
As they approached Galena, the voyageurs' depression vanished
with the anticipation of journey's end, and they broke into bois-
terous song. Galena proved to be "a dirty, wooden, ill-arranged
town." The men lost no time in getting abysmally inebriated
again, so it was not until 1 November that Featherston could pay
them off. He advised them to leave immediately for home, two
hundred miles away, but was not too surprised to see them get
wildly drunk again. With the icy water from the city pump, he

revived them sufficiently to take leave of them. He sold the canoe, and Mather, with no regrets, departed for the St. Louis Arsenal.[15] Featherston reflected that he had attained at least one of his objectives. He had traced the probable extent of the lead ore from the White River in Arkansas to the Minnesota, a distance of about two thousand miles. Although the breadth of the deposit was unknown, the possibilities for lead mining appeared fabulous.

He and John watched a steamer coming in, and Featherston could hardly believe his eyes. There on the quarterdeck, in an ancient white hat, stood the Honorable Charles A. Murray, the son of the earl of Dunmore. Featherston had met him the previous winter in Washington, where Murray had been the guest of Sir Charles Vaughan. Murray had spent the summer with the Pawnees, "as dirty a set of natives as are to be found on the continent," he said. He joined Featherston and John in their room for the night, and in the morning they all boarded Captain Throckmorton's *Warrior*. Pigs of lead ballast had to be off-loaded from the ship to a barge to make the *Warrior* light enough to pass over the Des Moines Rapids. While the ship was being reloaded below the rapids, Featherston found some interesing fossils in the river's limestone banks as well as some handsome geodes, filled with crystals.

Returning to the ship, he was delighted to find that George Catlin had boarded. He was returning from his fourth summer spent with the Indians, sketching their chiefs and collecting examples of their clothing, furnishings, and arms. He had accompanied Colonel Henry Dodge on a cavalry expedition to the tribes living in the Rocky Mountain area. Murray, Featherston, and Catlin had a fine time comparing notes. The two Englishmen were much impressed with the artist's sketches and collections. He had spent the winter in Washington painting portraits of such people as Dolley Madison, in order to finance his summer. He confided that he planned to spend several years on this project to preserve the customs and manners of the Indians, which he had begun in 1832. Featherston was enthusiastic over the idea, since he feared that the aborigines might become extinct before too long. He suggested that Catlin exhibit his collections not only in large cities in the

United States but abroad as well, for European interest might be helpful financially. In fact, Featherston thought on his return to Washington he would approach the government about buying Catlin's collections and financing a study of all the Indian languages.

The *Warrior* reached St. Louis on 5 November. The city was bustling, and there was not a room to be had. Featherston pleaded with the landlord of the National Hotel, where he had stayed the previous year. All the innkeeper could offer was a cellar room in which he kept firewood, but it was dry. The firewood was tossed out the window to make room for their buffalo skins and luggage. Murray could not but laugh at the accommodations but admitted that they were actually better off than the other hotel guests, who had to share a room with four or five men. Two beds, linen, two chairs, and a table were found for them, so they felt quite luxurious, especially after an excellent venison dinner. In the afternoon they walked to the Indian mounds Featherston had examined in 1834. They left John with one of Mrs. Bliss's friends, since they expected to be in St. Louis for several days.

When they visited the new Roman Catholic cathedral, one of the priests told Featherston that Joseph N. Nicollet was in St. Louis. Martha Coleman Bray has called him "a discoverer of comets, a surveyor of distinction, and a contributor to the fields of geodesy and magnetism." He had come to the United States from his native France in 1832, intent upon making a geographical study of the Mississippi basin. Extensive travels in the south, including a six weeks' stay at Nashville with Troost, had delayed his objective. Featherston, already familiar with his work, hastened to call on him. He found Nicollet "a most amiable and social person" and encouraged him with assurances of the importance of accurate topographical mapping to geology (2:50). Nicollet's equipment seemed to be of rather poor quality, but Featherston thought his observations would nevertheless be more accurate than any previous ones.[16]

Wisconsin Revisited

Featherston devoted much of the winter of 1835–1836 to preparing his official account of his geological reconnaissance of the previous year. He gave it to Colonel Abert on 22 April 1836, and Secretary of War Cass presented it to the Senate the following day. There were 168 pages, including diagrams, plates, and maps. Like his previous report, it contained not only specific details of observations but a good deal of discussion of broad geological principles. The report was generally well received by the Senate and was published later that year. When Silliman reviewed it in his journal, he commended it as containing "interesting facts which are presented in an attractive form," noting that the expedition must have required "no small share of hardihood and perseverance." He also remarked on the odd fact that, although W. W. Mather had taken part in the reconnaissance, he was not mentioned in the report, and he wondered if Mather intended to make his own report. Mather's absence from the report requires some explanation.[1]

Featherston and Mather's relations, never good, had deteriorated throughout the trip. At their parting, Featherston had asked for Mather's notes and the various sketches he had been directed to make, and Mather had declined to let him have them. They corresponded on the subject without result. Mather then wrote to Abert, detailing his grievances against Featherston. The colonel was not impressed. He replied that, after careful consideration, he could "adopt no other opinion than that you are essentially wrong in every position you have taken."[2]

In spite of his feelings toward Mather, Featherston thought he ought to try to bring in some of what Mather had done as favorably as possible. He knew that Abert had insisted that Mather send in his notes, sketches, and any report he cared to make. Since he had only been sent as an assistant to Featherston, no report had been required or expected. Featherston went to see Abert and was given the notes and sketches that he had directed and required but learned that the lieutenant had insisted that Featherston not be shown his report until after he had published his own. Whereupon Featherston decided it would be best simply to refrain from mentioning his assistant.[3]

On his return home, Featherston had expected to find a number of letters from his English geological friends but was disappointed to find none. He had written three times to Buckland since he had last heard from him. Buckland had finally written in November 1835 and his letter arrived some weeks later in the care of a doctor returning from England. His failure to write was understandable. In the interim he had lost two children to whooping cough. Several months later he had spent some time traveling in Germany. His publisher was now promising to produce his book in March 1836. Five thousand copies would be printed in England and another thousand in Germany, where it would be translated by Louis Agassiz. It was from Buckland that Featherston learned that his letters from Murchison, Sir Harry, the Royal Society, Murray, and others, had apparently been lost. The publisher wrote, agreeing to Featherston's specifications concerning his proposed book. Featherston devoted much time to preparing a manuscript, then decided to postpone completing it when friends persuaded him that he might offend many American friends because of his too-frank commentary on the United States.[4]

A visit of particular interest was one by the historian George Bancroft. Featherston had always had a strong interest in history. He had informed Bancroft the previous year that he had been collecting material on the early settlement of Virginia. He felt that no one had adequately written of the period, and he intended to do so. Whenever possible, he had visited county courts to study their records and he had painstakingly checked old family papers. He wanted to cover the colonists' transactions with the Indians and to trace the origins of their customs and manners in the period prior to the Revolution. Bancroft had written him concerning a diary of Governor Alexander Spotswood, lent to Featherston by Charlotte's relative John R. Spotswood. The historian had wanted to borrow it, but Featherston was not willing to chance its being lost in the mail. When Bancroft returned to Washington in 1836, Featherston permitted him to read it but still would not agree to lend it since he intended to use it himself before returning it.[5]

Featherston made a hasty geological reconnaisance for Abert that year. In late October the colonel directed him to examine the mineral resources of the Cherokee country. He was aware that the examination must be superficial this late in the year but thought it would lay the foundation for a more thorough survey. Congress had arranged a treaty under which the Cherokees would be resettled west of the Mississippi River. A detailed geological survey would be required for the United States geological map that Featherston planned. He was away until early December, but apparently no official report was published.[6]

There were many changes in Washington during the winter of 1836–1837. President Jackson, being far from well, was glad to hand over the office to Martin Van Buren in March. Featherston, who had known Van Buren for twenty-five years, considered him both prudent and discreet and thought he would make a good president.[7] A new arrival in the capital afforded Featherston particular pleasure. Henry Stephen Fox replaced Sir Charles Vaughan as British minister. Fox, a graduate of Eton and Christ Church, Oxford, had served at both Buenos Aires and Rio de Janeiro before coming to Washington. His wit and charming manners quickly made friends there and did much to improve Anglo-American relations. While Featherston had known Vaughan and liked him, he found Fox even more congenial. Another newcomer he found both amazing and disgusting. General Antonio Lopex de Santa Anna, who had been captured by General Sam Houston at the Battle of San Jacinto, was in Washington to promote recognition of the Republic of Texas. Featherston was equally repulsed by the Texans, whom he called "gallow-birds," and by Santa Anna, who was assisting them.[8]

General Gratiot told Featherston that Nicollet would be spending the winter in Washington, but soon afterward he learned that the Frenchman had settled instead at the home of Sibley, the American Fur Company factor at Fort Snelling. Featherston was surprised to learn that Nicollet intended to explore the headwaters of the Mississippi and hastened to send him his two maps and a copy of his report, which he thought might be helpful. He offered to have any of the Frenchman's accounts of his travels published in the *National Intelligencer*. He was not enthusiastic about Nicollet's intention of publishing a travel book, believing he should concentrate on the barometric field, in which he had so much expertise.[9]

As he comtemplated further field studies to be made during the summer of 1837 Featherston considered going as far as the Rocky Mountains and California. Abert, however, wanted him to return from his western trip early enough to complete his study of the Cherokee country. Featherston decided to compromise with a further investigation of the lead region, especially the Wisconsin Territory. He requested an increase in his per diem and was pleased to have it raised from six to eight dollars.[10]

His friends were confused about his summer plans. Senator Calhoun had expected a visit from him in South Carolina and wrote to him on 3 May that he understood Featherston had left Washington for the South and would be for some time in the vicinity of the survey of a railroad route. If this was true, he feared that he would not have the pleasure of the visit he had been anticipating. He was planning an excursion through the mountains of his neighborhood to the gold mines in Georgia and hoped that his friend would be able to join him.[11] Unfortunately, he did not receive the prompt reply he requested, for his letter did not reach Featherston until October. He had indeed left Washington, as Calhoun thought, but was well on his way to St. Louis at that time.

He reached St. Louis in mid-May, where he joined his friend, Richard Cowling Taylor.[12] Featherston found it pleasant to have the company of an English geologist. They traveled by steamer to Galena, Illinois. There they hired "a barbarous sort of wagon" drawn by two "lame and miserable horses" driven by "a droll Cockney Englishman." Prepossessing or not, this was the only available means of transport. From Galena they traveled to Mineral Point, some thirty-six miles away, which proved to be "an exceedingly miserable place." They were directed to two filthy taverns as possible places to stay but were not sorry to find both of them full. Court was in session in the town. They were happy to settle for sleeping on the floor of a room at the postmaster's house, which at least had the virtue of being clean.

The following morning was exceedingly cold, so Featherston got permission to make a fire. He had it burning well and had started his toilet, when "a dirty, unshaven, but confident-looking fellow, walked into the room with nothing but his nether garments on." The newcomer appropriated the fire and, somewhat to Featherston's discomfiture, proceeded to observe and comment on his toilet procedures. Featherston was tempted to throw him out but thought better of it, not knowing who he might be. It was a fortunate decision, for the man soon identified himself as "the court," or the presiding judge of the court that was in session. Featherston and Taylor were occupying the room usually reserved for him. Featherston soon found himself liking the judge, in spite of his first impression. He was highly amused by some of the judge's comments. He had never seen a nailbrush, for instance, and thought it a "considerable better invention than a fork," which he had seen some people use to clean their fingernails. He could not understand why Featherston carried so many toothbrushes. He had once owned one but found it a nuisance, except that the handle was useful for stirring brandy slings.

Featherston and Taylor spent ten days at Mineral Point, beginning their survey by visiting Kendall's copper diggings, which had been extravagantly acclaimed. They decided prospective purchasers would have to be very gullible indeed to invest in this mine stock. The deepest shaft was only thirty-seven feet and the assays showed only 5 to 8 percent copper. At Ansley's south copper diggings the yield was 50 percent, but the vein was small. Labor and provision costs, as well as lack of fuel, made these mines economically impractical. Later, the geologists visited the Iowa Copper Mining Company of Philadelphia, also near Mineral Point, in Wisconsin Territory. Featherston made three drawings and reported that the diggings were superficial and nothing positive could be stated.[13]

It was with little reluctance that the travelers left Mineral Point on 29 May, leaving their luggage with the apothecary. Five miles beyond town, they stopped briefly at the cabin of Governor Henry Dodge to pay their respects. They spent the night at John Messersmith's after visiting his diggings. By noon of the next day, they reached the Blue Mounds, two rocky outcroppings composed largely of siliceous hornstone like that Featherston had seen in the lead region of Missouri in 1834. The galena was very brittle and contained a great deal of sulphur. In early afternoon the geologists came to an area Featherston thought "one of the most exquisitely beautiful regions" he had ever seen anywhere. It was a land of ridges and rounded hills, separated by lovely valleys in which tributaries of the Sugar River had their origins. The clumps of handsome trees gave "an indescribable charm to the whole scene." No matter where he looked he was impressed by the beauty of the view: "Nature might be said to speak to you in a voice that must be listened to, and to tell you that she had here surpassed the most polished efforts of English park scenery, the most difficult of all her achievements. America will justly boast of this unrivalled spectacle when it becomes known" (2:88).

Featherston and Taylor followed an old Indian warpath that led from the Mississippi to Tychoberah (Four Lakes) and on to Lake Michigan. They had heard mention of Indian mounds along this trail but were completely unprepared for what they found. The first earthwork they saw was in the form of one man and seven buffalo. These mounds were about six feet in height above the level of the prairie but were covered with the same sod and appeared never to have been disturbed. The man, depicted as lying on his back with both arms and legs spread wide, measured 150 feet in length. Each of the seven buffalo, which formed a long line, measured 120 feet, including a 36-foot tail. Featherston made a careful sketch of them. They came across other mounds, some representing beaver, and were told of others like turtles. Featherston concluded that these mounds were the burying ground of ancient and important Indian tribes. The animals depicted represented tribal totems much like the lion, eagle, and horse totems of the Old World.

Having spent so much time at the mounds, the two men hurried to reach Madison before dark. A fellow boarder at Mineral Point had shown them engravings of seven large cities, close together, near the Four Lakes. Each had capacity for a population of 500,000, as portrayed on handsomely engraved plans showing streets, institutions, and squares. Cathedrals, theaters, cottages, and churches all appeared in great detail, along with elaborate descriptions of the excellent water, fine climate, and innumerable other advantages. The seven were Madison City; North, South, East, and West Madison; the City of the First Lake; and the City of the Four Lakes. Featherston and Taylor did not expect to see such lively, prosperous cities, but they did expect small villages.

It was late in the day when the two geologists finally reached the largest of the four Wisconsin lakes, and standing on its shore, they looked eagerly for the rising city across the water. They looked in vain, however, for not a house could they see. Since darkness was approaching and rain threatening, they must find one soon or prepare to camp in the rain. They scrambled through woods for a time and, missing the second lake, came to a third, still without finding a house or clearing. Featherston gave up and began collecting wood for a fire while Taylor scouted a little farther. Just as Featherston was about to light his fire, a shout from his companion announced his success. Featherston hurried to join him and found him at the door of a "hastily patched-up log hut, consisting of one room about twelve feet square. This was Madison City!" (2:94).

In spite of all of their expectations, both men were happy to have found a human habitation, no matter what its limitations. Featherston, having received a smart blow on his head from the five-foot doorway, was amused at the number of boxes and barrels that filled the small room. A "bustling little woman," Mrs. Eben

Peck, greeted them. "No male Peck was on the ground, but from very prominent symptoms that went before her, another half-bushel seemed to be expected." In spite of the shock of having two complete strangers arrive out of the darkness, Mrs. Peck proved "a very active and obliging person." She undertook to make them "as comfortable as it was possible for her to do" (2:95).

The next day Featherston and Taylor left Madison City, wondering how they had even half believed in the Seven Cities. Smart as he had thought the western Americans, Featherston still "had not thought them so systematically and callously fraudulent as to cause engravings to be made of cities, with all their concomitant appendages, in countries where not a single tree was cut down; and for the purpose of robbing their own countrymen. To rob strangers might, from the prejudice of education, be considered even meritorious; but to rob their own countrymen so remorselessly argued an absence of principle so universal and total," that he did not "know where it is to be paralleled in history" (2:97).

When the two men visited the shot tower on the Wisconsin River, Featherston was surprised by the improvements in the shot-making operation since 1835. He was impressed by the ingenuity of the men who had in such a short time developed "a well-conducted and prosperous manufactory" in this former wilderness. He revisited the colony of cliff swallows he had observed on his former visit and found that they too had prospered. Several hundred birds were now nesting in holes they had made in the soft sandstone and lined with clay. The heads of young birds were protruding from small holes all over the surface of the cliff begging food from the busy parents, "truly a very pretty sight."

Featherston and Taylor returned to Mineral Point on 2 June and left four days later for English Prairie on the Wisconsin River, to visit a lead furnace belonging to William S. Hamilton, a son of Alexander Hamilton. He was not there but his agent, Charles L. Stevenson, made them welcome and shared what food and shelter there was. The latter consisted of a small hut, which Hamilton occupied when he was there. In his absence, it was used by Stevenson and five or six workmen. They kept a fire going near the door in hope that the smoke would discourage mosquitoes, but the smoke had little or no effect, and the cabin swarmed with them.

On 8 June they passed through land of great farming potential by way of Lancaster to the Snake Diggings. Here galena was being very successfully mined. Some 800,000 pounds of first-quality galena had been removed from a small area only twenty-five feet below the surface. The digging had extended as deep as sixty feet. Leaving the mine, the travelers crossed the Platte River on a ferry to a settlement called Paris. After a visit to the Menominy Diggings, they reached the home of George Wallace Jones, delegate to Congress from the Wisconsin Territory, at Sinsinnaway Mound. Here they were welcomed by Jones, his wife, and his sister. The latter had been educated in Wales and had recently returned from a visit to England. Their gracious hospitality and interesting conversation were a pleasant relief from that which the two Englishmen had been enjoying.

Back in Galena on 10 June, they parted company. Featherston took a "dirty little steamer" from there to Dubuque and Prairie du Chien. The better steamers on the Mississippi he had found to be clean, comfortable, and well run, but there were many like this one, dirty, ill run, unseaworthy, and filled with gamblers. He thought that many of them lived on the boats and joined with the captains in various forms of villainy. At Prairie du Chien, he had to abandon his plan to visit the headwaters of the Iowa and Des Moines rivers and the Red Pipe-stone Quarry. He had hoped Nicollet might join him, but he was busy writing. There was no suitable interpreter-guide if he went alone.[14] Instead, he booked passage to St. Louis on the steamer *Burlington,* on which he had a large and comfortable stateroom. Much to his surprise he found as a fellow passenger the widow of Alexander Hamilton, "a lively old lady" of nearly eighty, who had come west to visit her son and to see the country. He was filled with admiration for her and greatly enjoyed her company. The Mississippi was very high and the current strong, so the steamer was carried swiftly downstream. He felt sad to be leaving "this beautiful country" and wondered if he would ever see it again. It disturbed him to see how rapidly the "selfish, vulgar" settlers were displacing the Indians and feared that "ere long, the whites will tread upon the graves of the whole red race."

After a few days at St. Louis, he traveled downriver to St. Genevieve. The village pleased him, for it reminded him of Normandy, from which most of the settlers had come. Their houses were much like those of their homeland. Every house had a flourishing garden and fruit trees, unlike most of the places were he had been traveling. There was rich bottomland nearby for good crops. Everyone raised both chickens and turkeys, for which there was an excellent market at New Orleans. The village, therefore, was prosperous. The few non-French settlers seemed to get along well with the French, despite the language barrier. Featherston hired a small pony and, leaving his baggage, set out for the lead-mining regions to the southwest. He revisited Mine La Motte and continued on to Fredericton.

Featherstonhaugh's sketch of "The Pilot Knob," Missouri, from his *A Canoe Voyage up the Minnay Sotor* [Courtesy of the Alderman Library, University of Virginia]

Wanting to visit Pilot Knob, he rode westward on 26 June to the home of Henry Pease who was planning an ironworks near there. After breakfast the next day, Featherston and Pease climbed Pilot

Knob. It proved to be "a well-wooded cone about 650 feet in height," consisting entirely of micaceous iron ore, yielding "from 50 to 65 per cent of pure iron." From the summit, Featherston was able to see that the knob "stood at the north edge of a basin, surrounded by mammilated hills, less lofty than itself." He hastened to make a sketch of the knob and its surroundings. Seeing that many trees had been struck by lightning, he suspected magnetism in the iron but could find no other evidence of it. Later, he rode with Pease to a waterfall on Stout's Creek where the latter "contemplated erecting some works" (2:144–46). Featherston felt some concern for the man. Although he had an abundant source of high-yielding iron ore, he might well find that it cost him too much to produce, as there was no scarcity of iron in the Atlantic states where demand would be the greatest.

Pease volunteered to guide him to Iron Mountain, which Featherston had wanted to visit again. Near there, he took Featherston to a brickyard where a man named Chapman was busily making bricks. Featherston was surprised to learn that Pease and J. L. Van Doren were planning to promote "an immense city" there, to be called the City of Missouri. Pease produced the typical engraved plan of such proposed cities. There was not yet one house, but at least bricks were being made. It seemed an unlikely spot for a city. There was no water near it, and there seemed no reason for even a village, but Featherston thought it best not to say so. The two men visited a curious formation of supposed statuary marble about twelve miles away. It proved to be Silurian limestone rather than marble, the exposed part of it covering about a thousand acres.

Dr. Lewis Fields Linn, United States senator from Missouri, whom Featherston had known in Washington, invited him to visit him at St. Genevieve. One of the Linns' dinner guests on 4 July was a former congressman, John Scott, who was adorned by a brace of large pistols and a bowie knife, which, Featherston was told, he always wore. The same was true of General Dodge, Linn's half brother, and many others in this part of the country. The frontier atmosphere was forgotten in the gaiety of the ball following dinner. The French Creoles danced "most vehemently," despite a temperature of a hundred degrees. While waiting for a steamer the next morning, Featherston was startled by the sound of pistol shots. He was even more startled to learn that Senator Linn had served as a second at a duel between two young men, one of whom was only nineteen. Fortunately, neither man was injured. When Featherston asked his host how he could bring himself to take part in such an affair, Linn explained that he did so only to show them how a duel could be conducted without injury.

During the three days that Featherston waited for a steamer, he had an opportunity to observe and reflect on the action of rivers in flood. The Mississippi, loaded with silt and debris, was rising an inch an hour. Banks caved into the stream as he watched. He realized that the phenomenon he was seeing was seldom observable in England or Europe, where rivers are not as long or as violent. Forest trees came down when the banks were eroded from under them and were eventually deposited, with tons of soil, in the ocean, forming deltas around the river's mouth.

When a steamer going south finally stopped, he went on board without even asking its destination. He was pleased to learn that it was bound for Louisville, for he wanted to disembark at Paducah. The ship tied up next morning at Bird's Point, Illinois, however, the captain never intending to go farther. He was returning to St. Louis with a load of lumber. He told his passengers that a ship would stop for them later in the day. When Featherston charged him with deliberately misleading the majority of his passengers, he readily admitted it but explained that he would never have gotten any if he had said he was going to Bird's Point. He added, "You can't get on no how on this river without lying a little" (2:166). The *Lady Marshall* arrived as promised, and everyone went on board. In a very few minutes they left the Mississippi for the Ohio, arriving at Paducah that evening.

On 14 July, Featherston embarked on a miserable old steamer going up the Tennessee River. To his surprise the food was excellent: coffee, dried beef, apple preserves, and good bread and butter, accompanied by "plenty of beautiful transparent ice." Even the tablecloth was spotless. He attributed these comforts to the influence of the captain's and clerk's wives, who were on board. That night it was cool on deck, and Featherston played a bit on an accordion. The clerk's wife was impressed, remarking to the captain's wife: "Well, if that ain't the leetlest piazzur-forte (pianoforte) I ever seed: don't it beat all, now don't it Miss Kittle?" Featherston entertained them with tales of Indians, storms at sea, and General Jackson, whom they venerated. He slept on deck, there being no unoccupied staterooms. A fifty-cent tip to the steward secured a mattress, clean sheets, and even a tub of water and two clean towels, which were used by the other passengers when he was through with them. They reached Tuscumbia, Alabama, three days later. The following morning, he caught a train to Decatur, forty-five miles away.

The breeze and the beautiful fields of cotton delighted him until he spied a "villainous-looking" overseer seated on a fence, armed with a whip with a knotted lash. Featherston again damned the whole Negro question when he wrote Abert: "It infects every thing, the whites won't do any thing for you because there are blacks to do it, and the blacks won't because you have not a whip in your hand."[15] Decatur consisted mainly of stores and taverns, and in one of the latter, he spent the next four days. Although he was only a hundred miles from the land of the Cherokees, he was unable to go by land because of his baggage but had to wait for another ship. Three boxes of minerals had been forwarded to Washington, but he still had a trunk and more specimens.

This forced delay gave him an opportunity to summarize his observations. Featherston had discovered that overturning an old theory was almost as satisfying as building up a new one. It had long been thought that the primary rocks extended "across the Mississippi and the inland sea of the Mississippi valley." In his travels, however, he had seen no primary rocks and had found the "tertiary and subcretaceous beds of lower Alabama" to be resting on carboniferous limestone beds. Thus, Alabama's bituminous coalfields were not independent but an extension of the great fields around Pittsburgh and the Cumberland Mountains. He still wanted to ascertain whether any primary rocks appeared in the state, for these might indicate an extension of the gold region.[16]

The steamer he boarded was able to go within fifteen miles of Ross' Landing, and Featherston hired a dugout canoe to take him the rest of the way. The town, now Chattanooga, consisted of three new log huts on a hill with a beautiful prospect, completely fascinating to a geologist: the limestone horizontal at the river, but the beds slanting above. This configuration did not surprise him, for the closer one came to the Alleghenies, the more marked was the influence of the great movement that had produced such flexures, or bands. At Ross' Landing he made arrangements to complete his study of the Cherokee lands, as ordered by Abert.

The Cherokees were an unusual and remarkable tribe, who had accepted many customs of the Europeans.[17] They had abandoned the life of the hunter, become successful farmers, and adopted the Christian religion. One, Sequoyah, having seen the books of the missionaries, had invented an alphabet for their language that was used to print hymnals, psalm books, and the Gospels. The alphabet was in some respects superior to the Roman, since there was a separate character for each of the eighty-five sounds of the language. Anyone who could pronounce the letters could automatically read their books.

The Cherokees had made many treaties with the United States government under which the Indians had ceded territory in exchange for promises of security in what remained. Such promises were doubtless meant to be kept, but unfortunately, greedy white Georgians and others continued to encroach on Indian territory, particularly after gold was discovered in several parts of their land. The eighteen thousand Cherokees were threatening to take action to stop this invasion, and the federal government was reluctant to use force against the citizens of Georgia. Tennessee militia and some federal troops had occupied Cherokee territory to keep the peace temporarily. Then, seeking a more permanent solution, the federal government offered to purchase the Cherokee lands and to provide the Indians with new lands west of the Mississippi. This offer was accepted by a small number of lesser chiefs, who had no authority to commit the entire nation, in what became known as the Schermerhorn Treaty. It derived its name from the Reverend John F. Schermerhorn, a Dutch Presbyterian minister, who had persuaded the lesser chiefs to accept it. Those chiefs who did have authority adamantly rejected the treaty. John Ross, an educated man (actually only one-eighth Cherokee), became the spokesman for the senior chiefs. It soon became evident that the vast majority of Cherokees would not leave their native land voluntarily. This was the state of affairs when Featherston visited them.

He had transportation problems in leaving Ross' Landing but was able to hire a horse and gig to take him to the stage road to Cleveland. The last forty-five miles, in the mountains, proved too much for the scarecrow horse, so Featherston walked thirty of them. Although it was extremely hot, he was glad of the opportunity to observe and talk to the great numbers of Cherokees, some on horseback, others on foot, on their way to the meeting that would decide their fate. Practically all of them spoke English. Most of them were from the North Carolina mountains, where they had retained more of their Indian customs than had those from Georgia and Tennessee and were consequently more independent. Featherston talked to missionaries, chiefs, militia officers, and tavern keepers, trying to assess how much influence Ross had exerted and whether the Indians would emigrate. His first impression was that they would, with little argument, given time.

Recognizing the potential danger, Featherston took it upon himself to apprise Joel Poinsett, now secretary of war, of his first-hand observations.[18] He stressed Ross's great influence. Although he had not yet met the man, from talking to his friends, Featherston gathered that Ross was a very proud and sensitive person who felt that ratification of Schermerhorn's Treaty by the Senate had deposed him as leader of the Cherokees. Whether he went west with them or stayed behind, his influence would be negligible. His life might even be in danger. For this reason, Ross had called the council meeting, hoping that they could agree that the treaty had not been authorized by the Cherokees and that a compromise was necessary. Featherston added that if force was used now, the Cherokees would retire to the mountains, where it would be almost impossible to dislodge them for many years. When this was finally accomplished, an embittered tribe would join the Sioux, the Winnebagoes, and other disgruntled Indians on the western frontier, "like sparks amongst gunpowder."

When he attended the meeting in early August, at the invitation of John Mason, Jr., the government's special agent, Featherston's ideas changed. Mason; General Nathaniel Smith, the Cherokee removal agent; and Colonel William Lindsay, commander of the United States troops, were to explain the government's orders. Arriving on 4 August, they had time to visit and to talk with the Cherokees. All of them were impressed with the arrangements that had been made for the meeting and the magnitude of the undertaking. The Cherokee Council was paying the huge cost of feeding three thousand Indians. The daily provisions alone, including fifteen beeves, cost three hundred dollars. Twenty-four families were employed to cook and serve three meals a day. All were allowed to eat as much as they wanted, helping themselves again and again. At night, the woods gleamed "with fires in every direction; several thousand Indians being scattered about in small groups, each with its fire, near to which a few sticks were set up, and a blanket or two laid over them to screen the women and children from the wind" (2:237). Featherston visited them often at night, chatting with the men and studying their pronunciation.

Some of the older chiefs and members of the council came to the hut that Featherston and Mason shared to pay their respects to the special agent. Featherston was especially impressed by two very dignified elders: eighty-year-old Innatahoolosah, or Going Snake, and Oonaykay, or White Path. The former had led a large army of Cherokees to help General Jackson in his war against the Creeks and had contributed to his victory over them at the Battle of Horseshoe Bend. The Cherokees felt, with reason, that they now deserved Jackson's protection. Instead, it was under his administration that arrangements for seizure of their land had been made. Featherston and Mason dined with Mrs. Walker, a fine old Cherokee lady, who spoke little English. There they met John Ross.

At divine services the next morning, there was a very long sermon by a Cherokee preacher and a second, in English, by the Reverend Evan Jones, an English missionary. Featherston had a long conversation with Jones after the service. He had lived with the Cherokees of the North Carolina mountains for many years and was cordially hated by the white Georgians and other settlers for the help and advice he had given the Indians in opposing attempts to grab Cherokee lands. Featherston found him very intelligent and well educated, even with a knowledge of Hebrew. He introduced Featherston to some of the Cherokees, who helped him with Cherokee vocabulary and the pronunciation of words. The Cherokees customarily gave names to white men with whom they had dealings. Having seen Featherston's interest in rocks, they called him Oostanaulee, which, he learned, meant "gravel or shingle brought down by floods." Colonel Lindsay, with a cavalry escort, called for Featherston at noon. They rode to Ross's house at Red Hill, where they waited in a room for two hours before dinner was served. The food was bountiful but ill cooked. According to Cherokee custom, neither Ross nor his wife ate with their guests. Ross's brother, Lewis, presided and everyone was extremely cordial.

Later Featherston visited the Reverend Elizur Butler, head of the Cherokee mission in that area, who gave him books and pamphlets printed in the Cherokee language. Meanwhile, Mason had been busy composing the principal address, which he was scheduled to deliver. A Cherokee interpreter came to look over the talk in advance. He told them anecdotes about Schermerhorn, who had "corrupted a few individuals to consent to emigrate and deliver up the Cherokee territory; and reported it to the Government as if it had been a solemn contract" (2:240).

From their informal talks with the Cherokees, General Smith, Colonel Lindsay, and Featherston realized that the majority had no intention of emigrating to Arkansas in May. Rumors of that state's unhealthful climate had already prejudiced them. They had been told cholera was endemic there. Rather than preparing to move, the North Carolina Cherokees were "repairing their houses, fencing in their gardens, etc." Many of them, recognizing Featherston's sympathetic attitude, asked his advice. He could only reply that there was little alternative but to obey. If the delay was too long, the impatient Georgians and Tennesseans would destroy the Cherokee nation.

As for the whites' attitude toward the treaty, Featherston found two classes. One group wanted to keep the Indians there, where the whites could profit from government expenditures on them. The other group wanted them to leave immediately so their land could be seized, and these stood about like "so many vultures." Most of them were poorer Georgians, whom Featherston described as "tall, thin, cadaverous-looking animals, looking as melancholy and cadaverous as boiled cod-fish . . . a striking contrast to some of the swarthy, athletic-looking Cherokees," who were hardworking and intelligent (2:226). Featherston felt that their inadequate diet had much to do with the wretched state of these Georgians, for the more prosperous were fine-looking people.

The last two days of the Cherokee gathering were conducted in a continuous downpour of rain. The hut Featherston and Mason occupied was thoroughly soaked. The Indian families, huddling under blankets and other flimsy shelters, were drenched. The chiefs, fearing serious illness might result, persuaded Mason to give his official speech on 7 August, before matters got any worse. Mason spoke from a stand erected for the purpose, to which Ross also conducted Colonel Lindsay, General Smith, and Featherston. Some eighteen hundred Cherokee men, dressed like the whites except for the red and blue turbans worn by men of pure Indian ancestry, stood in the rain to listen. They were attentive but heard nothing in the speech to suggest that President Van Buren had altered his determination to enforce the treaty. It would now be up to the true chiefs of the Cherokee Council to decide whether or not to resist. Featherston thought it likely that they would seek to gain time by another appeal to Congress and would attempt to get any concessions they could.

A few days later he wrote to Poinsett that he had been mistaken when he thought that the Cherokees would be willing to move west. When he finally heard from the secretary, he was relieved to learn that Poinsett had welcomed Featherston's letters rather than being annoyed. Featherston again made a strong plea for the Cherokees, stressing the fact that the majority of them had never been consulted about the treaty: "They are told they must leave for ever the beautiful country where they were born, the little Enclosures where their Huts are, with the orchard of Apples and peaches they planted, and the cool spring, because a treaty had been made to which not more than twenty in a thousand ever consented, and to which they are most bitterly opposed." In closing his letter, he added, "Mr. Madison told me with much feeling, almost on his death-bed, that no one thing made him more disconsolate than the treatment the Cherokees had met with. They had so earnestly adopted the arts of the whites on the faith that it would raise them to the same civilized condition and the same rights, only to be driven from their native land, and turned into a wilderness."[19]

Realizing the influence that gold mining was having on the Cherokee situation, Featherston was more anxious than ever to start his investigations. Leaving the Cherokees, he traveled to Dahlonega, Georgia, an attractive town situated in mountainous country, which was the center for the gold mining in the area. A welcome accumulation of mail greeted him, but he was disappointed to find no letter from Senator Calhoun. He felt greater respect for Calhoun than for any other man he had met in the United States: "His intellect is so active and comprehensive that he is able to grasp the most intricate subjects without an effort. He is also one of the most perfect gentlemen I ever knew, without any vice or vicious habit, and has at all times borne the most unsullied private character" (2:247).

Featherston was in his room, busily writing letters, when Calhoun walked in, having ridden across the mountains to see him. The two men settled down to a delightful evening, discussing a wide range of subjects. Having conversed about the gold-mining region, they moved on to protective tariffs and forms of government. Calhoun was adamantly opposed to any tariff on British manufactured goods, which he thought might lead Britain to purchase raw cotton from some other country. He considered the republican government of the United States to be the perfect form of government and that it would eventually "be imitated by all other countries. He would not admit that universal suffrage, which had been so successfully wielded by demagogues against himself, Mr. Clay, and other honorable men, would in the end exclude all *decent* men from power," Featherston noted (2:249). He disagreed and told Calhoun that he thought "he had formed too favourable an estimate of human nature."

Next day Featherston rode with Calhoun to visit the gold-mining operations at Cave Creek, Pigeon Roost, and other places. He was very much interested in the geological formations in which gold was being found, principally in decomposing "talcose slate" in a bed of gravel above the "talcose" rock, some twenty feet beneath the surface. He thought that the "Gold Region of North America, which extends about 700 miles from N.N.E. to S.S.W.," might continue into Canada, where he had observed similar geological formations. He speculated about the origin of the gold deposits. All appeared to have been formed under water. Gold, being the heaviest, had settled to the basal rock and had been covered by successively lighter materials, first gravel, then clay, and lighter materials above. He was interested in a log of what appeared to be pine wood, which was shown them at a washing operation on Pigeon Roost Creek. It had been found lying on the slate rock after the removal of the surface soil and gravel twenty-one feet deep. He assumed that it was a representative of the ancient forests of this continent but had never heard of one being found at such a depth in a mining operation.

Although he had been greatly interested in all of the geological examinations he had been able to make, his ecological observations disturbed him greatly. The beautiful wooded valleys around Dahlonega, through which the Indians had hunted without disturbing the environment, were being destroyed by the mining operations of the white man. The forests were being removed, soil washed and dumped in ugly mounds, the courses of streams diverted, and the result was a scene of complete desolation. "To obtain a small quantity of gold for the wants of the present generation, the most fertile bottoms are rendered barren for countless generations. And this must ever be the case in countries where the Government is not intelligent and strong enough to put the mining districts under regulations" (2:255).

The following day, Featherston and Calhoun made a long ride through more of the gold-mining region, stopping at various mines and collecting specimens. At the Eaton Diggings, they were told of "thirty-six ancient log huts, or pens," which had been found beneath the alluvial deposit next to the base rock. They appeared to have been cut and notched "with a metallic ax"

(2:257). Some sand crucibles and a rock trough had also been found. Featherston speculated that these might all have been used by de Soto's men and covered over by them. He and Calhoun finally reached Clarksville after dark.

Featherston talked with all the mine owners and other knowledgeable people he met, learning as much as he could about the location and general characteristics of the gold deposits. He was struck that "the general character of the surface" of the gold-mining regions, wherever he observed them, either in Georgia or Virginia, was always the same: "knolls and ridges intersected and divided by streams and valleys; and the conclusion to which a geologist is irresistably brought is, that the whole of the elevated mountain line from Georgia to Canada has been upraised at the same period. . . . there must have been some potent cause in action in ancient times to have so modified the surface of the earth, and whether it is dormant or not in our times is a problem of great interest" (2:259–60).

The two men parted company at Clarksville, for Featherston had to return his horse to Dahlonega, but he promised to visit Calhoun later at his home. At Dahlonega, he carefully packed all the specimens he had collected in cotton. He made additional expeditions to other mines, some of which would be very productive if worked with modern methods rather than by washing. At the Pickens courthouse two of Calhoun's servants met Featherston with a horse and a mule-drawn cart for his luggage. Calhoun's home, Fort Hill, delighted Featherston with its airy portico and charming rooms. At church the next day, he met many of the Calhouns' friends. There he saw Langdon Cheves for the first time since 1824. Cheves insisted that Featherston visit him before he left the area. The Calhouns had friends in to meet their guest, and Featherston found these southerners a contrast to the gentlefolk in the North. Conversation was far more liberal and intelligent.

Featherston left Fort Hill on 22 August, accompanied by William Sloane, a friend of the Calhouns. In North Carolina they found a local guide to take them up White Side Mountain, 4,930 feet in height. The mountain's name came from its snow-white appearance when seen from a distance. The eastern face was composed of almost pure white mica. Featherston made a careful sketch of this peak. Finally, they reached the Cherokee lands where the North Carolinians had already started a road. Sloane and Featherston considered it ironic that Cherokees were doing the manual labor on the road for the white men who had the contract and who had robbed the Indians. The travelers passed on into a valley of rich bottomland, with wigwams safely ensconced on knolls. These were surrounded by patches of corn, up whose stalks grew pole beans. There were squashes and pumpkins as well. There was also evidence of gold washing. Volunteer militia passed them, part of the state troops overseeing the Cherokees until they left. To Featherston they resembled Italian bandits in their torn and filthy clothes, but their manners were civil enough. At Fort Butler, a temporary army camp, they stayed at Hunter's comfortable tavern.

The missionary Preston Sterrit showed Featherston an open pit about fifteen feet deep and forty feet long. The ore slag was a mica slate embedded with garnets. Gold had been found in neighboring springs. The Indians denied any sort of mining; from tales handed down, they ascribed such workings to short white men many, many years before. As more and more white men had come, the Cherokee Council had become alarmed and massacred all of them. In one excavation, Featherston found skeletons in the bottom of a trench and presumed they were the bones of some of the miners murdered by the Indians. These mysterious excavations could only be explained, he thought, as the work of de Soto and his men, and he felt that someone could map the Spaniards' route from Tampa Bay by examining such remains.

By 5 September, Featherston and Sloane were back at Fort Hill. After a short visit to Cheves at Portman Shoal, Featherston returned the carriage to the Calhouns and took the stage to Greenville, South Carolina, and Asheville, North Carolina. There he climbed Mount Pisgah and visited Chimney Top and Painted Rock, both composed of sandstone, with shale strata dividing the "primary" rocks from those bearing fossils in eastern Tennessee. They were similar to the European beds named Cambrian by Sedgwick.

At Rutherford, North Carolina, Featherston called on the gold-smith Christopher Bechtler, pieces of whose gold coinage he had seen. A German immigrant, Bechtler and his son, Augustus, were renowned goldsmiths and gunsmiths. They provided an outlet for the settlers' gold, having made a die equivalent to the United States five-dollar gold piece. In fact, their coinage circulated more freely than that of the government. Bechtler's books showed his coinage to have been about two million dollars in the seven years he had been in the United States. He charged only 2 percent for his work and was known for his great honesty. The Bechtlers were equally skilled in the manufacture of guns and had invented one that fired eight times a minute. Featherston ordered a "pistol rifle," capable of killing at a hundred yards. He had the barrel inscribed with his name in some of their gold.

Not too far away was the land of a gold miner Major Abram Forney. It was desolate looking from the great hillocks of washed earth, but there Featherston found the first evidence of any attempt at restoring an area to its original fertility. Topsoil had been care-fully thrown to one side to be used later to cover the scars. When the trenches were refilled and leveled in the spring, corn was planted and yielded an excellent crop. Forney had already removed $200,000 worth of gold, using both white mountaineer and slave labor. In washing the gravel, other minerals were also found: tour-malines, rock crystal, platina (a crude form of platinum), and even some very small but brilliant diamonds. Featherston spent three days with the major, visiting various gold veins. Returning one night, they were shown a poplar branch that had been unearthed. Featherston was mystified, for unlike the usual lignite, it was waxy and could be cut with a knife, and yet every wood layer and fibre had been perfectly preserved. It exuded the odor of leather soaked in water. Lignite appeared in the Tertiary and upper beds but this had been found in the gold-bearing deposits. Recalling that John Ewing Colhoun had shown him an Indian pipe that had also been found beneath the gravel near Dahlonega, Featherston speculated that "the deposit of gold and gravel with wood in the valleys may have been produced by the *historic deluge*. In this view Mr. C——'s pipe is evidence of the existence of man here at that period. Has there not been too much haste in abandoning the opinion once generally entertained, that a great portion of what geologists have called diluvium, was a result of the Noahic Deluge?" (2:335–36).

Upon his return to Rutherfordton, Featherston labeled his new collections of very fine specimens, wrote letters and revisited the Bechtlers, from whom he acquired more rocks and his pistol. At Charlotte he was entertained by J. Humphrey Bissel, manager of a gold mine and owner of a copper mine. Featherston found both mines most promising. He stopped at Lexington to visit a gold mine on Conrad's Hill and Roswell King's copper mine, before traveling on to Richmond. Thence he went by train to Fredericksburg, where he boarded the Washington steamer. He reached home on 10 October, after a journey of five thousand miles. It had been five months since he had seen his wife and small daughter.

Libel at Home and Recognition Abroad **10**

Featherston had been home less than two weeks when he found himself involved in controversy. A friend showed him a copy of the September issue of the *Naval Magazine,* edited by the Reverend C. S. Stewart. It contained a scathing review by "An Officer of the U.S. Navy" of Featherston's *Report of a Geological Reconnaissance.* The entire tone of the review was malicious, and it contained a number of false statements reflecting very seriously on Featherston's integrity. It also incorporated a letter from Mather to the editor that the latter had inserted into the review. The review's author had set the tone by suggesting that Featherston's style might be good "were it not for the obscure sentences and grammatical errors with which he frequently frets the understanding and offends the ear of his patient reader. Let his *Murdered* English appear in judgment against him."[1]

This rather remarkable criticism Featherston could have ignored, but other comments were patently false and libelous. The reviewer praised the maps but added that he was "credibly informed that the map [of the St. Peter's River] was pirated from the notes of an American Geologist whose report on the geology of the same region has been smothered among the unpublished papers of the Topographical Bureau. Will the intelligent officer who is at the head of that Bureau inform the public why that report was not transmitted along with Mr. Featherstonhaugh's and why it was suppressed: and why, after its author had filed a letter at the War Department protesting against Mr. F's being allowed access to these notes this gentleman was suffered to filch from them." There were other similar comments: Featherston's "styling himself U.S. Geologist is a deliberate attempt to impose upon the public. He was merely a creature of the Topographical Bureau on per diem salary." Mather's protest said:

There is no such office recognized by the Acts of Congress as U.S. Geologist, a title assumed by Mr. F. in consequence of his having been a daily *employe* on geological duties under the orders of a Topographical Bureau, which is a sub-office of the War Department.

Mr. Featherstonhaugh and myself were associated under the orders of the Topographical Bureau, and were directed to make a geological survey of the country between Green Bay and the Coteau des Prairies, and were called on for separate reports. While engaged on that survey I made a sketch of the topography adjacent to the St. Peter's River, and took the bearings and comparative lengths of all the bends, so as to form a map of all the meanderings of the stream, with a view to illustrate the minute, as well as General geology, by references from my report. Mr. F. had no share in the original preparation of the materials for this map. In his published report of that survey is a topographical map of the St. Peter's by G. W. Featherstonhaugh. It is a copy of mine on a smaller scale, except that he had extended the courses of the streams far beyond where we saw them, and put on it topography of the Coteau des Prairies as he supposes it, for great distances north west, and south of where we saw it. The people will now understand, not my surprise at the course pursued by Mr. G. W. Featherstonhaugh, for I am not surprised, but my indignation that he should thus appropriate a portion of my labors *without acknowledgment.*

Under such circumstances, I deem it a duty to myself and the scientific public, to denounce Mr. Featherstonhaugh to the world, for this as one instance of his appropriating the labor of others to his own uses without acknowledgment. [2]

Featherston immediately fired off two letters, one to the editor, Stewart, and the other to Abert. To the former he declared various parts of the review and Mather's letter to be "malicious and false libels." To Abert he enclosed a copy of Mather's letter and requested a statement from him. Abert replied immediately, commenting specifically on each of Mather's principal points. First, Featherston had not "assumed the title of U.S. Geologist." The title had "always been bestowed upon" him "in all official communications." He had been "in fact the U.S. Geologist . . . a mere designation of" his "position and duties." Second, Mather's claim that he and Featherston "were associated under the orders of the Topographical Bureau and were directed to make a Geological Survey," implying that he "was associated as an equal on the duty . . . and was called on for a separate report" was ridiculous. "How he could have made such absurd premises . . . is to me inconceivable," wrote Abert. "Mr. Mather was not associated on the expedition. . . . his position as unequivocally subordinate. . . . he received no instructions from the Bureau directing him to make a survey . . . or a separate report, [and] he was not required to make any." It was only after their return and after Mather "had refused to make a report" to Featherston that he had been directed to make a report to the bureau. Mather's claim that "the map of St. Peter's which accompanied" Featherston's report was a copy of one furnished by him, and which Featherston had used "without acknowledgment" was equally without foundation. What Mather had submitted had been "a very loose and imperfect sketch of that River, without measurement of distances." Mather had been informed that it would be handed to Featherston "in order to enable him to compile a map to illustrate his report." It was not "customary to acknowledge the authorship of such papers." The compiler is "the greatest laborer in matters of this kind . . . and deserves the credit of the work." "The only acknowledgment which could have been made with propriety was to the Bureau." Mather's notes "were never delivered to" Featherston, "nor his report, because Mr. Mather" had "desired that they should not be." Abert had kept Mather's report "locked in a private drawer." When Featherston had been "desirous of presenting him in as favorable a light" as he could, he had been told that he could not see the notes because of Mather's request. Featherston had then remarked that "under such circumstances" it seemed best not to mention him. Having demolished every claim made by Mather and the reviewer, Abert added that all correspondence between the Topographical

Bureau and Mather was "open to the inspection of any person."[3]

Stewart attempted an apology in the November issue of the *Naval Magazine,* the last issue published. He regretted that "the position in which Mr. Featherstonhaugh has been placed by Professor Mather, compels us to introduce so much of mere personal matter in his reply." They had sought but were "inadvertently defeated" in the effort to expunge personal items from the review.[4] Stewart published Featherston's letter to Abert, the latter's reply, and other relevant materials. It was rather obvious that Featherston would be justified in suing for libel and defamation of character.

He decided to bring suit against the *Naval Magazine* and had every reason to expect success.[5] Yet he was aware that the reading public might learn little of the suit and saw the need to publicize the complete falsity of the statements that had been made about him. Not only had the *Naval Magazine* defamed him in the United States, but Silliman's *American Journal of Science,* which was widely read in Europe as well, had copied Mather's libel from the *Naval Magazine* in the September issue. When the December issue failed to pick up from the *Naval Magazine* Featherston's reply to Mather, Featherston published *Official Refutation of a Libel.*

The *Refutation* included Featherston's letter to Abert; Mather's statement in the September 1837 *Naval Magazine;* Abert's reply to Featherston; a certificate from Washington Hood, a draftsman for the Topographical Bureau; a certificate from General Macomb; and a summary of the entire affair by Featherston. Hood testified that Mather's sketch, when compared with observations made by "Mr. Calhoun in the time of Lieutenant Colonel Long's expedition . . . were found to be so erroneous that the sketch was not used." General Macomb certified that he had refused Mather permission to accompany Featherston and had been "induced solely upon the recommendation of Mr. Featherstonhaugh to reconsider my decision." Featherston indicated that he had preferred that his "justification with the public should be confined to the magazine where the libel first appeared" and that he had expected that other periodicals "which had given currency to the calumny" would have apologized at the first opportunity. They had not done so, and after three months of resisting the "importunities of many friends," he had decided to publish his refutation and to "have recourse to the just and impartial laws of the country which protect every man from defamation."

After reviewing Mather's conduct, which he found "not so surprising" in "an indifferently educated man," Featherston raised questions about the conduct of the editor, Stewart, and members of the "Advisory Committee" of the *Naval Magazine,* and of Silliman. He stated that Stewart had written him that he had delayed replying to Featherston's protest because "the responsibility of having published in the Naval Magazine for September *the article of which it is manifest you have just reason to complain,* does not rest with me but with the committee of publication." This committee was headed by Commodore C. G. Ridgely, to whom Featherston had written but had not received the courtesy of a reply.[6] The journal, though it published Featherston's reply to Mather and Abert's letter, had made not "a single expression which admitted that any wrong had been done" to Featherston.

During the fall and winter of 1837, while he was waiting for Stewart's refutation and apologies, Featherston was busy preparing an official report of his most recent survey. Abert was so anxious that all of the material which Featherston had collected should be well illustrated that he asked Poinsett to authorize the employment of a "very talented draughtsman," suggesting the paleontologist, Timothy Abbott Conrad, and requested an appropriation of five hundred dollars.[7] Although such an ambitious project was planned, no official report of Featherston's investigations has been located.

When Featherston had completed his report, he found time for other matters. He shipped an interesting collection of American fossils and minerals to the Scarborough Philosophical Society. A long letter from Murchison in January brought him up to date on geological matters in England and Europe. Murchison wrote from Uppark, where the little black pony and chaise that Featherston had given to Sir Harry conducted Murchison to the hunting field daily. Murchison had dined with Sir Charles Vaughan recently at the Travellers' Club, and they had chatted about Featherston.

Murchison was very much involved with preparing "the big Silurian System" for the press. He had not completed it when he wrote again in March, for he had had little time to devote to it. He had bought a new house and hastened to assure his friend that the painting of Featherston's former home was hanging in the same place in the new library as it had in the old.[8]

Sometime during that winter, Featherston had a conversation with James Garland, a Virginia representative in the House of Representatives, about the need for an international copyright law. The congressman asked him to write his views on the subject, which he did at some length in a letter on 23 March. He insisted that "Society has a great interest in protecting those who contribute so much to the happiness of mankind, for their whole lives being consecrated to its welfare, Society is placed under a moral obligation of protecting what it owes all its improvement to: so that no man shall appropriate to his own profit the property created by another without his consent. If Society is bound to protect persons in the use of their property, it is as much bound to protect the author in his right to his book as the farmer in the right to his farm." He later sent a copy of this letter to Henry Clay, who promised to study it when it came time for the Senate to take it up.[9] A bill had been introduced, but the committee acting on it had inexplicably delayed in reporting it. The idea of an international copyright was very unpopular with American publishers at Boston, Philadelphia, and elsewhere, who had often profited from pirating books from European authors. They presented numerous petitions against such a law to Congress. Not surprisingly, the committee reported the bill unfavorably.

In the early summer of 1838, the question of Featherston's next assignment arose. Abert suggested to him that he would be required to survey the territory long under dispute between the state of Maine and the province of New Brunswick. The need for a definitive settlement of this controversy was becoming increasingly urgent. This assignment raised serious questions for Featherston. He was still an English citizen. Though President Jackson had not considered his foreign citizenship a barrier to his appointment to a purely scientific post, the new assignment possessed an unexpected political aspect. He immediately told Abert that it would be highly inappropriate for him to make the survey and that he must decline to do so. This refusal evidently offended someone, but whether Abert, Poinsett, or Van Buren is not clear. In any event, afterward "a marked coolness took place," as Featherston later wrote. His completed report does not appear to have been published, and his proposed geological map of the United States seems to have lost its early support. He began to sense that his services were being treated in a "cold and neglectful manner." He suspected that Van Buren would like to make a political appointment to replace him. It seemed wise for him to submit his resignation, which he did, and it was accepted.[10]

With a family to support, Featherston could not long remain unemployed. He had often thought a geological study of the disputed territory would provide the best basis for a settlement. While he considered it inappropriate for him to represent the United States government in such a survey, he could see no objection to his doing so on behalf of the British. He thought he might be able to interest them in undertaking such a survey and appointing him to make it. The prospect of combining his love of geology with employment by the British government was exciting; the prospect of parlaying this job into permanent employment in England was everything that he could wish.

Before leaving Washington, he consulted Henry Fox on the subject. Fox was already much concerned about the boundary problem and was enthusiastic about the idea of a geological survey. He advised Featherston to go to Quebec and present his idea to Lord Durham, who had just become lord high commissioner of Canada. Lady Durham was the eldest daughter of Lord Grey and a niece of Lady Hannah, wife of Featherston's friend, Edward Ellice. Moreover, Durham had chosen Ellice's son, Edward, Jr., as his private secretary. Fox wrote a letter of introduction to Durham for Featherston, who then felt confident of receiving a thoughtful hearing, for he believed that in this world a man must help himself in everything.[11] If he was able to convince Lord Durham of the desirability of a geological survey, he could then go to England with the support of both Fox and Durham to present his ideas there. In addition, he might be able to see something of the country under dispute on his way to Canada.

He determined to take a month's vacation before leaving for Canada. Charlotte was at Brandywine Springs, west of Philadelphia, where he joined her on 1 August. They went on to New Brighton, where they joined Mrs. Carter and Charlotte's sister, Josephine, Countess Fransson. Two fast steamboats ferried passengers to New York City only twenty minutes away.[12] It had been eight years since Featherston had been in the city, and he was shocked by the changes. Where before he had known almost everyone, now he was lucky to see three or four acquaintances. The hot streets swarmed with recent immigrants: Germans, French, Spanish, and Italians. The fine houses of the old New York families were being converted into stores and hotels. The whole city appeared too bustling and vulgar for his taste. He spent the month examining the geology of Staten Island and of Schooley's Mountain in New Jersey, as well as devoting much of his time to his family.

On 31 August, he boarded the steamer for Troy, New York, on his way to Canada. On board, he met Fox's friend Thomas Turton, with his wife and daughter, who had just arrived from England. Turton was on his way to Quebec to become legal adviser to Lord Durham. The two ladies were left at Burlington, Vermont, planning to join Turton later. He and Featherston did not arrive at Quebec until 9 September, for the trip was no simple matter, requiring many changes, involving boats, stages, and a train.

There had been many improvements in the town in the thirty-one years since Featherston had been there. Then the Plains of Abraham had seemed unchanged since Wolfe and Montcalm had battled. Now there was an excellent road, lined by fine houses and attractive cottages, each in its own beautiful grounds. There was even a racecourse. The British military presence was very much in evidence. Their uniforms were well tailored and of fine cloth, yet cost half the price of American uniforms, which fact Featherston passed on to Abert.[13]

Two letters from Abert concerning the libel suit awaited Featherston in Quebec. His morale was improved by a notice in the

National Intelligencer, which Turton showed him. It was a lengthy lead editorial, taking note of the rumor that "Mr. Featherston-haugh, who has for some years held the appointment of U.S. Geologist, is no longer connected with the public service," expressing regret and the hope that his leaving would be temporary. It summarized his entire career in the United States and praised his many contributions and endeavors to advance the interests of the country.[14]

At breakfast with Turton the first morning, Featherston met the Buller brothers, Charles and Arthur, Lord Durham's secretaries and members of the Executive Council. He did not meet Durham until that evening, when both attended an exhibition of mesmerism, where several ladies were successfully hypnotized. Featherston had reservations about mesmerism, but he was favorably impressed by Durham. He was cordial and friendly, asking Featherston to arrange an appointment so they would have time for a lengthy talk.

They met a few days later, and Featherston sent Fox an account of the meeting. Lord Durham explained his views of the liberal colonial self-government he hoped to establish. He asked innumerable questions about the United States, on which he thought Featherston could advise him. The highlands that the United States claimed as the boundary line could be seen from Quebec. Featherston was pleased to learn that "the very idea of giving up an inch of them is derided here." Durham was cheerful in spite of attacks on him by Lord Brougham in the House of Lords for exiling Canadian rebels to Bermuda for four years. Featherston thought that Durham had been quite right in doing so, for he found every reason to believe that, at the moment, it would not be possible to get a Canadian jury to convict a fellow countryman for murder. Had Durham permitted the rebels a jury trial, they would certainly have been acquitted and would have continued to incite insurrection.[15]

The geology of the area around Quebec confirmed Featherston's theories of the similarity of North American geology to that of Europe. There were the slates and limestones of Sedgwick's Lower Cambrian, as well as horizontal carboniferous limestone.[16]

To Featherston's delight, a Mr. Price invited him to accompany him down the St. Lawrence to the Saguenay River, an important tributary on the left bank about 120 miles below Quebec. Price owned several sawmills on various streams and shipped lumber to Ireland and London; Great Britain had instituted a tariff on Norwegian lumber to protect Canadian wood. Price and Featherston started the trip on a sailing vessel, but when the wind failed after sixty miles, Featherston walked the next thirty, enjoying the geological formations and interesting fossils. There was an iron ore mountain similar to the one he had seen in Missouri, although far larger and higher. He found limestone containing fossils like those to be found in Georgia. When they reached the Saguenay, Mrs. Conally, wife of the Hudson's Bay agent, asked Featherston if he knew of a gentleman of his name who had married a Miss Duane. Prince and Featherston went up the Saguenay as far as La Baie de St. Jean. When it was time to return to the Conallys' the wind was against them, and they had to return by land, much to Featherston's disgust. He had hoped to cross the St. Lawrence to Madawaska in New Brunswick in the disputed boundary area.

Featherston dined with the Durhams a number of times before his departure. He was distressed to learn from Durham that he planned to return to England before the end of October to defend himself against Lord Brougham's attacks. The Whig prime minister, William Lamb, Lord Melbourne, had arranged Durham's appointment to his post by way of removing him as a rival.[17] He now appeared to have abandoned him to the attacks. Featherston thought that Durham might not only defend himself in England but might even replace Melbourne as prime minister. Durham sent for Featherston on several occasions and they had long conversations about the disputed territory and other matters. He had little difficulty in persuading Featherston to return to England, where Durham would use his influence to help Featherston obtain the appointment to survey the boundary line.

Should he fail to receive the appointment to conduct a survey, Featherston thought he might remain in England to write a book on United States geology. Then he might visit Mexico and California to continue his geological studies. Perhaps Audubon might accompany him.[18] He planned to leave on 7 October, but Durham asked him to remain another day to give him time to prepare some dispatches to Fox, which he wanted to send with Featherston. Durham wanted to see something of the United States himself before returning home. He asked Featherston to engage lodgings for him and his family in New York, Boston, and Washington and then to return to Troy to meet them on 2 November. There would be a rather large party: Lord and Lady Durham, their two daughters and a son, a secretary, and a physician, in addition to four or five servants.[19]

On a Lake Champlain steamer Featherston encountered General Henry A. S. Dearborn of Boston, a member of the United States House of Representatives, who had been appointed to negotiate with two New York Indian tribes for the purchase of their reservations. With so much time for relaxed conversation, the two men covered many topics, and the general was impressed by the range of the Englishman's knowledge. Featherston could not resist relating his Canadian experiences and his intimacy with Durham. Dearborn had long thought that there could be little improvement in the condition of the Canadians until their country became either independent or a part of the United States. Since capital there was in the hands of Englishmen and Scots, whose only idea was to make enough money to return home in triumph, there was little interest in the welfare of Canada as a country. The French Canadians were, on the whole, ignorant peasants who had remained unchanged. Dearborn felt strongly that the colony should be acquired by the United States, either at Canadian request or by purchase. Once Canada was part of the United States, such issues as navigation rights on the St. Lawrence, fishing rights, and many others would be automatically solved. Dearborn had even gone so far as to imagine four Canadian states, to be allocated eight senators and twelve representatives. He thought Canada would be worth a purchase price of a hundred million dollars. Since Featherston apparently knew Durham so well, he asked him to discover what the commissioner's thoughts on the subject might be. Would England be willing to sell the colony? If not, what kind of compromise could be reached on the boundary question?[20]

Featherston spent a few days in New York looking for lodgings for the Durhams. When he reached Philadelphia, he found his wife and "Georgy," as his daughter was called, both well. He caught the boat for Baltimore at six o'clock the next morning, delivered Durham's dispatches to Fox, and dined with him at ten that evening. His friend was so entertaining that Featherston did not leave until three in the morning, by which time he was in "quite a tottering state" and had to walk the two miles to his boarding-house in the rain. The capital seemed dull, though he dined again with Fox and "in Russian Style" with the French minister. He did see Abert and his friend W. W. Seaton but had to spend most of his time trying to locate a house for the Durhams. The problem was solved when Featherston learned that they would not be coming after all but were sailing to England. He returned to Philadelphia for a short visit but had to continue to New York where his lawsuit for libel was to be heard.

M. Pontois, the French minister, Mr. Andrew Buchanan, the British consul, and Henry Buckland all called on Featherston. A Colonel Clive delivered a letter from Murchison and told him that everything was reported to be quiet in Canada. Featherston was about to relay this information to Fox when an express reported an insurrection there on 3 November. Young Ellice had been taken prisoner and Sir John Colbourne had declared martial law in New Brunswick. To Featherston's disgust New York society was aiding the French Canadians. As many as three thousand people attended a meeting in support of them. Louis Joseph Papineau and Dr. Wolfred Nelson, who had been leaders of the earlier insurrection, had both been active in the United States. Nelson and others had been exiled to Bermuda by Durham, but Papineau had already fled to the United States, and Nelson joined him there. Henry Clay had told Featherston in Washington that both men had expressed to him their disappointment at not having received American support. Clay had assured them that they should not expect any unless the United States and Great Britain went to war. Yet he told Featherston that he hoped that ultimately the entire continent would be free of European dominion. Fox reported to Featherston that both John Quincy Adams and Caleb Cushing had criticized the government's neutrality. All of New England wanted control of the St. Lawrence.[21] Buchanan called again to tell Featherston that the rebels had been dispersed and young Ellice freed. The consul also said that Durham's proposed resignation had caused great consternation in England.

Continued postponements of his lawsuit kept Featherston in New York, much to his irritation. Night reading bothered his eyes but he did read James Fenimore Cooper's *Home as Found*. He thought it dull and pedantic but refrained from saying so when he had a lengthy visit with the author a few days later. His boredom was broken on 23 November by a message from his mother-in-law informing him of the birth of a son. He departed at once for Philadelphia, where he was happy to find Charlotte looking better than he had ever seen her and their son thriving. They decided to christen him Henry after the elderly baronet.

When Featherston returned to New York, frustrating delays continued. On 5 December he "offered not to go to trial if the adverse party would admit that I had been in the service of the U.S. as their geologist, but they refusing, the cause was put off until next term." Colonel Abert had been supposed to appear as a witness but did not arrive. Featherston was infuriated, writing in his journal that the only American upon whom he thought he could rely had failed to keep his promise. When Abert later apologized for missing the boat, he considered it a lame excuse, for he had to pay court costs because of Abert's laxness. By 12 December, Featherston had cooled down and was able to assure his friend that he had not meant to reproach him. He told him that the defendants, hearing that Abert had been subpoenaed, had decided not to use Mather as a witness. Whether or not this ended the suit is not clear.[22]

Featherston sailed on the *Great Western* on 25 February, taking with him Fox's dispatches. In addition to his luggage, he had sent on board two cases of gold ore, a package of dressed skins, the eight-hundred-pound specimen of leopardite, and a large box of books. Fox had also given Featherston letters of introduction to several people in England who, like himself, were concerned about the increasing friction between the state of Maine and the province of New Brunswick, and who might support Featherston's proposal for a geological survey to help settle the dispute.[23] Incidents occurring there had a distinct potential for leading to another war between the United States and Great Britain. Although the dispute had dragged on for a long time, it was obvious it could not be postponed much longer. Citizens of Maine, claiming far more territory than Great Britain was willing to cede, were openly building roads, cutting timber, and even surveying lots in the region.

The problem had its origin in the Treaty of 1783 and involved only the northeastern angle of Maine. Article 2 of the treaty read, in part: "And that all disputes which might arise in future on the subject of the boundaries of the said United States may be prevented, it is hereby agreed and declared, that the following are and shall be their boundaries, viz: from the north-west angle of Nova Scotia, viz: that angle which is formed by a line drawn due north from the source of the St. Croix River, to the Highlands, along the said Highlands which divide those rivers which empty themselves into the River St. Lawrence from those which fall into the Atlantic Ocean, to the north-westernmost head of the Connecticut River." This western boundary was not involved in the dispute, but the southern and eastern were. These were also delineated: "South— by a line to be drawn due east &c to the head of the St. Mary's river, and thence down along the middle of the St. Mary's river to the Atlantic Ocean:—East, by a line to be drawn along the middle of the river St. Croix from its mouth in the Bay of Fundy to its source directly north to the aforesaid Highlands which divide the rivers that fall into the Atlantic Ocean from those which fall into the River St. Lawrence."[24]

The treaty descriptions of the respective boundaries were perhaps as precise as could have been expected of those who drew them up and agreed to them, since there had never been a survey of the region concerned, but they contained terms easily subject to different interpretations. What constituted "the Highlands" or "the source of the St. Croix river?" Even which river is the St. Croix? Three different rivers had been called by that name at various times. The British claimed that the westernmost was the intended boundary; the United States claimed the easternmost. A later treaty, the Treaty of London, or Jay's Treaty, in 1794 sustained the United States claim, and a monument was erected at the source of this river to mark the boundary at this point. This still left undetermined "the northwest angle of Nova Scotia" in a wilderness never surveyed.[25]

Attempts to reach an agreement on the boundary line continued for twenty-nine years, during which the British colonial government maintained "a degree of possession and jurisdiction" over the disputed territory pending a final settlement of the question.[26] Failing to reach any agreement, the two countries finally decided to submit the problem to a neutral arbitrator for settlement and in 1827 chose the king of the Netherlands. It was not until 1831 that the king issued his decision. He declared that the Treaty of 1783 was too vague to permit a decision supporting the claims of either party and recommended a compromise. The United States Senate in 1832 rejected the king's decision on the grounds that he had not been empowered to reach a compromise. In 1835 Great Britain also declared its rejection. As Featherston went to England in 1839, the Senate was awaiting a reply from Great Britain to a United States proposal for the appointment of umpires to undertake a settlement of the boundary.

Featherston was convinced that an accurate geological survey of the disputed territory would support the British claims. A geological approach to the problem had not previously been considered and the joint survey now proposed by the United States would be geographical rather than geological. His problem would be to convince the foreign minister, Lord Palmerston, of the desirability of a geological emphasis in the survey. If he could do so, he would be the logical choice to make it. The letters given him by Fox were to John Backhouse, permanent undersecretary at the Foreign Office, and to William Thomas Fox Strangeways, under–foreign secretary. Featherston was thus assured of being able to present his proposal at the Foreign Office. When he reached London on 15 March he called on both men and presented Fox's letters. Following their meeting, Backhouse reported Featherston's arrival to Palmerston and reminded him that Fox had suggested his employment on the proposed commission. He noted to Palmerston that it was as a geologist, rather than an engineer, that Featherston viewed the boundary question and that he ardently supported British claims.

Having presented his letters at the Foreign Office and found lodgings, Featherston awaited developments. In the meantime he sought out old friends. The Murchisons gave him a hearty and affectionate welcome, and he dined with a number of people, including the Bullers, Durhams, and Turtons. He attended the marquis of Northampton's "Evening for Scientific Men" and addressed a meeting of the Geological Society, where he was pleased by enthusiastic applause. Both Ellice and Vaughan had commended him to the Foreign Office, so he called to express his appreciation. Vaughan now lived in Mayfair but also had chambers at All Souls, Oxford. When Featherston later dined with him there, he was impressed: "These fellows of All Souls lead famous lives—good quarters, a small income, excellent fare, and a beautiful college to live in all to themselves." Lord Durham not only invited him to dine but sought his advice about his political position. He and his staff were in the process of preparing for publication a two-volume *Report on the Affairs of British North America,* sometimes known as the Magna Carta of the Second British Empire. His recommendations, according to one biographer, were "so drastic and unprecedented that they amounted to a reversal of all the country's age long ideas of Colonial Government."[27] Featherston again discussed the problem of the disputed territory with Durham and made sketches to illustrate his points.

Featherston did not depend on his connections and good recommendations alone. His evenings were social, but he spent his days researching the history of the boundary dispute from its beginning and drawing up a detailed memoir concerning it, complete with maps. He pointed out that "the American Commissioners under Jay's Treaty of 1794 humbugged our Commissioners in the grossest manner. They not only got them to consent to abandon the ancient boundary between New England and Nova Scotia, which was the Penobscot, and what is now called the St. Croix, but persuaded them to take the Easternmost source instead of the 'most North West Source' according to the old boundary of Nova Scotia. This is the cause of all the embarrassment." On 25 March he gave one copy of the memoir to Lord Durham and another to Backhouse. The latter was delighted with it and promised to arrange an interview for him with Lord Palmerston. Featherston found some time for correspondence, keeping Fox informed of developments and telling him of the general approval of Fox's agreement with United States Secretary of State John Forsyth to withdraw all military forces from the disputed territory pending a settlement.[28]

The hoped-for interview with Lord Palmerston took place on the afternoon of 26 March. It was lengthy, for he discussed Featherston's memoir paragraph by paragraph. When the interview ended, the foreign minister told Featherston that he considered his views very important. A few days later, Featherston had to cancel a planned trip to Oxford with the Murchisons when Palmerston sent word that he would like to see him at home in the evening. Backhouse joined them for another lengthy discussion. Featherston was careful to avoid any intimation that he hoped to be appointed as a commissioner for the survey. The following day he joined the Murchisons at Oxford where they were visiting the Bucklands. Buckland had examined the section of leopardite Featherston had brought from Charlotte, pronounced it unique, and advised him to give it to the British Museum.[29]

Ten days went by without further word from anyone at the Foreign Office, but Featherston was still optimistic. On his birthday, 9 April, he reached the age of fifty-nine. He wrote in his journal that he was "not troubled with riches" but enjoyed good health and "valuable friends," and his "prospects for reputation" seemed good. He wanted to devote the remainder of his life to the welfare of his family and "to the acquirement of honest fame." While waiting as patiently as possible, he occupied parts of two days with operations by "Cartwright, the celebrated dentist." In spite of these he was able to dine at the Geological Society's prestigious Dining Club, of which he had become a member. The optimism expressed on his birthday was justified when Backhouse told him that Palmerston wanted to engage him in the government service "as Commissioner on the boundary survey." Needless to say, he readily accepted but asked permission to make a fortnight's visit to his mother at Scarborough. He would report immediately on his return.[30]

On his way to Scarborough he missed his stage connection at York. Taking advantage of the delay, he visited John Phillips and examined the fossil collection at the Philosophical Society. There was also time to write to Charlotte telling her of his appointment, enclosing her letter in a long one to Fox, in which he commented on the recent "Pine Log Heroics of the people of Maine." He added, "On this side the water, I must say both high and low appear singularly indifferent about the dignified position the Yankees have been endeavouring to lash themselves into. . . . he will not find ten persons in London who understand the case, or have any Curiosity about it."[31] At Scarborough he was relieved to find his mother, now eighty-seven, reasonably well. Her eyesight had failed badly but was not entirely gone. Featherston had brought her glasses from London with which she was able to distinguish many things. He took her to church services and to the spa. Much of her conversation concerned his father and what little she knew about his family.

The elderly William Smith visited him and sat for several hours discussing geological matters. Smith was now eighty but still quite active. They exchanged several visits and dined together, and so had ample opportunity to talk of geological questions and many other subjects. Smith gave him a copy of his paper "On the Culture of Wheat," in which he discussed the geological influence on wheat growing. In his youth, Smith told Featherston, he had been interested in the history of his country and was given books on English history. These seemed to deal only with kings, queens, and battles, so he read county histories but found these mainly concerned with churches, churchyards, and towns. This was not the kind of history he had in mind. He decided that if he was to learn anything about the earth and its history he would have to study it himself, and he proceeded to do so.

Discussing the origin of coal, Featherston was pleased to find that Smith was "of the opinion with me that the vegetable origin

William Smith [Courtesy of the Palaeontology Library, British Museum (Natural History)]

of coal is by no means clear." Featherston later made notes of their discussion on the subject: "Brongniart's theory is that these deposits of coal are the result of ancient insular tropical vegetation laid in basins. Now the line of the known coal fields being parallel to that of the other formations, it is much more simple to consider the coal formations a Series. . . . A casual drifting of ancient tropical forests into basins by no means accounts for the existing phenomena. The courses have been so exactly the same in both countries that it is manifest they have been general." After further notes on the similarity between the courses of the coal beds in England and those in North America, he added:

This subject, when it receives further consideration, will be considered more important than the leaders of the Geological Society, all vegetable origin men, are willing to consider now. My friend Smith carries his theoretical views beyond my approbation. He considers all the Series, or formations, to be Creations, in the sense of the original creation of matter. He resolutely rejects all the notions of Sedimentary rocks being the result of ancient abrasions. On the contrary, he considers the coal, equally with the Chalk, as separate creations. As to the fact of pebbles being found in the formations, he passed over, making light of it, as all theorists do of difficulties.[32]

Geological studies increasingly came into conflict with theological views during this period, as Daniels has pointed out: "It comes as no surprise to find that in the second quarter of the nineteenth century precisely the same kind of argument was taking place in geology as in physiology and with the same results. The earth was made for man, there had been purpose in the creation, and every topographic feature testified to the omnipotence of the Creator. While religion could with only minor adjustments accommodate the belief that the earth was formed in time, it could not with the same facility give up the proposition that the formation of the successive stages required the intervention of the Creator."[33]

After a very pleasant fortnight at Scarborough, Featherston reported for duty at the Foreign Office on 1 May, full of enthusiasm for his new post. His appointment would not be announced until Fox had "settled all the articles of the Convention" with the United States. In the meantime Palmerston assigned him an office and secretary at the Foreign Office, agreeing that he should prepare a summary of the disputed territory's history from the earliest times. During this interim period, until his appointment as commissioner, Featherston was to receive remuneration at the rate of twelve hundred pounds sterling per annum. When the appointment was made, the salary would be in accordance with the responsibility, possibly two thousand pounds. When Featherston reported this to Fox, he hastened to express his deep appreciation of all that Fox had done to make his appointment possible. It was true that his other friends had also supported him but the minister's influence had been the primary factor.[34]

Palmerston made all papers connected with the boundary question available to Featherston. These included those from the Plantation and Colonial offices, as well as many others. Sir Charles Vaughan lent him the journals of the United States Congress. Featherston was soon "up to the Chin in books, maps &c icarorum." He doubted that the United States government would agree to all the British proposals. The United States would insist on starting at the northwest angle of Nova Scotia. He felt that it had been a "trick on the part of the American Commissioners of 1783 to contrive the beginning of the boundary there. In all the original descriptions, the boundary was made to begin at the west, near the sources of the Connecticut, and running thence East. But this was reversed in 1783 by the astute management of Franklin, and the line directed to run from East to West. Our Commissioners must have been exceedingly stupid, and in fact overlooked the preposterous absurdity of directing a line to be run from *an unknown point to a known point,* a reversal of rule and Common Sense." The British cause had been greatly damaged by such "thick-wittedness" from 1783 on, but they still had a "capital case."[35]

Featherston wrote Fox that a point covered by Palmerston in his official letter to Fox was one Featherston himself had stressed. This was that it should be insisted that the United States "literally . . . execute the words of the treaty and run the line *to* the highlands." The Americans wanted the line run to the most northerly edge of the highlands, twenty miles from the St. Lawrence, but the treaty said "to" the highlands, a point, Featherston said, eighty miles from the St. Lawrence. He urged Fox to "make a most manful fight" against another proposal he felt sure the United States would make, namely that American and British commissioners should receive the same compensation. "The Americans want to do everything Cheap. None of our ablest Geometricians will consent to serve on this Commission for less than £2,000 a year, and Government is prepared to give that." Featherston, of course, had a personal interest. "Whenever they are boring you about this," he wrote, "just fancy you see me with my hat in my hand to you, saying 'Pray remember a poor man and two small children.'"[36]

Featherston was barely settled at the Foreign Office when he found his appointment in jeopardy. Lord Melbourne resigned his post as prime minister on 7 May, following a key vote on which he obtained a majority of only five. Rumors flew about London as to who would succeed him, what cabinet members would be replaced, and by whom. Featherston wondered whether or not his appointment would be confirmed by a new foreign minister if Palmerston were replaced. Since his appointment was not a political one, he thought he might be kept. He could only wait and see. Eventually it became known that Queen Victoria had sent for the duke of Wellington, who advised her to ask Sir Robert Peel to form a ministry. This she had done, and Peel had made his potential appointments, but his "reign was not quite as long as King David's," as Featherston expressed it. Peel and his advisers thought it would be wise to replace some of Victoria's "Ladies of the Bed Chamber," who were "wives and sisters of the political enemies of the Tories" and "known to be political managers." They had underestimated the queen, however; when approached by Peel on the subject, she "told him she should not give him any trouble with her maids, as she had not the remotest intention of changing any of them." Peel sought help from Wellington who accompanied him back to the palace. The queen informed him that "neither he nor Sir Robert Peel should have anything to do with her Women." He replied "that in that case they could have nothing to do with her." That evening Lord Melbourne was sent for by the queen and informed that the "Peel Ministry was 'still born.'" Featherston had mixed feelings about all of this. He thought that Victoria had gained stature with the general public, although conceding that it would have been difficult for a Peel ministry to have done its work as long as its political enemies were allowed to remain at court. Featherston's own position would be unchanged, for Palmerston continued in office.[37]

In spite of all the political upheaval, Backhouse and Palmerston had been exchanging views concerning Featherston's appointment as one of the commissioners for the proposed boundary survey. Backhouse reminded Palmerston that the last commission had consisted of a chief commissioner and an "agent." He thought it was important for Palmerston to consider the relationship between the two commissioners: "The value of Mr. Featherstonhaugh's services might be entirely nullified if a colleague of equal authority were joined to him." Sir Hussey Vivian, master general of the ordnance, had recommended Lieutenant Colonel Richard Zachariah Mudge, of the Royal Engineers, and Backhouse thought that he would be a "safe man." Palmerston agreed but thought it might be wise for Mudge to be the chief.[38]

Featherston considered it unwise to disturb the area before the proposed joint survey, but Palmerston disagreed. He wanted Featherston and Mudge to make a preliminary cursory examination. He did not expect Featherston and Mudge to make any "extensive or detailed topographical Survey," just "barometrical and other measures of land elevation, Highlands, etc." He wanted the information "to guide him somewhat in the final settlement of the details of the Convention." In spite of this need for information, however, there were continuing delays.[39]

Featherston was temporarily distracted by Charles Lyell, who wrote that he had been so much interested in all that Featherston had told him of United States geology that he wanted to hear more. He sought a meeting where they might have maps to study as they talked. In view of Featherston's present involvement at the Foreign Office, Lyell saw little prospect of his "communicating even an outline of" his "views to the scientific world" any time soon. Nevertheless, he suggested that Featherston prepare a "broad outline" of his observations for the Birmingham meeting of the British Association for the advancement of science.[40]

Lord Anglesea invited Featherston to dinner to discuss the boundary question, in which he was extremely interested. He gave Featherston a copy of a pamphlet on the subject by David Urquhart, diplomat and author. When Featherston read it, he was surprised to find "so voluminous a work quite barren of information." Urquhart seemed to be "quite ignorant of the history of the Case he affects to write the Exposition of." Featherston expressed his views on the subject to Sir Charles Vaughan, whose opinion he sought concerning the validity of the settlement made in 1798 to correct a defect in the Treaty of 1794. It was his own opinion that "the proceedings of the Commissioners of 1794–1798 are all void, except in the single article of the decision of which was the river St. Croix." He believed that the commissioners had exceeded their authority in erecting a monument and that one of the commissioners was never sworn. More important, they had erred badly in selecting the north branch of the St. Croix instead of the north-westernmost branch. He thought that it was the latter at which the two governments should look. "If we can manage to begin the St. Croix business over again, it will be a great advantage. Old Consul Barclay was regularly done brown at that Commission. He was a native of New York, Howell, the American Commissioner, was an acute New Englandman, Judge Benson, the Umpire, was a native citizen of New York, and the Secretary was a Yankee. A pretty mess!"[41]

With the coming of June, Featherston became increasingly concerned about the slow pace of developments at the Foreign Office. If even a cursory survey was to be made during the current year, it could not be delayed much longer. It seemed strange that Lieutenant Colonel Mudge, who was to be the other commissioner, had not yet reported to help plan the survey. Mudge had been educated at the Royal Military Academy at Woolwich. His father, William Mudge, had been a major general in the Royal Artillery, a first-rate mathematician, and a fellow of the Royal Society. The son, who had been trained under his father, had for some years been in charge of the drawing department at the Tower of London. He had taken part in various surveys and had seen service near Lisbon in 1809. In 1823 he had been elected to the Royal Society.[42] Although he seemed well qualified for this assignment, Featherston had no reason to suppose that Mudge was particularly well informed concerning the boundary question.

While waiting for action by the Foreign Office, Featherston

wrote a reply to an American article on the subject of the boundary. He asked Backhouse to request Palmerston's approval of publishing it in a newspaper or as a pamphlet. Backhouse sent it to Palmerston with the comment that he thought its publication could not fail to have a favorable influence. Featherston told Backhouse he thought he should meet with Mudge immediately, and he asked for authority to purchase instruments and other necessary equipment. He suggested that the authorities at Fredericton, New Brunswick, should be requested to secure flour, pork, tents, and other supplies. These requests, too, were forwarded to Palmerston for approval. When Backhouse suggested that Featherston was impatient for a decision on the publication of his article, Palmerston replied that Featherston seemed to think that he had nothing else to do. He vetoed another suggestion by Backhouse that Featherston and Mudge should be made joint commissioners. Mudge would be the chief, since Featherston's appointment was based only on his scientific attainments and his knowledge of the country. Palmerston asked Backhouse to inform Fox that he should tell the United States that the sending of Mudge and Featherston was not intended to prejudge the proposed settlement. Featherston was less optimistic than Palmerston about American reaction to their coming. He even thought it possible, he wrote Fox, that he and Mudge might begin their reconnaissance "within the walls of the jail at Bangor."[43]

Finally he was able to locate Mudge at Sir Hussey Vivian's on 17 June and took him to the Foreign Office. Next day, they met with Palmerston to discuss what he expected of them. It was agreed that Mudge would find four or five capable sappers to accompany them and would obtain the necessary surveying equipment, for which he would be responsible. Featherston would complete all preparations at the Foreign Office. He arranged their passage on the *British Queen*, scheduled to sail on her maiden voyage on 1 July. If Palmerston made it clear that Mudge would be the chief commissioner, Featherston did not so indicate when he wrote to Fox on the same day: "Col. Mudge, a crack Engineer, accompanies me as associate Commissioner and we shall have a party with us" consisting of several young officers, "practical working and scientific persons." He thought they might be hard to find for most such men were employed by the railroad and other enterprises.[44]

The *British Queen*'s "ponderous machinery" seemed to be baffling those who were trying to put it together, and she would be unable to sail before 10 July. In fact, Featherston wrote Fox, he thought it quite possible that they might "spend a great part of the summer on the Atlantic and then turn back." In view of the delayed sailing, he suggested to Palmerston that it might be well for him and Mudge to make a trip to Paris to look into French archives for evidence of old boundaries. Palmerston approved and, at Featherston's request, provided a letter of introduction to Lord Granville, the British ambassador.[45]

The two new commissioners spent a week in Paris, where they examined French records and attended a formal dinner with Lord and Lady Granville. They called on Brongniart, visited the Jardin du Roi and the zoo, walked in the Tuileries gardens, and spent some time at the Louvre and at the Chamber of Peers, where Featherston was reassured to find the members "quite respectable looking." He enjoyed a visit with his friend and former boss, General Cass, now minister at Paris, with whom he discussed the boundary question.

Back in London, they reported their return at the Foreign Office and began preparations for their departure. Featherston was amused and a little annoyed by an attack on his appointment in the London *Morning Herald,* written by Moses Perley, a New Brunswick lawyer, who did not think Featherston a proper person to represent British interests. Featherston informed Palmerston that both Perley and Senator Daniel Webster owned land in the disputed territory.[46]

As their ship would sail from Portsmouth on 12 July, Featherston decided to visit Sir Harry and Lady Fetherstonhaugh at Uppark. He breakfasted with them and spent several hours there. Uppark was still a "terrestrial paradise," he wrote in his journal. Sir Harry seemed well and was clearly "enjoying a charming green old age." His wife seemed a "most interesting and pleasing person, admirable on every account." The great happiness of both was obvious and "beyond all description." Colonel Mudge joined Featherston at Uppark and they continued on to Portsmouth.

The Boundary Reconnaissance and Its Aftermath

While the *British Queen* anchored off Sandy Hook to await a pilot on 28 July, Featherston wrote a personal letter to Fox asking his assistance with a problem. It was a matter about which he could not say much in his official letter. Palmerston had declined Featherston's request that he ask the United States to provide the party with a safe-conduct since he thought that it might be construed as conceding American rights in the disputed area. Featherston was more concerned that they might be arrested by some officious local militiamen and so have their entire objective defeated. They must of necessity trespass on some territory occupied by the United States. He was not sure just what Fox might be able to do to help but thought something might be done unofficially.[1]

Much of Featherston's first day was occupied in making arrangements for the party that accompanied them and for their luggage and equipment. It was not until the next morning that he was able to join Charlotte and the children at Long Branch for three days. James came down from Springfield, Massachusetts, for the first two days but George, Jr., was too far away to come. He had moved to some of his father's land in Wisconsin, planning to settle there.[2]

James's arrival suggested to his father a possible solution to a problem. He and Mudge needed a secretary and draftsman with

228

some knowledge of engineering. They knew it would be difficult to find one in the time at their disposal. James would suit them admirably, but he was already in the employment of the United States government, and Featherston had some hesitation in suggesting that he leave it. James had no such reluctance. The exploration with his father would be a great experience. He was therefore employed at the rate of three hundred pounds per annum and returned to Springfield to settle his affairs, joining the party at Boston on 5 August. They sailed next day for Bangor, and from there, they traveled by coach over roads made nearly impassable by artillery wagons.

Their route took them up the Penobscot River through various small towns west of the St. Croix River to Houlton, an American settlement where an infantry garrison had been established. They were told that two companies were stationed there. The town was only twelve miles from the New Brunswick village of Woodstock, across the St. John River. From there they continued another seventy-two miles to Fredericton, arriving late on 9 August. Sir John Harvey, deputy adjutant general of Canadian forces and lieutenant governor of New Brunswick, welcomed the party. Featherston thought him the "very model of an English general," tall, slender, and handsome. Harvey assigned them comfortable bedrooms in Government House and arranged a meeting for them with Chief Justice Ward Chipman, Jr., and Mr. Odell, the former surveyor general of the province. When Perley had again attacked Featherston's appointment, with editorial support, in a St. John newspaper, Judge Chipman had answered the criticism, supporting Featherston's qualifications for the post. He and Odell had a long session with Featherston, who used maps to show what he believed to be the boundary line intended by the Treaty of 1783 and presented Palmerston's instructions to them for conducting a reconnaissance. He found Chipman and Odell well informed about the boundary question and impressed by his views. They met again on 12 August to plan the organization of their party.³

In a report to Palmerston, Featherston attempted to give him some grasp of the difficulties they might expect, feeling that he probably had little or no conception of what would be involved.

The group had agreed that they would have to make much of their way through wilderness so dense that horses would be useless. They would have to cut their way through jungles and swamps, carrying all instruments and provisions on their backs. If they were fortunate, they might average four miles per day. They would begin at the Grand Falls of the St. John River and continue to the sources of the Chaudière River, which empties into the St. Lawrence at Quebec, a distance they estimated to be 180 miles. Featherston thought they might reach their goal in forty-five days, taking perhaps another twenty to return. If they could get started by 25 August, they would be back by 1 November, when winter might be expected in that region. The delay in getting started was caused by the necessity of locating woodsmen suited to the undertaking. Parties would be sent by water to make caches of pork and biscuits at certain points near the sources of the Aroostook and St. John rivers. Featherston had some concern about the pilfering of these provisions by citizens of Maine now occupying territory along the Aroostook and the mouth of Fish River, near Madawaska, but thought it a chance they must take. Both Fox and Harvey had written friendly letters to Governor John Fairfield of Maine, informing him of the proposed reconnaissance. This was the first of a numbered series of reports from the two commissioners to Palmerston, signed by both men but written by Featherston.[4]

Next day Featherston wrote to officially inform Palmerston of Harvey's agreement that his proposal for a boundary settlement in an April letter to the marquis of Normanby should be put aside pending the completion of their reconnaissance. Harvey agreed with Featherston that any further consideration of a purely conventional settlement, without a survey, should be postponed. Should the reconnaissance discover a natural boundary consistent with that described in the Treaty of 1783, the British could control any proposed revision of that treaty. Featherston was not content with official reports to Palmerston. He also wrote a rather lengthy personal letter, in which he could say things he thought unwise to include in an official report. Everything he had heard since their arrival had further convinced him of the correctness of the views he had expressed in London. If nothing interfered with their proposed exploration, he felt confident that they would find a natural boundary entirely consistent with that described in the 1783 Treaty.[5]

There were, however, reasons for serious concern. In spite of an agreement Harvey had made with the governor of Maine and Major General Winfield Scott, Americans were rapidly occupying the disputed territory. A Maine citizen named Nye, acting as a deputy for one of Maine's land agents, had a party of 150 men at the mouth of Fish River. A permanent, well-constructed road was being built there from the Aroostook River. Featherston thought it probable that after harvesttime this party would be greatly enlarged. Americans had displaced Indian tribes and, more recently, had occupied the Mexican territory of Texas in the same way. Since the British had no military post at Madawaska there would be nothing to stop them from not only occupying the territory but interrupting normal British communication lines with Quebec. Once well established, they would only be removed by force. There would probably be no agreement upon a joint survey of the line for several years. By that time the settlers would be firmly established and would certainly have the sympathy of United States citizens elsewhere, which would leave the federal government with little or no ability to remove them. Featherston did not presume to suggest how Palmerston might prevent the problem from worsening but evidently believed that a British garrison at Madawaska would help.[6]

Featherston, Mudge, and the men who had come with them spent almost a fortnight at Fredericton, assembling the rest of their party and supplies both there and at St. John on the coast. All needed rest and recreation before beginning what they knew would be an exhausting experience. Featherston had been concerned about a weakness in his legs that had bothered him recently. He was alarmed on 19 August by the report of a disastrous fire at St. John, which destroyed 150 houses, warehouses, and stores. He accompanied Harvey to the coast the next day and was relieved to find that their storehouse had not been burned.[7] Featherston was not impressed by either the town or its people, finding it much like most American small towns; he believed that the better class of immigrants went to farms rather than towns.

During their stay at Fredericton, Featherston took time to bring their accounts up to date. He had been given £400 by the Foreign Office for contingency expenses. He and Mudge were jointly authorized to sign for additional expenses that might become necessary. They had spent £37 on the trip to Paris. Passage to New York for three engineers, several sappers, and themselves had cost an additional £188. They had purchased a barometer for £20. There had also been expenses in New York, travel to Fredericton, and board there, as well as the purchase of special clothing. Before leaving they had spent £553.[8]

The party that finally took shape included more than forty men. A man named Wilkinson was appointed commissary and put in charge of the local men they had hired. Another member of the party, Hansard, was sent to Maine with a letter from Harvey to Governor Fairfield, bespeaking freedom from interference for the party. The complete group, including those who would come from St. John, would assemble at Grand Falls, on the St. John River. There they would be subdivided. Those leaving from Fredericton began their travels on a towboat on 23 August, spending their nights at taverns along the way. Hordes of blackflies made life miserable all day, and their progress was not rapid, for the horses could pull the boats at an average of only three and a half miles an hour.

On 28 August, Featherston, Mudge, and James left the boat. They hired horses to ride to Mars Hill, where they left them in order to climb the mountain. The elevation there had been said to be 1,500 feet but Mudge's determination made it only 1,285. Featherston thought that the mountains, of which Mars Hill was a part, were extensions of the Alleghenies. They had been worn down by aqueous action, forming and enriching the bottomland along the Aroostook and other streams in the disputed territory. From Mars Hill they made their way to the Tobique settlement and then another twenty-five miles to Grand Falls. Their route took them through a limestone valley that reminded Featherston of Virginia's Shenandoah Valley. At Grand Falls, Featherston enjoyed a visit with Sir John Caldwell. Thirty-two years had passed since he and Edward Ellice had visited him at Chaudière Falls. Sir John had reason to be concerned about the boundary settlement, for he owned a number of lumber mills in the disputed territory.[9]

Featherston spent ten busy days at Grand Falls waiting for all the men, equipment, and supplies to assemble, making preparations, and organizing parties. Captain J. A. McLaughlin, warden of the disputed territory, arrived with two highly trustworty men, very familiar with the country between Grand Falls and the headwaters of the Chaudière and Connecticut rivers. Featherston was most favorably impressed by the warden and learned as much from him as he could. Hansard returned from Maine with a letter from Fairfield requesting his land agent, his deputies, all magistrates, and citizens, to avoid any interruption of Featherston, Mudge, and their party and to assist them if possible. The governor apparently thought the party was there only to confirm the state's claim. He told Hansard that Maine was claiming the whole of the disputed area and that the federal government supported her. A fleet of canoes that had been ordered finally arrived, as did the remainder of their supplies and equipment.[10]

There were three separate parties for the reconnaissance. One would travel northeast to examine the terrain between Grand Falls and the western tip of the Bay of Chaleurs. A second would proceed up the St. John River to its sources. The third, to include Featherston, Mudge, and James, would go southwest across country toward the headwaters of the St. John and the Chaudière, joining the second party in that area. Caches of food would be made for them at certain strategic locations.[11]

Colonel Jarvis, Maine's superintendent of the roads being built in the disputed territory, came to see Featherston, who had long had a cordial relationship with the Jarvis family. He found the colonel, a political leader in Maine, an attractive and intelligent man. He would be a member of the next legislature, due to convene in January. It was soon evident to Featherston that the colonel was on a fishing expedition to learn what he and Mudge were preparing to do. They quickly achieved a mutual understanding and were able to speak frankly. Jarvis confirmed what Featherston had already heard rumored, that the forthcoming session of the legislature would almost certainly pass a resolution authorizing state authorities to seize the entire territory under dispute. Every candidate for the legislature had promised his constituents to support such a measure. Featherston pointed out to him that no matter what results he might report to the British government, it would not be possible to send them to Washington in time for the legislators of Maine to be informed of them. The action they proposed would put them clearly in the wrong. He had no great difficulty in convincing Jarvis that they would be making a great mistake, and the latter promised to use his influence to try to prevent such precipitate action. It was evident to Featherston after talking with Jarvis that the situation in Maine was quite as tense as he had thought. Any unfortunate incident might trigger an explosion by Maine citizens eager to acquire the land involved.[12]

Only a few days after his meeting with Jarvis, Featherston learned of just such an incident as he feared. A few lumbermen from New Brunswick had seized arms from a depot near the Tobique settlement and had attacked the American military post at Fort Fairfield but had been repulsed. Featherston and McLaughlin hastened to the fort to express their regrets to the commander, Captain Parrott. To their infinite relief he told them that the incident could not be taken seriously. The few men involved had fled when the first shot was fired by a guard, leaving behind three hats, boots, five bayonets, and an axe. Featherston apologized to Governor Fairfield, and McLaughlin had the arms depot moved to Grand Falls.

In spite of Featherston's relief over Parrott's attitude, he could not help being sympathetic to the "vagabonds." He was shocked by the calm assurance with which the Americans had established Fort Fairfield six miles from the Aroostook's mouth in territory he considered British. Well fortified, it had five hundred "stand of arms," field guns, and a regular garrison. Going up the Aroostook a few days later, he examined the road being built between the Fish River fort and Bangor in direct contravention of the agreement with Major General Scott. This was no hasty, temporary road, but one done systematically, with tree roots removed and well-defined ditches dug. Other roads were being established and surveyors were busy running township lines. Lands that were in English territory were being sold, with titles from the Maine government. New settlers arrived daily. Featherston reported these encroachments, and Fox wrote to Strangeways about it. Palmerston consulted Lord John Russell, saying that it was imperative to prevent the gradual American occupation of an area that the commission might prove to be British land. If the Americans had already settled there, it would be very difficult to persuade the United States to agree. Russell advised that Fox be asked to make an immediate protest to Secretary of State John Forsyth, pointing out that the building of roads and barracks in the disputed territory was directly contrary to the agreement made by Scott and Harvey and might have very grave consequences. Fox was to request that Forsyth take steps promptly to have all construction stopped and Maine troops and other citizens withdrawn to the lines agreed upon.[13]

The weather was already getting chilly, with heavy frosts in the mornings, when the survey party made its start on 11 September. Featherston's penchant for covering some distance before breakfast was not popular. Even he soon conceded that early morning fog made it impractical. The country was beautiful, with fine mountains and many lakes reminding him of the Tyrol, but the going was difficult. There were lengthy portages between lakes, and trails to be cleared. Cold rains were frequent and at night the party spent much time around fires trying to dry clothing and equipment. Colonel Mudge, unused to such conditions, was anything but enthusiastic, enduring the hardships only by reminding himself that each day brought them nearer to Quebec. He quickly lost all concern about his appearance, not bothering to shave and looking generally sloppy. Featherston, on the other hand, reveled in camp life. Although he was fastidious, exploring excited him. Mudge did enjoy hunting and fishing, and at times, they fared very well. Wilkinson, although a good clerk, proved a disappointment in dealing with the rough canoe men. They consumed most of the meat and potatoes provided for them in the first few days. Fortunately, Featherston was able to purchase another barrel of pork and eight bushels of potatoes.[14]

One day, Featherston, James, Wilkinson, and Mudge set out

with axemen to climb a mountain. It was steep but not dangerous; yet Mudge stopped when they were only halfway up. Featherston wondered if he was bothered by heights. When the others reached the top they cleared away trees until they could see Mt. Katahdin, some thirty miles away. When he rose the next day, Featherston was stiff and sore and not in the best of humor. He reflected in his journal that an expedition of this sort should have only one man in charge. He was already tired of getting up at six and waiting until eight for Mudge to get up. The men tended to follow Mudge's example, so they were always slow getting started. Mudge was beginning to complain of the cold, wondering if he could hold out until they reached Quebec, and Featherston volunteered to do all the work himself. When they were underway, the colonel lagged as much as half a mile behind the others. Featherston began to wish Mudge was in Quebec. On 29 September he noted that the "colonel takes no interest in anything but his meats, makes no observations, and is so totally mindless and passive that he would not only be utterly incapable of finding his way back but would let me carry him to China without concerning himself about any occurrence foreign to his wants. . . . I have just told him that he must make some observations for longitude here, now that we have leisure, but he will not do it. Neither have we had the variation once ascertained, so that my general map is in danger of being regulated by approximation." One day Mudge returned to camp with his canoe half full of water and their barometrical register soaked. Featherston dried it as carefully as he could before returning it to Mudge. Soon afterward he found it by the fire, which threatened to burn what barometrical records they had.

While the colonel fished or hunted, Featherston, with James and Wilkinson, explored and took elevations as they climbed the ridges. Featherston made geological notes, collected specimens, and occasionally carved "VR" (Victoria Regina) on a birch tree. Often he had to shelter under his cloak to check his compass in a pouring rain. As he studied his survey notes and summarized them at night he was exultant. They completely bore out the hypothesis he had proposed in his memoir to Palmerston before leaving England. The highlands clearly ran from northeast to southwest, exactly along the line he had projected, fully supporting the British understanding of the Treaty of 1783. Convinced that no court could doubt the validity of their claim, he was more than ever conscious of the value of this new science, exclaiming in his journal: "This is the triumph of Geology."

The party had been remarkably free of accidents until 29 September, when one of the canoes overturned on Lake Wattasoquon. Featherston and Mudge's servants, Parsons and Thomas, having had little experience with canoes, were sitting on the thwarts instead of the bottom of a large canoe. They lost their balance and tipped themselves and others into the icy water. They were rescued, but an Irishman named Curran was drowned. The following day Hansard and one of the Indian guides overturned a canoe while duck hunting but managed to get ashore after a half hour in the water.

On 30 September, Featherston decided to reduce the size of the party. He discharged twenty-two men, who would make their way back to Fredericton. He would direct a group consisting of Wilkinson, James, the Indian Peter, Parsons, and seven other men. They would take three birch canoes, two tents, and ten days' supply of food, making their way south to Wallastoquagum. Hansard would take charge of the third party, which was to follow Allagash River to its mouth. Then they would go up the St. John until they could rejoin Featherston's group at Wallastoquagum. This would be the safest and least difficult route, so the colonel would go with Hansard.

The groups separated on 1 October. Featherston's party made its way toward the area where there was a division of waters between the Penobscot and the Allagash and where Lake Obscurus emptied into the Penobscot. The region was a real wilderness, with rapids, portages, and swamps, and so the going was extremely difficult. They reached the point where they expected to join Hansard and Mudge on 10 October but found no one. They had to wait three days for their arrival. By that time their food was gone, it was raining, and worse weather seemed likely. Hansard's group had been delayed by shallow water near the sources of the St. John. When at last they arrived, the colonel, still unshaven and unkempt, looked wretched. He asked no questions about observations made by the other party. Featherston was worried but found his apathy "inconceivable." Mudge made it plain that he had no intention of returning to Fredericton. He had already sent his luggage on to Quebec. The combined party continued on to that city, through snow and rain, arriving there on 21 October. Their feet were so swollen that they had to buy moccasins for they were unable to wear shoes.[15]

They reported to the newly appointed govenor general, Charles Edward Poulett Thomson; Sir John Colbourne, commander of the forces; and his replacement, Sir Richard Jackson. Thomson told Featherston that Palmerston's instructions were for him to return from Fredericton at completion of the investigation and meet the governor at Montreal to work out what measures were to be taken in accordance with additional orders. Featherston was a trifle startled at Palmerston's offhand instruction for such lengthy travel. He realized, however, that the foreign secretary thought in terms of the distance from South Audley Street to Great Stanhope Street. Featherston told the governor that it would not be possible to comply with the order, and Thomson agreed.[16]

It had been ten years since Featherston had seen Colbourne. Finding that Sir John was sailing on the *Pique* the next day, he called on him privately to discuss the whole boundary question. Colbourne thought that Harvey's "somewhat menacing note" to the governor of Maine the previous spring had contributed much to the disturbance Maine had been creating since. Featherston, although he liked Harvey very much, thought that he had been very hasty in signing the agreement with General Scott. Harvey thought that Scott had agreed that the Americans should occupy the Aroostook Valley and the British the St. John Valley, pending a final settlement. Flattered by Scott's letter accompanying the written agreement, Harvey had signed it after a very quick reading. Later, he realized that it limited the occupancy of the British to the settlement of Madawaska and allowed the Americans to occupy almost all the disputed territory south and west of the St. John River. Colbourne and Featherston both wrote to Harvey. Featherston advised that if a circumstance occurred that would authorize or justify the use of force, Harvey should take advantage of it to seize the main points now occupied by Maine and drive the Americans out. The settlers were still so few that it would not be difficult, but if there was too long a delay it would be impossible. He also suggested to Fox that he try to get the United States government to admit that the Maine people were violating the agreement.[17]

Paper work—accounts, letters, and the fourth official dispatch to Palmerston—occupied Featherston. There were purchases for the coming travel. The colonel had not changed his mind and refused to complete the last part of the expedition. Featherston had mixed feelings about the refusal. He had found Mudge to be of little assistance; yet his absence would make things difficult, since both commissioners were supposed to sign bills of exchange. He wondered how the Foreign Office would react to Mudge's action.[18]

Featherston accepted Captain Stewart's offer to take his party as far as Rimouski on the sloop of war *Ringdove*.[19] Stewart delayed his departure to enable Featherston to complete his preparations. On 25 October, after parting with Mudge, he went on board, having had only two days to recover from his earlier travels but determined to complete his work, weary or not. The party was put ashore at Bic Island, near Rimouski. A pilot boat took them to Old Bic, where they hired a cart to take them to Remainster, twelve miles away. During the next two weeks, Featherston, James, and their men made their way to Lake Metis and explored the area under very difficult conditions. The weather was abominable, alternating between snow and rain. The party traveled as much as possible in canoes manned by hired Indians. They contended with leaking canoes, ice in the water, disgruntled paddlers, portages, and mocassins torn to ribbons. Reaching the St. Lawrence on 7 November, they paid off the Indians. Since it was snowing heavily, they remained where they were until the following day, when they set out in hired sleighs for Rivière du Loup, arriving there on 10 November. During the next three days, they made their way back to Grand Falls, which they reached with great thankfulness.

Although thoroughly exhausted, Featherston had no intention of lingering there. Disgusted to find no communication from Fox, he gathered enough energy to write to him, wanting to express his anxieties to someone. He told Fox that he hoped to reach Fredericton on 16 November; there he would be greatly embarrassed in settling the expenses of the expedition without having Mudge to cosign the vouchers as their instructions commanded. Mudge should have stayed with him to the end. The colonel had been very imprudent in abandoning Featherston at Quebec and might find it mortifying to explain at the Foreign Office. Featherston and his party had succeeded with great difficulty in examining what the Americans had claimed to be the northwest angle of Nova Scotia. There was absolutely nothing to support their absurd claims, and there would be no problem in convincing the world of that. [20]

While Featherston and his party were exploring along the St. Lawrence watershed, Harvey had written to Thomson that he assumed Featherston would have fully informed the governor general while at Quebec both of their success in determining the correct boundary line and of the extent to which Maine lumbermen and others had occupied the disputed territory. Harvey had the highest regard for Featherston and his group and no question about the accuracy of their findings. If England should use them to justify a joint survey and all the delay that would involve, however, he strongly feared that it would lead to war. There was no doubt in his mind that the boundary settlement must now be made on the basis of an arbitrary conventional agreement. Harvey hoped that this reconnaissance might provide a favorable climate for such a settlement. [21]

On 20 November, Featherston was recuperating from his travels at Fredericton. He was grateful to Harvey for having sent a special messenger to the high sheriff, requesting that a posse be provided to protect him on his return from a threatened tarring and feathering by some of the Maine intruders along the St. John. Featherston thought it probable that a fast current for their canoes had helped but doubted that he would have been safe in the territory another year. Since he could not send an official dispatch in Mudge's absence, he wrote a personal letter to Backhouse, expressing pleasure in the confirmation of his theories. Before returning he would go to Washington to see Fox, who had "every talent but locomotion." He added that Fox had sent a copy of the latest American counterproposal for a joint survey to Harvey, asking his and Featherston's opinion. Featherston found the preamble objectionable and had mixed feelings about making Mitchell's map official. Maine's newspapers were beginning to criticize the reconnaissance. Both he and Harvey thought it might be well for Featherston to write an article for the Fredericton *Royal Gazette,* answering some questions that were arising in New Brunswick. When he did so, he pointed out that not one American had ever been over the disputed area. At St. John, he made a speech on the same subject, which appeared in the newspaper and was widely reprinted.[22]

On his way south, Featherston was appalled to see the Maine papers predicting that the governor's annual message would recommend an immediate invasion of the land in question. He stopped to visit Governor Fairfield, who received him cordially. He, like his guest, wondered if it was not possible to settle the dispute in a friendly way. Featherston thanked him for the safe-conduct the governor had provided for his party. Fairfield assured him that most Maine citizens had been pleased by his appointment, feeling convinced that he would be fair and honest. Land speculators were causing most of the trouble. Featherston had little difficulty in convincing the governor of the importance of maintaining the existing state of affairs until the two governments could receive his report and evaluate it. An agreement could then be reached for either a joint survey or a conventional settlement. Fairfield promised to say nothing in his address that might precipitate any action on the border question. He felt sure that he could keep things calm during January and February. Featherston made prompt reports of his visit to both Backhouse and Harvey, advising the latter to suspend all troop movements for the time being.[23]

In Boston, Featherston had a good visit with his friend Edward Everett, former editor of the *North American Review* and now governor of Massachusetts, bringing him up to date on the boundary situation. Following a short visit with his family in Philadelphia,

Featherston hastened to Washington. After a long consultation with Fox, Featherston wrote to Harvey on 7 December that they had agreed upon the best course to pursue. The immediate necessity was to make sure the frontier was quiet. Fox did warn Featherston not to place too much confidence in Fairfield's assurances, but the lack of hostilities during the next few months was certainly due, in great part, to Featherston's diplomacy.[24]

Featherston, Charlotte, their two young children, James, and Colonel Mudge sailed 28 December on the *Siddons*. Featherston was cheered by the president's statement that England was as determined on an amicable settlement as was the United States. In fact, many were saying that Maine was "humbugging" and need expect no support. The *Siddons* reached St. George's Channel on 14 January.[25]

Featherston and Mudge made an oral report to Palmerston. Featherston then began the process of assembling everything he would need to prepare their official report. He anticipated little assistance from the colonel, other than in the preparation of some tables of elevations. There were still papers to come from Harvey. While waiting for them, Featherston traced the history of the disputed territory from its inclusion as part of a grant from James I to Sir William Alexander in 1621. He would need to consult the queen's legal adviser about a part of this original grant, which he believed had been misinterpreted. He spent some time at the British Museum consulting old maps. One of these, brought to his attention by Anthony Panizzi, keeper of printed books there, was a 1689 map by the Venetian geographer Marco Coronelli. Featherston thought that parts of it would be helpful in illustrating points he wanted to make, and he received permission from Palmerston to borrow it and have copies made. Although Mitchell's map of 1755 was excellent, it contained errors and thus caused confusion. For example, the Bay of Chaleurs was shown one degree, forty minutes too far to the north and this location had possibly confused American negotiators in 1783.[26]

Writing had always come easily to Featherston. He had some experience, too, in the writing of official government reports, but this one would almost certainly be controversial. A great deal might depend on its accuracy and the way in which he expressed himself. He knew that every line would have to satisfy both Backhouse and Palmerston before it was completed, and perhaps the queen's legal advisers as well. It would be scrutinized by many people on both sides of the Atlantic when it was printed. He therefore spent much of the winter preparing it, conferring frequently with Backhouse and Palmerston. He was very much gratified that they never actually struck out any passage, although they often suggested minor changes. There was a predictable delay for Mudge to complete tables of elevation and a log of barometric observations. Featherston's final product was presented to Palmerston on 16 April. Both he and Backhouse professed to be delighted with it. Palmerston wanted to present it to Parliament as soon as Mudge's tables were completed and it could be printed.[27]

Palmerston asked Featherston to evaluate the political situation in the United States as related to the boundary dispute and to advise him concerning procedure when the report was ready. Featherston gave him a written memorandum on the subject, making some ten to twelve points to be kept in mind. Maine relied upon national sympathy. Van Buren would need Maine's vote if he was to be reelected, but Featherston doubted that he would be reelected anyway. His probable successor, General William Henry Harrison, would be more difficult to deal with. The American public, in general, supported the claims of Maine; wherefore Featherston thought it would be advisable to get the report to the president as soon as possible, hoping for a wide circulation of it. Since Congress did not want to adjourn before receiving Britain's reply to its proposal, he thought it would be well to agree to it, but Britain should not agree to start a survey at the incorrectly placed monument. Any joint survey party would disagree, and he therefore believed umpires would be necessary. The line of the highlands should be clearly established and Featherston maintained that, since both countries had rejected the decision of the king of the Netherlands, they should return to the Treaty of 1783, as a basis for negotiations. He urged the evacuation of the disputed territory until a decision could be reached. The land that Britain should receive had excellent agricultural potential but the value of its timber had been exaggerated. Still, its incorporation into Lower Canada should have the beneficial effect of diluting the French influence in the province.[28]

Concerned about the importance of making his report public before some unfortunate incident ignited conflict between Maine and New Brunswick, Featherston was extremely impatient at the delay of publication for over a month. He protested several times to Palmerston, who finally told him that there was a limit to how much he could do. Featherston realized that Palmerston did have more then he could handle. In fact, the whole cabinet did. At the moment they were involved with Parliament over the corn laws and the opium trade. The minister replied to Sir Robert Peel on the opium question at three o'clock one morning with a hundred members sound asleep. They were awakened by his stirring words and even cheered his speech. Featherston thought the ministers led a dreadful existence, rather like defenders of a besieged town.[29]

Letters were a welcome relief from Foreign Office affairs for Featherston. Murchison was at Paris in mid-April, thoroughly enjoying himself as usual. His fellow scientists, Brongniart, Elie de Beaumont, other friends, and even the British Embassy had been entertaining him royally. He felt tempted to abandon the fogs of London and what he regarded as its snobbish aristocracy and to emigrate to Paris, where his scientific interests and accomplishments were considered a social asset rather than a bore.[30]

While waiting for Mudge to finish his computations, Featherston made a brief trip to Scarborough. Upon his return in early June, he was pleased to learn that Palmerston had appointed James and Lieutenant W. E. D. Broughton of the Royal Engineers joint surveyors to make a number of surveys in the disputed territory for which Featherston and Mudge had insufficient time. Palmerston consulted Featherston about the preparation of their instructions, and the latter made a number of suggestions, Palmerston's instructions, if carried out, would provide all the information desired but could not all be accomplished in a single season. The most important project, the determination of levels of elevation between the St. John and Metis rivers, could be done. The survey, however, would take them through very difficult wilderness. All supplies and equipment would have to be carried.[31]

Although he was not ready to present the report to Parliament, Palmerston decided to send a copy to Van Buren on 3 June. Thinking that the president might present it to Congress promptly, Featherston suggested that some additional copies be sent to Fox, to be given to key members of the Senate and House. The first should go to Henry Clay, to whom Featherston wrote an accompanying letter saying that he knew it would meet with some prejudice. He frankly wished the disputed area at the bottom of the ocean rather than that friendly relations should be endangered, since it "would be a serious injury to nobody but the Moose Deer." Nevertheless, he hoped that Clay would continue to promote a friendly settlement. Another to whom an advance copy was sent was Sir Charles Vaughan, who had, of course, been involved with the boundary problem when he was British minister at Washington. It was his enthusiastic approval that pleased Featherston the most, for Vaughan knew all the difficulties involved. He thought Featherston had succeeded brilliantly and complimented him. He was amazed by Featherston's circumspection in writing since he was inclined to talk so "warmly."[32]

It was now time to print the bulk of the copies of the report for distribution to members of Parliament. It would take two weeks to have twelve to fifteen hundred copies printed and stitched. Only fifty maps a day could be made from the copper plates. Featherston suggested that these should be put in cases since they would be on thin paper and easily torn. The dotted orange line representing their route from the Bay of Chaleurs southwest had been poorly engraved and showed inadequately on some; he hoped this problem would be corrected. He drew up a list of people not in Parliament who should receive copies, including societies and embassies in other countries, for he considered it wise to enlist the sympathy of Europeans as the United States was already doing. American ministers at European courts had circulated a paper signed "A Citizen of the United States," giving all the American arguments for their claims, and Galignani had published it in 1839. It was the work of a young lawyer from Massachusetts then living in Europe, Charles Sumner. Featherston had written a reply, refuting Sumner's arguments. The Foreign Office now instructed him to send two copies of his and Mudge's report to each British embassy, one of which would be retained and the other circulated. Later, he translated it into French for distribution on the Continent.[33]

"Overworked and overwalked," Featherston was completely exhausted by late June. Charlotte was six months pregnant with their son, Albany, who would be born in September. Featherston thought it advisable that he and his family retire to Scarborough for the summer. He told Palmerston that he would be happy to return on short notice if needed. On their way north, Featherston wanted to show Charlotte Blenheim, the duke of Marlborough's famous estate in Oxfordshire. Buckland suggested that they come up for the Oxford commemoration on 30 June and 1 July, and stay with his family. Not long after reaching Scarborough, Featherston was distressed to learn of the death of Lord Durham. Of all the English noblemen he had met he had formed the highest regard for Durham, both intellectually and personally. Durham had invited Featherston to visit him at Lambton in September on his way to the Glasgow meetings.[34]

All during the summer, Featherston passed on any information he thought might be of value to Palmerston. In mid-July he expressed his surprise that Van Buren had not given his report to Congress immediately. Fox had handed it to Forsyth on 22 June. Both the president and his cabinet had read it and studied the maps. Featherston suspected that they wanted to suppress it because of the upcoming election. Such a blackout could not be continued much longer, however, because the report was being released in Canada and would be picked up in the United States from papers in New Brunswick and Lower Canada.[35]

Palmerston placed the report before Parliament in late July. On 31 July the London *Times,* which had more than once attacked Featherston for being biased toward America, astonished both him and Palmerston by not only approving the report but praising it highly, saying it was "among the most important documents" that they had ever read and "the most decisive as to the merits of a great national question." At this time the report still had not been widely circulated in the United States. The president's reaction was measured; he hinted that the English cabinet had not publicly adopted it, a remark that infuriated Featherston since "not a phrase went to press" without his superiors' sanction. Ridding himself of some spleen to Fox, Featherston referred to Van Buren as "a very pleasant little person . . . yet a more thoroughly and affectionately single mindedly devoted person to *dear self,* I never knew." He felt sure that Van Buren would lose the coming election and, having done so, would not "care a single damn" what became of the boundary question. Featherston hoped that a compromise settlement could be reached without a long-drawn-out survey that might take eight to ten years. He supposed, however, that if the Americans insisted on one, he could "afford to be the Queen's Commissioner the remainder of my life."[36]

The report soon received support from British journals such as *Blackwood's* and *Fraser's.* The former had strongly advocated an "equal partition of the contested territory. . . . Even while reading the present report we were somewhat reluctant to be persuaded of the full strength of our own title lest this should interfere with our favourite project of mutual concession; but after an attentive perusal of this report we cannot escape from the conviction, that our own claim is now placed on such grounds as render it quite incontrovertible." After giving a careful analysis of the report for the benefit of readers who avoided official documents, the editor called attention to the difficulties under which the reconnaissance was made: "It was no common survey they undertook; and in making their numerous observations, they must necessarily have undergone much labour and fatigue, the narrative of which, like high-minded men, they have suppressed."[37]

Featherston had reason to feel proud. He had used his knowledge of the geology and physical geography of North America to conceive that it should support the British claims. He had presented his ideas to Lord Palmerston, convinced him of their importance, and received an appointment as commissioner. At Palmerston's request, he had planned, organized, and conducted an extremely difficult and strenuous reconnaissance that supplied complete factual support for his beliefs. He had made himself thoroughly familiar with the history of the dispute and had written a clear and convincing report of his findings. Well aware of his British bias, he had made every effort to be fair and accurate. He had, beyond question, placed Great Britain in a strong position to settle this troublesome question. It was no small achievement. If he felt any irritation that Mudge, who had been a handicap to him throughout the affair, must receive equal public acclaim, he kept it to himself, knowing that a number of people officially connected with the undertaking could not help but be aware of what the situation had been.

When Murchison returned from Russia in early September, he told Featherston that, after reading his report, the Russians in St. Petersburg were all in Britain's favor. Since arbitrators for the boundary settlement might well be chosen from men on the Continent, Featherston thought he should attend the meeting of the British Association for the Advancement of Science to explain England's case to those foreigners present. The meeting, which was held in Glasgow, was the first he had attended. He enjoyed it immensely, particularly since both the Bucklands and the Murchisons were there. The distinguished company included many members of Parliament, some dukes and other nobles, with the marquis of Bredalbane presiding. Some of the MPs asked Featherston to describe the disputed area, so he set up diagrams, charts, and maps for his lecture in the Physical Section, explaining in more detail to the foreigners. After the meeting adjourned, he visited the duke of Hamilton, where he met a number of distinguished gentlemen from the Continent who questioned him and to whom he gave copies of the report and maps. All were interested in being appointed to a board of arbitration if one was set up. Featherston felt that his untiring efforts must soon make the whole of Europe cognizant of the boundary problem, especially when the French translation of the report was completed.[38]

American reaction to his report was predictable but came more slowly than Featherston had expected. The government had sent its own surveyors to verify the Featherston-Mudge findings, or perhaps to question them. Meanwhile, Maine had let it be known that if any joint survey was to be undertaken, Maine residents should be either a part of it or present as observers. Featherston felt it would be inadmissible to allow them to be present on a negotiating survey. He wrote Fox, "If they want to inform themselves correctly about a Conventional line, let them go and ascertain one—nobody will oppose them. As to the English Commissioners dragging a pack of Ragamuffins along with them for forty or fifty years as the Lord did Moses and the Israelites, that miracle was not intended to be played over again." He suspected that the citizens of Maine had been watching with interest some friction developing between England and France. A war between the two would provide another opportunity not only to complete the occupation of the disputed territory but to encourage revolt in Canada and to seize additional land. He thought that he had helped prevent their doing either by convincing Lord John Russell of the importance of giving Sir John Harvey military command of New Brunswick. He applauded the proposal to build blockhouses at Madawaska and opposite Fish River.[39]

Confirmation of Featherston and Mudge's findings came from James in mid-November. The survey he and Broughton had made had been stopped by snow at the end of October, but it had already fully substantiated Map A of Featherston's report, which hitherto had been conjectural. They had met some of the American party but had thought them poorly equipped for their task. Broughton was returning to England with their data while James reconnoitered the Chaudière country to get an impression of what they would encounter the following year. James would then go to Washington to report to Fox. It was in November, too, that his father was highly amused by an item that appeared in both the *Times* and the *Globe*. It was reported that the emperor of Russia had sent Featherston a million rubles. He informed Backhouse that he was prepared to give half of that sum to anyone who could tell him where to find it.[40]

By December, American reaction was finally being received in England. Caleb Cushing, who, like Daniel Webster, had been a land speculator, wrote a letter to an American paper denouncing Featherston in vitriolic terms, calling him a traitor. Featherston wrote Backhouse of a previous clash when Cushing had accused Fox of joining the Mexican minister in insulting the United States government. Knowing that Fox was completely innocent, Featherston had threatened to expose Cushing as the author of articles encouraging Americans to help the Canadian insurgents; whereupon Cushing had decided to retract his statements about Fox. Webster, likewise, was organizing the opposition.[41]

One American whose criticism especially irked Featherston was his former friend James Renwick. He referred to Renwick as a teacher at Columbia College, "a sort of school for big American boys." Although Featherston had long been intimate with the whole Renwick family, James had not bothered to call on him when he and Mudge had been in New York. Renwick, an engineer, had been one of those appointed by the United States to check the accuracy of the Featherston-Mudge report. Earlier, a friend of Renwick's knowing that he planned to visit Sir John Harvey, had assured the latter that Renwick not only had been born in England but shared the English point of view. Featherston wrote Fox that he had hastened to disillusion Sir John, telling him that Renwick might be British in August but would definitely be a patriotic American in October, since he wanted to be appointed United States commisioner; he would do everything that he could to confuse the issue. Learning of his report later in the year, Featherston found his prediction had been well founded. Renwick had managed to avoid seeing any of the highlands reported by Featherston and Mudge, except at Grand Falls, the lowest point. He had reported a mountain from the Bay of Chaleurs around all the heads of the tributaries of the St. John. Featherston was doubly thankful for James's and Broughton's confirmation of his conjecture.[42]

The first serious attempt to refute the report was made by the eighty-one-year-old Albert Gallatin. Backhouse sent Featherston a copy of his *Right of the United States to the North-eastern Boundary Claimed by Them* in late December. Gallatin had been one of the United States negotiators of the Treaty of Ghent, as well as the United States ambassador to England, so he was well qualified to comment on the boundary question. He emphasized at the beginning of his paper that he had always found the British conciliatory and anxious to maintain peaceful relations with the United States. He expressed his conviction that a desire for peace, particularly peace with England, was almost universal in the United States. For any breach of the peace to occur over the boundary question would be a disaster. Featherston heartily shared these sentiments but took exception to most of the other assumptions Gallatin had made. He was particularly irked by Gallatin's assertion that Palmerston's having presented the report of the commissioners to Parliament was proof that he had been too busy to investigate the matter personally. Featherston knew that Gallatin was too experienced a diplomat to believe this, although he might well not have conceived what a great deal of time Palmerston had spent with him working on every detail. Gallatin's principal thesis was that the case the United States had presented to the king of the Netherlands was eminently just and must eventually be admitted. Featherston could hardly have been expected to agree. While he admitted that Gallatin was a "long headed man," he thought him a "tricky person, worthy of the country of his adoption." He was amused that no British newspaper even commented on Gallatin's work.[43]

Featherston appended his remarks on Gallatin's essay to a forthcoming work of his own, *Historical Sketch of the Negociations at Paris in 1782.* This study and the research involved kept Featherston busy for many months after his return to London the end of January. Lord Palmerston had asked him to compose a detailed history of these negotiations. He was able to discover several unpublished documents on the subject. Lord Sydney lent him the papers of his grandfather, Lord Townsend, who had been head of the Foreign Office at the time. Sir Henry Strachey made the papers of his grandfather, also Henry Strachey, Lord Melbourne's agent and undersecretary of state, available to Featherston. Strachey had been given "secret instructions to control Mr. Oswald, whose easy manner of yielding to the pretensions of American Commissioners was not approved of." The marquis of Lansdowne lent Featherston three of the manuscripts of William Petty Fitzmaurice, second earl of Shelburne. Since he had concluded the Treaty of Paris, these were most important.[44]

From these papers, Featherston drew up a précis for Palmerston. The American representatives had never even hinted at a boundary north of the St. John, and Great Britain had refused the American suggestion to make the St. John the boundary to its source. With these two points, it could be shown that Great Britain wanted not only the area south of the St. Lawrence but also that south of the St. John—in other words, the old French boundary. Featherston talked to Anthony Barclay, who had been English commissioner, but he could not give any detailed information. Featherston's completed work was to be published in December so it would be available to the British negotiator in 1842. However, reviewing the information streaming in from the United States, in addition to writing the history, Featherston felt the need of assistance; Palmerston approved his request for a secretary-draftsman.[45]

Featherston continued to keep Palmerston informed of any important developments in the United States that had a bearing on the boundary question. A joint committee of the Maine legislature proclaimed that the state was entitled to the entire disputed territory. The United States commissioners appointed to check the accuracy of the Featherston-Mudge report made their own report. Featherston thought that it proved nothing whatever and found it rather amusing in parts, one of which he quoted for Palmerston: "That the ground dividing the Rivers is necessarily more elevated than those rivers and their banks, is sufficient to entitle it to the designation of 'Highlands,' in relation to those Rivers."[46]

In February there was a rumor that Sir John Harvey was being recalled because of a letter he supposedly had written to Governor Fairfield, in which he had opposed the governor general's sending troops to Madawaska. Featherston could not believe that Harvey, an old soldier, could have written such a letter. He thought that the whole affair was an American newspaper chimera. He investigated the accusation as far as he could, writing Harvey what he learned and doing everything he could to aid his friend. At this point, the Foreign Office intervened and forbade him to pursue the affair any further.[47]

The boundary question had come to a standstill at the Foreign Office, pending the inauguration of the new United States president, for it was difficult for Great Britain to predict the reactions of the new administration. Harrison, the first Whig president, had died of pneumonia a month after taking office in March and was succeeded by the vice-president, John Tyler. Daniel Webster, Harrison's secretary of state, continued in that office under Tyler. Fox thought that Webster would deal reasonably with the British but doubted that he would have any more control over Maine than Forsyth had had. Fox and Webster had quite an exchange of letters when two companies of United States soldiers were ordered to the Aroostook and Fish rivers in Maine. Webster said they had been sent without his knowledge and would be withdrawn. Later, he explained that it had been a routine move and had no relation to the boundary question. Featherston, having some personal acquaintance with Webster, was skeptical.[48]

Great Britain, too, had a change of administration. In the summer elections Viscount Melbourne was replaced as prime minister by Sir Robert Peel, and Palmerston gave way to George Hamilton-Gordon, fourth earl of Aberdeen, at the Foreign Office. Featherston was not disturbed in his duties and found Aberdeen pleasant and congenial. He informed the earl about his history of the 1782 negotiations, which would be published in time for the convening of Congress in December. Again there was unwelcome news from the disputed territory. The Americans had cut a canal from the Allagash to the Penobscot.[49]

Charles Lyell was about to sail to the United States in July, where he would give the Lowell Lectures in Boston. Featherston spent many hours with the younger man, who was very appreciative of information given him. Featherston even made a trip to Scarborough to bring up a large number of his North American fossils, which he, Lyell, and William Lonsdale, curator of the Geological Society, spent a day examining. Lonsdale had no hesitation in agreeing that they were mountain limestone, Silurian and Devonian. Most of them had certain differences from their European counterparts but some were identical.[50]

The Webster-Ashburton Treaty 12

Not long after Aberdeen replaced Palmerston, Lord Ashburton was appointed to represent the British in the new boundary negotiations of 1842. He had been a member of the Baring Brothers banking firm from 1810 to 1832 and president of the Board of Trade in Peel's ministry of 1834–1835. He had spent several years in the United States in his youth, where he had married a daughter of Senator William Bingham of Pennsylvania, who owned land in northern Maine. Ashburton had visited the disputed territory at that time. On his return from the United States he had served in the House of Commons from 1806 to 1835, when he had been created a peer. Featherston was not surprised that the new foreign minister had chosen a man more politically prominent than himself, but he was not enthusiastic about the choice. He thought that Ashburton's parliamentary record had been characterized by saying one thing and voting another. Featherston's preference would have been for Fox, whom he considered brilliant and who he felt sure would not give up anything that rightfully belonged to Britain. He recognized, however, that Fox would find it difficult to play up to the American representatives in such fashion as to achieve the reasonable compromise that would almost certainly be necessary. Ashburton, eager for an earldom, would not have difficulty in doing so. He sailed for the United States on 9 February

1842, but having chosen to travel on a sailing frigate rather than a steam packet, he did not arrive there until 4 April. [1]

It was not until mid-May that Featherston was given an opportunity to see Ashburton's instructions. He was disturbed to find them so indefinite on some geographical points and so incorrect on others as to be likely to cause new problems and confusion if accepted by the United States. For example, a branch of the river St. John, having its source in a small lake, was mentioned, but which branch was not specified. The St. John has several branches arising from small lakes. No lake was commonly known by the name applied to it in the instructions. Featherston discussed the problem with Aberdeen, advising that the instructions should be revised to make them conform to the maps and sent to Ashburton as quickly as possible. [2]

Ashburton's negotiations were delayed for nearly two months in Washington before the United States commissioners, three from Massachusetts and four from Maine, could be assembled. Agreement on a treaty was not reached until 9 August, but it was soon afterward ratified by the United States Senate. Featherston had very mixed feelings about the treaty when he learned its terms. He had always been torn between the determination to clearly establish British legal rights with respect to the territory and the recognition that compromise would certainly be necessary to effect a settlement. He had long feared that the dispute might lead to another war, which, he felt sure, France would eagerly promote. He therefore accepted the terms of the Webster-Ashburton Treaty much as he would take "Castor oil, very much disliking it, but with Confidence that it will do good." Although he had been completely absorbed in the boundary dispute for several years, he recognized that most British people knew little about it and cared even less. The country was at peace and prosperous. Everyone was content to have it so. He thought that the essential point was that the British had preserved everything necessary to the welfare of her Canadian colonies and that they had received nothing to which they were not honorably entitled, while he could not say the same for the United States. [3]

He returned from Scarborough in mid-September to meet Lord

Aberdeen, who had been attending the queen in Scotland. Ashburton, who was now back in England, asked Featherston to come to see him. When he did so, he found another visitor, John Wilson Croker. A native of Ireland, Croker had attended Trinity College, Dublin, and studied law at Lincoln's Inn. He was a politician, a member of Parliament, and a well-known essayist who had written articles about the boundary dispute for the London *Quarterly Review*. Aberdeen and Ashburton thought it would be politically expedient to forestall some of the criticism that would almost certainly be raised against the treaty in parliament and elsewhere. They encouraged both Featherston and Croker to do so.[4]

In early October, Featherston attended a meeting of the Cornwall Polytechnic Society at Falmouth, where the chairman, Sir Charles Lemon, proposed a toast to him. He was warmly applauded and took advantage of the opportunity to explain the basis for the treaty and what it had accomplished, refuting some of the criticism he had read in the papers. He declared at the outset that he could say without hesitation of both the present and preceding administrations that "the Queen's Ministers have uniformly acted with the most loyal regard to the honour and interests of Great Britain, and have never preferred a claim to any territory coterminus with the United States which was not founded on the clearest right." He then gave a brief history of the boundary dispute, summarized the situation when Ashburton was sent to the United States, and explained what had been accomplished by the treaty. The American claim had been abandoned. The disputed territory had been divided more or less equally. The part received by Great Britain "secures to us every object that was essential to the welfare of our colonies, all our communications, military and civil, are forever placed beyond hostile reach, and all the military positions on the highlands claimed by America are without exception secured for ever to Great Britain." All this had been accomplished while preserving the peace. The British had given up only some territory south of the St. John River that had never been important to them and a right of way on the river, subject to regulations of New Brunswick. His speech was reported in full by the *West Briton* and copied by the London *Times* on 10 October. Featherston was gratified to learn from Aberdeen that Sir Robert Peel had complimented it highly.[5]

Featherston next undertook to correct misapprehensions on the continent like those that appeared in an error-filled article by a French writer in the *Revue des Deux Mondes*. His pamphlet would serve the dual purpose of informing British opinion as well. He corresponded with Ashburton while composing it, showing it to no one until Aberdeen read and approved it. He had tried to anticipate and answer any questions that might be raised against the treaty either by members of Parliament or by others. The pamphlet was completed and approved in January and appeared under the title *Observations upon the Treaty of Washington Signed 9th August 1842*. Featherston signed himself as "Late Commissioner" to give it the appearance of a private publication.[6]

All during the fall, while working on the *Observations,* he had been wondering if he would be offered the appointment of executing the treaty. Whether such a position would tempt him or not, he still did not know. Since Bangor had been named the meeting place, he felt a great reluctance, but then he would not necessarily be expected to remain there the whole time. Actually, he would prefer going to the Rockies to settle the Columbia River Boundary. In early December the question was settled. The new permanent undersecretary for foreign affairs was Henry Unwin Addington, a particular friend of Mudge's. He, with Aberdeen's reluctant blessing, offered the colonel the post of chief commissioner, which Mudge declined on 30 November. Informing Featherston of the offer and refusal Addington told him he would not be considered for the position. Featherston was understandably very upset. In a letter to Addington on 5 December, he enquired how he might have offended Aberdeen, who had always been so personally kind to him. He did not think that the secretary "would inflict what would be an incurable wound" to Featherston's reputation. If Mudge was thought worthy and Featherston not, was it not reasonable that he should be alarmed?[7]

Addington talked to Featherston the next day, reminding him that Mudge had been chief commissioner and an officer of "scientific distinction," while Featherston had once been employed by the United States government. Moreover, in defending the British claim so vigorously, he had incurred much hostility in the United States. Although this might seem to increase his claim for consideration, it was a bar to appointment, for it would endanger any harmony that had been achieved. Addington said that Aberdeen had taken it for granted that Featherston would understand or he would have written him on the subject. In fact, he had expressed to Addington a high opinion of Featherston's work on the boundary.[8]

On 10 December, Addington gave his and Featherston's letters to Lord Aberdeen, who was so distressed that he sat down immediately to write and reassure Featherston. The secretary said that at the treaty completion he had not even considered appointing the two former commissioners to execute it, since this was such a simple affair in comparison to their previous work. It could easily be accomplished by someone less qualified, and he was convinced that they would not be interested. When Addington offered it to the colonel, Aberdeen had stipulated that, should Mudge accept, Featherston would likewise be appointed. Since the colonel refused, the affair had proceeded no further. Aberdeen had taken for granted that Featherston had understood the situation but apologized for not being explicit. The foreign secretary added that he wished to retain Featherston's services for some time to come and that Addington had mentioned that his "great zeal, activity, and talent" in the boundary controversy had made him "obnoxious" to the Americans. Featherston appreciated the genuine kindliness and respect expressed by Lord Aberdeen. In his letter of thanks, he offered to assist the new commissioner and suggested that he be a man "of an active and resolute character and somewhat accustomed to privation."[9]

Featherston's irritation was somewhat alleviated when the new commissioner, Lieutenant Colonel James Bucknall Estcourt, included James Featherstonhaugh in his party. By May 1843, James, a Captain Robinson, and a Lieutenant Pipon were in Fredericton, whence Estcourt ordered them to Great Falls. James was in charge of general arrangements for the party. At Great Falls the two army officers surveyed one area, and James, with an American counterpart, surveyed the St. John River northward, mapping the islands, the channel, and the depth until they met Captain Broughton. Addington informed Featherston several times of Estcourt's unqualified satisfaction with his son's work and ability.[10]

After his *Observations* had been approved and advertised for sale, Featherston, like many others in England, was shocked to read an article in the *Washington Globe* quoting a speech made in secret session to the United States Senate on 17 August 1842 by Senator William Cabell Rives of Virginia, chairman of the Foreign Relations Committee. The speech had been made in an attempt to persuade the Senate to ratify the Webster-Ashburton Treaty. Rives had revealed that the Boston historian Jared Sparks had informed the Department of State that he had found in Paris, among archives relating to the American Revolution, an original letter from Benjamin Franklin to the comte de Vergennes, the chief French representative at the negotiation of the Treaty of Paris. Franklin wrote that he was returning to him a map on which he had "marked with a strong red line according to your desire the limits of the United States, as settled in the preliminaries between the British and American plenipotentiaries."[11] The letter had been written six days after the preliminaries were signed. Knowing that such a map could provide clear evidence of the intentions of the commissioners, so long since debated, Sparks had tried to find it. After some searching with the aid of the French map curator, he found a map of North America by d'Anville, dated 1746, "on which was drawn a *strong red line* throughout the entire boundary of the United States, answering precisely to Franklin's description." Sparks had been startled to see that the line in the disputed territory differed from present British claims only in that it conceded even more territory than the British were claiming. Sparks had marked a map of Maine exactly as the D'Anville map was marked and sent it to Daniel Webster. Rives indicated to the Senate that, whether or not they accepted the red-line map as Franklin's, should the boundary question again be submitted to arbitration, the map would argue powerfully for British claims.[12]

Senators opposed to the treaty had produced a map from Jefferson's papers that they thought would invalidate the one found by

Sparks, but Rives informed the Senate that this map, when carefully examined, showed a red line coinciding exactly with the boundary traced on Sparks's map. This map had been printed at Paris in 1784 by Lattre, engraver of maps to the king, and was entitled *Map of the United States of America According to the Treaty of Peace of 1783*. Since it had been dedicated to Franklin, who was still in Paris, Rives felt no doubt that it had been done with Franklin's knowledge and approval. After ratifying the Webster-Ashburton Treaty, the Senate had authorized the release of Rives's speech to the press.[13]

The indignant British government decided to inform its countrymen of the American subterfuges and asked Featherston to write a supplement to his *Observations*. In it, he traced the history of the actual negotiations and listed the papers Ashburton brought with him but never bothered to show Secretary of State Webster, since they might be considered controversial. Featherston and others had relied upon a map drawn in 1785 by William Faden, English map engraver and publisher of the *North American Atlas*. On Faden's map was a red boundary line drawn along the highlands south of the "St. John's River and from there to the Lake of the Woods," supporting the British claim. Not long after Ashburton had left England, Featherston had discovered an earlier map in one of the public offices that confirmed this claim but could not be authenticated, since it was unsigned. Yet another map, found in the State Paper Office, also substantiated the English claim. Webster had performed an exacting and clever juggling act. He had concealed knowledge of the French maps from Ashburton but revealed them to the intractable men of Maine, persuading them to agree to the proposals lest they end up with far less land. In the *Supplement,* Featherston attacked Webster's duplicity in concealing the maps while maintaining his complete conviction of the integrity of the American claims.

Featherston's *Supplement* stirred up a great deal of indignation in the press. Even Tory papers, which were fond of referring to the opposition as "the war party," assumed a belligerent attitude. The *Morning Chronicle* dealt with the subject at great length under the heading "The Ashburton Capitulation," taking great pleasure in deriding its opponents: "The Tory Press—the *Times* and the *Herald*—may with reason complain of this 'scandalous swindle,' and cry out 'let us henceforth put no confidence in American protestations, or in Webster's vows: let us not negotiate with a people devoid of the commonest principles of honour: we must act (Lord Aberdeen must act). And before we have any tricks played on us in the Oregon, let us send a fleet of heavily armed and well-manned steamboats, to protect our rights in the fertile and valuable Valley of the Columbia River.' Brave talking this. . . . A fleet of heavily armed and well-manned steamboats' indeed! Not, certainly, so long as yielding and cringing can postpone the necessity of any such energetic display."[14]

Croker, in a lengthy article in the March issue of the *Quarterly Review,* dealt not only with Featherston's *Observations* but also with Senator Rives's speech and another by Senator Thomas Hart Benton of Missouri, opposing its ratification. Croker praised Ashburton's accomplishments highly but took a much more charitable view of Rives's and Webster's suppression of the red-line map found by Sparks: "Mr. Featherstonhaugh remarks that 'We are unavoidably brought to a conviction that whilst the highest functionaries of the American Government were dealing with Lord Ashburton with a seeming integrity, they were, in fact, deceiving him; and that whilst they were pledging the faith of their Government for a perfect conviction of the justice of their claim to the territory which was in dispute, they had the highest evidence in their possession which the nature of the case admitted of, that the United States never had the slightest shadow of right to any part of the territory which they had been disputing with Great Britain for near fifty years.'" Croker continued, "Now we cannot quite concur in Mr. Featherstonhaugh's censure of the American functionaries. We doubt in the abstract how far a public minister or a private advocate is bound to produce to his adversary evidence hostile to his own case, particularly when that evidence had been confided to him in his capacity of minister or advocate. Our readers will recollect Sir Henry Wotton's punning definition of an ambassador, made when he himself was an ambassador:—'An honest man sent to *lie* abroad for the good of his country;' and there is some difference in such matters between the *suggestio falsi* and the *suppressio veri;* but we need not discuss these nice cases, because Mr. Webster cannot, we think, be justly charged with either."[15]

Webster himself was not disturbed by Featherston's comments. He wrote to Edward Everett: "With respect, Sir, to the publication of Mr. Featherstonhaugh, and the tone of sundry articles in the London press, concerning the Paris map, I hope nobody supposes, as far as the government of the United States is concerned, that these things are exciting any sensation at Washington. Mr. Featherstonhaugh does not alarm us for our reputations. . . . It was always surprising to me that the Government of Great Britain employed Mr. Featherstonhaugh. It did not know him as well as you and I know him. He is shallow, conceited, with quite a lurch towards mischief."[16]

During the controversy aroused by Rives's revelations no one mentioned at least two additional red-line maps, purportedly showing the line established by Richard Oswald, the chief British negotiator of the Treaty of Paris, both of which strongly favored the United States. One had been offered to the British consul in New York by John W. Mulligan who had inherited it from Baron Friederich Wilhelm von Steuben. The other was known as the King George map, for that monarch had supposedly signed it (now known not to have been the case). It had been found in the British Museum, whose librarian passed it on to Lord Palmerston in early 1839. Webster accused Featherston of having suppressed it. Although Featherston never mentioned this map, he probably had seen it. When he found Fitzmaurice's and Strachey's instructions to curb Commissioner Oswald's bias, he must have recognized the King George map as purely tentative and thought no more about it.[17]

The inference that Featherston had withheld the map apparently came from a letter from his old friend, the United States minister in London, Edward Everett, to the State Department, 31 March 1843. In it, he described his interview with Lord Aberdeen, who showed him the map and told him that neither he nor Ashburton had known of it during the negotiations. Ashburton, as a trustee of the British Museum, had discovered the map upon his return to England. Aberdeen told Everett its history and said both Lord Palmerston and Featherston knew of it. Everett was not told in whose custody it had been, but he suspected "in that of Mr. Featherstonhaugh himself, who has been employed until lately, as a sort of general Agent for the Boundary question." The revelation about the map did much to tone down criticism of Ashburton's treaty. Three years later, in a caustic mood, Featherston remarked to a friend, "I have had a great deal to do with 'red Lines' in the old Boundary affair and take to them naturally." He was bitter and disillusioned. He had not even considered concealing anything and was deeply convinced that Ashburton had let England down, destroying all the work he had so laboriously done to make clear the justice of Britain's claims. To John Backhouse, then in Rome, he expressed his indignation:

Only think of the trouble that you and I and others have had to bring our British case up to its proper proportions, against such a load of obstinate argument and grave assertion, from a set of knaves who knew *from the first* that they were lying, and relying at all times upon our ignorance and indolence for their ultimate success. You will observe that the map alluded to in the quotation from Mr. Rives' Speech, was taken from Jefferson's Collection which was purchased by the Congress 35 years ago, and was undoubtedly seen by Gallatin and the whole of them. This added to Dr. Franklin's map found by Sparks, and to Faden's Map found by myself, and the old Map at the State Paper Office, furnishes all the Documentary Evidence Honesty would require, if the Case had not been triumphantly made out by the Report of 1840, which is now universally admitted.[18]

Although Aberdeen had written of his desire to retain his services, Featherston was, of course, aware that he had been employed by the government only in connection with the boundary problem. With the signing and ratification of the Webster-Ashburton Treaty his usefulness came to an end. It therefore came as no surprise to him when Lord Addington informed him in February 1843 that his services would not be required beyond the end of March. Once more he must seek a new career. He realized that he had so thoroughly enjoyed his work at the Foreign Office that it had spoiled him for anything else. He felt reasonably confident that the services he had rendered there entitled him to expect some permanent government employment in recognition of them. Addington had implied that Aberdeen would want to do anything he could to promote his wishes in that regard. Five weeks passed with no word from Aberdeen, and so Featherston wrote him a personal letter on 22 March, explaining his situation. Having spent more than half his life abroad and with three young children to educate in English schools, he would much prefer an English post. He was, however, well qualified to assume a consulship. He was knowledgeable about business as well as "men and books." He also spoke and wrote fluent French, Italian, and Spanish, while having some understanding of other languages.[19]

Charlotte was called home by the death of her father. She and Georgiana sailed in April and spent six months in the United States. Featherston and his family had been renting a house from Backhouse, but now, with only the two little boys left at home and no salary, he went to live with his ninety-two-year-old mother in Scarborough. He occupied his time writing an account of his expedition through the southern states to the Ozarks, the book he had abandoned while still employed as United States geologist. It was mainly a matter of organizing his journal into chapters, for he did not change the words or descriptions, although he sometimes substituted initials for names. At his request, Murchison approached John Murray, who expressed interest and asked to see a quarter of Featherston's work. Murchison advised Featherston to send, too, some of the views he was having lithographed in Scarborough. He added that he had no doubt Murray would be "happy to be your accoucheur," since he admired Featherston's style of writing.[20]

On 3 February 1844 Featherston sent the publisher eight chapters of the proposed work, estimating that the completed work would require two octavo volumes of approximately three hundred pages of large type each; he planned to include four or five drawings and a small map. He stressed to Murray that his work would describe "the Manners and Customs, the Geology and Natural History, of a part of America *which has not been described*." He

St. Nicholas Cliff, Scarborough [Courtesy of the Scarborough Public Library]

had tried to make the scientific aspects of his account appealing to the general reader as well, and he had taken care that there should not be "a thought or expression in it unfriendly to the Americans, though I hope there is a good deal in it to make people laugh at them." One of the two drawings enclosed was a "view of the Alleghaney Mountains" and the other of a "Slave driver's Camp. . . . The account of the domestic Slave trade carried on in the interior of the United States is *quite new* to the world." Aberdeen had been surprised to learn of it from him. He asked Murray's opinion of his idea of dedicating the work "by permission to the Earl of Aberdeen" and also of the possible title: "Trans Potomac Sketches, with Geological Notices and Personal Narratives appertaining to a Tour between Baltimore in Maryland and the Frontiers of Mexico."[21]

Pleased with Featherston's writing, Murray agreed to publication, and so Featherston went to London to see the publisher in early March. Murray had not liked the proposed title, so Featherston suggested "An Excursion through the Slave States," to which Murray agreed, with some modifications. He returned the eight chapters to the author with penciled suggestions that Featherston incorporated in his revision. As advised, he had shortened his description of White Sulphur, "taking a great deal off the shoulders of the Landlord, including his white Pig Tail." He was able to keep ahead of the printer handily and sent a dozen more chapters in a few days.[22]

By the end of April he had finished the introduction, most of which he had read to Sir Charles Vaughan, "who knows so well what it would be right and prudent to say at this particular juncture on the subject of the U. States," and Sir Charles had praised it highly. The only other advice he sought was that of Richard Owen. Featherston wanted to know if Linnaeus's *Vultur aura* was the proper scientific name for the American buzzard, which he thought must be Cuvier's *Cathartes*. Owen replied the same day that the accepted nomenclature was *C. aura,* which he thought was the subject of Audubon's experiments in regard to the vulture's sense of smell. After such kindly help from Owen, Featherston was encouraged to send him several proof sheets on a zoological passage, asking Owen's opinion of it. He approved of it, making a few alterations in pencil.[23]

Excursion was published in the last week of May in two volumes and priced at twenty-six shillings. Backhouse received one of two prepublication copies. John Lockhart, editor of the *Quarterly Review,* heartily approved of the work, as did Owen, who remarked that "the travels of one who combines so much science with the more essential requirements of an observer of the social & political characters of the American People, are more than usually instructive and interesting to me." He could not put the book aside until he had finished it. He praised the "natural simplicity, clearness and truthfulness of its style"; since Defoe, he had found no work that pleased him so much. Buckland thanked Featherston for his copy on the day he received it. In dipping into it, he was surprised to find that his friend had "ever been meddling with Agriculture."[24]

"The Perils of Buffalo Hunting," Frontispiece of Featherstonhaugh's *Excursion Through the Slave States,* II [Courtesy of the Alderman Library, University of Virginia]

Someone even told Featherston that his book had "been relished at the Palace." The *Morning Chronicle* wrote of it: "The hearty determination with which the author encountered the perils and hardships of a journey through so wild a country, the fund of true English humour, and right feeling with which he tells his adventures and the manly directness with which he speaks out his opinions, induce us to follow him in his long course with an interest rarely inspired by modern travellers." The *New Monthly Magazine* was equally complimentary, and Featherston was touched by a letter from her majesty's minister in Lima, Peru: "I have just finished reading your charming book on the Slave States in America. It was most happily sent out here to our literary Society as a standard work."[25]

The *Foreign Quarterly Review* commented, in a lengthy review: "In running through these clever and entertaining volumes, we have, as we promised in opening, confined ourselves to the social traits developed here and there by our intelligent traveller; but it is proper to inform the reader that he will find much more matter of the same kind in the work, besides a variety of curious and interesting sketches concerning the people and the resources of the soil. The publication is honourable alike to the judgment and the feelings of the writer; and may be truly ranked amongst the most impartial works that have ever appeared upon the subject of America and her institutions."[26]

Harper and Brothers brought out an American edition later that year in New York. They printed it in one volume of double columns of very small print and did not include any illustrations or the map. Reviews in the United States were a contrast to the British ones, as exemplified by a vicious article in the *New York Evening Post:* "This Featherstonhaugh, if we remember rightly, when in the United States, did not have a very high reputation, and was known to have engaged in some mean and rascally tricks. It is certain that he is a very superficial man, altogether unqualified to write a trustworthy book on any subject."[27]

Featherston had not completely abandoned geology. He presented a paper before the British Association for the Advancement of Science, "On the Excavation of the Rocky Channels of Rivers by the Recession of Their Cataracts," which was subsequently published in their *Report* and was reprinted in *Floriess Notizen.* He also prepared an article, "On the Lead & Copper Deposits of Missouri & Wisconsin," to be read before the same society in York the following September but had to leave that city before the meeting and so withdrew the paper.[28]

Featherston was delighted to hear of James's engagement to Emily Chapman, daughter of General Sidney F. Chapman of Virginia. He regretted his inability to be present at the fashionable wedding in Washington on 18 January 1844, where "President Tyler was a guest and Dolley Madison stood beside the bride." A week after the wedding James sent his father some information he had requested, having spent a morning researching in the news-paper files of Gales & Seaton. Featherston's old friend Seaton had told James to inform his father that he might as well write to Henry Clay and "congratulate him on his *election.*" George, Jr., was now living in Duanesburg and reported that his Aunt Kitty was partially paralyzed.[29]

It was well that Featherston had the distraction of his writing, for he was seriously worried about his finances and his future. Thinking it wise not to harass Aberdeen about his request for an appointment, he had not communicated with the foreign secretary for nearly a year when he wrote on 12 March 1844. In his letter, he reviewed his life as "the Cultivator" of a large estate in New York, as an investigator of United States geology, encouraged by Buck-land and other geologists, and as United States geologist. His reasons for resigning this post had been well understood by such friends as Henry Clay. Even newspapers had praised his action. He had "left America in good odour with every body," and until his 1840 report was presented to Parliament, he had "continued to be very popular in America." Many of the public papers there had said that he could be "relied upon for an honest statement of the merits of the dispute." As soon as he had made what he believed to be just such an honest statement, he had been subjected to "the most unqualified and rancorous abuse." He had then abandoned all thought of returning to the United States and had given up his estate there to his elder sons. He therefore found himself in an embarrassing position. He had "a family of small children to edu-cate, and although blest with health and energy," he had neither occupation nor income. He believed that Aberdeen would agree that he had just claims on the government and, he trusted, an ability to serve it. He was reluctant to trespass on Aberdeen's time, and he had confidence that Aberdeen's reputation for fairness and justice was well founded.[30] It was most embarrassing to take hat in hand in this way, but Featherston's need was becoming urgent. If he had any hope that his letter would produce an immediate re-sponse, however, he was disappointed. It may have been acknowl-edged in some way, but more than six months passed without any letter from Aberdeen.

For better or worse, the boundary between Maine and New

Brunswick had been agreed upon, and although divergent opinions about it would continue to be expressed for a long time, it would not be changed. The western boundary was yet to be agreed upon, however, and Featherston continued to be concerned about it. In June, while waiting at Scarborough hoping for some word from Lord Aberdeen, he wrote to John Murray in London: "The English public has much less information than the American, concerning what these last call the 'Oregon' dispute, and yet it is of great importance and will engage universal attention in this Country as soon as the now Presidential Election in the U. States is determined; for it will be only after the inauguration of the new president that the negociations will be resumed, and rapidly *brought to a Crisis.*" He felt that ignorance on the part of the public in both America and Britain concerning "the nature of the British title in the old Boundary Affair, was very disadvantageous to a favorable Settlement of it" for Britain and feared that the same might be true in "the Columbia territory dispute." He had been considering publishing a pamphlet on the subject but now thought that an article in the *Quarterly Review* might be more effective. If it could appear in the October number, "it would be republished in America before Congress met in December" and might make negotiation easier for the British. His article would be in the form of a review of a recent book. He asked Murray to query Lockhart about his interest in publishing the review. If he was willing to do so, Featherston asked Murray to send him a copy of the book.[31] Actually, the essay appeared as a review of not one but eleven books on the subject, under the title "The Oregon Question," in Volume 77 of the *Quarterly Review.*

The Life of a Diplomat 13

Featherston's faith in Aberdeen was becoming extremely strained when he finally received a letter from him written 9 October 1844. Aberdeen recalled that he had assured Featherston it would give him great pleasure to appoint him to some suitable office, but he had not had any at his disposal. Now, however, Gilbert Gordon, the consul at Havre, had died. Aberdeen wrote that he would be happy to appoint Featherston as Gordon's replacement if he was interested. He knew few details about the consulship, but they could be easily obtained at the Foreign Office. He doubted that any similar opportunity would occur in the near future. Featherston lost no time in accepting the appointment and expressing his appreciation, saying that France would be particularly congenial since those of the literary and scientific world were held in esteem there. He knew, too, that Havre and Marseilles were the two most important consulates in France.[1]

Much of the month of November and part of December he spent at the Foreign Office, learning as much as he could about the responsibilities and problems of the Havre consulship. It had been in the hands of one family for twenty-four years, for Gilbert Gordon had succeeded his father, Archibald. The salary was not munificent—four hundred pounds per year, plus an average of two hundred pounds in shipping fees—but Featherston thought it would be adequate, combined with his small personal income and perhaps some book royalties. The consul was also permitted to engage in commercial activities.[2]

His friends were delighted and relieved for him. Sedgwick wished him "happiness in his new dignity" and enclosed a copy of his "phiz." Some of his friends thought it a fair likeness, but others suggested it resembled "a drawing of a red Indian with a string of bloody scalps in his right hand." It had been made while he was "pounding at the Dean of York." Featherston was "delighted with the Indian Chief." He intended to have it framed "with the inscription beneath it in the Nacotah tongue: Ta-tonka Dacono O-de-anha, 'The great Chief that pounded the Dean.'" He urged Sedgwick to take on a new opponent. He should obtain a copy of a book just published anonymously entitled *Vestiges of the Natural History of Creation*. The author was Robert Chambers, Scottish author and publisher, with his brother William, of the *Edinburgh Journal* and *Chambers's Encyclopedia*. According to Morgan Sherwood, *Vestiges* contended that "life originated through a chemico-electric process by which primitive germinal vesicles were produced. All the various forms of life 'developed' or evolved from the primitive germ, from the simplest to the next more complex, and so on." Not surprisingly, the work quickly became highly controversial. It was attacked quite as vigorously by scientists as by churchmen; in fact, Daniels contends that "of all the bad reviews this book and its evolutionary theory received, the most intemperate came from scientists."[3]

Featherston had found *Vestiges* brilliantly and eloquently written, but by the time he finished reading it, he had "felt something like Contempt that so gifted and instructed a person should have made so bad a use of his power." The author's thesis would "cut off all accountability betwixt the Created and the Creator." He elaborated the shocking beliefs of the author at some length, urging Sedgwick to provide an antidote to what many were already calling a "revolt against the Church." Sedgwick had not seen the book when he replied, but he maintained his hatred and abhorrence of all the views Featherston had told him the book expressed. He was in no mood for more controversy himself, being exhausted by his long-continuing battle with the dean of York.

Soon afterward, however, he read the book and wrote a scathing review of it, much to Featherston's delight.[4]

It was mid-December when Featherston sailed for France. He spent five weeks in Paris becoming acquainted with the British ambassador, Henry Richard Wellesley, the first earl Cowley, nephew of the duke of Wellington, as well as other English and French officials with whom he would be associated. He was introduced to the royal family and found King Louis Philippe most cordial. The king recalled with pleasure the days he had spent at Uppark as the guest of Sir Harry, who was also a great friend of his father's. To Featherston's surprise, he had read and enjoyed the *Excursion*. Featherston received an invitation to a grand ball and supper at the Tuileries. On 17 January 1845 he arrived at Havre to assume his duties. Thirty years before, weary of his problems as a New York farmer, he had expressed a wish to retire to southern France, where he might have "leisure for Literature." Whether his new post in northern France would provide such leisure remained to be seen.[5]

He found Havre much like a small Liverpool. It was one of France's principal ports and would become even more important when a railway to Paris was completed the following year. Havre's docks, capable of berthing 250 ships at a time, were crowded with shipping. The piers were a scene of great activity, where all manner of goods were in transit. He found no obvious beggars, but there were other sorts of mendicants doing tricks with mice, monkeys, and even alligators.[6]

Beyond the city gates there was a hill with southwest exposure, "covered with gay pavilions and Gardens," where the gentlefolk lived. There Featherston found a house in a suburb known as Injoinville. It was the one that had been leased by the Gordon family for the past twenty-four years. He took over the unexpired lease with a rent, including taxes, of £170 per year. He also assumed the lease of the consular office in Havre from the Gordons. Although the house needed a few improvements, it was quite commodious, and the walled gardens all he could wish for. They contained a superb variety of the fruit for which the region was famous: apricots, plums, figs, peaches, and pears. To make the list complete, he asked James to send him cuttings of Catawba and Isabella grapes. Both the house and the town seemed to provide everything that he needed for his wife and children. He was given a month's leave to move them and went back to England on 24 February.[7]

Lyell, having heard that Featherston was in London for a few days only, quickly sought his assistance in modifying the map Murray had made for *Excursion* for use in Lyell's forthcoming *Travels in North America*. Murray had reengraved the map to add some names and dotted lines for colors. Lyell had added the geological colors he had shown Featherston at the York meeting of the British Association for the Advancement of Science and had now extended them into Canada. He was able to show the tertiary and chalk as far southwest as New Orleans and hoped that Featherston could help him carry it north into Arkansas. He promised that anything added by Featherston would be suitably acknowledged. He would either send a blank map or would meet him at Somerset House. The publication of *Excursion* had been very helpful to Lyell, and he gave Featherston full credit in his own volume: "From this work, and verbal communication, I have obtained much valuable information respecting the Allegheny Mountains, the Arkansas, and other Western territories, likewise in regard to the line of junction of the Primary and Silurian rocks on St. Peter's River, Missouri, and around the Ozark mountains. On Mr. F's authority I have extended the Cretaceous Colour for a considerable distance along both banks of the Arkansas River; and he informs me that he had seen the same formation characterized by the abundance of *Exogyra costata* extending all the way to the sources of the Yellowstone river."[8]

Featherston returned to Havre on 28 March, but Charlotte, being unwell, did not join him for another month. Murchison was so involved in completing his *Geology of Russia* that he did not even see her in mid-April when she called on his wife on her way to France. He apologized to Featherston when he wrote a few days later. He had just received thanks for a medal that was to be presented to Emperor Nicholas of Russia to commemorate his visit to England in May 1844 and had been assured that he would always be welcomed in Russia. He told Featherston how grateful he was for "these little words from a truly great man to a man who never had a kind word or even thanks of any sort from his own Sovereign." Murchison was becoming very sensitive on this subject.[9]

When Charlotte and the children finally joined Featherston, she was not too happy with her new home but hoped that the French climate would be more favorable to her health.[10] With his family together again, Featherston was able to concentrate on the duties of his new post. As the principal representative of Great Britain at a major French seaport, he was concerned with a great number of routine matters, on the one hand, and a fair number of unpredictable and extremely variable nonroutine matters, on the other. The former included such things as port dues; coal certificates; trade returns; agricultural prices; problems of British ships, British seamen, and other British subjects; the allocation of funds to British churches; rewards to foreign ships for saving English crews; and regular reports to various offices of the British government. His responsibilities as consul for the Departments of Calvados and Seine Inférieure included general supervision of vice-consulates at other ports besides Havre, including Caen, Dieppe, Honfleur, Rouen, and others. British–French relations were always sensitive. French internal political affairs were in a very uncertain state, and the consul had to proceed with considerable caution in his handling of unusual problems. Having a very limited background in diplomatic affairs, Featherston had a lot to learn.

Although they had been unable to settle in England, as they would have preferred, the Featherstonhaughs were not completely isolated from their friends. In fact, there was a great deal of coming and going between England and the Continent via Havre. Often Featherston was called upon for advice, assistance, or both, particularly during his first summer there. In May, Charlotte Murchison wrote about their summer plans. She had decided not to accompany her husband to Sweden in July or to Russia in August but hoped to visit Havre and southern France in the late summer. Although the Featherstonhaughs invited her to stay with them, she insisted on going to a hotel. Her niece would be with her, as well as a maid. Moreover, they would spend quite a bit of time visiting other places, including a month's tour of Normandy. She wanted Featherston's advice on hotels and on lodgings for the Bucklands, who would also vacation in Havre, with the children and their governess. They would prefer less expensive accommodations. Charlotte Murchison promised to go herself to Somerset House to look for the box of American fossils Featherston had taken there for Lyell to study. She concluded her letter with the news that Sedgwick's review of the *Vestiges* had appeared in the *Edinburgh Review* and that it would delight Featherston, since Sedgwick's opinions coincided with his.[11]

The late summer seemed like a house party. Mrs. Murchison and her niece arrived 15 August for six weeks and the Bucklands about the same time. In September, Buckland spent some time in Paris, where he, Richard Owen, and some other friends had attended a meeting. Owen had given a paper on the fossil monkey recently found in Essex. Two papers dealt with the potato murrain, which was causing great losses in France, Belgium, and Ireland. Mrs. Buckland and the younger children were still at Havre, but her husband lingered at Paris to show his eldest son the city. He suggested that Featherston and Charlotte permit Georgiana to join them for three days to see the sights. Owen also visited the Featherstonhaughs at Havre.[12]

Featherston had not been in his new post very long before he realized that he would soon be in serious financial difficulties unless some changes were made. He had thought that the salary and fees of the office, with his small private income, would surely be adequate, but he soon learned that the fees totaled much less than he had been told. Living expenses at Havre, too, were higher than he was accustomed to. The town was known as the most expensive in France. For instance, coal was double the London price, and fires were needed seven months of the year. The Havre consulate was an extremely busy place with seven vice-consulates under its supervision. The consul was really performing the duties of a consul general without the rank or salary. The right to indulge in commercial pursuits that went with the office was an empty one, since the consul had no time to undertake any. Rather than being supported by the consulate, Featherston found himself supporting it. The consulate took in £160 that year, while the expenditures were £187, leaving £27 for him to pay. By the time rents, taxes, stamps, and office expenses were paid, Featherston was left with only £200, barely enough to cover three months's expenses for his family and "private charity." He wrote Lord Aberdeen these discouraging economic facts on 10 July, but the minister was in Germany at the time, and so it was not until 30 September that Featherston had a reply. Aberdeen agreed that the importance of Havre as a port was increasing and that it required the full services of the consul. Permission for commercial pursuits was therefore withdrawn, and the salary was raised from £400 to £650 a year, still a great deal less than Featherston had received as a commissioner.[13]

The increased salary would certainly help, but he would still have to exercise very strict economy. His vegetable garden and fruit trees became important as well as enjoyable, and he gave thought to other agricultural undertakings in which he had not indulged for some years. He asked Buckland to purchase a Hampshire sow for him as a start toward raising pigs. Buckland, who considered himself something of an authority on the subject, was happy to do so but first urged the great superiority of pigs from Berkshire. Having pointed out their larger size and larger litters, he added that he supposed Featherston would say, "I do not want a side of bacon 5 feet long." That might be, but he could kill half-grown pigs and have "double the number that a sow from Hants w'd give you for the same money."[14]

Several people consulted Featherston on the current relations between the United States and Great Britain. During his first year at Havre, friction had been mounting between the two countries over the Oregon Territory. He and his friends corresponded about the likelihood of another war. In the spring, the United States Congress, after a bitter debate over the slavery question, passed a resolution annexing Texas to the Union. President Tyler signed the resolution in March. His successor, James Knox Polk, who had narrowly defeated Henry Clay, had approved it. Texas became a state in December. The proposal to annex the Oregon Territory as well had become a political issue at the same time. The platform of the Democratic party, which had elected Polk, had called for the annexation of the entire territory. The campaign slogan "Fifty-four Forty or Fight" became increasingly popular. The British had long wanted the boundary to be established along the Columbia River. They had proposed arbitration in January 1845, but the United States had rejected the proposal. By July, however, Polk, anticipating war with Mexico, offered to compromise with Britain and accept a boundary line drawn along the forty-ninth parallel. The British minister at Washington, Richard Packenham, rejected the offer at once, and Polk indignantly withdrew it. For almost a year afterward the situation remained tense and war distinctly possible. Soon after rejoining his wife at Tours, Murchison wrote to Featherston from Paris, asking if he thought war likely and requesting advice about how best to sell the Pennsylvania stocks he owned. He doubted that war would come but did not feel comfortable owning American stocks. He expected to take a loss in disposing of them but thought that he could compensate for it by making favourable investments in England and France.[15]

Sir Charles Vaughan also raised the Oregon question, and Featherston replied at great length. When he had first heard of Polk's election, a great disappointment to one so long devoted to Henry Clay, he had written Addington that he knew Polk personally, "that he was a vulgar shoemaker looking fellow incapable of acting in a lofty manner. . . . he would give the Foreign Office a great deal of trouble." He now predicted that the slave states and free states would battle each other in Congress until July 1846. They would then vote to give the British twelve months' notice for ending joint occupancy of the territory as provided for by treaty. There would be no direct conflict before July 1847, and the matter might be resolved in the meantime. Featherston suggested that Polk and his Democratic party would continue to bluff and to swear they would not budge from fifty-four degrees, forty minutes. He noted, however, that he had been with Henry Clay in the Senate in 1838 when "solemn resolutions" had been passed proclaiming the right of the United States to the entire Northeast Territory. Yet Congress had ultimately agreed to divide the territory "they had so deeply pledged themselves they would never surrender an inch of." Featherston concluded, "So in the end it will be with the Oregon affair. They will consent that the Columbia shall be the boundary. I am of the opinion that under no Circumstances will her Majesty's present Government permit them to cross that River."[16]

Featherston expressed his concern about the long-range protection of British interests on the Pacific coast. He was not eager to see Britain risk war by the acquisition of new territories, but he thought it should be recognized that "our country can only be sustained hereafter by an almost universal Commerce; and not only will ports on the North Pacific, be soon of much value to Great Britain for the purpose of maintaining a thorough communication across our North American Provinces, but it will be essential to her power that she should have the best ports there, from which to sweep the Pacific Ocean with her fleets upon all necessary occasions. And I trust if Mexico will not let us occupy Port San Francisco—which is the grandest harbour almost in Christendom—that the Americans will never be permitted to establish themselves there." He hoped "never to see more ample Concessions made to a people who are already cherishing the mad and idle thought that they are destined to turn us out of Canada ere long." He regretted that he could not write as freely to Lord Aberdeen as he did to Vaughan, but he did not think Aberdeen wanted for advice. Featherston was concerned about current political attacks on the government. "As an Englishman ardently attached to my Country I should be unhappy if I perceived any danger ahead of the Government being wrested from the aristocracy and intelligence of England, by the Cotton Lords of Manchester."[17]

In mid-November Featherston received a letter from Buckland, saying that he had been offered the deanery of Westminster and had accepted. Now he would have to wear a silk apron, straight coat, and a St. George and dragon round his neck on a red ribbon, to which he would add a small icthyosaurus and a suckling hyena or a pregnant Berkshire sow. Not long after, Owen reported on the dignity with which the new dean had presided at the Westminster boys' Latin play. He thought it would not be long before fossils would be found in Westminster stalls.[18]

The king invited Featherston for a visit to St. Cloud on 18

December, where he spent the evening with the royal family. When the king introduced him to his sister, Princess Adelaide, he referred to Featherston as one of the family who had been so kind to their father. Louis Philippe was worried about what changes might be made by the new prime minister, Lord John Russell. "I assure you Mr. Featherston," he said, "that if Lord Aberdeen, *whose heart and head are amongst the very best in Europe,* goes out of office, it may turn out to be an universal misfortune." Featherston replied, "Your Majesty remembers that in 1841 when Lord Melbourne resigned, things did not turn out exactly as politicians at one time expected. We have an old saying that 'betwixt the Cup and the Lip, things are often apt to slip.'" Looking arch, the king whispered in Featherston's ear, "My dear Sir, I shall not be the first to cry, if it all slips together." In parting, he told Featherston that he was always welcome at the palace without an invitation. Featherston lost no time in reporting the conversation to Lord Aberdeen.[19]

On 23 December the Featherstonhaughs dined at the Tuileries, where they met all the ambassadors and other distinguished members of Parisian society. Elegant in his blue uniform, Featherston was chatting with Benjamin Disraeli, equally elegant in red. Louis Philippe came up to them and enquired if there was any news. Disraeli replied that Baron Rothschild had received an express stating that William Gladstone would take the Colonial Office. "Then Sir Robert Peel is going to be stronger than he ever was," said the king. Disraeli prophesied a long period of instability, during which there would be a rapid turnover of ministries, and that Richard Cobden would sweep everything before him. The king looked to Featherston for confirmation, but he said, "What Mr. d'Israeli states to your Majesty would make a very amusing dream, but does not appear to me to have the semblance of reality in it." The king laughed and remarked, "Gentlemen your opinions appear to differ as much as the Colour of your Coats." Later, he told Featherston that he did not agree with Disraeli.[20]

Soon after, Featherston received a request for assistance from Murchison in a matter about which he had long been concerned. Two years previously, Sir Robert Peel had declined to recommend to the queen that Murchison be permitted to wear decorations received from foreign governments. The czar had just presented

Murchison with the Great Cross of St. Stanislaus and had appointed him to the Imperial Academy of Sciences, which carried a rank between colonel and general. Now Murchison decided to appeal to the queen for permission but would not do so directly. He asked Featherston to write one of his "best & most judicious letters" to Addington, emphasizing Murchison's hard work investigating western Russia, which was more than half of Europe. Not long after Peel's government resigned, Murchison received the queen's permission to wear his decorations.[21]

The next two years were largely routine insofar as Featherston's consular duties were concerned. There were a number of events in his personal affairs which were less so. In early 1846 he was preparing a manuscript describing his last two expeditions as United States geologist. He again approached John Murray in February and was gratified to have him reply that he was very eager to publish the new work. Murray suggested that Featherston might adopt the style of another writer then popular, to which he replied, "If I were condemned to write 'A *Continuation* of Mr. Simpkins' Travels in the Low Countries,' then indeed the idea of hanging myself would occur as something exceedingly refreshing, but as I feel remarkably Anti-suicide just at present, I propose not to appear as a Continuator of any thing, but to describe after my own way Countries and folksesses not yet described, and to narrate stories not yet narrated." He was much more concerned about a title, "for if the author cannot easily suit himself how may he be expected to suit his Publisher 'Who fain would fish with such a bait / As Codfish like as well as Skate.'"[22]

Featherston had been told that if he included in his book what he knew of the lead mines in the western United States, it would sell well to British mining people, but mention of the mines must be included in the title. Featherston thought his tentative title—"A Canoe Voyage, To the North Western Sources of the Mississippi, with a Geological Account of the Wisconsin Lead Region, and Sketches of the Manners of Red and White Americans"—might satisfy the purpose. He promised Murray some new and interesting illustrations but thought they could use the map from *Excursion*. If Murray would send him two copies of this he would return one with the routes of his travels traced on it. He asked Murray to be sure to send the right maps as, when he had recently requested some for another purpose, they had sent him copies of the map used in Lyell's recent book, on which there were black patches showing the mineral deposits and an accompanying explanatory column. He had been able to use one of them, but they were not what he wanted. In spite of his instructions, he received more copies of the map amended by Lyell. Again, he asked for copies of the original map used in his own work. Evidently, they were no longer available, however, and he was reluctantly forced to use those that were sent. He did not consider it "a very pretty thing to father another's labours," but after all, it was Lyell who had "laid his Egg in my nest." Thus, Featherston felt no compunction in appropriating the map originally his.[23]

The completed manuscript and several drawings were forwarded to London on 22 April. To Featherston's amazement, Murray was not happy with the drawings, particularly the one of Pilot Knob and that of the Falls of the White Water, both illustrating interesting geological formations. The latter, on a large scale, had been exhibited at the British Association for the Advancement of Science, where it had aroused much favourable comment. Moreover, Murray felt that little in the manuscript appeared "novel and striking," and apparently he was far from enthusiastic. Featherston reminded him that he had felt the same way about *Excursion,* in which opinion Featherston had joined him, but that had been a success. He felt that there was "nothing pedantic or Conventional" in his writing. He wrote with a natural "effusion of heart and mind," which had been the reason for the "high Commendations which the *Spectator* and other periodicals gave to the 'Excursion,'" and which was "by no means wanting in the 'Canoe Voyage.'"[24]

He was in bed with a nasty sore throat when he received Murray's letter of 14 May. It did nothing to lower his temperature, and he did not reply until he had recovered ten days later. Murray had intimated that he would lose money on the book, but he refused to frankly state that he had changed his mind about publishing. Instead, he suggested that "Considerable Omissions and Curtailments" would be necessary, giving no specific examples. Feather-

Featherstonhaugh's sketch of "Whitewater Falls," from his *A Canoe Voyage up the Minnay Sotor* [Courtesy of the Alderman Library, University of Virginia]

ston was perfectly willing to cut, for he thought there was more material than needed for two volumes, but Murray would have to give him specific ideas. The publisher had also insinuated that Lyell's *Travels in North America* had made another such book less desirable. Featherston objected to any comparison, noting that Lyell's work would have little appeal to the general public. In fact, Featherston and a number of his friends were agreed that, although Lyell's book contained valuable geological information, "it was a dull book not to be read with pleasure." The part of Featherston's manuscript that dealt with railway communication between the Atlantic ports of Canada and Lake Erie had aroused the interest of a number of people in government, including Sir Robert Peel, Lord Stanley, and others. If the book was published, Featherston had friends who would call the attention of the public to these ideas of national importance. He would be truly sorry if it became necessary for him to seek another publisher. To his disappointment, he was forced to do just that.[25]

There was another disappointment that spring when Edward de Verneuil was unable to visit Featherston. He had invited the French geologist to come 29 April on his way to Liverpool, whence he would sail to North America. Verneuil had accompanied Murchison on two of his Russian expeditions. He was now going to study American rock formations to determine if there were any similarities in stratification to those in Europe. He particularly wanted to see the map Featherston had prepared for "A Canoe Voyage," but there was not time. Featherston did send him letters of introduction to his sister-in-law Mrs. Willing, the paleontologist Timothy Abbott Conrad, and others.[26]

In early July, Aberdeen resigned, and Palmerston returned to the Foreign Office. Featherston used the occasion to write the latter a long letter, sending him a "memoir" on the subject of the British Empire in North America and the desirability of internal improvements there. His travels in the American Middle West had impressed him with the tremendous potential for highly successful agricultural and mineralogical development in that region. His knowledge of railroads and his familiarity with eastern Canada had convinced him that rail and water transportation must be developed in Canada to compete with the United States for the vast amount of shipping that must soon arise between the American grain-raising central and middle western states and the East Coast. There would be a great demand for the manufactured goods of Europe in exchange for grain, meat, and minerals. During the previous summer, he had corresponded with W. Bridges, who had sought his advice concerning a proposed railroad between Halifax and Quebec. Earlier he had corresponded with Peel about the colonies, and Lord Cowley had requested that he send a copy of the correspondence to the duke of Wellington. When preparing the manuscript for the account of his canoe voyage, he had included a chapter entitled "Reflections on the Policy to Be Observed for the Development of British North American Commerce, and for the Protection of Our Colonies." The memoir that he was sending Palmerston was a copy of this chapter of his book, which he still intended to have published.[27]

In the memoir he expressed concern about the importance of securing an amicable relationship and lasting peace between England, the United States, and Canada. In his accompanying letter to Palmerston he urged that a railroad, under British government control, should be constructed following the most direct route from one of the Atlantic ports of Nova Scotia or New Brunswick, through Canada to a point adjacent to the great grain-producing region of the United States. He had discussed this at length with Lord Durham in 1838, but at that time railroads were less fully accepted. He enclosed a map for Palmerston, on which he had marked a possible route for a railroad from St. John to the St. Lawrence River and thence to Lake Erie. The lake and various canals provided connection to shipping ports for the export of the grain and other products and for the reception of imports of European manufactured goods. He predicted a population expansion in the region to twenty million people by 1896. Such a number would cause Britain much concern if the two countries were not on a friendly footing. He called Palmerston's attention to official reports to the United States Congress for 1844, which estimated the commerce of the Great Lakes for that year as amounting to a hundred million dollars. He also noted the extensive construction of canals and railroads in the United States to provide for the shipment of goods to and from the central region and the importance of providing a Canadian alternative. Not only would such a rail and water transportation system as he proposed promote Canadian and English commercial prosperity, but it would also contribute to the security of the Canadian colonies by providing rapid movement of troops and military equipment should they be needed. Featherston quoted a recent American newspaper article that claimed the vast majority of Canadian citizens favored annexation by the United States.

During the summer of 1846, Featherston was again worried about a weakness in the muscles of his legs. The Murchisons urged him to try the waters at Buxton in Derbyshire, which they were enjoying in late July. Their enthusiasm persuaded him to ask Palmerston for a month's leave starting in August, which would allow him to attend the British Association meeting at Southhampton. Although the Murchisons were no longer at Buxton, Lady Murchison (whose husband had recently been knighted) had sent Featherston detailed instructions. She had even drawn a sketch of the buildings comprised in the Crescent. They had been designed by the architect, John Carr, for the fifth duke of Devonshire around 1784. Both Murchisons thought the presence of iodine in the waters more beneficial than the traces of nitrogen, soda, and salts and the merely tepid temperature. Whatever the mysterious ingredient was, Lady Murchison found it "caused a quicker circulation, a glow of excitement most delicious to the feelings." The waters did seem to help Featherston. He spent a few days with his mother at Scarborough before joining the Murchisons at Southhampton for the meetings. Murchison, the current president, had succeeded in obtaining the names of Lord Palmerston and the duke of Wellington as vice-presidents of the association, and even Prince Albert attended.[28]

When Featherston went to England for his holiday, he brought along his manuscript of "A Canoe Voyage" and the drawings for it. These he submitted to the publisher Richard Bentley. He had been back home only ten days when he received Bentley's agreement to publish. After all costs had been paid, he and Featherston would divide the profits equally. *A Canoe Voyage up the Minnay Sotor* came out in two handsome clothbound volumes, containing two folding maps and a dozen woodcuts and lithographs based on

Featherston's sketches, engraved by the well-known firm of Hulmandel and Walton. The first printing of four hundred copies came out on 26 December 1846 (although the publication date appeared as 1847). It sold for twenty-eight shillings. Bentley's report of orders from booksellers as of 23 December 1846 showed 211 books, far more than most of the books on Bentley's list.[29]

The *Spectator* reviewed the book most favorably on 6 January 1847:

> This character of the interest and largeness of geology for the traveller is better impressed by Mr. Featherstonhaugh than by any other writer we

Featherstonhaugh's Map of the United States, from his *A Canoe Voyage up the Minnay Sotor* [Courtesy of the Alderman Library, University of Virginia]

have met with. Like the *Excursion Through the Slave States,* strip the book of its scientific particulars, and speculations, and we have a *story* rather than a narrative of travels. The cares and bustle of preparation for a canoe voyage, the characters of the Voyageurs, the freshness of life of the daily incidents, whether enjoyment, privation, hope or depression are given with as much effect as in Washington Irving's description of prairie adventure but with more force from their greater closeness, and perhaps with more reality from the apparent absence of art—though now and then some touches of coarseness might have been spared.[30]

There were other complimentary reviews. The *Westminster Review* was impressed by the author's remarks on the probable effect of universal suffrage in the United States, especially the possibility of an eventual attempt to incorporate Canada into the Republic: "Recent events have, indeed in some measure, justified the author's anticipations of the inevitable tendencies of 'universal suffrage, and the government of an uncontrolled democracy.'" The reviewer was pleased that, "instead of being a mere dry detail of mining operations and geological deposits, interesting and valuable to the geologist and the mineralogist, but to them only, Mr. Featherstonhaugh has produced a book which cannot fail to be acceptable to every reader." The popularity of *A Canoe Voyage* was sufficient to justify a second printing of 260 copies in 1849. It was not published in the United States, since its reception was predictable. Featherston expected no fortune from his book, but it produced a welcome dividend from time to time. Even as late as the two-year period 1854–1856, he received his half of the profits, which amounted to £10.9.6.[31]

Word came from England in late October 1846 that Sir Harry had died on 24 October at the age of ninety-two. He had been in declining health for some time. The Murchisons, who saw him frequently, had kept Featherston informed. Sir Harry had left Uppark and all his property to his wife, Mary Ann. This bequest came as a great surprise to Colonel Mudge, who wrote to Featherston soon afterward: "If I mistake not you were his natural heir, and if as I have heard he has left the whole of his prospect to Lady F it is in every way a most unjust and cruel dispersal." Featherston would certainly have been delighted to inherit Uppark, but it is most unlikely that he had expected to do so.[32] The death of his friend Fox in Washington at the age of fifty-five about the same time probably came as a greater shock.

Verneuil returned from his summer's work in the United States and, in late November 1846, reported his experiences to Featherston. He was extremely appreciative of all that Featherston had done. Mrs. Willing had entertained him at Philadelphia, and he had been elected a member of the Academy of Natural Sciences. Troost had welcomed him in Tennessee. From Nashville he had gone to St. Louis, Dubuque, Chicago, Mackinac, Lake Superior, Sault Ste. Marie, and parts of Canada. He promised to see Featherston soon at Havre to study his American fossil collection and would then explain his "ideas on the correspondence of the formations between America and Europe." He had not seen anything that did not confirm Featherston's ideas and European classifications. This news was gratifying to Featherston, who had long contended that the geological formations of the United States conformed to those of Europe and had been criticized in the United States for saying so, even though, as Leonard Wilson has pointed out, Maclure as early as 1809 "had attempted to classify the strata of North America in terms of Werner's four groups of primitive rocks."[33]

Few of the old geological crowd came to the Continent in 1847, but Featherston managed to keep abreast of news through his friends' letters. He was shocked to learn of the rift that had developed between Sedgwick and Murchison and ended their long association. When the latter had written in January, he had described at some length his clash with Sedgwick at a recent meeting of the Geological Society. For Featherston and many others who considered both men good friends, this rupture was distressing. Both had served as presidents of the society and had made major geological contributions. They had done fieldwork together before each had specialized in the study of a particular geological system. Sedgwick had become the leading authority on what he had named the Cambrian System, from the Latin name for Wales, where much of his work had been done. This series of rocks contained early fossil forms, and Sedgwick thought it might contain evidence of the beginning of life on earth. Murchison had concentrated on a younger series of rocks, lying above Sedgwick's

Cambrian, which he had named Silurian, after the Silure, a "Romano-British" tribe that had lived in the Welsh border area. Both men were concerned with the fossil fauna of the respective systems. Sedgwick now gave a paper in which he claimed certain lower levels of Murchison's Silurian system as more properly belonging to his upper Cambrian. Murchison was outraged and said so to Featherston at great length: "It was nothing more or less than a proposition to smash my Lower Silurian & to baptize it Cambrian!!!" He did not mention his own attempts to annex some of Sedgwick's upper Cambrian. Many other geologists at the meeting had been, he said, astonished by Sedgwick, particularly Buckland, Greenough, de la Beche, Fritton, Warburton, Owen, and Darwin.[34] Murchison was always eager for recognition for his accomplishments; apparently the honors he had recently received were making him increasingly intolerant of the geological views of others.

Early in the summer of 1847 Charlotte and Georgiana traveled to the United States for an extended visit with her family. Throughout much of this year, Featherston had anticipated a hurried communication from Scarborough. His mother, then in her ninety-sixth year, had failed noticeably. He had obtained permission to leave on short notice, doing so on 24 September. He arrived in time to be with her several days before she died. Dorothy Featherstonhaugh was buried on 4 October in the same grave with her parents at the old church of St. Mary the Virgin, where she had attended services for the greater part of a century. Featherston ordered a finely polished stone and sought Buckland's assistance in preparing the Latin inscription. Her will had been drawn up in 1842, leaving five hundred pounds to each of her five surviving grandchildren. Her two Cliff Houses and the remainder of her estate were left to her son.[35]

The bequests were very welcome not only to Featherston but also to his adult children. The younger ones would have to wait until they came of age, but income from their invested inheritance could be used for their support and education. Featherston was able to seek a tutor for them and asked Buckland's help in finding one. James had been highly praised by Colonel Estcourt for his work on the Boundary Commission and had hope of obtaining employment in the construction of the proposed Canadian railroad but was still unemployed. In the meantime, he, Emily, and their children had been living with Featherston and Charlotte.[36]

Revolution and Its Aftermath 14

The year 1848 began with a request from the Foreign Office that Featherston enquire about the attempts of the French navy to distill sea water and, if possible, that he acquire one of the so-called ship kitchens for the Admiralty. He duly forwarded the desired information, including a list of the French ships employing the process and a price list for the mechanism. Similar business posing no great necessity for his decisions or presence, he felt that he could safely leave the office in the hands of William Jones for two weeks while he returned to Scarborough to settle his mother's estate. Jones, his confidential clerk, had recently been made vice-consul. Featherston had found it necessary the previous year to request that the former vice-consul, George Hutton, be replaced for he brought too many people into the consulate who had no right to be there, endangering the confidentiality of the consular records. Hutton had understandably protested that it was unreasonable to expect a married man to work seven hours a day for five pounds a month, but he was reluctant to give up the title. Jones was appointed with no salary whatever. In February, Featherston requested and received permission to leave Jones in charge temporarily. Before he could pack for the trip, however, alarming news began to filter through from Paris. The revolution that had been threatening for several years was finally under way.[1]

Beginning 25 February, Featherston for some time lived a life of perpetual exhaustion. Early on that morning, hundreds of English refugees from Paris poured into Havre. They had fled on the last train out of the capital before the bridges were burned. Most of them came penniless and without baggage. There were French refugees also, including many attached to the court. Four thousand English and Irish workers at Rouen alone needed to be repatriated. Housing for those awaiting transportation to England was severely taxed. Rich and poor alike sought the consul's assistance, and all expected him to perform miracles. He was in frequent communication with the Foreign Office about ships for refugees and other problems. Fortunately, Palmerston was extremely understanding and helpful. He gave permission for the issuance of passports to any in danger, authorizing Featherston to draw money on the treasury to assist the destitute.[2]

Dire accounts of conditions in Paris were reported. Military posts had been burned, and everywhere there were drunken mobs. Even "the trees on the Boulevard" had been cut down. All post offices and banks were closed, and for a few days, there was no discernible government. Featherston reported to the Foreign Office that there was complete anarchy. He suggested that steamers be sent daily to evacuate the refugees, for Havre was a madhouse of homeless people. The queen's messenger brought word from Paris that the rails of the Paris station had been torn up to keep the army out. The next day, the provisional government in Paris proclaimed a republic, and Havre and other cities followed suit on the following day.[3]

Featherston was soon exhausted, not just from the incredible labors of his office. At night his sleep was interrupted by the bell ringing at the gate of his home when messengers arrived with government dispatches. He confessed to the Foreign Office that he was worn out from talking, running around, and writing. To his relief, two steamers arrived for the refugees, but then the French refused permission for the vessels to leave. It was only through his cordial relations with the mayor that the ships were finally allowed to sail. He asked the Foreign Office to have the Admirality send a man-of-war to prevent another such incident. Instead, the Admi-

ralty sent an old steamer, the *Monarch,* the slowest of the Southampton line.[4]

During all the early confusion Featherston was extremely worried about the fate of the royal family and their relatives but could
learn little or nothing about their supposed whereabouts. He
hoped to be able to help them escape to England if he could get in
touch before they were arrested. The king had abdicated in favor
of his grandson, the comte de Paris. The royal family had no
sooner left the Tuileries than the mob burst in and sacked it.
Having heard a rumor of the hiding place of the duchess of Orleans and her two sons, the comte de Paris and his brother, Featherston sent James to Paris to bring them to Havre. James took with
him a dress belonging to the Featherstonhaughs' governess and
clothes of their two small sons, who were the same age as the royal
children, to be used as a disguise. Beds had been prepared for them
at the consul's home, but James was unable to locate them. In the
meantime, Featherston asked Captain Paul, master of the *Express,*
to call on him. Paul was also a commander in the Royal Navy and
Featherston had more confidence in navy men than in mercantile
captains. Moreover, Paul's ship was the fastest of the line to which
the *Monarch* belonged. Favorably impressed by the young man and
certain that he could be trusted, Featherston confided that he
wished to save the royal family. He urged Paul to return as quickly
as possible after delivering the refugees now on the *Express.* While
he was gone, Featherston arranged that the shipping line exchange
the *Monarch* for the *Express* as the ship under his command. He
gave the agent his personal guarantee that he would not be held
responsible by the company.[5]

Again the night bell rang, at two o'clock in the morning on 29
February. This time the messenger brought a confidential dispatch
from Palmerston. He had heard that the French king and queen
would be near Havre, and he had asked the Admiralty to send the
Monarch in case they needed to escape. The commander, although
ostensibly there to rescue English families, would be subject to
Featherston's orders. If he heard that the royal family was nearby,
he should arrange their escape. If this was impossible, refugees
could return on the packet, but it could be delayed for several days.

Cherbourg was also informed. Featherston immediately interviewed some ladies of the court, but no one knew where the royal family might be. He had already written to the marquis of Normanby, hoping that he might be able to get in touch with the king. He even sent a steamer to Dieppe and Treport, whose mayor was the king's favorite, to pursue inquiries but with no success.[6]

At last Featherston learned that the king was hiding at Trouville and the queen at Honfleur. He first planned to have the king board a fishing boat that would meet the *Express* at sea after dark on 1 March. A severe storm with very rough seas made this plan too dangerous, however. The situation was rapidly becoming critical, since it had become known locally that someone was hiding at Trouville. A party would soon be sent to discover if it was the king and to arrest him. The former mayor of Trouville took Louis Philippe through secret courtyards and back alleys to his own home just as the house in which the royal party had been staying was about to be invaded by the authorities. There they waited until the lateness of the hour emptied the streets and walked six miles before the carriages caught up. It was just as well they were walking, for three guardhouses had to be avoided. It was half past six on the morning of 2 March when the king and his party reached the cottage at Honfleur where they had left the queen. The usual occupant of the isolated cottage, the gardener Racine, had been told that the royal couple were the Lebruns, uncle and aunt of his master, M. Perthius. The cottage consisted of four small apartments, only one of which had a fireplace, and was furnished with rickety chairs and tables.[7]

Featherston did not know all this, but he was becoming extremely apprehensive. Whatever he could do to rescue the king and queen must be done very soon. He decided on a hazardous move, hoping that its very boldness might avoid suspicion. He would try to bring the royal couple to Havre on the regular 7:30 P.M. ferry run from Honfleur and have the *Express,* which had returned 1 March, ready to sail immediately after they went on board. Success would require very careful planning and a great deal of good luck. He did not like the element of risk but could think of nothing safer. He took Vice-Consul Jones into his confidence and asked if he was willing to undertake the dangerous mission of delivering a letter to the queen at daybreak on 2 March, not then knowing exactly where the king was. Jones readily agreed to take the 4:45 A.M. ferry to Honfleur, deliver the letter to the queen at the cottage belonging to Perthius, whom Featherston knew, and bring back a message. Featherston provided him with a diagram of the roads to take and a sketch of the house, which was three-quarters of a mile from the ferry, so he need not attract attention by asking directions. In his letter to the queen, Featherston outlined his plan. The royal couple, provided with English passports in the names of Mr. and Mrs. William Smith, made out by Featherston, would come by public ferry to Havre where they would immediately embark on the *Express*. He asked the queen if she could get word to her husband, for Featherston would need to know whether they thought they could follow his idea exactly.[8]

Jones crossed over to Honfleur early the next morning and found not a soul stirring in the town. The gardener's cottage appeared equally deserted, with shades drawn and not a wisp of smoke. The king opened the door, saying that he had only arrived two hours earlier and without any baggage. Though weary, he was surprisingly cheerful. The king and queen, after some discussion, told Jones to inform the consul that "they would wait where they were until they again heard" from him and would then do whatever he advised.[9]

Knowing full well how easily something unexpected could disrupt any plan, Featherston was doing everything he could think of to provide for the unforeseen. By half past seven that evening, Captain Paul was to have the water hot in the boilers but not actually producing steam, which might attract a crowd to the ship. He would have his vessel secured to the quay only by a light rope that could be cut quickly if need be. Featherston informed several of the town's known gossips that he had learned of the king's safe arrival in England and gave out some excuse why the *Express* was delayed in sailing. He engaged some young men he knew well, members of the National Guard who had no liking for gendarmes, to assist him with the crowd while he was embarking some friends for England. Should there be an unusual number of gendarmes present or if they gave him any difficulty about embarking his friends, he arranged for two of the young men to simulate a fight a little distance away to draw both the crowd and the gendarmes away from the ship. If those on the ferry should question the king's passport, Jones was to tell them that Mr. Smith was the consul's uncle, whom he had been told to conduct to Havre. Featherston could think of nothing else to do as he nervously awaited the arrival of the ferry. His greatest fear was that he was being watched and might draw the entire royal family into a trap.[10]

The first of the unanticipated problems to arise could have wrecked the whole plan. The master of the Honfleur ferry, the *Courier,* told M. Bresson, a loyal French naval officer who knew Featherston's plans, that he doubted that he would make the evening run to Honfleur and return, for he did not expect enough passengers to justify the trip. Featherston asked Bresson to promise the captain that he would make up any loss of funds on the trip on the grounds that it was important for him to get to Honfleur to prevent the protest of some bills of exchange. The master was persuaded to go, and Bresson and Jones went with him.[11]

At Honfleur, Bresson walked from the landing slip to the gardener's cottage, leaving Jones where the ferry docked. Jones was horrified when two gendarmes appeared and asked to see the passports of some of the passengers already on the ferry. He was even more disturbed when seven o'clock came and no king had arrived, although the queen was already on board. She had come with Bresson, and her husband was to follow with General Dumas. The remainder of the royal party came on board, one by one. Just as the ferry was about to leave, the king appeared, muffled in a heavy brown coat, a Norman peasant's cap, large green spectacles, and a scarf that concealed half of his face; he hardly resembled a monarch.[12]

Jones asked him if he was Mr. Smith, and Louis Philippe replied, "Ah, how do you do, how is my good friend, the Consul?" He continued to play the part of a typical Englishman with no knowledge of French. When the steward collected fares and a gratuity for the band, the king shook his head as if he did not understand, and Jones paid for them both. It was almost dark when the ferry arrived at Havre, but Featherston could just make out the white pocket handkerchief Jones was waving to signal that all was well. When half the passengers had debarked, the queen came down the ladder. Featherston shook her hand as she moved off with Bresson. Finally the king appeared, stumbling, for he was half blinded by the goggles. "Oh, my dear Uncle, I am delighted to see you," Featherston greeted him. "My dear George, I am glad you are here," the king replied, continuing to talk so loudly that the consul tried to quiet him as he led his "uncle" through the crowd toward the steamer.[13]

Just as they started up the *Express* gangway, an army officer approached. The half-blind king, being unable to see that the gangway was a little high, Featherston had to lift his right leg to help him, whispering to him to move on. The officer enquired who the old gentleman was. Featherston half opened his coat to display his half-dress uniform and, looking his inquisitor in the eye, replied, "Ce monsieur est mon oncle et je suis le Consul D'Angleterre." Obviously skeptical, the officer declared incredulously, "Est-ce que M. le Consul, dit que ce Monsieur est son oncle?" Fearing that the man had recognized his sovereign, Featherston was relieved to see those whom he had engaged for just such an emergency move in between them so that he was free to hurry the king on, knowing that the young men would corroborate his relationship to the elderly gentleman. He put his hands on Louis Philippe's shoulder to steady him as they walked down the gangplank. At the foot they were met by Captain Paul, who reported, "All's right." He led them to a small stateroom, and Featherston locked them in. There he exclaimed, "Thank God, Sir, you are safe." He informed the royal couple that the duchess of Montpensier and her husband were in London and the duchess of Nemours and her two sons were in Jersey. There was no word from the duchess of Orleans and her two children.[14]

The suspicious officer finally got on board. He questioned Captain Paul closely as to his apparent readiness to sail. Paul told him he was hurrying home with dispatches. The officer asked to see the cabins but was told that it would have to be next time. As the ship began to move, the officer had to scramble to get ashore. Paul hurried to the king's cabin and told the consul, "All's ready, Sir." Featherston gave the king the key, rushed to the gangway, telling everyone if they did not go ashore immediately they would be carried to England. At the foot of the gangway, the officer came up to him, saying, "Pray who was that whom you put aboard the *Express*?" Again, Featherston answered, "My uncle." "Your uncle," said the officer incredulously, shaking his head sadly, "Ah! Monsieur le consul." Featherston joined Jones in the carriage waiting for them and drove to the outer jetty, where they watched the *Express* steaming safely away. Speculation about the hurried departure of the steamer was so widespread that Featherston finally had to confess that his uncle was actually one of the brothers of the king of Naples. He had been so badly frightened, needlessly, that he had engaged the *Express* for himself and his family. [15]

On the following day, Featherston dined with Bresson and Perthius, who told him that only an hour after the king and queen left the Honfleur cottage for the ferry the republican *procureur* had arrived with three gendarmes to arrest the king. Louis Philippe would have been murdered if they had seized him. In fact, the king had told him as much. Featherston reflected on how lucky they had all been but realized that his careful planning deserved a lot of credit also. Bresson brought a friend, Adolphe d'Houdetot, to meet Featherston. He had been a receiver of taxes for the district under the old regime and had a brother who was an aide to the king. Featherston had told no one of what they had done, but evidently Bresson had, for d'Houdetot complimented him lavishly. The *Journal de Havre* for 5 March announced the royal party's safe arrival in England two days previously. They reached London on 6 March and Louis Philippe and his wife eventually settled in a villa in Surrey. [16]

Featherston wrote a detailed report of the king's escape to Palmerston. He highly commended both Jones and Captain Paul (and the latter in a letter to the Admiralty as well) for their conduct throughout the affair. In referring to the fidelity and intelligence exhibited by Jones, he pointed out that, as vice-consul, Jones had no salary, yet had run great risks. He hoped that the young man would have a suitable reward. On the day Palmerston received his report, he sent it to Queen Victoria, noting:

Viscount Palmerston was sure that your Majesty would read with interest Mr. Featherstonhaugh's account of the manner in which he managed the escape of the King and Queen of the French. It is like one of Walter Scott's best tales, and the arrangements and the execution of them do great credit to Mr. Featherstonhaugh, who will be highly gratified to learn, as Viscount Palmerston proposes to inform him, that your Majesty has approved his conduct. Mr. Featherstonhaugh has also probably rendered a good service to the Provisional Government who would have been much embarrassed if their Commissioner had arrested the King and Queen.[17]

It was customary to reward British subjects for services rendered to foreigners, but Featherston received only a letter from the Foreign Office approving his conduct in the affair. Palmerston's recommendation to Lord John Russell that Featherston should be commended "in handsome Terms" was not acted upon. King Louis Philippe presented Featherston with a gold snuff box, encrusted with diamonds, accompanied by a card inscribed: "A M. G. Featherstonhaugh, Souvenir de Havre, Le deux Mars 1848. Louis Philippe."[18]

Although Featherston was intensely relieved to see the royal family safely away, his problems were far from over. On 3 March he went to Rouen to see three hundred British flax workers, who were reported to be in "desolate condition." They had been driven aboard an English ship by indignant French workers who had not allowed them to take any luggage or to be paid their due wages. Featherston sent a strong remonstrance to M. Deuxchamps who was in charge of keeping the peace in the department of Seine Inférieure. By 10 March calm had apparently returned in Havre, although commerce was at a standstill. One bank might have to close its doors, and vessels with American cotton were being diverted to Liverpool. English refugees were no longer trying to leave now that there were plenty of available berths. Unfortunately, this peaceful interval was all too temporary. By 20

March, Havre was again crowded with British workers coming from all over France. Although many complained, Featherston found that the majority had received their wages and bank depos-

Gold snuff box presented to Featherstonhaugh by King Louis Philippe, belonging to James D. Featherstonhaugh. Duanesburg, New York. [Print courtesy of the McKinney Library, Albany Institute of History & Art]

its. There had been hardships, but there were no more than one would expect in a revolution. Physical violence from the French workers was the main threat. English mill owners were leaving too, and the French government had issued no orders for payment of deposits in the Caisse des Epargnes to British subjects in spite of Lord Normanby's appeal. The Foreign Office complied with many of Featherston's suggestions, sending the *Pasha* to Havre to bring workers home. The Foreign Office also made available funds supervised by the social reformer Lord Ashley. Some of this money Featherston used to pay the eighteen pence charged for the passage of workers on colliers, and some for the relief of various penniless refugees.[19]

Eventually, it began to look as if quiet would last at least until the election on 20 April. In spite of all the alarms, anxiety, and late nights, the Featherstonhaughs were all well. At last Featherston was able to take the two weeks' leave that he had requested in January, and he traveled to Scarborough, returning 10 April. He found Havre still peaceful, though business was inactive. The main difficulty was the great number of unemployed. Within two days he dispatched 150 workers back to England. Money was becoming scarce even though he had accomplished miracles with what he had been given. He had relieved two thousand people with Ashley's two hundred pounds.[20]

By August, the consulate was back to normal. On the whole it was a reasonably peaceful summer, but in September, Featherston again found himself involved in a problem with international implications. The Havre police arrested one John Cavanaugh, who had arrived by ship from England without a passport. His violent behavior was such that he was placed in jail overnight. Next morning he was brought to the consulate. The police agreed to permit him to go to a hotel while Featherston investigated his story and background. His inquiry to the Home Office produced a reply to the effect that Cavanaugh was an Irish citizen accused of treason and wanted by the Dublin police. Featherston was asked to try to have him returned to England. He attempted to arrange for the police to place Cavanaugh on an English vessel so he could be arrested on his arrival at Southampton. Unfortunately, they had not kept him under observation. When they went to the hotel to pick him up, they found that he had never slept there and was missing. Next morning an Irishman named Miles Byrne appeared at the consulate and threatened to "blow any man's brains out who would arrest Cavanaugh." Byrne had long been attempting to persuade the French to aid the Irish against England. Featherston asked the Havre police to arrest both him and Cavanaugh, but they declined to do so unless authorized by the government in Paris.[21]

In the meanwhile, a third Irishman called on Featherston. John O'Connell, member of Parliament for Youghal, was opposed to the violence of the Young Ireland party, which Byrne and Cavanaugh supported. He came to warn the consul that the many young Irishmen at Havre were threatening to attack both him and Captain Paul. The following day the Irish editor of the *Journal de Havre* attacked Featherston in his editorial, accusing him of having bribed the commissioner of police at Havre, a twenty-year veteran in that post. Fearing that the commissioner, whom he respected, might lose his job, Featherston decided to answer the accusation. He did so, and so convincingly that he turned public sentiment against the Irish. Meanwhile, Cavanaugh boarded a sailing vessel bound for New York. When Featherston reported all his experience with Cavanaugh to Lord Normanby, the latter was both outraged and embarrassed. Featherston's attempt to have Cavanaugh arrested violated the Convention of 1843, under which both France and England maintained the right to grant asylum to political refugees. Featherston could only express his regret and be thankful that the Irishman had evaded arrest.[22]

Another turbulent event, for which there was little precedent to guide him, involved him in October 1848. Two vessels bound for Portsmouth had been loaded with potatoes and were preparing to leave the quay when a hungry mob boarded them and prevented their departure. The cargo of one vessel had been unloaded on the pier. Featherston sought the aid of his friend the mayor. The latter quickly summoned police assistance, and he, Featherston, and a number of other armed men dispersed the mob and had the vessel reloaded. Featherston expressed his appreciation for both the attitude and the actions of the French authorities both to them and to

Lord Normanby, who this time approved Featherston's actions.[23]

Having missed a proper month's vacation in the summer of 1848, Featherston joined the Murchisons at Buxton in early July 1849. There he found the usual congenial and stimulating company. He was reluctant to leave them all in early August, but he had to spend a few days in London on business. While there, he wrote a short article about passports for the *Times*. He also met his old friend George Catlin. The artist had followed his suggestion and had been exhibiting his paintings of American Indians in Europe for the past several years with considerable success. He now sought advice in connection with a new and different undertaking. He was preparing to head an expedition to hunt for gold in the foothills of the Rocky Mountains. Sir William Stewart had reported seeing gold on both the northern fork of the Platte River and the Colorado River. The expedition also intended to start a new colony in Texas. A company had been formed to raise a hundred thousand pounds to support the venture and, among its patrons, was the earl of Derby. Featherston gave such information as he could and later corresponded with Catlin about the project.[24]

Featherston went to London again for a short time in late January and early February 1850. While there, he learned that Buckland had developed a mysterious ailment that had affected his brain; clearly his mind was failing. Thinking that Sedgwick might not have heard of this, Featherston wrote to him and found that he had not. He, too, was deeply shocked. Buckland had always seemed so robust and vigorous, and no member of the geological fraternity was more beloved by his fellows. When Sedgwick replied, he apologized for not having invited Featherston to visit him and see his museum. He, too, had been having problems. He had suffered a serious fall on Christmas Eve, breaking his right arm, crushing the right elbow, and dangerously bruising his entire right side. Now six weeks later he was slowly recovering but by no means back to normal.[25]

Since Featherston, in his position, was not free to write an account of the rescue of Louis Philippe for public consumption and since the British government would not want to do anything that might be embarrassing to the French, he assumed that he had heard the last of the affair. He was, therefore, surprised to read in the April 1850 issue of the *Revue Britannique* a translation of an article that had appeared in the London *Quarterly Review,* giving an account of the escape. On the several occasions that people had asked him about the rescue, he had always declined to discuss it. Fearing that he might be suspected of having provided information to the author of the article, he wrote to Palmerston to assure him that he had not done so. Palmerston asked Addington to write Featherston that it was believed that the information had been provided by Louis Philippe himself. Addington sent him copies of several papers dealing with the escape that had been privately printed for the Foreign Office for a very limited circulation. To Featherston's complete astonishment, one of them had been written by his vice-consul, William Jones. He recalled that Jones had spent a short time in London not long after the event and supposed Jones had left his account for Palmerston at that time. He was highly annoyed, not only that Jones should have done this without consulting him but that the account contained a great many misrepresentations. He had asked Jones to write a report of his part in the affair at the time, and the two accounts differed.[26]

The article in the *Quarterly Review* had been written by John Wilson Croker. It was a review of treatises about the escape, written by François Guizot, Alphonse M. L. de Lamartine, and Louis Blanc. Featherston received his own copy of the *Review,* and he and his family were gratified to read Croker's footnote identifyng him: "Mr. Featherstonhaugh—the representative (we are told) of the once powerful family of that name in the north of England (whose ancient castle was so skilfully repaired and embellished by the late Lord Wallace)—is well known as, we believe that we may say, the founder—certainly the first successful teacher and active promoter—of geology in the United States. His travels in that part of the world, still more extensive than those of his royal *uncle,* have been narrated in pages of singular liveliness."[27]

Soon after reading the review, Featherston exchanged several letters with Croker about it. He liked Croker's account but called his attention to a few errors he might wish to correct. Croker did so in June when he commented on a reply Lamartine had made to his review. Featherston also stressed to Croker how much Palmerston had done to support him during the crisis. Not only Jones but Paul and even d'Houdetot promulgated their own versions of the affair. It all got so badly out of hand that Featherston had little choice but to fire Jones, whose protests to Palmerston made an unpleasant ending to the entire incident.[28]

During the summer of 1850, George, Jr., visited his father and stepmother and met his half brothers and half sister for the first time. In August, Featherston went to England to return his sons Albany and Henry to their English schools. He intended to spend two weeks at Buxton catering to his arthritic knees and to pay a visit to Lady Fetherstonhaugh at Uppark. While he was still at Buxton, word came of the death of Louis Philippe, and Featherston accepted an invitation to attend his funeral. He was preparing to continue to Uppark when he learned that President Louis Napoleon would be visiting his consular district; he felt he should return to Havre.[29] France's Second Republic, founded when Louis Philippe abdicated, was now firmly established. Napoleon's nephew, now president, was becoming more autocratic and dictatorial. Two years later he would proclaim himself emperor of France.

The Late Years at Havre   15

All the repercussions arising from Featherston's rescue of Louis Philippe eventually subsided, and his life settled into a routine. From time to time some unusual development at Havre, London, Paris, or elsewhere created a diversion. Palmerston was replaced by the earl of Granville. The new foreign secretary was interested in French military preparedness and queried the British consuls about it. In replying, Featherston pointed out the difficulty of transmitting such information. He suggested a telegraph code to be used in sending intelligence in an emergency and recommended a fifty-pound fund that he might use in acquiring it. At the moment he could see no indication of either offensive or defensive military preparations in his district. He listed the French merchant ships and small craft that might be used in time of war, giving statistics concerning them. He added that only a small force would be needed to capture Havre.[1]

By far the most serious problem with which Featherston became involved during his remaining years as consul ended in strained relations with the Foreign Office. It began in a most unlikely and unexpected way over a seemingly trivial matter. He had befriended an Italian Swiss named Leopoldo Boffi, who was married to an Englishwoman and living in Havre. Boffi acted as a night watchman for ships in the port. Featherston felt sorry for the man, who had many children and very little money, and he gave him old clothing and any odd jobs he could. Featherston also managed to get him appointed sexton for the church and found him a nice black coat to wear on Sundays. Feeling that he had done enough for poor Boffi, for whom he had no actual responsibility, Featherston declined to make him a rather large loan that he had requested. Soon afterward he had occasion to send Boffi on an errand to obtain the address of an Englishman whose well-to-do brother had died at Havre. The address was obtained and Featherston wrote to the brother. When the latter replied, he enclosed a letter he had received from Boffi, saying that he would meet him when he arrived but not to let the consul know that he had written. Just what Boffi had in mind was not evident, but Featherston, who was completely astounded, was forced to stop employing him.[2]

Not very long after this incident, Featherston was again amazed when Addington wrote from the Foreign Office, asking for an explanation of charges brought against Featherston by Boffi. He had represented himself as an interpreter and messenger for the consulate, claiming that he was owed two pounds, which the consul refused to pay him. Addington considered the charges "unworthy of credit" but thought they should be explained. They could not be considered official, since they had not been submitted through the Swiss consul general. A check of consular records revealed that Boffi had made his original claim for some services in 1850, and the Foreign Office had rejected it. He later claimed to have made three trips to England to try to collect the two pounds.[3]

Now, years after the original claim, Boffi had decided to bring charges in the French courts against the consul. Both the French procurator general at Rouen and Featherston's lawyer advised him not to appear in court when the case was heard before a police tribunal on 25 February 1854, on the grounds that, as consul performing official duties, he should have some sort of immunity. The French *procureur impérial* agreed and addressed the tribunal, opposing such a trial. The tribunal disagreed and found in Boffi's favor. They were apparently swayed by the Swiss consul, Wanner, a violent socialist, who attended the trial and supported Boffi. It later appeared that Wanner had been encouraging and financing Boffi. Featherston recalled that Wanner had been infuriated by Louis Philippe's escape. On one occasion, when Wanner had publicly criticized the Havre police, Featherston had risen to their defense.[4]

Featherston discussed the case with the *garde des sceaux,* who assured him that it would be quashed on appeal. He soon learned, however, that there was no immunity for French consuls in England and hence none for British consuls in France. He could not only be fined but jailed, on the word of Boffi. There was an even more important ramification: if this case were not defeated, it could set a precedent that might result in British consuls being brought before petty tribunals on all manner of trumped-up charges. For this reason he felt confident that he would have the solid backing of the Foreign Office. He soon learned, notwithstanding, that Lord Clarendon seemed little concerned, considered Featherston too sensitive, and thought that he should have appeared in court. Featherston began to be seriously disturbed not only for himself but for his family. Charlotte had recently undergone two serious operations in Paris and was very much upset by the threat to him. He appealed the case in May but again the decision went against him. His next legal remedy was to take the case to the Court of Cassation at Paris in late December. He did so but again lost. The case would go to a jury trial in February 1855.[5]

Absurd though it might seem, the Boffi affair had ceased to be an irritation and had become a serious threat. Featherston had no illusions about French juries or French jails. Unless the Foreign Office exerted its influence, he might well spend a year in one of the latter because of a two-pound claim that the Foreign Office had disallowed. It occurred to him that if the Foreign Office could think of nothing else to do, they might ask Queen Victoria to confer some special mark of her favor on him that might help to protect him. He wrote at length to Clarendon, attempting to rouse him to some action on his behalf. Sixteen days passed without any reply. Featherston was now not only desperate; he was furious. He wrote again, making no attempt to hide his indignation. He intended to take any steps that he must to protect his good name, including, if necessary, laying his case before the queen and Parliament. Many members of Parliament knew him well and would have no hesitation in coming to his defense. If doing this cost him the loss of the consulate and consequent bankruptcy, so be it. His family fully supported him in this decision.[6]

When Clarendon's undersecretary, Thomas Staveley, passed this letter on, he noted that he had not yet sent the letter Clarendon had composed. In it, the secretary had regretted Featherston's "trouble and vexation." He did not question Featherston's conduct but did not feel justified in requesting some mark of the queen's favor. He had noted for Staveley's information that it was not possible to ask the queen to knight Featherston. Staveley drafted a new letter, saying that it was not possible to put his request before the queen but that Featherston was to rest assured that his reputation and honor had not suffered in the eyes of her majesty's government. This was small comfort to Featherston, who now did not really have time to place his case before either the queen or Parliament. He decided that he must take his chances in court. Fortunately, his attorney was able to prove that Featherston was in England on the day Boffi claimed he had been promised the two pounds. Featherston was acquitted, and Boffi was ordered to pay court costs. Whereupon Boffi promised Featherston to "pursue him to the death."[7]

One might suppose that this would have been the end of this ridiculously prolonged case, but it was not. Boffi was granted an appeal by a court at Rouen in March. The case was to be heard in May. His counsel was now a Monsieur Deschamps, who had been the head of Rouen's Republican party in the 1848 provisional government. It was evident that the case had now become thoroughly involved in French politics. Featherston felt really desperate. He wrote to Lord Cowley, asking him to apply for Boffi's expulsion from the country. Boffi's threats were making it difficult for him to perform his duties. Cowley proved more sympathetic than Clarendon. He could not request Boffi's expulsion, but he did persuade the French minister of foreign affairs to have Boffi placed under surveillance. Finally, Clarendon, possibly influenced by Cowley, began to take the matter seriously. He wrote to the Swiss government, protesting Wanner's actions. Cowley asked the French government to relieve Featherston of any further legal proceedings, but they declined. The prefect of the Lower Seine did agree to take steps for his protection. Finally, on 10 May 1855 the case was again heard in court. Boffi's lawyer described Featherston as "an unremitting persecutor" of his client, but the court confirmed the previous judgment against Boffi. The absurd affair had cost Featherston more than peace of mind. His attempts to defend himself had cost in excess of 3,000 francs, of which only 2,436 were reimbursed by the Foreign Office. For Featherston, now seventy-five, the entire affair had been an ordeal.[8]

He always found as much time as he could for his family, yet he was a bit startled the following year to realize that their daughter was now a handsome, talented young lady, whose popularity assured her of innumerable invitations. That September, she and a friend visited far north of Aberdeen before returning to Edinburgh. After visiting in London, she went on to Uppark, where a large house party, including Lady Murchison, had assembled for a week. Harry was now eighteen and had elected to pursue an army career, studying engineering at the Military College, Addiscombe. His father had worried about him, for Harry was often thoughtless and too often impatient with his professors, who penalized such behavior with extra drills. After graduation, his first military assignment was with the Madras Artillery. Albany was two years younger and, according to his father, "prudence and discretion itself." He was studying for the Indian Civil Service at Wimbledon but later went to the Royal Military Academy at Woolwich.[9]

James, having failed to establish himself at any permanent career in England, decided to return to the United States. He and Emily had moved from Havre to Ealing in 1852 and both of them had become very much involved in the current fad of mesmerism. James had published at least one paper on the subject, and Emily performed many experiments, claiming to be able to cure a variety of ailments. Featherston found many of their experiments difficult to explain. He was not quite prepared to debunk mesmerism, but he was quite sure that James's involvement in it would do nothing to help him find employment. At one time he conceived the idea that James might be appointed to succeed him as consul, but nothing came of this. In 1855 James inherited his Aunt Kitty's house, and he and his family returned to the United States where they made their home at Duanesburg. Two years later, his father gave him title to all his lands in New York state.[10]

Featherston continued his longtime interest in his family origins. He was pleased when he received a letter from a Joseph Fetherstonhaugh, who had been digging into old court records, intending to draw up a family genealogy. He told Featherston that the *a* had crept into their family line around 1800 but that this corruption had subsequently been dropped. Not knowing Featherston's age or background, he wrote that if it had been his father who had been involved in settling the land dispute in the United States, they were certainly related, for his mother had told him so. He and his brother lived at Hopton Court in the Malvern Hills. The family line he was tracing began with Albany, lord of Barhaugh, in 1638, who was a cousin of the last Albany of Fetherston Castle. Joseph and Featherston exchanged a number of letters on the subject, and Featherston and his daughter visited Joseph and his brother at Malvern.[11]

Buckland's continued illness and his death in 1856 were sad blows to Featherston. Like all who knew Buckland, he had valued the friendship of this brilliant and kindly man. Featherston continued to keep in touch with a number of other members of the scientific community. He saw as many of them as possible when his vacations and other affairs took him to England. The mutual devotion between himself and the Murchisons continued unabated throughout his life. They maintained a continuous correspondence. He visited them and vacationed with them at Buxton, Tunbridge Wells, and elsewhere almost every year. He kept in touch, to some degree, with Sedgwick also. Another scientific friend to whom he became increasingly close was Richard Owen, who had left the College of Surgeons to become superintendent of natural history at the British Museum. Owen often had specimens passing through Havre that Featherston was able to care for, and Owen visited him on occasion.[12]

In February 1857 Featherston welcomed a formal inquiry into

Richard Owen [Courtesy of the Palaeontology Library, British Museum (Natural History)]

the consulate system from the Foreign Office, having been reluctant to volunteer any complaints. He added a separate statement to his reply, emphasizing the huge increase in prices since his appointment. He was now forced to use most of his private income to maintain the efficiency of his office. With a big family this was not easy. He again pointed out that the Havre consulate was actually equivalent to a consulate general since it included the commercial operations of the ports of Lecamp, Dieppe, Rouen, and Caen, in addition to those of Havre. The only other consulate with similar responsibilities was that of the United States, yet Featherston received £620 in 1856, while the United States consul received £1,350. In spite of these protests, it was six years before Featherston's salary was raised to £700, with an allowance of £200 for office expenses.[13]

The Crimean War caused him some concern in his official capacity. He worried about the large amounts of saltpeter and other materials of potential military importance that passed through the port, fearing that much of it might be destined for Russia rather than France. No sooner had peace been established than the Sepoy Rebellion began, in February 1857, and almost all of northern India had fallen. In October, Featherston was approached by a number of French soldiers who had been recently discharged. They wished to join the British army to fight in India against the mutineers. Cawnpore and Delhi had just been retaken by the British, however, so the Foreign Office directed Featherston to thank the Frenchmen but inform them no foreigners were being employed at the moment. He started a subscription in Havre for the victims of the mutiny and recommended that his vice-consuls do the same. By November, he was able to send them £423.[14]

When civil war broke out in the United States, Murchison once more panicked about his American investments. After the battle of Bull Run he wrote to Featherston, seeking advice about whether to sell his Massachusetts state bonds and his Boston city bonds. Murchison found it impossible to predict the outcome of the war and was incensed by the undisguised bias of the London *Times* toward the Confederacy, which he believed might help to provoke a declaration of war against Great Britain by the United States government. He reported that many in England thought the United States might split into separate governments, united only if at war with a European power. During the long-drawn-out conflict in the United States, Featherston was concerned about the recruitment of British seamen by Confederate ships, but there was little he could do to prevent it. During the early part of the war there was increased activity at Havre, with 417 ships from North America in port in 1861, adding considerably to his work. Gradually, the reverse effect set in, until in 1864 only 29 American ships called there.[15]

Murchison finally sold all of his investments in the United States and found the nervousness from which he had been suffering greatly relieved. Featherston assured him that this peace of mind was worth any financial sacrifice he might have had to make. He had seen too many of his friends suffer in their old age from a variety of ailments brought on by shattered nerves. While on the subject of old age, Featherston commented that nothing gave him more satisfaction as he looked back over his eighty-one years than his association with the rise of geology as a science and his association on the fringes of this great movement with such principal performers as Buckland, Fitton, Greenough, Murchison, Sedgwick, Warburton, and others.[16]

As his work load lightened, Featherston felt more relaxed. Although he had some problems, he was reasonably healthy for a man in his eighties still holding a full-time consulship. Some time had passed since he had last done any serious writing, and he felt inclined to undertake a work that he had long thought of. In the past he had tried a variety of literary forms: poetry, a play, essays, reviews, translations, and lengthy travel accounts. Now he had in mind a novel. He had once casually mentioned to Murchison that he thought of writing one, but he discussed it seriously only with Owen when he saw him one day in London. Having heard nothing more about it for a long time, Owen enquired what had become of it when he wrote about another matter on 23 March 1865. The occasion of his writing was to request that Featherston inspect twelve boxes of fossils that had been shipped to Havre by the count de Montravel of Monte Video, who hoped to sell them to the British Museum. Owen doubted that he could buy them unless they were very rare. Space had become scarce at the museum. Featherston had been ill when he received Owen's request, but he managed to examine the fossils. His report did not justify Owen in requesting a special grant from the treasury to purchase them.[17]

Featherston still considered himself an invalid when he wrote a month later, glad that he could be of assistance to Owen. He asked a favor in return. He had indeed written a novel and had sent it to John Chapman, of the publishers Chapman and Hall. They had corresponded about it several times while it was being printed. He had corrected the proofs and had returned the last of them several months before but had heard nothing since. They had agreed that Chapman would manage the sales, charging 10 percent for this service. A French translation was planned. Although he thought he had no reason to be ashamed of it, Featherston had elected to publish it anonymously. He would appreciate Owen's asking Chapman about its status. Owen wrote a few days later that he had conferred with Chapman and was glad to be able to report that the book would appear during the following week. Featherston replied at once, expressing his thanks and confessing to some "solicitude as to the opinions that may be pronounced of this child of my old age." He hoped that the book would be "considered as a wholesome one, and that the writing of it at 84 years of age was not time entirely thrown away."[18]

In all this correspondence about the book neither Featherston nor Owen mentioned either its subject or title. It was a two-volume novel of 802 pages entitled *Langleyhaugh: A Tale of an Anglo-Saxon Family,* which sold for twenty-one shillings. Like many Victorian romances, good and evil were well defined. There were innumerable incidents involving deceit, cruelty, theft, pomposity, avarice, treasonable activity, and even bigamy. Inevitably, right triumphed in the end; seemingly unrelated plots and subplots were ultimately drawn together. The Langleyhaugh family background was exceedingly similar to that of the Featherstonhaughs, including a castle in approximately the same location, the beheading of an ancestor after the battle of Worcester, and the loss of family fortune from horse racing. The childhood and education of Cuthbert, the hero, closely paralleled Featherston's. He, too, had an elder sister to whom he was devoted. There were fine descriptions of Scarborough and of the schools of Featherston's youth. Cuthbert's European travels, too, bore a striking resemblance to Featherston's. The author, however, used this backdrop only as a setting for purely imaginary events. Curious cases that had come to his attention as consul were woven into his tale, as were a number of his personal prejudices.[19]

Although Featherston's health had improved somewhat in April, his illness had served as a warning to him that he should get his affairs in order. On 9 May he drew up or revised his holograph will in accordance with French laws. To Charlotte he left the silver, china, linen, furniture, and all the pictures except two, which he specified were to go to Georgiana. These were the two scenes embroidered by his sister Ann in 1795, one representing the death of General Wolfe on the Plains of Abraham and the other Daniel in the lion's den. To Albany and Georgiana jointly were left all his books, including rare editions of the Italian poets and other valuable volumes, and his papers, among which were many letters from famous people. Featherston directed that all family letters were to be destroyed. The gold snuff box given him by Louis Philippe also went to Albany. To Henry his father left his extensive collection of minerals and other geological specimens.[20]

Featherston attended to his consular duties throughout the following summer until September, when he became ill again. His illness develped into pleurisy, of which he died on 27 September 1866. In the absence of his sons, his funeral was arranged by his assistant, E. C. Parker-Rhodes. It was an impressive affair, attended by a number of Frenchmen prominent in public life. His six vice-consuls served as pallbearers, and his cortege included civic and military authorities, ship captains, merchants, and many of Havre's citizens. A French journal described the graveside eulogy as eloquent, "commemorating the eminent qualities and high character which had distinguished the honorable dead."[21]

Notices of his death appeared in a number of publications in Europe and America. The London *Times* wrote that Featherston was "distinguished by his acquirements in science and letters, as well as by the efficient performance of his public duties." They considered his North American exploration to have been a fine preparation for his services as boundary commissioner and described his writings on "statistical and political subjects" as "clear and vigorous." His "geological memoirs merited the warm approval of his attached friends Buckland and Murchison." This article was copied in its entirety by the *Gentleman's Magazine*. Murchison wrote a short piece for the *Times* concerning Featherston's publications, not all of which were known to him. Publications of the Royal Society and the American Philosophical Society took note of his passing. The *Geological Magazine* contained a short article by Warburton concerning Featherston's geological accomplishments and the *Journal of the Geological Society of London* carried a long article, in which the closest of his friends, Murchison, reviewed his entire life. Unfortunately, the article contained some errors concerning the part of it with which Murchison had been less familiar. Characteristically, he concluded, "Let me say that those who remember Mr. Featherstonhaugh will dwell upon those genial social qualities and telling anecdotes which rendered him so agreeable and instructive a companion."[22]

The various accomplishments of Featherston's life are not easy to evaluate. Perhaps his greatest contribution was as a catalyst to stimulate others by his example and by his persistent promotion of causes in which he believed. This gift was evident during the approximately twenty years he devoted to agriculture in his continuous attempt to improve not only his own farming practices but those of his region and the whole of New York state. During this period, he realized how important railroads could become to United States development, studied what was being done in England, convinced the New York legislature of the soundness of his views, organized the Mohawk and Hudson Rail Road, and pushed it to completion. When circumstances forced him to seek a new career, and he turned to a longtime interest in geology, he became deeply convinced of its potential importance to the public. He promoted interest in the subject by every means at his command: public lectures and demonstrations, articles and reviews, a geological journal, and personal appeals to legislators, both state and federal. Having convinced the Congress and President Jackson of the importance which a geological survey could have for the entire country, he obtained their approval and conducted several surveys as United States geologist. Having long believed that a geological survey could provide a basis for settling the boundary dispute between Maine and New Brunswick, he set out to convince others. He persuaded Lord Palmerston to authorize the survey, planned it, organized it, conducted it, and so provided a sound basis for the Webster-Ashburton Treaty.

It must be emphasized that his formal education was limited, that he was not the Oxford graduate some have thought him. Featherston was fundamentally a scholar by inclination. Throughout his life he was driven by an intense desire to apply his able brain to a study of the world around him, interested in both its past and its future. In the course of his life he demonstrated competence in a surprisingly diverse array of undertakings. He ever believed himself mentally qualified to belong to the intellectual elite of any society in which he found himself. That he was able to convince others of this is amply demonstrated by his election to membership in the American Philosophical Society, the Geological Society of London, and the Royal Society of London, as well as by the enduring friendship he formed with such able scientists as Buckland, Murchison, Owen, and Sedgwick. Although he believed himself to be a descendant of English nobility, it was intellectual accomplishment and recognition that he respected and coveted and that drove him to literary attainments and to unrelenting labor in many fields.

In summary, it may be said that Featherston was a man of unusual ability, bordering brilliance, who made important contributions to several fields of human endeavor. He was a man of compassion, genuinely concerned about the inhumanity shown the Negro and the Indian. He was affectionately devoted to his family and friends and to his native country. He earnestly strove to use his God-given ability to improve the lot of humanity. Little more can be asked of any man.[23]

Notes

Abbreviations

AJS	*American Journal of Science and Arts*
APS	American Philosophical Society
ASC	All Souls College, Oxford University
BL	British Library
Bod	Bodleian Library, Oxford University
CO	Colonial Office records, British Public Record Office, Kew
CU	Cambridge University
DAB	*Dictionary of American Biography*
DNB	*Dictionary of National Biography*
DSB	*Dictionary of Scientific Biography*
FFP	Microfilm reels of Featherstonhaugh Family Papers, Minnesota Historical Society, cited by roll and frame number. The papers are housed at the Albany Institute of History and Art.
FO	Foreign Office records, British Public Record Office, Kew
GSL	Geological Society of London
GWF	George William Featherstonhaugh
HSP	Historical Society of Pennsylvania
MAJ	*Monthly American Journal of Geology and Natural Science* 1 (July 1831–June 1832). Reprinted with an introduction by George W. White. New York, 1969.
MHS	Missouri Historical Society
NYHS	New-York Historical Society

NYPL   New York Public Library
NYSL   New York State Library
PRO   British Public Record Office, Kew
TB   Topographical Bureau of the United
        States War Department
UM   University of Michigan, William L.
        Clements Library
YUL   Yale University Library

Preface

1. White, Introduction to *MAJ,* xiv.

1. Early Life

1. The following account of Featherstonhaugh's birth and the death and family background of his father is based primarily on his own notes, entitled "Memorandum Given Me by My Mother in 1827," FFP 2.
2. Yorkshire Parish Register Society, *Publications* 85 (1928): 121.
3. *York Courant,* 16 May 1780, p. 3.
4. *Kent's London Directory for the Year 1780.*
5. PRO, PROB 11/1066, 65, 8.
6. Yorkshire Records, North Allerton.
7. *Universal British Directory of Trade and Commerce* (1798), p. 384.
8. Bush, *Scarborough Castle,* pp. 1–24.
9. Page, ed., *A History of Yorkshire, North Riding,* 2:538–60.
10. Ibid.; *Universal British Directory,* p. 381; Ainsworth, *The Scarborough Guide,* pp. 2–89; Hinderwell, *History and Antiquities of Scarborough,* pp. 168–200.
11. See Dorothy Featherstonhaugh to John Rowles, 23–24 November 1812 (Dp. p. 469), deed 608, R. Courteen to Dorothy Featherstonhaugh, 14 March 1791, Memorial of Indenture CH 144/191, Yorkshire Records.
12. [GWF], *Langleyhaugh,* 1:129–30. This novel is partly autobiographical.
13. Ibid.
14. GWF, *A Canoe Voyage up the Minnay Sotor,* 2:158.
15. GWF, *Excursion through the Slave States,* p. 44.
16. Rountree, ed., *History of Scarborough,* pp. 255–56.
17. Page, ed., *History of Yorkshire, North Riding,* 2:554–55.
18. Ainsworth, *Scarborough Guide,* pp. 21, 101–3. Could this have been "Dru Drury"?
19. GWF, Jr., mentions the school in a letter to his father, 21 June 1823, FFP 6.
20. [GWF], *Langleyhaugh,* 1:138, 140–42.
21. Rountree, ed., *History of Scarborough,* p. 264.
22. James Duane Featherstonhaugh, "Memoir of Mr. G. W. Featherstonhaugh," p. 217.
23. [GWF], *Langleyhaugh,* 1:217–21.
24. Ainsworth, *Scarborough Guide,* p. 47.
25. [GWF], *Langleyhaugh,* 1:169–70.
26. The relative was probably the sister of Timothy Fysche of Scarborough, for

she lived at Fysche Hall at one time. Her father-in-law had once been equerry to the Duke of Clarence before he became William IV. See GWF to Hammond, 27 April 1857, FO 27/1209. Except where noted, the account of Featherston's travels is taken from his *Langleyhaugh*.

27. GWF, *Excursion*, p. 58; [GWF], *Langleyhaugh*, 2:1–4.
28. GWF, *Langleyhaugh*, 2:16.
29. Testimony of Philip Jaume in lawsuit, October 1823, FFP 6:176–78.
30. GWF to Ann, 12 November 1803, FFP 2:88–92; GWF 1838 Journal, 8 September 1838, FFP 2.
31. GWF to Ann, 1 August 1802, FFP 2:49–50.
32. Eyles, "The Extent of Geological Knowledge in the Eighteenth Century," pp. 159–80.
33. *DNB*.
34. GWF to Ann, 1 August 1802, FFP 2:53–54.
35. Ibid.; W. R. Courteen to GWF, 30 October 1802, R. Courteen, Jr., to GWF, 24 May 1803, FFP 2:65, 73.
36. GWF to Ann, 12 November 1803, FFP 2:108; John Bielby to GWF, 15 May 1815, FFP 4:62–63.
37. Buried 13 February 1804, Scarborough Burials, Yorkshire Records.
38. Mrs. Belcombe to GWF, 13 January 1806, FFP 2:139; GWF to mother, [?] 1806, FFP 2:137.
39. GWF to Ann, 26 February 1806, NYHS; George Simpson's will, dated October 1800, Borthwick Institute of Historical Research, University of York; GWF, *Excursion*, pp. 145–46; Tom Dickason to GWF, 24 April 1806, FFP 2:154–56; GWF to GWF, Jr., 18 August 1826, FFP 7:263–64.
40. W. H. Nevitt to GWF, 10 December 1806, FFP 2:178–80.
41. GWF to Ann, 30 September 1813, FFP 3:499–505.
42. Roberts, *Old Schenectady*, p. 188; Alexander, *A Revolutionary Conservative*, p. 215. Sally's sister Mary married General William North, Adelia married Alfred Pell, and Catherine, or "Kitty," was unmarried.
43. Greene and Burke, *The Science of Minerals in the Age of Jefferson*, p. 65; Greene, *American Science in the Age of Jefferson*, p. 173. For further discussion of Bruce and MacNeven as mineralogists, see Brush, *A Sketch of the Progress of American Mineralogy*, pp. 8–10.
44. MacNeven to GWF, 23 April 1807, FFP 2:190–92; GWF Journal, 10 March 1815, FFP 4.
45. GWF to Lord Addington, 18 January 1854, FO 27/1031 (PRO).
46. GWF, Memorandum N.A. Boundary Commission, 9 September 1838, FFP 8:6; GWF to Lt. Col. Abert, 16 September 1838, MHS; GWF Memorandum, 29 August 1839, FFP 8:125.
47. GWF, *A Canoe Voyage*, 1:384; GWF, *Excursion*, p. 88.
48. Charles Wilkes to GWF, [?] February 1808, FFP 2:203–4; GWF, "On the Excavation of the Rocky Channels," p. 45.
49. Ellice to GWF, [?] October 1807, FFP 2:201–2.
50. Nott to GWF, 7 October 1808, Allen to GWF, 12 December 1808, Reynaud to GWF, 18 December 1808, FFP 2:217, 233–34, 236–38; GWF, *A Canoe Voyage*, 1:65n.
51. Marriage Articles, 5 November 1808, FFP 2:222–24.

52. North to GWF, 15 January 1809, 23 December 1808, FFP 2:257, 239–40.
53. Reynaud to GWF, 18 December 1808, Allen to GWF, 12 December 1808, FFP 2:236–38, 233–34; William Johnson to GWF, 19 February 1817, FFP 4:273; Benjamin Morgan to GWF, 14 March 1810, FFP 2:471–72.
54. Peter S. DuPonceau to GWF, 21 May 1809, FFP 2:331–32; GWF to Mahlon Dickinson, 20 June 1809, APS; DuPonceau to GWF, 13 June, 21 July 1809, FFP 2:342, 353.
55. DuPonceau to GWF, 21 May 1809, FFP 2:331–32; GWF to Ann, 30 September 1813, FFP 3:499–505; North to GWF, 18 May 1809, Robert E. Griffith to GWF, 19 July 1809, FFP 2:320, 356–59.
56. Ann to GWF, 18 September 1809, Dr. Bruce to GWF, 23 September 1809, GWF to mother, 19 November 1809, FFP 2:372, 375, 393.
57. GWF Journal, 8 October, 21 June 1814, FFP 3, 8 August 1815, FFP 4; GWF to mother, 13 March 1817, FFP 4:280–81.
58. GWF to Ann, 10 December 1813, FFP 3:532–33.
59. Ibid. Very little remains of the fort today.
60. GWF to mother, 7 March 1813, Johnson to GWF, 5 January 1813, FFP 3:431–33, 420–21; Bruce to GWF, 26 February 1813, NYHS; GWF to mother, 5 May 1813, Sally to Mrs. Featherstonhaugh, [?] August 1814, FFP 3:463–64, 601–2.
61. GWF to Ann, 30 September 1813, FFP 3:499–505.
62. GWF Journal, 3 February 1814, FFP 3; Samuel Bard to GWF, 10 June 1811, FFP 2:130–32; *American Farmer* (Baltimore) 5 (29 August 1823): 177.
63. *Plough Boy* 2 (16 December 1820, and 24 February 1821), 4 (31 December 1822).
64. Ibid. 3 (25 May 1822).
65. GWF to mother, 9 December 1820, FFP 5:217–19.
66. GWF Journal, 14 February 1815, FFP 4; GWF to mother, 4 April 1815, 5 June 1816, FFP 4:56–58, 208–10; GWF Journal, 1 January 1816, FFP 4; GWF to Courteen, 26 December 1818, Bielby to GWF, 15 May 1815, mother to GWF, 26 April 1818, FFP 4:452, 62–63, 387–88.
67. Sally to GWF, [?] 1820, GWF to mother, 6 March 1820, FFP 5:7–10, 50–52.

2. New Interests and Undertakings

1. Greene, *American Science,* p. 106.
2. GWF Journal, 1816, FFP 4; Merrill, *The First One Hundred Years of American Geology,* pp. 7, 39; Brush, *A Sketch of the Progress of American Mineralogy,* pp. 11, 12; Greene, *American Science,* p. 295. Colonel Gibbs's cabinet was exhibited at Yale University in 1810 and purchased by Yale in 1825 (Smallwood, *Natural History and the American Mind,* p. 332).
3. Report of Surgeon Wood, FFP 3:626–27; GWF to mother, 4 April 1815, FFP 4:56–58.
4. GWF Journal, 22 September 1814, FFP 3.
5. Ibid., 9 December 1814, FFP 4. For further discussion of Cooper, see Malone, *The Public Life of Thomas Cooper.*
6. GWF, "Refutation of Opinions Contained in Two Papers of the Irish Language." An evaluation of the validity of Featherston's arguments is beyond

the scope of this biography.

7. Caldwell to GWF, 23 February 1815, FFP 4:29–30; GWF, "Observations on a Paper in the *Port Folio,*" pp. 519–27.

8. Armytage, "G. W. Featherstonhaugh."

9. GWF Journal, 5 March 1815, FFP 4; GWF to Edward Everett, 3 September 1821, Massachusetts Historical Society; Peter DuPonceau to GWF, 20 January 1823, FFP 6:10.

10. *Plough Boy* 1 (25 September 1819): 134, 2 (10 February 1821): 295, (27 January 1821): 373.

11. Ibid. 1 (15 January 1820): 262–63 (22 January 1820): 265, 2 (20 January 1821): 270.

12. GWF to Stephen Van Rensselaer, [?] December 1820, University of Kentucky Libraries; GWF to Madison, 7 December 1820, NYPL; Madison to GWF, 23 December 1820, Madison Papers 68, Library of Congress.

13. GWF, "Essay on Rural Economy," reprinted in *American Farmer* 5 (25 July 1823): 137–39.

14. Resolution of the Board of Agriculture, 16 January 1821, FFP 5:239, reprinted in *Plough Boy* 2 (10 February 1821): 295; *American Farmer* 5 (18 July 1823): 136.

15. *Plough Boy* 4 (23 July 1822): 59; GWF to Jesse Buel, 21 October 1822, College of Physicians, Philadelphia, reprinted in *American Farmer* 5 (29 August 1823): 177–79; GWF to Buel, 3 November 1822, NYSL; GWF to Buel, 16 November 1822, HSP.

16. Dan Bradley to GWF, 27 May 1823, John Hare Powell to GWF, 10 June 1823, note on Judge Hayden's letter to GWF by Van Rensselaer, 15 March 1824, L. Suydam to GWF, 5 June 1824, Lewis C. Beck to GWF, 20 May 1823, FFP 6:72–73, 78–79, 262, 306, 67. Buel was largely responsible for the third volume.

17. Everett to GWF, 17 August 1821, FFP 2:410.

18. GWF, "The New York Canals," pp. 233–34, 235–36. He was reviewing *Public Documents Relating to New York Canals* (1821), *History of the Rise, Progress, and Existing Condition of the Western Canals in the State of New York* (1820), and Robert Troup, *A Vindication of the Claim of Elkanah Watson, Esq., to the Merit of Projecting the Lake Canal Policy* (1821).

19. Mother to GWF, 1 December 1815, FFP 4:151–52; Sally to mother-in-law, [?] September 1820, mother to GWF, [?] December 1820, FFP 5:168A, 230–31.

20. GWF to mother, [?] May 1821, FFP 5:340–42.

21. George to father, 20 July 1821, Miss Buchanan to GWF, 21 July 1821, mother to GWF, 1 August, 27 October, 7 December 1821, Herbert Phillips to GWF, 22 February 1822, FFP 5:377, 378–79, 400, 481, 500, 560–61.

22. GWF to Edmund Kean, 1 October 1821, FFP 5:450–52; George to father, 31 December 1825, FFP 6:563–65.

23. Van Rensselaer to GWF, 10 February 1824, NYSL.

24. GWF Journal, 1–19 January 1823, FFP 6; indenture dated 8 January 1823, FFP 6:1–3.

25. GWF Journal, 28–31 January 1823, FFP 6.

26. Ibid., 1–3 February 1823; Cheves to GWF, 8 March 1823, FFP 6:35–36.

27. GWF Journal, 3–5 February 1823, FFP 6; GWF to mother, 26 March 1823, FFP 6:40–41; GWF Journal, 12–22 February 1823, FFP 6.

28. GWF Journal, 1–29 March, 17 May, 13 June 1823, FFP 6.

29. Ibid., 8 August 1823; GWF to mother, 18 December 1823, FFP 6:221–23; GWF Journal, 9–10, 8–13 September 1823, FFP 6; Van Rensselaer to GWF, 20 October 1823, FFP 6:187.

30. Beverley Robinson to GWF, 13 September 1823, FFP 6:149–50; GWF to mother, 9 September 1821, FFP 5:431; John Wells to GWF, 8 October 1821, FFP 6:460.

31. GWF to Bielby, 8 August 1821, GWF to mother, 9 September 1821, Wells to GWF, 8 October 1821, FFP 5:404–8, 431, 460.

32. GWF Journal, 18, 26 September 1823, FFP 6; Peter A. Jay to GWF, 16 December 1823, FFP 6:219.

33. GWF to E. P. Livingston, 15 February 1823, FFP 6:24; GWF Journal, 4, 6, 18 March 1823, FFP 6; Lewis Eaton to GWF, 10 January 1824, Wadsworth to GWF, 22 December 1823, GWF to Clay, 24 April 1824, FFP 6:235–36, 226–27, 295.

34. GWF to Clay, 24 April, 12 May 1824, FFP 6:295, 303; Clay to GWF, 26 May 1824, University of Kentucky.

35. GWF to Cheves, 13 November 1824, postscript added 16 November, HSP; Clay to GWF, 10 October 1824, Kylof, Filson Club; GWF to Van Rensselaer, 29 November 1824, HSP.

36. Van Rensselaer to GWF, 13 December 1824, NYSL; GWF to Van Rensselaer, 20 February 1825, HSP; GWF to Clay, 31 January 1825, FFP 6:435; Renwick to GWF, 24 December 1824, FFP 6:16; GWF to Van Rensselaer, 30 December 1824, HSP.

37. GWF to Van Rensselaer, 4 January 1825, HSP.

38. Roberts, *Old Schenectady*, pp. 188, 145.

39. Jenkins to GWF, 10 June 1820, FFP 5:2. For further details, see GWF, "Estimate of Timber and Carpenter Work of the Rail Road," Memoranda, "Principles of Traction for Railroad and Canals," all FFP 6:414–28; GWF to Van Rensselaer, 4 January 1825, HSP.

40. GWF to Van Rensselaer, 30 January 1825, FFP 6:409–13.

41. GWF to Van Rensselaer, 13 April 1825, HSP; GWF to George, 16 May 1825, FFP 6:458–59; GWF to Thomas Cole, 12 December 1825, NYSL; GWF to mother, 16 June 1825, FFP 6:470–71.

42. New York Common Council, *Minutes of the Common Council,* 18 July 1825, vol. 14, p. 677; Duane to GWF, 11 July 1825, North to GWF, 6 July 1825, GWF to George, 30 November 1825, FFP 6:489, 494, 553–55.

43. Bryant, *Orations and Addresses,* pp. 9–11; GWF to Cole, 7 April 1826, 12 December 1825, NYSL.

44. *DAB;* GWF to Van Rensselaer, 14 January 1826, HSP.

45. GWF to Cole, 7 April 1826, NYSL; GWF to Van Rensselaer, 14 January 1826, HSP; GWF to Cole, 8 November 1826, NYSL; Noble, *The Life and Works of Thomas Cole,* pp. 37–38. There seems to be little or no justification for the comments of William Cullen Bryant, repeated by Noble, that Cole was ill treated by GWF.

46. GWF to Van Rensselaer, 25 February 1826, HSP; GWF to Major Dallaby, 15 March 1826, FFP 7:81–83; Harlow, *The Road of the Century,* p. 6.

47. GWF to Van Rensselaer, 12 March 1826, HSP.

48. Van Rensselaer to GWF, 15 March 1826, in Stevens, *The Beginnings of the New*

York Central Railroad, p. 2; GWF to Van Rensselaer, 20 March 1826, HSP.

49. Stevens, *New York Central Railroad,* pp. 2, 10–11.

50. GWF to Van Rensselaer, 2 March 1826, HSP; Stevens, *New York Central Railroad,* pp. 8–9; James Renwick to GWF, 22 March 1826, FFP 7:104.

51. James to brother George, 8 June 1826, FFP 7:209–10.

52. Hazen, Preface to his *North American Geology,* p. 2;[GWF], "Geology" (June 1830): 365.

53. Daniels, *American Science in the Age of Jackson,* p. 7.

54. Robert Edmiston to GWF, 25 November 1826, Andrew Edmiston to GWF, 28 March 1826, GWF to George, 18 August 1826, Robert Campbell to GWF, 4 September 1826, FFP 7:351–53, 111–12, 263–64, 283–84.

55. Stevens, *New York Central Railroad,* p. 10; GWF to Van Rensselaer, 14 November 1826, HSP.

3. Old and New Friends in England

1. GWF to [Van Rensselaer ?], 6 December 1826, HSP; receipt for coat, waistcoat, trousers, jacket, etc., from Megraw & Heron, and shirtings, etc., from Armstrong & Hall, Liverpool, [?] and 7 December 1826, FFP 7:363–65.

2. GWF to [Van Rensselaer ?], 6 December 1826, HSP; GWF to General Theodore Sill, 18 December 1826, FFP 7:377–78.

3. Receipt for exchange, 5 December 1826, FFP 7:361; GWF to [Van Rensselaer ?], 6 December 1826, HSP; GWF to Sill, 18 December 1826, FFP 7:377–78.

4. GWF to Fish, 14 February 1827, Columbia University Libraries.

5. GWF to Charles Babbage, 27 April 1827, Add. Mss. 37184, f. 18, BL; Murchison, "Mr. George W. Featherstonhaugh," xliii–xlv.

6. GWF to Fish, 14 February 1827, Columbia University Libraries.

7. Ibid.; Sinclair to GWF, 8, 10, 13, 26, 29 January, 1 February 1827, FFP 7:396–418.

8. GWF to Adam Sedgwick, 13 December 1831, Add. Mss. 7652, IF24, CU.

9. [GWF], "Geology" (June 1830): 368–70. For a full discussion of this topic, see Greene, *Geology in the Nineteenth Century,* pp. 19–45.

10. Schneer, ed., *Toward a History of Geology,* p. 13; Eyles, "William Smith, Sir Joseph Banks and the French Geologists," p. 37.

11. Thomas Miles Richardson to GWF, 16 March 1827, FFP 7:466–67.

12. Phillips, *Memoirs of William Smith,* pp. 110–12; *MAJ* I (July 1831): 31; Eyles, "G. W. Featherstonhaugh," p. 382.

13. GWF to George Brettingham Sowerby, 20 April 1827, FFP 7:516.

14. GWF to Gallatin, 21 July 1827, NYHS.

15. GWF to Babbage, 27 April 1827, Add. 37184, f. 18, BL.

16. Geikie, *Life of Sir Roderick Murchison,* p. 115; Fitton to GWF, 19 May 1827, FFP 7:543–45.

17. Geikie, *Murchison,* p. 103; [GWF], "Geology" (June 1830): 364.

18. William Buckland to GWF, 1 June 1827, Add. 7652/II, LL1, CU.

19. Ibid., and 2 June 1827, Add. 7652/II, LL2, CU.

20. See Geikie, *Murchison,* p. 85.

21. [GWF], Review of *Geological Text Book,* pp. 472–73.

22. GWF to Buckland, 17 June 1827, Devon Record Office, Exeter, according to Joan Eyles, "G. W. Featherstonhaugh," n. 11; Murchison's account in Geikie, *Murchison,* p. 135.
23. Audubon Journal, 22 June 1827, quoted in Maria R. Audubon, *Audubon and His Journals,* p. 257.
24. Buckland to GWF, 5 July 1827, Add. 7652/II, LL4 and 5, CU; Eyles, "Featherstonhaugh," p. 383; *DNB*; GWF to Mantell, 21 [19 ?] July 1827, Alexander Turnbull Library, N.Z., as quoted in Eyles, "Featherstonhaugh," pp. 392–93. All further GWF letters to Mantell are from the same source.
25. GWF to Mantell, 28 July 1827; Buckland to GWF, 24 July, 3 August 1827, Add. 7652/II, LL8 and 9, CU.
26. GWF to Mantell, 4 August 1827; Buckland to GWF, 20 September 1827, Add. 7652/II, LL14, CU; museum catalogue (503, p. 147) description of idol formerly in the Ashmolean Museum, now in the Pitt Rivers Museum.
27. GWF to Mantell, 19 August 1827.
28. Ibid.
29. Eyles, "Smith, Banks and the French Geologists," p. 37.
30. Buckland to GWF, 8, 20 September 1827, Add. 7652/II, LL13 and 14, CU.
31. Murchison to GWF, 6 October 1827, GWF to Murchison, 22 October 1827, Add. 7652/II, KK2 and 1, CU.
32. GWF to Murchison, 22 October 1827, Add. II, KK1, CU.
33. Ibid.; St. Aubyn, *St. Michael's Mount,* pp. 19–20; *MAJ* I (May 1832): 485; GWF, introductory letters, [?] August 1825, FFP 6:496–99; St. Aubyn to GWF, 15 January 1826, FFP 7:23–24.
34. GWF to Murchison, 22 October 1827, Add. 7652/II, KK1, CU; Forde, *Mary Anning.* This, or another she found, measured twenty-four feet in length. Her later discoveries included a *Plesiosaurus* and the first *Pterodactylus,* all now in the British Museum (Natural History), many prepared by her.
35. GWF to Murchison, 22 October 1827, Add. 7652/II, KK1, CU. Today Uppark is beautifully maintained by the National Trust.
36. *Uppark* (the National Trust, 1981), p. 12; Aspinwall, ed., *Correspondence of George, Prince of Wales,* 7:1047n, 1204, 1386, 1789, 1797, 2328, 2589.
37. The parish register of All Saints, Norwich, under George Featherstonhaugh's burial entry, to which a note was added: "visited by his only surviving son George Wm. Featherstonhaugh" (according to Jean Kennedy, County Archivist, 9 July 1979); *Proceedings of the Geological Society of London* (1827–28): 35.
38. Buckland to GWF, 2 November 1827, Add. 7652/II, LL16, CU; Nevitt to GWF, 10 January 1810, FFP 2:439; Law to GWF, 18 January 1822, NYHS.
39. Dr. Bell to Sally, [?] November 1827, FFP 7:587.

4. Tragedy and Disillusionment

1. Murchison to GWF, 10 February 1828, Add. 7652/II, KK4, CU; bill for lodging at Park Place House, 9–19 January 1828, FFP 7:620; Murchison to GWF, 11 April 1828, Add. 7652/II, KK5, CU.
2. Greene, *American Science,* p. 103; "Proceedings of the Lyceum of Natural History, New York," for January 1828, *AJS* 14:193–97; GWF to Benjamin Silliman, 16 March 1828, YUL.

3. Greene and Burke, *The Science of Minerals,* pp. 103–4; GWF to Silliman, 16 March, 14 April 1828, YUL.

4. GWF to Madison, 28 February 1828, NYPL; Madison to GWF, 13 March 1828, Jasper E. Crane, Nemours Building, Wilmington, Delaware (courtesy Madison Papers, University of Virginia).

5. Clay to GWF, 18 February 1828, University of Kentucky Libraries; Buckland to GWF, 25 February, 24 June 1828, Add. 7652/II, LL18 and 19, CU.

6. Murchison to GWF, 8 December 1827, 10 February 1828, Add. 7652/II, KK3 and 4, CU.

7. E. Hitching's receipt for $118, for attending Sally from November 1827 to 6 May 1828, FFP 7:631; Buckland to GWF, 10 October 1828, Murchison to GWF, 26 October 1828, Add. 7652/II, LL20 and KK8, CU.

8. GWF to Madison, 1 March 1829, NYPL.

9. *AJS* 15:194, 16:206.

10. Murchison to GWF, 26 December 1828, Add. 7652/II, KK9, CU; GWF to Eaton, 13 June 1829, HSP; Eyles, "Featherstonhaugh," p. 385. Featherston's paper appeared in the *Proceedings of the Geological Society of London* in 1834 and then as a two-page abstract.

11. Buckland to GWF, 10 October 1828, Add. 7652/II, LL20, CU; *AJS* 15:400; Greene, *American Science,* p. 235.

12. Buckland to GWF, 23 March 1829, Add. 7652/II, LL21, CU.

13. Stevens, *New York Central,* pp. 3, 13-17.

14. Ibid., pp. 18–19; GWF to Fish, 18 November 1829, 24 December 1830, Fish Family MSS, Columbia University Libraries; Hedrick, *History of Agriculture in New York,* p. 255.

15. *AJS* 16 (January 1829): 355; GWF to Silliman, 29 April 1829, YUL; GWF to Buckland, 12 July 1830, copy at National Museum of Wales, the original at Devon Record Office (183M/F 264).

16. GWF to Silliman, 29 April 1829, YUL.

17. Silliman to Delafield, 4 May 1829, Silliman to GWF, 5 May 1829, YUL.

18. GWF to Silliman, 13, 26 May 1829, Silliman to GWF, 28 May 1829, Hare to GWF, 24 May 1829, Silliman to Hare, 28 May 1829, all YUL; GWF to Silliman, 1 June 1829, HSP.

19. GWF to mother, 30 September 1829, FFP 7:675–76.

20. [GWF], "Geology" (September 1829). His authorship of this unsigned article is acknowledged in his review of two geological books in the June 1830 issue of the same journal (p. 361). Everett quoted in Daniels, *American Science in the Age of Jackson,* p. 63.

21. Buckland to GWF, 23 March 1829, Add. 7652/II, LL21, CU.

22. Murchison to GWF, 7 November 1829, Add. 7652/II, KK16, CU; Wilson, *Charles Lyell,* 1:294–96.

23. GWF to Buckland, 27 June 1829, Royal Society of London Archives; GWF, "On the Ancient Drainage of North America," MAJ (1831), pp. 13–21.

24. GWF, "On the Series of Rocks in the United States," pp. 91–93; GWF, "On the Ancient Drainage of North America," p. 17.

25. Buckland to GWF, 6 November 1829, Murchison to GWF, 13 May, 20 June 1829, Mrs. Murchison to GWF, 13 July 1829, Add. 7652/II, LL23, KK10, 11, and 14, CU.

26. Murchison to GWF, 7 November 1829, Mrs. Murchison to GWF, 13 July 1829, Add. 7652/II, KK16 and 14, CU.
27. Published by Carey and Lea; Review in *American Quarterly Review* 8 (September 1830): 156–58; GWF to Murchison, [?] May 1830, GSL.
28. GWF to Madison, 3 January 1830, NYPL; *Register of Graduates and Former Cadets, United States Military Academy,* p. 161; Murchison to GWF, 21 April 1830, Add. 7652/II, KK20, CU.
29. GWF to Murchison, 22 February 1830, GSL. See APS, "Old Minutes of the Society from 1743 to 1838," *Proceedings of the American Philosophical Society* 22 (July 1885), pt. 3. For more on the academy, see Smallwood, *Natural History,* pp. 155–65; or Greene and Burke, *The Science of Minerals,* pp. 38–44; academy records, courtesy of Carol M. Spawn, Archivist/Manuscript Librarian.
30. [GWF], "Geology" (July 1830). Brande was coeditor of the *Quarterly Journal of Science and Art.*
31. Ibid., p. 403; GWF to Sedgwick, 9 January 1831, Add. 7652/II, IF15, CU.
32. GWF to Sedgwick, 12 July 1830, Add. 7652/II, IF16, CU; Sedgwick to GWF, 28 October 1830, Add. 7652/III, A1, CU.
33. Murchison, "Memorial Address by the President," *Journal of the Geological Society of London* 23 (1867): xliii–xlv; Buckland to GWF, 28 February 1831, Add. 7652/II, LL26, CU.
34. Murchison to GWF, 7 November 1829, 18 January, 21 April 1830, Add. 7652/II, KK16, 18, and 20, CU.
35. GWF to Buckland, 12 July 1830, National Museum of Wales, Cardiff; Buckland to GWF, 28 August 1830, Add. 7652/II, LL25, CU; Lyell to Rev. Dr. Fleming, 6 February 1828, Lyell, *Life, Letters and Journals,* 1:178.
36. GWF Journal, 3 August 1838, FFP 10; Steinmeyer, *Staten Island,* pp. 46–47. The wedding was announced in the *Richmond Inquirer,* 16 September 1831, p. 3, col. 5.
37. GWF to Nicholas Fish, 24 December 1830, Fish Family MSS; GWF to Isaac Hays, 11 February 1831, APS; 18 February 1831, APS, *Proceedings* 22:614; GWF to Hamilton, 15 March 1831, Faculty Correspondence, 1824–65, Records of the Committee on Instruction, Franklin Institute; GWF to Sedgwick, 9 January 1831, Add. 7652/II, IF15, CU.
38. GWF to Edward Everett, 5 May 1830, Massachusetts Historical Society.
39. [GWF], Review of *Geological Text Book,* pp. 482–90; Van Rensselaer's letter in *AJS* 20 (1831): 419.
40. GWF to Sedgwick, 9 January 1831, Add. 7652/II, IF 15, CU; Lyell to Mantell, [?] March 1831, in Lyell, *Life, Letters and Journals,* 1:317; Buckland to GWF, 28 February 1831, Add. 7652/II, LL26, CU.

5. New Developments in American Geology

1. GWF to Sedgwick, 9 January 1831, Add. 7652/II, IF15, CU; Smallwood, *Natural History,* pp. 57–61; Daniels; *American Science,* p. 14.
2. GWF to mother, 18 April 1831, FFP 8:146–48; GWF to Carey, [?] April 1831, NYPL.
3. GWF to Sedgwick, enclosing copy of the prospectus, 22 May 1831, Add. 7652/II, IF18, CU; Smallwood, *Natural History,* p. 162; GWF to Sedgwick,

13 December 1831, Add. 7652/II, IF24, CU.

4. GWF to Sedgwick, 22 May 1831, Add. 7652/II, IF18, CU; Buckland to GWF, 23 August 1831, Add. 7652/II, LL29, CU.

5. See the Minnesota Historical Society's reprint of the journal, with an introduction by George W. White, who commented that it "contains much more of importance in American geology and history than is indicated by its 576 pages and 12 numbers."

6. White, "History of Geology and Mineralogy," p. 213.

7. Ford, *John James Audubon*, p. 280.

8. Ibid., p. 282; *MAJ* (September 1831): 136–39.

9. GWF, Review of *Birds of America* and *Ornithological Biography*, *MAJ* (April 1832): 460–61.

10. 7 December letter in February 1832 issue, 31 December letter in March 1832 issue, and 12 January 1832 in June issue, *MAJ*; Audubon, *Letters*, p. 166.

11. Ford, *Audubon*, p. 288.

12. GWF, "Audubon's Biography of Birds," pp. 364–65.

13. Ibid., p. 366.

14. Ibid., pp. 369, 370.

15. Ibid., p. 404; Audubon, *Letters*, pp. 194–95.

16. Croghan Journal in December 1831 issue; letter published in the October 1831 issue, pp. 175–76.

17. Daniels, *American Science*, p. 208. For further details of this controversy, see statement by Richard Harlan, Isaac Lea, A. D. Bache, et al. to GWF, [?] May 1831, Hays to GWF, 2 August 1831, G. W. Smith to GWF, 3 letters dated 3 August 1831, GWF to Smith, 2 letters dated 3 August 1831, GWF to Smith, 4 August 1831, all APS.

18. GWF to Murchison, 3 April 1831, Add. 7652/II, LL28, CU.

19. Buckland to GWF, 23 August 1831, Add. 7652/II, LL29, CU.

20. *MAJ*: 278–80; GWF to Sedgwick, 13 December 1831, Add. 7652/II, IF24, CU; Buckland to GWF, 3 May 1832, Add. 7652/II, LL31, CU.

21. *MAJ* (March 1832): 425–30; records of the GSL; GWF to Murchison, 18 March 1832, GSL.

22. GWF to Prof. J. T. Ducatel, University of Kentucky Libraries; GWF to Buckland, 15 May 1832, Royal Society of London Archives.

23. Kastner, *A Species of Eternity*, pp. 240–53. For a recent study of Rafinesque, see Fitzpatrick, *Rafinesque*.

24. *MAJ* (May 1832): 508–15.

25. Rafinesque, *A Life of Travels*, p. 333; Rafinesque to Torrey, 7 November 1832, New York Botanical Garden. Harlan had no part in the publication of *MAJ* though he often wrote for it.

26. Audubon to GWF, 15 April 1832, Gunther Collection, Chicago Historical Society; Buckland to GWF, 3 May 1832, Add. 7652/II, LL31, CU; GWF to Buckland, 15 May 1832, Royal Society of London Archives.

27. Moore, *The Madisons*, p. 499; GWF, *Excursion*, p. 38.

28. GWF, *Excursion*, p. 162; untitled poem, MS in the collection of Mr. and Mrs. George B. Cutts, Brookline, Mass., copy in the Madison Papers, University of Virginia Library.

29. GWF to Sedgwick, 12 July 1830, Add. 7652/II, IF16, CU; [GWF], "Gold

Districts," GWF to Rhea, 27 May, 26 June 1832, Tennessee Historical Society.
30. [GWF], "Geology" (June 1830): 366; Daniels, *American Science,* p. 44.
31. Taylor, "Section of the Allegheny Mountain . . . ," *MAJ* (April 1832), 433–38; [GWF], "Geology" (September 1831): 128–34.
32. *Sen. Doc.,* 22d Cong., 2d Sess., no. 35, pp. 1–7.
33. GWF to Livingston, 28 December 1832, National Archives, copy from State Historical Society of Wisconsin.
34. GWF to Murchison, 2 September 1833, GSL; Abert to Cass, 11 March, [?] 1833, TB, Letters Received, #266 (12 February 1829–29 August 1835), pp. 269, 27.
35. GWF to Editor, *Farmers' Register* 1, no. 2 (1834): 152–55; Sheridan, "Mineral Fertilizers in Southern Agriculture," p. 76. Merrill has called attention to geological aspects of Ruffin's later (1843) report of his agricultural survey of South Carolina (*The First Hundred Years,* p. 239).
36. GWF, *Excursion,* p. 160; GWF, "Mineral Resources of Virginia," pp. 520–23.
37. GWF to Maclure, 20 September 1833, New Harmony Workingmen's Institute Library, New Harmony, Indiana.
38. *U.S. Telegraph,* 4 December 1833; GWF, "Mineral Resources of Virginia," pp. 520–23.
39. GWF to Cabell, 4, 22 January 1834, Virginia Geological Survey Collection, #3073, Manuscripts Department, University of Virginia Library; William Alexander to Polk, 26 January 1834, Polk, *Correspondence,* 2:278.

6. The First Geological Survey Begins

1. Abert to GWF, 8 July 1834, TB, Letters Sent 1:385; GWF to Abert, TB, Letters Received, 1:80.
2. Abert to GWF, 16 July 1834, TB, Letters Sent, 1:388–89.
3. Ibid.
4. GWF, *Excursion,* U.S. edition, pp. 11–12. Unless otherwise noted, the account of the Featherstonhaughs' travels is based on this book; page numbers of quotations are given parenthetically in the text. Illustrations are from the English edition.
5. GWF to Madison, 1 September 1834, NYPL.
6. The previous year, Murchison had written his friend about his studies of classification of the transition formations. He had finally reduced them to their natural order and had named the earlier system Silurian. Featherston had used this information in his own studies. See GWF, *Excursion,* p. 13n.
7. Porter, *The Eagle's Nest,* pp. 109–10.
8. Corgan, "Early American Geological Surveys and Gerard Troost's Field Assistants, 1831–1836," in Corgan, ed., *Geological Sciences in the Antebellum South,* p. 62.

7. A New Mode of Travel

1. See [GWF], "Geology" (June, 1830): 368–74.
2. GWF to mother, 14 November 1834, FFP 8:156–57.
3. GWF, *Geological Report of an Examination Made in 1834.*
4. Hendrickson, "The Western Academy of Natural Sciences of St. Louis"; *AJS*

28 (1835): 379; Madison to GWF, 3 July 1835, Jasper E. Crane, Nemours Building, Wilmington, Delaware; Buckland to GWF, 29 November 1835, Add. 7652/II, LL33, CU.

5. Eyles, "Featherstonhaugh," p. 388.
6. GWF to Cabell, 2 March, 8 June 1835, Cabell Collection; Troost to GWF, 2 April 1835, FFP 8:160–61.
7. GWF to Madison, 15 July 1835, NYPL; Gordon, "Old Homes on Georgetown Heights."
8. Buckland to Murchison, 5 February 1835, National Museum of Wales.
9. GWF to Murray, 17 June 1835, Archives of John Murray, Publishers, London.

8. Canoeing Up the Minnay Sotor

1. Abert to GWF, 7 July 1835, TB, Letters Sent, 1:511; GWF to Madison, 15 July 1835, NYPL.
2. Abert to Cass, 24 June 1835, Abert to GWF, Jr., TB, Letters Sent, 1:510, 501; GWF to mother, 19 August 1835, FFP 8:165–66.
3. Abert to Macomb, 9 June 1835, Abert to Mather, 3 July 1835, TB, Letters Sent, 1:508, 510. Unless otherwise indicated, the following account of GWF's travels is based on his 1835–36 journal, FFP 8 and 9; GWF, *A Canoe Voyage.* Page numbers of quotations from *A Canoe Voyage* appear parenthetically in the text.
4. GWF to Abert, 2 August 1835, MHS.
5. Ibid.
6. Ibid.
7. *DAB.*
8. GWF to Abert, 1 September 1835, MHS.
9. Ibid.
10. Ibid. Mather's original orders to rejoin his regiment at Fort Gibson, Arkansas, prevailed (Abert to GWF, 8 September 1835, TB, Letters Sent, 2:35).
11. GWF to Abert, 13 September 1835, MHS.
12. On Renville, see Ackerman, "Joseph Renville of Lac Qui Parle."
13. GWF to Abert, 5 November 1835, MHS.
14. Bliss, "Reminiscences of Fort Snelling," p. 352.
15. Later he was transferred to Fort Gibson, Arkansas.
16. Bray, "Southern Influences on the Career of Nicollet," p. 105. See also Bray and Bray, *Joseph Nicollet on the Plains and Prairies.*

9. Wisconsin Revisited

1. *Sen. Doc.* 24th Cong., 1st Sess. no. 333; *AJS* 32 (1836): 185–86.
2. Abert to GWF, 25 October 1836, Abert to Mather, 21 December 1835, TB, Letters Sent, 2:395, 1:35–36.
3. Abert to GWF, 24 October 1837, ibid., 2:395.
4. Buckland to GWF, 29 November 1835, Add. 7652/II, LL33, CU; GWF, *Excursion,* p. v.
5. GWF to Bancroft, 3 March 1835, Massachesetts Historical Society, Boston; Bancroft to GWF, 5 April 1836, FFP 8:182.

6. Abert to GWF, 25 October 1836, TB, Letters Sent, 2:185.
7. GWF to Nicollet, 17 January 1837, bookseller's catalogue of the Rendells, Newton, Mass.
8. Ibid.
9. Ibid.; GWF to Abert, 19 May 1837, MHS.
10. GWF to Nicollet, 17 January 1837, the Rendells; Abert to GWF, 29 April, 10 March 1837, TB, Letters Sent, 2:313, 275.
11. Calhoun to GWF, 3 May 1837, HSP.
12. Unless otherwise noted, the following account of his travels is taken from GWF, *A Canoe Voyage,* 2:64–351 (page numbers of quotations given parenthetically in the text); and GWF Journal, FFP 8.
13. FFP 8:129, 65–103; Report to Iowa Copper Mining Company of Philadelphia, draft at Albany Institute, FFP 8:188.
14. GWF to Nicollet, 3 November 1837, the Rendells.
15. GWF to Abert, 19 July 1837, MHS.
16. Ibid.
17. For more information on the Cherokees, see South, *Indians of North Carolina;* and Swanton, *Indians of the Southeastern United States.*
18. GWF to Poinsett, 29 July 1837, HSP.
19. GWF to Poinsett, 11 August 1837, HSP; GWF to Poinsett, 30 September 1837, Quaker Collection, Haverford College, Haverford, Pa.

10. Libel at Home and Recognition Abroad

1. An Officer of the U.S. Navy, "Report of a Geological Reconnaissance," p. 481.
2. Ibid., p. 482; GWF, *Official Refutation of a Libel,* pp. 2–3.
3. GWF to the editor *Naval Magazine,* GWF to Abert, 21 October 1837, Abert to GWF, 24 October 1837, all *Naval Magazine* (November 1837): 2, 3–6. Unless otherwise noted, the following account is based on GWF, *Official Refutation of a Libel.* The original of Abert's letter is in TB, Letters Sent, 2:395.
4. *Naval Magazine* (November 1837): 569.
5. It is not known whether his lawsuit included Mather or any other journals.
6. Other members were Captain Matthew Calbraith Perry, then commander of the *Fulton,* the navy's first steamboat; C. O. Handy; M. G. Delaney; Lieutenant W. L. Hudson; Professor E. C. Ward; and Passed Midshipman R. J. Moeller.
7. Abert to Poinsett, 31 December 1837, TB, Letters Sent, 2:441–42.
8. Eyles, "Featherstonhaugh," p. 390; Murchison to GWF, 4 January, 21 March 1838, Add. 7652/II, KK19 and 23, CU.
9. GWF to James Garland, 23 March 1838, FFP 8:225–32; Clay to GWF, 2 June 1838, University of Kentucky Libraries.
10. GWF to Lord Aberdeen, 12 March 1844, Add. 43240, BL; Dearborn, "The Dearborn Journals," p. 171.
11. GWF to Abert, 16 September 1838, MHS.
12. See Steinmeyer, *Staten Island;* and pamphlet by the New Brighton Association, published in 1836, NYHS. GWF Journals (FFP 10), unless otherwise

indicated, are the source of information for his activities from August 1838 through November 1839.

13. GWF to Abert, 16 September 1838, MHS.
14. Ibid.; *National Intelligencer,* 7 September 1838.
15. GWF to Fox, 14 September 1838, Bod.
16. GWF to Abert, 16 September 1838, MHS.
17. Dearborn, "Journals," p. 170.
18. See Cooper, *Radical Jack; Macmillan Dictionary of Canadian Biography;* GWF to Fox, 22 January 1839, Bod; Dearborn, "Journals," p. 171.
19. GWF to Fox, 2 October 1838, Bod.
20. Dearborn, "Journals," pp. 170, 175–78.
21. GWF to Fox, 9 January 1839, Bod; Clay to GWF, 10 February 1839, Henry Clay Collection, University of Virginia Library.
22. GWF Journal, 5 December 1838, FFP 10:36; GWF to Abert, 12 December 1838, MHS.
23. GWF to Fox, 9, 22 January, 2 May 1839, all Bod.
24. "United States Boundary Question," p. 505. Also see Bemis, *A Diplomatic History of the United States,* pp. 253–59.
25. Sparks, "The Treaty of Washington," pp. 453–54.
26. "United States Boundary Question," p. 506.
27. Cooper, *Radical Jack,* pp. 291, 289.
28. GWF to Fox, 17 April 1839, Bod.
29. Ibid.; Buckland to GWF, [?] April 1839, Add. 7652/II, LL34, CU.
30. GWF Journal, 9 April 1838, FFP 9:60; GWF to Fox, 17 April 1839, Bod.
31. Ibid.
32. GWF Journal, 23 April 1839, FFP 10:65–66. Featherston was familiar with fossil plants in coal and had promised to send some to Mantell when he was last in England. See also his commentary on Brongniart and the origin of coal, GWF, *Excursion,* p. 163n.
33. Daniels, *American Science,* pp. 159–60.
34. GWF to Fox, 2 May 1839, Bod.
35. Ibid., 9, 2 May 1839.
36. Ibid., 2 May 1839.
37. Ibid., 9, 15 May 1839.
38. Backhouse to Lord Palmerston, 3 May 1839, Palmerston to Backhouse, 9 May 1839, FO 97/15, pp. 24–27, 33–34.
39. Ibid.; GWF to Backhouse, 11 May 1839, Minute of Mudge's and GWF's interview with Palmerston, FO 97/15, pp. 39–40, 49–50; GWF to Fox, 18 June 1839, Bod.
40. Lyell to GWF, 14 May 1839, Add. 7652/II, OO3, CU.
41. GWF to Vaughan, 30, and 24 May 1839, ASC.
42. *DNB.*
43. Backhouse to Palmerston, 8 June 1839, Memorandum, 10 June 1839, FO 97/15, pp. 43, 44–46; GWF to Fox, 23 June 1839, Bod.
44. Minute of Mudge's and Featherston's interview with Palmerston, FO 97/15, pp. 49–50; GWF to Fox, 18 June 1839, Bod.
45. GWF to Fox, 23 June 1839, Bod; GWF to Backhouse, 25 June 1839, FO 97/15, p. 71.

46. GWF to Backhouse, 3 July 1839, FO 97/15, pp. 72–73; GWF to Fox, 23 August 1839, Bod.

11. The Boundary Reconnaissance and Its Aftermath

1. GWF to Fox, 28 July 1839, Bod. As noted in Chapter 10, unless otherwise specified, the source of information for GWF's activities is his 1839 journal, FFP 10–11.
2. GWF to Fox, 28 July 1839, Bod; biographical sketches, Writers' Section Files, 3 December 1940, State Historical Society of Wisconsin.
3. GWF and Mudge to Palmerston, 14 August 1839, FO 6/13, pp. 533–42; GWF to Fox, 23 August 1839, Bod. Later, while at St. John, GWF met the editor, who apologized and promised to publish a retraction.
4. GWF and Mudge, Dispatch #1, to Palmerston, 14 August 1839, FO 6/13, pp. 533–42.
5. GWF and Mudge, Dispatch #2, to Palmerston, 15 August 1839, GWF to Palmerston, 17 August 1839, FO 6/13, pp. 545–49, 557–64.
6. GWF to Palmerston, 17 August 1839, FO 6/13, pp. 557–64.
7. GWF to Fox, 23 August 1839, Bod.
8. Boundary Commission Accounts, GWF Journal, FFP 12:237–44.
9. GWF to Harvey, 2 September 1839, FO 6/13, pp. 924–26; GWF to Fox, 3 September 1839, Bod.
10. Fairfield to Harvey, 25 August 1839, FO 6/13, p. 923; GWF to Fox, 3 September 1839, Bod; McLaughlin to Harvey, 21 August 1839, FO 6/13, pp. 920–21.
11. GWF to Harvey, 2 September 1839, FO 6/13, pp. 924–26.
12. GWF to Fox, 4 September 1839, Bod; GWF and Mudge, Dispatch #3, to Palmerston, 4 September 1839, FO 6/13, pp. 573–77.
13. Captain Parrott to McLaughlin, 9 September 1839, FO 6/13, p. 928; GWF to Fox, 24 October 1839, Bod; GWF to Harvey, 10 September 1839, Strangeways to James Stephens, 17 September 1839, Palmerston to Fox, 14 October 1839, FO 6/13, pp. 928, 517–19, 587–89.
14. GWF to Fox, 28 September 1839, Bod.
15. GWF to Fox, 22 October 1839, Bod.
16. Ibid.
17. GWF to Fox, 24 October 1839, Bod.
18. Dispatch #4, FO 6/13, pp. 613–19; GWF to Fox, 22 October, 13 November 1839, both Bod.
19. GWF to Fox, 24 October 1839, Bod.
20. GWF to Fox, 13 November 1839, Bod. Later, when GWF talked to some members of the Maine commission of 1838, he understood the discrepancy between his report of the northwest angle and their claims. The Maine commission had never actually gone there, since the weather was too severe and their provisions had given out.
21. Harvey to Thomson, 6 November 1839, FO 6/13, pp. 661–73.
22. GWF to Backhouse, 17 December, 20 November 1839, FO 97/15, pp. 142–54, 130–35.
23. GWF to Harvey, 12 December 1839, FO 6/13, pp. 966–67; GWF to Back-

house, 13 December 1839, FO 97/15, pp. 140–41.

24. GWF to Harvey, 7 December 1839, FO 6/13, p. 963; GWF to Fox, 8 December 1839, Bod.

25. GWF to Fox, 17, 28 December 1839, Bod; GWF to Backhouse, 14 January 1840, FO 97/15, pp. 158–60.

26. GWF to Palmerston, 1, 26 February 1840, FO 97/15, pp. 168–70, 188–89; GWF to Palmerston, 16 April 1840, CO 6/14, pp. 9–29. There is a manuscript "General Map of the Disputed Territory, Showing Line Surveyed by Featherstonhaugh and Mudge," in the National Archives (Records Relating to the U.S. Claims against the Central Powers, part of Record Group 76—Records of Boundary and Claim Commissions and Arbitrations, # 1–2.)

27. GWF to Vaughan, 9 June 1840, ASC; Backhouse to Palmerston, 17 May 1840, FO 97/15, pp. 200–203; Palmerston to Fox, 3 June 1840, CO 6/14, pp. 325–30; (London) *Times,* 11 August 1840, p. 5; Palmerston to Backhouse, 19 April 1840, FÖ 97/15, pp. 190–91.

28. GWF to Palmerston, 27 April 1840, FO 97/15, pp. 194–99.

29. GWF to Fox, 15 May, 14 April 1840, Bod.

30. Murchison to GWF, 15–18 April 1840, Add. 7652/II, KK27, CU.

31. Backhouse to Mudge, 26 May 1840, FO 97/15, pp. 212–14; Palmerston to Broughton and James Featherstonhaugh, 1 June 1840, CO 6/14, pp. 265–66; GWF Memorandums re expedition, 7, 8 June 1840, FO 97/15, pp. 237–40, 276–77.

32. GWF to Clay, 3 June 1840, FFP 8:253–55; GWF to Vaughan, 9 June 1840, ASC.

33. GWF to Backhouse, 6 June 1840, FO 97/15, pp. 274–75; GWF to Fox, 3 June 1840, Bod; GWF to Vaughan, 9 June 1840, ASC; GWF to Fox, 2 December 1840, Bod; GWF to Vaughan, 9 June 1840, ASC; GWF to Fox, 2 December 1840, Bod.

34. GWF to Fox, 30 July 1840, Bod; GWF to Palmerston, 21 June 1840, FO 97/15, pp. 280–82; Buckland to GWF, 21 June 1840, Add. 7652/II, LL35, CU; GWF to Fox, 9 September 1840, Bod.

35. GWF to Palmerston, 18 July 1840, FO 97/15, pp. 280–92; GWF to Fox, 30 July 1840, Bod.

36. GWF to Fox, 9 September 1840, Bod.

37. "The Boundary Question."

38. GWF to Backhouse, 12 September 1840, FO 97/15, pp. 297–98; GWF to Fox, 2 December 1840, Bod.

39. GWF to Fox, 2 December 1840, GWF to Fox, 3 January 1841, Bod.

40. GWF to Backhouse, 20 November 1840, FO 97/15, pp. 307–10; GWF to Fox, 5 November 1840, Bod.

41. GWF to Backhouse, 23 December 1840, FO 97/15, pp. 323–32.

42. Renwick was of Scottish descent, born in Liverpool. GWF to Fox, 3 January 1841, Bod; GWF to Backhouse, 23 December 1840, FO 97/15, pp. 323–32.

43. Backhouse to GWF, 21 December 1840, FO 97/15, p. 319; GWF to Fox, 3 January 1841, Bod; GWF to Backhouse, 21 December 1840, FO 97/15, pp. 321–22.

44. GWF to Palmerston, 14 December 1840, GWF to Lord Aberdeen, 3 September 1841, FO 97/15, pp. 313–16, 425–27.

45. GWF to Palmerston, 14 December 1840, 8 March 1841, GWF to Backhouse, 13 March 1841, Backhouse to GWF, 20 July 1841, FO 97/15, pp. 313–16, 345–48, 349–52, 421. A Mr. Scott was appointed at two hundred pounds a year.
46. GWF to Palmerston, 10 May 1841, GWF to Backhouse, 19 March 1841, FO 97/15, pp. 418–19, 356–59.
47. GWF to Fox, 3 February 1841, Bod.
48. Fox to Palmerston, 8 August 1841, CO 6/19, pp. 148–51; Fox to Lord Sydenham, 1 September 1841, CO 6/19, pp. 261–66.
49. GWF to Aberdeen, 3 September 1841, FO 97/15, pp. 425–27; Viscount Canning to James Stephens, 15 December 1841, CO 6/19, pp. 371–72.
50. Lyell to GWF, 15 July 1841, Add. 7652/II, OO4, CU.

12. The Webster-Ashburton Treaty

1. GWF had met Ashburton at Quebec in 1838. GWF to Fox, 17 September 1842, Bod; Mills, "The Ashburton Treaty," p. 690. Also see Miller, ed., *Treaties and Other International Acts of the United States,* 4:383–403.
2. GWF to Aberdeen, 19 May 1842, Add. 43239, BL.
3. GWF to Fox, 17 September 1842, Bod. See Bemis, *A Diplomatic History,* pp. 261–66. The treaty signing was endangered by the slavery question (Carman and Syrett, *A History of the American People,* 1:391).
4. GWF to Fox, 17 September 1842, Bod; GWF to Backhouse, 13 February 1843, Duke University.
5. (London) *Times,* 10 October 1842, p. 5; GWF to Aberdeen, 12 March 1844, Add. 43240, BL.
6. GWF to Aberdeen, 13, 26 January 1843, Add. 43240, BL.
7. GWF to Fox, 17 September 1842, Bod; Addington to Mudge, 28 November 1842, Mudge to Addington, 30 November 1842, GWF to Addington, 5 December 1842, FO 97/15, pp. 431–33, 453–54, 455–56.
8. Addington to GWF, 7 December 1842, ibid., pp. 457–58.
9. Aberdeen to GWF, 10 December 1842, GWF to Aberdeen, 12 December 1842, Add. 43240, BL.
10. Estcourt's orders to Capt. Robinson, Lt. Pipon, and James Featherstonhaugh, 25 May 1843, FFP 8:276–78.
11. GWF to Fox, 3 February 1843, Bod; Croker, "Treaty of Washington."
12. Croker, "Treaty," pp. 579, 580.
13. GWF to Backhouse, 13 February 1843, Duke University; Sparks, "The Treaty of Washington," p. 471.
14. *Morning Chronicle,* 6 February 1843.
15. Croker, "Treaty," pp. 581–82.
16. Webster to Everett, 25 April 1843, quoted in Curtis, *Life of Daniel Webster,* 2:171.
17. Consul Buchanan to Palmerston, 6 April 1838, FO 5, vol. 325; A. Panizzi to Palmerston, 29 March 1839, FO 5, p. 340; Miller, ed., *Treaties,* 3:342–45. Also see Berkeley and Berkeley, *Dr. John Mitchell,* pp. 263–67.
18. Jones, *To the Webster-Ashburton Treaty,* p. 108; GWF to Murray, 20 April 1846, Murray Archives; GWF to Backhouse, 13 February 1843, Duke University.

19. GWF to Aberdeen, 22 March 1843, Add. 43240, BL; GWF to Backhouse, 27 November 1843, Duke University; GWF to Aberdeen, Add. 43240, BL.

20. GWF to Backhouse, 22 November 1843, Duke University; Murchison to GWF, 24, 28 January 1844, Add. 7652/II, KK34, CU.

21. GWF to Murray, 3 February 1844, Murray Archives.

22. GWF to Murray, 5 March, 25 April 1844, ibid.

23. Ibid.; GWF to Owen, 4 May 1844, Owen to GWF, 4 May 1844, Add. 7652/II, JJ11 and 10, CU; GWF to Owen, 16 April 1844, British Museum (Natural History).

24. GWF to Backhouse, 23 May 1844, Duke University; Owen to GWF, 23 May, 3 August 1844, Buckland to GWF, 31 May 1844, Add. 7652/II, JJ9 and 8, LL40, CU.

25. GWF to Murray, 22 June 1844, Murray Archives; advertisement for GWF, *Excursion,* in *Edinburgh Review* 80 (July 1844): 5, quoting the *Morning Chronicle* and the *New Monthly Magazine;* GWF to Murray, 23 February 1846, Murray Archives.

26. Review of GWF, *Excursion, Foreign Quarterly Review,* American edition, 34 (October 1844): 70.

27. *New York Evening Post,* 21 June 1844.

28. GWF Journal, 30 September 1844, FFP 8:279–84.

29. Roberts, *Old Schenectady,* p. 200; James to GWF, 27 January 1844, GWF to James, 31 January 1845, GWF, Jr., to James, 3 October 1844, FFP 8:297–99, 323–26, 314.

30. GWF to Aberdeen, 12 March 1844, Add. 43240, BL.

31. GWF to Murray, 22 June 1844, Murray Archives.

13. The Life of a Diplomat

1. Aberdeen to GWF, 9 October 1844, GWF to Aberdeen, 12 October 1844, both Add. 43240, BL.

2. GWF to Aberdeen, 29 August 1845, FO 27/732; GWF, 21 February 1849, answering queries re *Expenses of British Consular Establishments,* FO 27/851; GWF to Aberdeen, 10 July 1849, FO 27/732.

3. Sedgwick to GWF, 12 November 1844, Add. 7652/II, A4, CU; GWF to Sedgwick, 16 November 1844, Add. 7652/II, IE105, CU; Sherwood, "Genesis, Evolution, and Geology before Darwin,'" p. 310; Daniels, *American Science,* pp. 57–59.

4. GWF to Sedgwick, 16 November 1844, Add. 7652/II, IE105, CU; Sedgwick to GWF, 24 November 1844, Add. 7652/II, A5, CU.

5. GWF to James, 31 January 1845, FFP 8:323–26; GWF to Vaughan, 29 January, 8 February 1846, ASC; GWF Journal, 20 May 1815, FFP 4.

6. Bourdin, ed., *Voyage de Paris,* pp. 124–26; Weed, *Letters from Europe,* pp. 259–61.

7. GWF, 21 February 1849, answering queries, FO 27/851; GWF to James, 31 January 1845, FFP 8:323–26; GWF to Aberdeen, 24 February 1845, FO 27/732.

8. Lyell to GWF, 26 February 1845, Add. 7652/II, OO7, CU; Lyell, *Travels in North America,* 2:241.

9. GWF to Aberdeen, 28 March 1845, FO 27/732; Mrs. Murchison to GWF, 29 May 1845, Murchison to GWF, 17 April 1845, Add. 7652/II, KK37 and 38, CU.

10. Mrs. Murchison to GWF, 15 July 1845, Add. 7652/II, KK40, CU.

11. Ibid., 29 May, 1, 15 July 1845, KK38 and 39.

12. Buckland to GWF, 6 and 11 September 1845, Add. 7652/II, LL42 and 43, CU; Owen to GWF, 19 December 1845, Mrs. Murchison to GWF, 14 September 1845, Add. 7652/II, JJ7, KK43, CU.

13. GWF to Aberdeen, 10 July 1845, Aberdeen to GWF, 30 September 1845, FO 27/732.

14. Buckland to GWF, 14 October 1845, Add. 7652/II, LL46, CU.

15. Murchison to GWF, 26 November 1845, Add. 7652/II, KK47, CU.

16. GWF to Vaughan, 4 December 1845, ASC.

17. Ibid. Featherston's son Albany, who became a colonel in the Royal Engineers, served on the Boundary Commission of 1872–1876, which settled the marine portions of the boundary. See his *Narrative of Operations of the Boundary Commission.*

18. Buckland to GWF, 11 November 1845, Owen to GWF, 19 December 1845, Add. 7652/II, LL47 and JJ7, CU.

19. GWF to Aberdeen, 29 December 1845, Add. 43240, BL. See GWF to Vaughan, 29 January 1846, ASC.

20. GWF related the incident in the letter to Aberdeen, 29 December 1845, Add. 43240, BL.

21. Murchison to GWF, 27 and [?] December 1845, 12 January 1846, Add. 7652/II, KK53, 49, and 50, CU; Geikie, *Murchison,* 2:11–12.

22. GWF to Murray, 23 February 1846, Murray Archives.

23. GWF to Murray, 23 February, 20 April, 30 March 1846, ibid.

24. GWF to Murray, 22 April, 2 May 1846, ibid.

25. GWF to Murray, 25 May 1846, ibid.

26. Verneuil to GWF, 14 April, and 20 November 1846, Add. 7652/II, OO8 and 9, CU.

27. GWF to Palmerston, 20 July 1846, FO 27/759.

28. Murchison to GWF, 27 July 1846, Lady Murchison to GWF, 22 July 1846, Add. 7652/II, KK57 and 58, CU; GWF to Palmerston, 3 August 1846, FO 27/759; Lady Murchison to GWF, 7 August 1846, Murchison to GWF, 18 August 1846, Add. 7652/II, KK60 and 61, CU.

29. Memorandum of an Agreement between Richard Bentley and GWF, 26 September 1846, Bentley Papers, 46,614, vol. 55, f. 336, BL; Bentley's report of orders, Bentley Papers 46,670, vol. 111, ff. 163–64, BL. As this is written (1985) a first edition of the *Canoe Voyage* is being offered for sale at £325 by Remington (Barnet, Hertfordshire) Cat. 9 (1984).

30. Review of GWF, *A Canoe Voyage, Spectator,* 6 January 1847, pp. 62–63.

31. Reprint from *Westminster Review* in the *Daguerrotype* (Boston) 1:36, 38. Cries of outrage over the *Excursion* would linger in the United States for generations. It was finally reprinted in 1968 by the Negro Universities Press and *A Canoe Voyage* in 1970 by the Minnesota Historical Society. Archives of British publishers on microfilm, compiled by Allison Ingram, Cambridge, 1981, 2d ser., frame 185.

32. Mudge to GWF, 2 January 1847, Add. 7652/II, KK66, CU.
33. Verneuil to GWF, 20 November 1846, Add. 7652/II, OO9, CU; Wilson, *Lyell*, p. 77.
34. Murchison to GWF, 15 January 1847, Add. 7652/II, KK68, CU.
35. GWF to marquis of Normanby, 17 May, 24 September 1847, FO 146/325; Buckland to GWF, 15, 19 October 1847, Add. 7652/II, LL50 and 51a, CU; will at Borthwick Institute; FO to GWF, 5 February 1848, FO 27/818; GWF to Normanby, 26 March 1848, FO 146/350.
36. Buckland to GWF, 15 October 1847, Add. 7652/II, LL50, CU; Estcourt to James, 19 September 1846, Spencer Ponsonby, FO, to James, 26 April 1847, FFP 8:340–42, 353.

14. Revolution and Its Aftermath

1. Addington to GWF, 7 January 1848, GWF to FO, 12 January, 28 January 1848, FO to GWF, 5 February 1848, all FO 27/818; GWF to FO, 3 May 1847, Hutton to GWF, 1 May 1847, GWF to FO, 5 June 1847, all FO 27/785.
2. GWF to FO, 25, 26 February, 1 March 1848, FO 27/818; GWF to Croker, 9 May 1850, UM.
3. GWF to FO, 25, 26 February 1848, FO 27/818.
4. GWF to Buckland, 8 March 1848, Royal Society of London Archives; GWF to FO, 26–29 February 1848, FO 27/818.
5. Palmerston to GWF, "Confidential," 27 February 1848, GWF to FO, 29 February 1848, GWF to Palmerston, 4 March 1848, all FO 27/818; GWF to Croker, 9 May 1850, UM.
6. Palmerston to GWF, 27 February 1848, FO 27/818. GWF to Normanby, 29 February 1848, FO 146/350. GWF, of course, already had made arrangements with Captain Paul.
7. GWF to Palmerston, 3 March 1848, sent by Palmerston to Queen Victoria, in Victoria, *Letters*, 2:184–88; Croker, "Escape of Louis Philippe," pp. 576–78; d'Houdetot. "Eight Days of a Royal Exile," pp. 323–28.
8. GWF to Palmerston, 3 March 1848, Victoria, *Letters*, 2:184; GWF to Croker, 10, 12, 24 June 1850, UM.
9. GWF to FO, 3 March 1848, enclosing Jones's account, FO 27/818; GWF to Palmerston, 3 March 1848, Victoria, *Letters*, 2:185.
10. GWF to Palmerston, 3 March 1848, Victoria, *Letters*, 2:185–86; GWF to Croker, 12 June 1850, UM.
11. GWF to Croker, 24 June 1850, UM.
12. Jones's account in GWF to Palmerston, 3 March 1848, FO 27/818.
13. Ibid.; Croker, "Escape," p. 578; GWF to Palmerston, 3 March 1848, Victoria, *Letters*, 2:186–87.
14. GWF to Croker, 24 June 1850, UM; Croker, "Escape," pp. 578–79.
15. Croker, "Escape," p. 579; GWF to Croker, 24 June 1850, UM; GWF to Palmerston, 3 March 1848, Victoria, *Letters*, 2:188.
16. GWF to Croker, 12, 24 June 1850, UM.
17. GWF to Palmerston, enclosing Jones's report, 3 March 1848, FO 27/818; Palmerston to Victoria, 5 March 1848, Victoria, *Letters*, 2:193.

18. FO to GWF, 14 March 1848, FO 27/818. The snuff box is still in the possession of his American descendants.
19. GWF to Normanby, 4, 10 March 1848, FO 146/350; GWF to FO, 20 March 1848, FO 27/818; GWF to Normanby, 21, 22 March 1848, FO 146/350; FO to GWF, 22 March, 20 March 1848, GWF to FO, 25 March 1848, all FO 27/818.
20. GWF to Normanby, 26 March, 10 April 1848, FO 146/350; GWF to FO, 12 April 1848, GWF to Palmerston, 24 May 1848, both FO 27/818.
21. FO to GWF, 22 September 1848, FO 27/818; GWF to Normanby, 29, 30 September, 3, 7 October, Normanby to GWF, 30 September, 2, 6 October 1848, all FO 146/350.
22. GWF to Normanby, 29 September, 3, 7 October 1848, FO 146/350; GWF to Palmerston, 2 October 1848, FO 27/818; Normanby to GWF, 6 October 1848, FO 146/350.
23. GWF to Normanby, 19 October 1848, Normanby to GWF, 22 October 1848, FO 146/350.
24. FO to GWF, 3 July 1849, FO 27/851; Murchison to GWF, 14 August 1849, Add. 7652/II, KK69, CU; *Times,* 11 August 1849, p. 4, col. 2; Catlin to GWF, 14 September 1849, FFP 8:371–72.
25. Sedgwick to GWF, 6 February 1850, Add. 7652/III, A6, CU.
26. GWF to Palmerston, 29 April 1850, Addington to GWF, 7 May 1850, GWF to Addington, 20 May 1850, all FO 27/878.
27. Croker, "Escape," 578n.
28. GWF to Croker, 9 May, 10, 12, 24 June 1850, all UM; d'Houdetot, "Eight Days of a Royal Exile," pp. 320–32.
29. GWF to Croker, 3 October 1850, UM.

15. The Late Years at Havre

1. GWF to Granville, 5 February, 8 March 1852, FO 27/941.
2. GWF to Addington, 10 July 1853, FO 27/981.
3. Addington to GWF, 29 October 1853, GWF to Addington, 5 November 1853, FO to GWF, 14 July 1853, all FO 27/981.
4. GWF to earl of Clarendon, 17 April 1854, FO 146/548; GWF to earl of Cowley, 3 March 1855, FO 146/606.
5. GWF to Clarendon, 17 April 1854, FO 146/548; GWF to Thomas Staveley, 27 April 1854, FO 146/548; GWF to Staveley, 17 April 1854, FO 27/1031; GWF to Cowley, 6 May 1854, FO 146/548; GWF to Clarendon, 30 December 1854, FO 27/1031; GWF to Cowley, 25 February 1855, FO 146/606.
6. GWF to Clarendon, 30 December 1854, FO 27/1031; GWF to Staveley, 15 January 1855, FO 27/1084.
7. Clarendon to GWF, 19 January 1855, Staveley to GWF, 24 January 1855, GWF to Clarendon, 26 February 1855, all FO 27/1084; GWF to Cowley, 12 May 1855, FO 146/606.
8. GWF to Cowley, 13, 19 March 1855, FO 146/606; Wodehouse to GWF, 26 March 1855, FO 27/1084; Cowley to GWF, 13, 24 April 1855, GWF to Cowley, 12 May 1855, all FO 146/606; Wodehouse to GWF, 17 July 1855, FO 27/1084.

9. GWF to James, 28 October 1856, FFP 8:419–23; Murchison to GWF, 10 September 1858, 11 February 1859, Add. 7652/II, KK80 and 82, CU; Georgiana Featherstonhaugh to George Featherstonhaugh (James's son), 4 February 1901, Albany Institute of History and Art.

10. Roberts, *Old Schenectady,* p. 200; James to GWF, 16 January 1854, GWF to James, 28 October 1856, FFP 8:384, 419–23. GWF's assignment to James of all interest in New York lands, 12 June 1857, NYHS.

11. Joseph Fetherstonhaugh to GWF, 19, 27 July, 9 September, 3 November 1854, FFP 8:394–415.

12. Owen to GWF, 22 June, 7 July 1857, Add. 7652/II, JJ6 and 5, CU.

13. GWF to Cowley, 24 February 1857, FO 146/746; FO to GWF, 19 January 1855, FO 27/1505.

14. GWF to Cowley, 15 January 1855, FO 146/606; FO to GWF, 3 October 1857, GWF to FO, 10 November 1857, both FO 27/1209.

15. Murchison to GWF, 10, 27 August 1861, Add. 7652/II, KK86 and 85, CU.

16. GWF to Murchison, 20 September 1861, GSL.

17. GWF to Owen, 24 April 1865, British Museum (Natural History); Owen to GWF, 23 March, 5 April 1865, Add. 7652/II, JJ2 and 3, CU.

18. GWF to Owen, 24 April 1865, British Museum (Natural History); Owen to GWF, 28 April 1865, Add. 7652/II, JJ1, CU; GWF to Owen, 30 April 1865, British Museum (Natural History).

19. We had considerable difficulty in locating a copy of this work, since it was anonymous and the subject unknown. Having examined the only four anonymous publications by Chapman and Hall for 1865 at the British Library, we were convinced beyond question of Featherston's authorship of *Langleyhaugh.*

20. Holograph Will, 9 May 1866, Somerset House, London.

21. Rhodes to FO, "private," 28 September 1866, FO 27/1631; J. D. Featherstonhaugh, "Memoir," p. 223.

22. *Times,* 4 October 1866, p. 10, col. 5; *Gentleman's Magazine* 220 (November 1866): 700; *Proceedings of the Royal Society of London* 14 (1866–67): 269; *Proceedings of the American Philosophical Society* 10 (1867): 308; *Geological Magazine* 30 (December 1866): 528; *Journal of the Geological Society of London* 23 (1867): xliii–xlv.

23. Charlotte died at Tunbridge Wells and was buried there 15 September 1879, as were her sons, Henry (April 1881) and Albany (1902). The vault there was originally inscribed: "To the cherished memory of our father George William Featherstonhaugh, F.R.S., Her Majesty's Boundary Commissioner for the Ashburton Treaty, and afterwards, until his death, H.M.'s Consul at Havre. He died September 27th at his post, where he now lies buried." An addition to the inscription was made as follows: "His remains were removed from France and deposited below on April 11th 1889." Georgiana outlived all her family. If she, too, was buried at Tunbridge Wells, nothing so indicates.

Bibliography

Manuscript Collections

Albany, New York

The Albany Institute of History and Art. Featherstonhaugh Family Papers (filmed by the Minnesota Historical Society)
The New York State Library

Ann Arbor, Michigan

William L. Clements Library, University of Michigan, Miscellaneous Collection

Boston, Massachusetts

Massachusetts Historical Society, Bancroft, Everett, Pickering, and Sedgwick Papers

Cambridge, England

University Library, Sedgwick Collection

Cardiff, Wales

National Museum of Wales

Charlottesville, Virginia

Manuscript Department, University of Virginia Library, Virginia Geological Survey Collection, #3073

343

Chicago, Illinois

Chicago Historical Society, Gunther Collection

Durham, North Carolina

William R. Perkins Library, Duke University, Backhouse Papers

Haverford, Pennsylvania

Haverford College Library, Quaker Collection

Lexington, Kentucky

University of Kentucky Libraries, the Papers of Henry Clay

London, England

Archives of John Murray (Publishers) Ltd.
British Library, Lord Aberdeen Papers
British Museum (Natural History)
Geological Society of London
Public Record Office, London and Kew
Royal Society of London

Louisville, Kentucky

The Filson Club

Nashville, Tennessee

Tennessee State Library/Archives, Rhea Papers, from Texas Historical Society

New Haven, Connecticut

Yale University Library, Silliman Family Papers

New York, New York

Columbia University Libraries, Fish Family Papers
New-York Historical Society
New York Public Library, Miscellaneous Papers

Oxford, England

Codrington Library, All Souls College, Sir Charles Vaughan Papers
Bodleian Library, MS Eng. lett. c. 234

Philadelphia, Pennsylvania

Academy of Natural Sciences of Philadelphia

American Philosophical Society
College of Physicians of Philadelphia
Historical Society of Pennsylvania

St. Louis, Missouri

Missouri Historical Society

Washington, D.C.

Library of Congress, Madison Papers
National Archives, Topographical Bureau

Wellington, New Zealand

Alexander Turnbull Library

Yorkshire, England

Borthwick Institute, University of York
Yorkshire Records, North Allerton

Published Sources

Ackerman, Gertrude W. "Joseph Renville of Lac Qui Parle." *Minnesota History* 12 (September 1931): 231–46.
Adams, Alexander B. *John James Audubon.* New York, 1966.
Adams, Frank Dawson. *The Birth and Development of the Geological Sciences.* Baltimore, 1938.
Ainsworth, William. *The Scarborough Guide.* York, 1806.
Alexander, E. P. *A Revolutionary Conservative, James Duane of New York.* New York, 1938.
American Philosophical Society. "Old Minutes of the Society from 1743 to 1838." *Proceedings of the American Philosophical Society* 22 (July 1885), pt. 3, no. 119.
Armytage, W. H. G. "G. W. Featherstonhaugh, 1780–1866, Anglo-American Scientist." Royal Society of London, *Notes and Records* 11 (March 1955): 228–35.
Aspinwall, A., ed. *The Correspondence of George, Prince of Wales 1770–1812.* Vol. 7. London, 1965.
Audubon, John James. *Letters of John James Audubon, 1826–1840.* Ed. Howard Corning. Boston, 1969.
Audubon, Maria R. *Audubon and His Journals.* Notes by Elliott Coues. 2 vols. New York, 1960.
Bailey, Thomas A. *A Diplomatic History of the American People.* New York, 1969.
Barnard, Daniel D. *A Discourse on the Life, Services and Character of Stephen Van Rensselaer.* Albany, 1939.
Bemis, Samuel F. *A Diplomatic History of the United States.* New York, 1947.

————, ed. *The American Secretaries of State and Their Diplomacy.* Vol. 4. New York, 1928.

Berkeley, Edmund, and Dorothy Smith Berkeley. *Dr. John Mitchell: The Man Who Made the Map of North America.* Chapel Hill, 1974.

Bliss, John H. "Reminiscences of Fort Snelling." *Minnesota Historical Society Collections* 6 (1894): 336–53.

"The Boundary Question." *Blackwood's Magazine* 4 (September 1840): 331–37.

Bourdin, Ernest, ed. *Voyage de Paris a la Mer par Rouen et le Havre.* Paris, 1845.

Bray, Edward C., and Martha Coleman Bray, eds. and trans. *Joseph Nicollet on the Plains and Prairies.* St. Paul, 1976.

Bray, Martha Coleman. "Southern Influences on the Career of Joseph Nicollet." In *Geological Sciences in the Antebellum South,* ed. Corgan, pp. 105–18.

Brush, George J. *A Sketch of the Progress of American Mineralogy.* Montreal, 1882.

Bryant, William Cullen. *Orations and Addresses.* New York, 1873.

Bush, R. *Scarborough Castle.* London, 1981.

Buxton History Notes. Pamphlet published by Osborne Publicity Services, Buxton, n.d.

Carman, Harry J., and Harold C. Syrett. *A History of the American People.* Vol. 1. New York, 1955.

Carter, Bernard Moore. *The Dying Bard: A Poem for My Album.* London, 1829.

————. *A Medley: A Poem.* London, 1823.

————. *Miscellaneous Poems.* Philadelphia, 1820.

————. *Poems.* London, 1824.

————. *A Poem to William E. West, Esq., of the United States, on his Portraits of Lord Byron and of Mrs. M. A. Patterson of Maryland.* Paris, 1825.

Clay, Henry. *The Papers of Henry Clay.* Ed. James F. Hopkins, Mary W. M. Hargreaves, Robert Seagar II. Lexington, Ky., 1972–.

————. *The Works of Henry Clay.* Ed. Calvin Colton. 10 vols. New York, 1904.

Cockerell, T. D. A. "Dru Drury, an Eighteenth Century Entomologist." *Scientific Monthly* 14 (January 1922): 67–82.

Cooper, Leonard. *Radical Jack.* London, 1959.

Corgan, James X., ed. *The Geological Sciences in the Antebellum South.* University, Ala., 1982.

Croker, John Wilson. "Escape of Louis Philippe." (London) *Quarterly Review* 86 (March 1850): 526–85.

————. "Treaty of Washington." (London) *Quarterly Review* 71 (March 1843): 560–95.

Curtis, G. T. *Life of Daniel Webster.* 2 vols. New York, 1872.

Daniels, George H. *American Science in the Age of Jackson.* New York, 1968.

Dearborn, Henry A. S. "The Dearborn Journals." Ed. Frank H. Severance. *Publications of the Buffalo Historical Society* 7 (1904): 169–79.

D'Houdetot, Adolphe. "Eight Days of a Royal Exile." Trans. Leon Besson. *Bentley's Miscellaney* 28 (1850): 320–32.

Eyles, Joan M. "G. W. Featherstonhaugh (1780–1866), F.R.S., F.G.S., Geologist and Traveler." *Journal of the Society for the Bibliography of Natural History* 8, no. 4 (1978): 381–95.

————. "William Smith, Sir Joseph Banks and the French Geologists." In *From Linnaeus to Darwin: Commentaries on the History of Biology and Geology,* pp. 37–50. Society for the History of Natural History. London, 1985.

Eyles, Victor A. "The Extent of Geological Knowledge in the Eighteenth Century." In *Toward a History of Geology,* ed. Schneer, pp. 159–80. Cambridge, Mass., 1969.

Featherstonhaugh, Albany. *Narrative of the Operations of the British–North American Boundary Commission, 1872–76.* Woolwich, 1876.

Featherstonhaugh, George William. "Account of the Travertine Deposited by the Waters of the Sweet Springs in Alleghany County, in the State of Virginia, and of an Ancient Travertine Discovered in the Adjacent Hills." *Transactions of the* (Pennsylvania) *Geological Society* 1 (1835): 328–34.

————. "Audubon's Biography of Birds." *North American Review* 34, no. 75 (April 1832): 364–405.

————. *A Canoe Voyage up the Minnay Sotor.* London, 1847. Reprinted by the Minnesota Historical Society. St. Paul, 1970.

————. *The Death of Ugolino.* Philadelphia, 1830.

————. "An Essay on the Principles and Practice of Rural Economy, with an Introductory Letter to the Hon. Stephen Van Rensselaer, President of the Board of Argiculture of the State of New-York." *Memoirs of the Board of Agriculture of the State of New-York.* Vol. 1:51–97. Albany, 1821. Reprinted in the *American Farmer* 5 (25 July 1823): 137–39 (29 August 1823): 177–79 (5 September 1823): 185–86.

————. *Excursion through the Slave States.* London, 1844. Reprinted New York, 1968.

————. *Geological Report of an Examination Made in 1834 of the Elevated Country between the Missouri and Red Rivers by G. W. Featherstonhaugh, U.S. Geologist. House Doc.,* 23d Cong. 2d Sess., vol. 4, no. 51. Washington, D.C., 1835. (Copy presented by author to the "University of Charlottesville, Va.")

[————]. "Geology." *American Quarterly Review* 6 (September 1829): 73–104.

[————]. "Geology." *American Quarterly Review* 7 (June 1830): 361–409.

[————]. "Gold Districts." *American Quarterly Review* 11 (March 1832): 66–102.

————. "G. W. Featherstonhaugh to Colonel J. J. Abert," Mrs. Dana O. Jensen, ed., *Missouri Historical Society Bulletin* 8 (April 1952): 271–92.

————. *Historical Sketch of the Negociations at Paris in 1782, from Inedited Documents; with remarks on Mr. Albert Gallatin's "Right of the United States of America to the North-eastern Boundary Claimed by Them."* London, 1842.

————. "Lampoon on the Baron." A few sheets printed privately in 1819, probably at Albany. Apparently it does not survive but has been confused with the later publication, "Baron Roorback's Tour," printed in 1839, which was mistakenly attributed to Featherstonhaugh.

[————]. *Langleyhaugh: A Tale of an Anglo-Saxon Family.* 2 vols. London, 1865.

————. "Mineral Resources of Virginia." (A letter to Madison dated 4 December 1833, published in the *United States Telegraph,* 23 December, and later in the *Richmond Inquirer* and *Farmers' Register* 1 (1834): 620–23.

————. *Monthly American Journal of Geology and Natural Science.* Edited by Featherston and containing many of his own contributions, vol. 1 (July 1831–June 1832). Reprinted by the Minnesota Historical Society with an introduction by George W. White. New York, 1969.

[————]. "The New York Canals." *North American Review* 14 (January 1822): 230–51.

————. "Observations on a Paper in the March Number of the *Port Folio,*

Touching the Peopling of the Continent of America." *Port Folio* (June 1815): 519–27.

———. *Observations upon the Treaty of Washington Signed August 9, 1842: With the Treaty annexed. Together with a map, to illustrate the Boundary Line as Established by the Treaty between Her Majesty's Colonies of New Brunswick and Canada and the United States of America.* And *Supplement to the Observations.* Both published in London, 1843.

———. *Official Refutation of a Libel.* Washington, D.C., 1837.

———. "On a Beloved Sister." *Port Folio* 6 (August 1816): 204–5.

———. "On the Ancient Drainage of North America and the Origin of the Cataract of Niagara." *Monthly American Journal of Geology and Natural Science* 1 (July 1831): 13–21. Abstract in *Geological Society of London Proceedings* 1 (1834): 91–93, under the title "On the Series of Rocks in the United States."

———. "On the Excavation of the Rocky Channels of Rivers by the Recession of Their Cataracts." *British Association Report*, pt. 2 (1844): 45–46. Reprinted in *Floriess Notizen* 33 (1845): col. 214–16.

———. "On the Series of Rocks in the United States," *Geological Society of London Proceedings* 1 (1834): 91–93.

[———]. "The Oregon Question." (London) *Quarterly Review* 77 (1846): 563–610.

———. "Refutation of Opinions Contained in Two Papers on the Irish Language, Preserved in the *Port Folio* for October and November 1814." *Port Folio* (April 1815): 333–49.

———. *Report of a Geological Reconnaissance in 1835, from Washington, by Way of Green Bay and the Wisconsin Territory, to the Coteau de Prairie.* Washington, 1836.

[———]. Review of *Geological Text Book*, by Amos Eaton. *North American Review* 32 (April 1831): 471–90.

———. "To the Editor of the *London Times*, 8 Jan. 1842." *Times*, 12 January 1842.

———. Portions of his writings reprinted in *Alabama in the 1830's as Recorded by British Travelers*, ed. Walter Brownlow Posey. Birmingham, 1938. Also in *Travels in the Old South*, ed. Thomas D. Clark. 3 vols. Norman, Okla., 1959.

———. trans. *The Betrothed Lovers (I Promessi Sposi)*, by Alessandro Manzoni. Washington, D.C., 1834.

———. trans. *The Republic*, by Cicero. New York, 1829.

Featherstonhaugh, George William, and Richard Zachariah Mudge. *Report of the British Commissioners Appointed to Survey the Territory in Dispute, between Great Britain and the United States of America, on the Northeastern Boundary of the United States.* London, 1840.

Featherstonhaugh, James Duane. "Memoir of Mr. G. W. Featherstonhaugh." *American Geologist* 3 (April 1889): 217–23.

Fitzpatrick, T. J. *Rafinesque: A Sketch of His Life, with Bibliography.* Revised and enlarged by Charles Boewe. Weston, Mass., 1984.

Ford, Alice. *John James Audubon.* Norman, Okla., 1964.

Forde, H. A. *Mary Anning—the Heroine of Lyme Regis.* A pamphlet, unbound and undated. British Library 010827.

Gallatin, Albert. *The Right of the United States of America to the North-eastern Boundary Claimed by Them.* New York, 1840.

Geikie, Archibald. *Life of Sir Roderick Murchison.* 2 vols. London, 1875.

————. *The Founders of Geology.* London, 1905.

Geisse, Harold L. "Featherstonhaugh and His Critics." *Wisconsin Magazine of History* (Spring 1962): 164–71.

George IV. *The Correspondence of George, Prince of Wales, 1770–1812.* 8 vols. Ed. A. Aspinwall. London, 1965.

Goetzman, William H. *Army Exploration in the American West, 1803–1863.* New Haven, 1959.

Gordon, William M. "Old Homes on Georgetown Heights." *Records of the Columbia Historical Society* 18 (1915): 70–191.

Gouverneur, Marian. *As I Remember.* New York, 1911.

Greene, John C. *American Science in the Age of Jefferson.* Ames, Iowa, 1984.

Greene, John C., and John G. Burke, *The Science of Minerals in the Age of Jefferson.* Philadelphia, 1978.

Greene, Mott T. *Geology in the Nineteenth Century.* Ithaca, 1982.

Harlow, Alvin F. *The Road of the Century.* New York, 1947.

Hazen, Robert M. *North American Geology: Early Writings.* Stroudsburg, Pa., 1979.

Hedrick, Ulysses Prentiss. *A History of Agriculture in the State of New York.* New York, 1933.

Hendrickson, Walter B. "The Western Academy of Natural Sciences of St. Louis." *Missouri Historical Society Bulletin* 16 (January 1960): 114–29.

Hinderwell, Thomas. *The History and Antiquities of Scarborough.* Scarborough, 1832.

Hunt, Harold Capper. *A Retired Habitation.* London, 1932.

H. W. C. "Featherstonhaugh in Tycoberah." *Wisconsin Magazine of History* (Spring 1962): 172–85.

Jackson, Gordon. *Hull in the Eighteenth Century.* New York, 1972.

Jones, Howard. *To the Webster-Ashburton Treaty.* Chapel Hill, 1977.

Kastner, Joseph. *A Species of Eternity.* New York, 1977.

Kent's London Directory for the Year 1780. London.

Lyell, Sir Charles. *Life, Letters and Journals of Sir Charles Lyell, Bart.* 2 vols. Ed. by his sister-in-law, Mrs. Lyell. London, 1881.

————. *Travels in North America.* London, 1845.

Malone, Dumas. *The Public Life of Thomas Cooper, 1783–1839.* New Haven, 1926.

Meisel, Max. *A Bibliography of American Natural History.* New York, 1924.

Merrill, George Perkins. *The First One Hundred Years of American Geology.* New Haven, 1924.

Miller, Hunter, ed. *Treaties and Other International Acts of the United States.* Vol. 4. Washington, D.C., 1931.

Mills, Lt. Col. Dudley A. "The Ashburton Treaty: Development of the Boundary Line." *United Empire* (Royal Colonial Institute journal) 11, n.s. (1911): 684–712.

Monthly American Journal. See Featherstonhaugh, George W.

Moore, Virginia. *The Madisons: A Biography.* New York, 1979.

Munsell, Joel. *The Annals of Albany.* 10 vols. Albany, 1857.

Murchison, Sir Roderick Impey. "Mr. George W. Featherstonhaugh." *Journal of the Geological Society of London* 23 (1867): xliii–xlv.

New York Board of Agriculture. *Memoirs of the Board of Agriculture of the State of*

New York. 3 vols. Albany, 1821, 1823, and 1826.

New York Common Council. *Minutes of the Common Council of the City of New York, 1784–1831.* New York, 1917.

New York Lyceum. "Proceedings of the Lyceum of Natural History, New York." *American Journal of Science and Arts* 14 (July 1828): 193–97.

Noble, Louis Legrand. *The Life and Works of Thomas Cole.* Ed. Elliot S. Vesell. Cambridge, Mass., 1964.

North, F. G. "Paviland Cave, the 'Red Lady,' the Deluge, and William Buckland." *Annals of Science* 5 (December 1942): 91–128.

An Officer of the U.S. Navy. "Report of a Geological Reconnaissance." *Naval Magazine* (September 1837): 473–503.

Page, William, ed. *A History of Yorkshire, North Riding,* vol. 2. *The Victoria History of the Counties of England.* London, 1914–1923.

Phillips, John. *Memoirs of William Smith, LL.D.* London, 1844.

Polk, James K. *Correspondence of James K. Polk.* Ed. Herbert Weaver. Nashville, 1972.

Porter, Charlotte M. *The Eagle's Nest: Natural History and American Ideas, 1812–1842.* University, Ala., 1986.

Proceedings of the Geological Society of London (1827–28): 35.

Rafinesque, C. S. *A Life of Travels and Researches in North America and South Europe.* Philadelphia, 1836.

Register of Graduates and Former Cadets, United States Military Academy, 1802–1951. N.p., 1951.

Roberts, George S. *Old Schenectady.* Schenectady, N.Y., 1904.

Roberts, Joseph K. *Annotated Geological Bibliography of Virginia.* Richmond, 1942.

Rountree, Arthur, ed. *History of Scarborough.* London, 1931.

St. Aubyn, John. *St. Michael's Mount.* St. Ives, Cornwall, 1978.

Schneer, Cecil J., ed. *Toward a History of Geology.* Cambridge, Mass., 1969.

Sheridan, Richard C. "Mineral Fertilizers in Southern Agriculture." In *Geological Sciences in the Antebellum South,* ed. Corgan, pp. 73–82.

Sherwood, Morgan B. "Genesis, Evolution, and Geology in America before Darwin." In *Toward a History of Geology,* ed. Schneer.

Sibley, Henry H. "Reminiscences." *Minnesota Historical Society Collections* 1 (1894): 374–96.

Smallwood, William Martin. *Natural History and the American Mind.* New York, 1941.

South, Stanley A. *Indians of North Carolina.* Raleigh, 1972.

Sparks, Jared. "The Treaty of Washington." *North American Review* (April 1843): 452–96.

Steinmeyer, Henry G. *Staten Island, 1524–1898.* New York, 1950.

Stevens, Frank Walker. *The Beginnings of the New York Central Railroad.* New York, 1926.

Swanton, John R. *The Indians of the Southeastern United States.* Washington, D.C., 1946.

Turner, Michael L. *Index and Guide to the Lists of Publications of Richard Bentley & Son, 1829–1898.* Teaneck, N.J., 1975.

"United States Boundary Question." (London) *Quarterly Review* 67 (March 1841): 501–41.

United States Military Academy. *Register of Graduates and Former Cadets, United States Military Academy . . . 1802–1951.* N.p., 1951.

Universal British Directory of Trade and Commerce. 5 vols. London, 1790, 1791, and 1798.

Victoria, Queen. *The Letters of Queen Victoria, 1837–1861.* Ed. Arthur Christopher and Viscount Esher. 9 vols. London, 1908.

Ward, George. *New Brighton Association.* Pamphlet, n.p., 1836.

Waterman, Thomas Tileston. *The Mansions of Virginia, 1706–1776.* Chapel Hill, 1946.

Weed, Thurlow. *Letters from Europe, 1843–52.* Albany, 1866.

White, George W. "The History of Geology and Mineralogy as Seen by American Writers, 1803–1835: A Bibliographic Essay." *Isis* 64 (June 1973): 197–214.

Wilson, Leonard G. *Charles Lyell.* Vol 1: *The Years to 1841: The Revolution in Geology.* New Haven, 1972.

Yorkshire Parish Register Society. *Publications* 85 (1928).

Index

352